MW00810815

RENEWAL WITHIN TRADITION

SERIES EDITOR: MATTHEW LEVERING

Matthew Levering is the James N. and Mary D. Perry Jr. Chair of Theology at Mundelein Seminary. Levering is the author or editor of over thirty books. He serves as coeditor of the journals *Nova et Vetera* and the *International Journal of Systematic Theology*.

ABOUT THE SERIES

Catholic theology reflects upon the content of divine revelation as interpreted and handed down in the Church, but today Catholic theologians often find the scriptural and dogmatic past to be alien territory. The Renewal within Tradition Series undertakes to reform and reinvigorate contemporary theology from within the tradition, with St. Thomas Aquinas as a central exemplar. As part of its purpose, the Series reunites the streams of Catholic theology that, prior to the Council, separated into neo-scholastic and *nouvelle theologie* modes. The biblical, historical-critical, patristic, liturgical, and ecumenical emphases of the Ressourcement movement need the dogmatic, philosophical, scientific, and traditioned enquiries of Thomism, and vice versa. Renewal within Tradition challenges the regnant forms of theological liberalism that, by dissolving the cognitive content of the gospel, impede believers from knowing the love of Christ.

PUBLISHED OR FORTHCOMING

Reading the Sermons of Thomas Aquinas: A Beginner's Guide
Randall B. Smith

The Culture of the Incarnation: Essays in Catholic Theology
Tracey Rowland

Self-Gift: Humanae Vitae and the Thought of John Paul II
Janet E. Smith

On Love and Virtue: Theological Essays
Michael S. Sherwin, O.P.

Aquinas on Beatific Charity and the Problem of Love
Christopher J. Malloy

Christ the Logos of Creation: Essays in Analogical Metaphysics
John R. Betz

The One Church of Christ: Understanding Vatican II
Stephen A. Hipp

O Lord, I Seek Your Countenance:
Explorations and Discoveries in Pope Benedict XVI's Theology
Emery de Gaál

The Trinitarian Wisdom of God:
Louis Bouyer on the God-World Relationship
Keith Lemna

ONE OF THE TRINITY HAS SUFFERED

ONE OF THE TRINITY HAS SUFFERED

—— • ——

Balthasar's Theology of Divine Suffering in Dialogue

JOSHUA R. BROTHERTON

EMMAUS
ACADEMIC

Steubenville, Ohio
www.emmausacademic.com

EMMAUS
ACADEMIC

Steubenville, Ohio
www.emmausacademic.com
A Division of The St. Paul Center for Biblical Theology
Editor-in-Chief: Scott Hahn
1468 Parkview Circle
Steubenville, Ohio 43952

Library of Congress Cataloging-in-Publication Data
Names: Brotherton, Joshua R., 1984- author.
Title: One of the Trinity has suffered : Balthasar's theology of divine
   suffering in dialogue / Joshua R. Brotherton.
Other titles: Reclaiming Hans Urs von Balthasar's theodramatic eschatology
Description: Steubenville, Ohio : Emmaus Academic, [2019] | Series: Renewal
   within tradition | Revision of author's thesis (doctoral)--Catholic
   University of America, 2015, titled Reclaiming Hans Urs von Balthasar's
   theodramatic eschatology : revisions from Jacques Maritain, Joseph
   Ratzinger, and Bernard Lonergan. | Includes bibliographical references.
   | Summary: "The goal of this volume is to revise Hans Urs von
   Balthasar's theology of divine suffering, that is, his disputed
   discourse on the descent of Christ into hell and its implications for
   the Triune God, according to a robust contemporary Catholic theology. In
   order to accomplish such an appropriation, I have recourse not only to
   twentieth-century Thomistic theology, but also to the thought of Pope
   Emeritus Benedict XVI (Joseph Ratzinger) and Pope St. John Paul II. I
   seek to engage the best of the vast relevant secondary literature on
   Balthasar and to offer a balanced assessment of his work on the topic of
   divine suffering, both critical and appreciative in different respects.
   I argue for a peculiar interpretation of Balthasar's take on Holy
   Saturday and for a more refined use of language in theological discourse
   than is typical of his sometimes-hyperbolic style. Recognizing his
   laudable attempt to integrate mystical spirituality and systematic
   theology, I seek to distinguish valid insights from confused mixtures of
   metaphorical, meta-symbolic, and philosophical (metaphysical) discourse
   on God, particularly, with respect to the classical problem of how the
   Creator who willed to become incarnate may be said to suffer. Truly,

"One of the Trinity has suffered," and yet this is mystery of faith that ought to be carefully explained and understood in conformity with sustained Catholic reflection on divine immutability and simplicity, the dual nature and unique personhood of Christ, the Trinity of divine subsistent relations, the freedom of God in creating and becoming man, the analogy of being, the problem of evil, and the immensity and infinite value of Christ's redemptive suffering"-- Provided by publisher.

Identifiers: LCCN 2019033113 (print) | LCCN 2019033114 (ebook) | ISBN 9781949013580 (hardcover) | ISBN 9781949013597 (paperback) | ISBN 9781949013603 (ebook)

Subjects: LCSH: Balthasar, Hans Urs von, 1905-1988. | Jesus Christ--Descent into hell. | Catholic Church--Doctrines. | Suffering of God. | Trinity | Holy Saturday.

Classification: LCC BT470 .B76 2019 (print) | LCC BT470 (ebook) | DDC 232/.8--dc23

LC record available at https://lccn.loc.gov/2019033113

LC ebook record available at https://lccn.loc.gov/2019033114

Cover image: *Holy Trinity* (1504–1559) by Jan Cornelisz Vermeyen, Museo del Prado, Madrid, Spain
Cover design and layout by Emily Demary

To my wife and my beautiful little girls, Gabriella and Lucia

Unus ex Trinitate passus est

Unknown

TABLE OF CONTENTS

Acknowledgments.. xvii

Introduction..1

Abbreviations..11

PART I: THE DESCENT-SUFFERING OF CHRIST

Chapter One: The Infinite Solidarity of Divine Love:
    Balthasar on the Redemptive Descent..15

Chapter Two: A Response to Critiques of Balthasar's
    Theology of Descent-Suffering 41

Chapter Three: The Mystery of Christ's Beatific Suffering:
    Whether Christ Lost the Beatific Vision in
    His Descent-Suffering..79

PART II: TRINITARIAN UNDERGIRDING

Chapter Four: Theodramatic Impassibility and Divine
    Affectivity after Balthasar..143

Chapter Five: Trinitarian Suffering and Divine Receptivity:
    Dialectic and Metaphor...177

Chapter Six: Theodramatic Self-Surrender and
    Analogical Discourse in Balthasar's
    Trinitarian Theology 213

Conclusion..265

Appendix: Crucial Differences between
    Balthasar and Ratzinger...277

Bibliography 307

Index 341

ACKNOWLEDGMENTS

I COULD NOT HAVE COMPLETED THIS PROJECT without the aid, encouragement, and suggestions offered by many during both my dissertation research and post-doctoral independent research. There are too many such figures to count, including William Loewe, Chad Pecknold, Thomas Joseph White, OP, Robert Joseph Matava, and to the editorial staff at Emmaus. I was particularly pleased to be able to count on steady support from such renowned theologians as Michael Root and Matthew Levering, who also provided a keen editorial eye. Of course, my family—immediate and extended—remain at the forefront of my mind throughout all of my work, academic or otherwise. I thank my parents for supporting me always in my ambitious endeavors, including this one. I also owe a debt of gratitude to my wife for supporting me while I spent countless hours on research for this project and others, as we began our family, and for manually completing the index of names for me. I pray that this small contribution to theological scholarship may affect at least one person for the good in a lasting manner, for which I may thank the Lord for assistance on the last day. I dedicate this work especially to my wife, Veronica, and my beautiful little girls, Gabriella and Lucia.

Parts of Chapters One and Two were previously published in "Hans Urs von Balthasar on the Redemptive Descent," *Pro Ecclesia* 22, no. 2 (Spring 2013): 167–188, and the section on "timeless descent" (in Chapter One) appears in "The Possibility of Universal Conversion in Death: Temporality, Annihilation, and Grace," *Modern Theology* 32, no. 3 (Summer 2016): 307–324. Part of Chapter Three appears in *Nova et Vetera* vol. 17, no. 4 as "The Mystery of Christ's Beatific Suffering: Whether Christ Lost the Beatific Vision in His Passion." Another version of Chapter Four was published as "God's Relation to Evil: Divine Impassibility in Balthasar and Maritain," *Irish Theological Quarterly* 80, no. 3 (August 2015): 191–211. Another version of Chapter Five has been published as "Trinitarian Suffering and Divine Receptivity after Balthasar" in vol. 82, no. 2 of *The Thomist*. Part of Chapter Six is published in "Towards a Resolution to Balthasar's Aporia: The Problem of Moral Evil and Theodramatic Hope," *Josephinum Journal of Theology* 25, no. 1 (Winter/Spring 2018). Finally, a version of my previously published article, "Damnation and the Trinity in Ratzinger and Balthasar," *Logos* 18, no. 3 (Summer 2015): 123–150, appears with relatively significant revisions in the Appendix.

June 8, 2018
Solemnity of the Sacred Heart of Jesus
Eve of the Feast of the Immaculate Heart of Mary
Joshua R. Brotherton

Introduction

WHY BALTHASAR?

RIK VAN NIEUWENHOVE offers the following insightful commentary on the state of theology today concerning the salvation wrought by the passion of Jesus Christ: "Whereas Protestant theologians such as Moltmann and Jungel developed an interesting *theologia crucis* (and in doing so drew a close link between soteriology and theodicy), major Catholic theologians such as Schillebeeckx and Rahner fail—or refuse—to attribute any intrinsic salvific significance to the Cross of Christ. Indeed, the Cross has become somewhat problematic in modern Catholic theology."[1] But this is indubitably not true in the case of Hans Urs von Balthasar. The Cross features at the very center of his theology. While it might be argued that this is one of many aspects of his theology that make it superior to those of other prominent twentieth-century theologians, his theology is not thereby rendered immune to criticism, as will become more evident in the latter half of the present work.

Both the influence and controversy aroused by the theology of Hans Urs von Balthasar, particularly in the areas of eschatology, Trinitarian theology, and soteriology, are well known. It will certainly take many decades for Balthasar's thought to be sifted through effectively.[2] It is most pressing

---

[1] "Bearing the Marks of Christ's Passion: Aquinas' Soteriology," in *The Theology of Thomas Aquinas*, ed. Rik van Nieuwenhove and Joseph Wawrykow (Notre Dame: University of Notre Dame Pres, 2005), 277–302, at 277.

[2] For probably the most comprehensive, albeit preliminary, attempt to sum up Balthasar's theology overall, see Aidan Nichols, OP, *Scattering the Seed: A Guide through Balthasar's Early Writings on Philosophy and the Arts* (Washington, DC: Catholic University of America, 2006); *Divine Fruitfulness: A Guide through Balthasar's Theology beyond the Trilogy* (Washington, DC: Catholic University of America, 2007); *A Key to Balthasar: Hans Urs von Balthasar on Beauty, Goodness, and Truth* (Grand Rapids, MI: Baker Aca-

to evaluate the work of Balthasar because he—among all recent theological writers—has dealt most extensively, provocatively, and influentially with such complex issues as the origin and significance of evil in salvation history, the relevance of the Trinitarian God to suffering humanity, and the way these realities are to be understood with respect to the ultimate end of all things.

My goal here is to sift out legitimate from illegitimate critique of Balthasar's project, particularly with respect to divine suffering, so that his true weaknesses might be corrected and his perceived weaknesses might be shown to be more insightful than his critics have acknowledged. James J. Buckley aptly observes:

> [T]he failure in the dialogue between students of Thomas and predecessors of Balthasar may have been a contributing cause to the success of quasi-traditionalisms in the first part of the twentieth century, just as the current paucity of dialogue has been a contributing factor in the dominance of quasi-modernist theologies in the second part of the twentieth century. Both traditionalisms and modernisms, I tend to think, derive their strengths from unsettled issues between Balthasar and Aquinas.[3]

Thus, I propose to do this by analyzing the coherence of his thought in light of broadly Thomistic metaphysical reasoning (in which the volumes of his *Theo-Aesthetics* and the first volume of the *Theo-Logic* show he was well versed), asking questions about the rationale for his assertions, and proposing interpretive moves that may help Balthasar's readers to reap

---

demic, 2011); and especially Nichols's trilogy on Balthasar's fifteen volume trilogy (excluding the separate *Epilog* [Einsiedeln: Johannes Verlag, 1987], ET, *Epilogue*, trans. Edward T. Oakes [San Francisco: Ignatius, 2004]) in *The Word Has Been Abroad: A Guide through Balthasar's Aesthetics* (Edinburgh: T&T Clark, 1998); *No Bloodless Myth: A Guide through Balthasar's Dramatics* (Washington, DC: Catholic University of America Press, 2000); *Say It Is Pentecost: A Guide through Balthasar's Logic* (Edinburgh: T&T Clark, 2001).

[3] Buckley, "Balthasar's Use of the Theology of Aquinas," *The Thomist* 59, no. 4 (1995): 517–545, at 520. He also suggests that Balthasar's criticisms of Aquinas may not be consistent with each other (see 540). For analysis of Balthasar's use of Aquinas that is more favorable to Balthasar, see Angelo Campodonico, "Il pensiero filosofico di Tommaso d'Aquino nell'interpretazione di H. U. Von Balthasar," *Medioevo* 18 (1992): 187–202; ET (english translation); "Hans Urs von Balthasar's Interpretation of the Philosophy of Thomas Aquinas," *Nova et Vetera* 8, no. 1 (2010): 33–53. The latter acknowledges "moderate" influence from Hegel, Schelling, Heidegger, and twentieth-century Jewish dialogical thought.

maximal benefit from his work without compromising philosophical rigor and precision.

INTRODUCING BALTHASAR'S PROJECT: CENTRAL ELEMENTS

While many theologians acknowledge the ingenuity and depth of Balthasar's theology, the following three theses, which play pivotal roles in his project, are sometimes designated as dangerously innovative: (1) a so-called *ur-kenosis* constitutes the Trinitarian processions, (2) Christ's passion extends to the very depths of damnation itself, and (3) hell may in fact be forever empty of human beings.[4] Thomas Joseph White, OP, who has written several articles critical of Balthasar's theses, notes the inter-connectedness of these proposals:

> [I]t is necessary to emphasize that Balthasar's goal in *Dare We Hope*, as in *Theo-Drama* V, is to envisage salvation from within the parameters of his own dramatic theology of Trinitarian self-emptying. This portrayal of redemption hinges especially upon Christ's descent into hell on behalf of the salvation of all persons.[5]

A Jesuit Balthasar scholar much more sympathetic to his project similarly states:

> This requirement that the Trinity be actively and fully involved in the death of Jesus and above all in his descent into hell leads to two other conclusions, equally controversial in contemporary theology: a very strong (and perhaps dark?) theology of the atone-ment and a quasi-Origenist (and perhaps overly optimistic?) vision of the possible redemption of all humans at the end of time.[6]

---

[4] Concerning the third thesis, I hope to publish a book soon called *Grace Abounds More: Balthasar's Universalism in Dialogue*. The first thesis will be engaged later on in the present tome.

[5] Thomas Joseph White, "Von Balthasar and Journet on the Universal Possibility of Salvation and the Twofold Will of God," *Nova et Vetera* (English Edition) 4, no. 3 (2006), 633–666, at 646. He continues: "Because such a narrative structures his theology, this same narrative consequently conditions his understanding of the role of human freedom and its final 'resolution' in light of the Incarnation and Paschal mystery" (646–647).

[6] Edward T. Oakes, SJ, *Infinity Dwindled to Infancy: A Catholic and Evangelical Christol-*

While I contest many of Oakes's assertions elsewhere, he is right on point in his hesitations.

Distinct from both of these respected theologians, however, I will follow what I think is the logical course of thought in Balthasar or, at least, the *via inventionis*—that is, the descent of Christ as a divine economic event, revealing something for Balthasar about the immanent identity of the Trinitarian God. The proper context in which to approach a "theory of redemption" in Balthasar is his understanding of God's very being as self-surrender, one of the freely chosen goals of which is the effective conversion of all men to His love.[7] I will evaluate the precise meaning of the soteriological element of his project first before addressing the Trinitarian dimension, as the for-

---

ogy (Grand Rapids, MI: Eerdmans, 2011), 368.

[7] Balthasar quotes the powerful testimony of St. Teresa Benedicta of the Cross: "All-merciful love can thus descend to everyone. We believe that it does so. And now, can we assume that there are souls that remain perpetually closed to such love? As a possibility in principle, this cannot be rejected. *In reality,* it can become infinitely improbable— precisely through what preparatory grace is capable of effecting in the soul" (*Dare We Hope "That All Men be Saved"? With A Short Discourse on Hell*, trans. David Kipp and Lothar Krauth [San Francisco: Ignatius Press, 1988], 219 [*Kleiner Diskurs* über die Höll, *Apokatastasis* (Reprint, Freiburg: Johannes Verlag, 2013), 67–68]).

German versions for the texts comprising the English version of this text are the following: *Was dürfen wir hoffen?* (Reprint, Einsieldeln: Johannes Verlag, 1989), and *Kleiner Diskurs* über die Höll, *Apokatastasis*. *Kleiner Diskurs* über *die Höll* (or *A Short Discourse on Hell*) was written in response to criticism of his *Was dürfen wir hoffen* (changed in the English to *Dare We Hope*), and a subsequent response concerning *apokatastasis*, originally published in *Trierer Theologische Zeitschrift* 97 (1988): 169–182, appears as the final part of *Dare We Hope "That All Men Be Saved"? With A Short Discourse on Hell* and *Kleiner Diskurs* über *die Höll, Apokatastasis*.

Concerning the text Balthasar quotes from Stein, Richard Schenk, OP, and Manfred Hauke point out how disingenuous a citation this is, based on the context and Stein's later reflections (see Schenk, "The Epoche of Factical Damnation?: On the Costs of Bracketing Out the Likelihood of Final Loss," *Logos: A Journal of Catholic Thought and Culture* 1, no. 3 (Fall 1997): 122–154, at 150n35; Hauke, "'Sperare per tutti?' Il ricorso all'esperienza dei santi nell'ultima grande controversia di Hans Urs von Balthasar," *Rivista teologica di Lugano* 6, no. 1 [2001]: 195–220, at 207–208).

Concerning citations, when referencing Balthasar's major works and a few other writings: whenever possible, I will cite the page numbers in the English version followed by the corresponding pages in the German version referenced in the first citation of the work, appearing within brackets after the letter 'G' with no mention of the respective volume. In general, when there is an English translation available for any foreign text referenced, I will cite the English version followed by brackets containing the page numbers of the corresponding text in the original language after a capitalized letter that indicates the name of the foreign language in English (e.g., French originals will be cross-referenced in the form: [F ##]).

mer precedes the latter in the *ordo cognoscendi* (as Balthasar was well aware).

At the heart of Balthasar's project is the desire not to leave God unaffected by the great moral evils of the fallen world, which were put in relief in the twentieth century especially. But this concern is obviously perennial, and thus Balthasar harnesses the power of resources throughout history. Characterizing Balthasar's perspective on the problem as both faithful to the tradition and going beyond it, Nicholas J. Healy notes Origen's influence and states:

> During the Theopasichite [sic] controversy in the sixth century, the statement "one of the Trinity has suffered" was declared orthodox. It is possible on the basis of the *communicatio idiomatum* to interpret this statement as referring solely to the Son's mode of existence in the Incarnation. However, this line of interpretation leaves unanswered the question of how the suffering of the Son reveals the eternal love of the Father. Furthermore, if one of the persons of the Trinity has "suffered," surely the other two persons are not indifferent to this suffering.[8]

These are the kinds of concerns with which the present work will be preoccupied, utilizing a host of secondary literature on Balthasar and interlocutors, both actual and proposed. The question of the nature of the descent of Christ into hell functions for Balthasar as a cipher into the question of the radicality of redemption, that is, the profound nature of God's relationship to evil. For Balthasar, the only answer to this question is a kenotic Trinitarian Christology:

> Here the God-man drama reaches its acme: finite freedom casts all its guilt onto God, making him the sole accused, the scapegoat, while *God allows himself to be thoroughly affected by this, not only in the humanity of Christ but also in Christ's trinitarian mission.* The omnipotent powerlessness of God's love shines forth in the mystery of darkness and alienation between God and the sin-bearing Son.[9]

---

[8] *The Eschatology of Hans Urs von Balthasar: Being as Communion* (New York: Oxford University Press, 2005), 133n109. For a rigorous and precise exposition of such Christology, Healy defers to Gerard F. O'Hanlon, SJ's magisterial book, *The Immutability of God in the Theology of Hans Urs von Balthasar* (New York: Cambridge University Press, 2007), 133.

[9] *Theo-Drama: Theological Dramatic Theory*, vol. 4, *The Action*, trans. Graham Harrison

While there are benefits to this kind of approach, it is also prone to certain pitfalls, which will be parsed in this volume.

THE SCOPE AND CENTRAL THESIS OF THIS VOLUME

This volume addresses the Trinitarian soteriology that appears concomitantly in Balthasar's *Trilogy*, especially the last four volumes of his *Theodrama* and the second volume of his *Theologic*. His Trinitarian soteriology and theodramatic eschatology together comprise what he calls his "trinitarian eschatology," which he offers as an alternative to Karl Rahner's and others' attempts to integrate the various departments of systematic theology. Such alternatives (e.g., Rahner's) cannot be treated with any detail here. But I do hope to spark more profound dialogue between the increasing number of Balthasarians, on the one hand, and representative members of other schools of Catholic theology— particularly, Thomists of various stripes. Although I will make many points both supportive and critical of Balthasar's soteriology and Trinitarian theology, the overall result from examining his treatment of divine suffering will be to recognize both insight (particularly in the former sphere) and defect (particularly in the latter) and to prescribe remedies for the latter.

Rather than approach the question of evil and salvation here from the perspective of theological anthropology, that is, the relationship between supernatural grace and natural freedom in the human being (the *imago Dei*), I will come at the same problem from an angle with which Balthasar is more explicitly fixated, namely, the suffering of Christ and what it reveals about God Himself as Trinity (*amor ipsum*). While no doubt many (including this reader) have gained insight into the compassionate heart of God-made-man, "like us in all things except sin," from Balthasar's reflections on Christ's suffering, his theoretical interpolations with regard to the divine life, in particular, engender confusion that must be dispersed through sober and refined analysis. Balthasar's response to the problem of evil goes beyond the salvific meaning accorded to suffering through Christ's ultimate solidarity with the human condition—the suffering into which the God-man willingly descended on that holy night (the threshold between Good Friday and Holy Saturday) functions for Balthasar as a cipher into the Trinitarian "undergirding" of all evil.[10] This response, while

---

(San Francisco: Ignatius, 1994), 335 (emphasis added); *Theodramatik*, Band III: *Die Handlung* (Einsiedeln: Johannes Verlag, 1980), 312.

[10] For instance, see *TD* V, 152, 279, 283 [G 132, 253, 258–259]; *TD* IV, 324 [301]. The

understandable given the contemporary dialogue partners of the Swiss theologian, is problematic for a number of reasons that should become clearer as the book progresses (particularly in the second part).

Structure of the Present Work

Thus, I will examine in detail the strengths and weaknesses of Balthasar's soteriological and Trinitarian attempt to reconcile divine love and moral evil. Given that there are principally two parts to my central thesis, namely, the passion of Christ (particularly, what I will call His descent-suffering), and the Trinitarian undergirding of all suffering and evil, there are two principal parts to the book. In the first part, I will offer a peculiar interpretation and defense of Balthasar's controversial theology of Christ's suffering, particularly the most profound suffering of His death and descent, sometimes called his "theology of Holy Saturday." I will seek to clarify what I believe Balthasar intended to convey with his several treatments of this issue against critiques that are either textually myopic or not sufficiently generous. For Balthasar, the suffering of Christ reveals to us something even deeper about the very nature of God as love. For this reason, the second part will focus on God Himself in relation to the Christological economy and the evil suffered by Him, beginning with what the events of Christ's passion reveal or do not reveal concerning God's inherent susceptibility to suffering and ending with questions about what may or may not be extrapolated from this economy concerning the very identity of God as eternally tri-hypostatic. Thus, the question of divine impassibility in Balthasar inevitably involves the problem of proper theological predication and the role of metaphor, mysticism, and analogical speech in systematic theology.[11] The Conclusion will bring the entire discussion back to

---

original German term in Balthasar's text is *Unterfassung.* He also uses the term in conjunction with überholt ("overtaken") in the context of what God does with resistant human freedom through Christ's passion (see *Explorations in Theology* 4, *Spirit and Institution*, trans. Edward T. Oakes [San Francisco: Ignatius, 1995], 422; *Pneuma und Institution: Skizzen der Theologie*, Band IV [Einsiedeln: Johannes Verlag, 1974], 408–409).

[11] Balthasar is resistant to the notion of systematic theology insofar as it connotes scholasticism (see, e.g., "Another Ten Years 1975," trans. John Saward, in *The Analogy of Beauty: The Theology of Hans Urs von Balthasar*, ed. John Riches [Edinburgh: T&T Clarke, 1986], 226), but he certainly wishes to shed light on the classical topics of systematic treatises, e.g., Trinity, Christology, redemption, eschatology.

One cannot treat such topics in language that is at times more philosophical and at times more mystical and yet claim immunity to systematic critique. Attempting to synthe original purpose of the two parts, namely, whether Balthasar responds aptly to the problem of evil and, if not, how best to do so in systematic theology, given all the analyses that have been made. In the Appendix, I will offer an excursus to the claim argued in the first part, especially the first two chapters, that seeks to complement the treatment there of the similarity between the articulations of Balthasar and Ratzinger on the descent with an exposition of how their respective reflections contrast on various related issues.

Therefore, beginning with his chief soteriological claim—that Christ descended into a hellish suffering beyond all telling for our sakes—I will offer a nuanced interpretation of this conception of Christ's passion on theoretical, rather than exegetical, grounds, in Chapter One. Furthermore, in Chapter Two, I will defend the position there proposed on the descent-suffering that characterizes the pinnacle of His passion, buttressed by the support of the former Joseph Ratzinger, now Pope Emeritus Benedict XVI. In Chapter Three, I will force the reflections of Balthasar-Speyr on Christ's descent-suffering into dialogue with Thomistic Christology concerning the particularly vexing question of how Christ could have ex-

---

thesize spirituality and theology may be laudable, but discussion about such topics cannot be exempt from the demand for precision that is essential for intelligent discourse.

I think, nonetheless, that his instinct to resist the kind of systematization characteristic of thinkers like Karl Rahner, who is more Kantian-Heideggerian than neoscholastic, is not misguided. Michelle A. Gonzalez rightly points out that Balthasar resisted "methodology" in theology, which to an extent is understandable, because he objected to "systematization" (see "Hans Urs von Balthasar and Contemporary Feminist Theology," 576). However, it is impossible to engage in any rigorous endeavor without some implicit or operative methodology—the question is whether that methodology is thought through or not—and whether methodology becomes the singular determinative feature of that theology (as it arguably does for Bernard Lonergan in his later writings).

Balthasar certainly does not pursue "systematics" in the sense understood by Lonergan, as Hilary Mooney recognizes but perhaps overstates (see her *The Liberation of Consciousness: Bernard Lonergan's Theological Foundations in Dialogue with the Theological Aesthetics of Hans Urs von Balthasar* [Frankfurt: Josef Knecht, 1992], 251). As Robert Doran says, "If Balthasar speaks of 'theological dramatics theory,' we must inquire into his meaning of the word 'theory.' If its explanatory potential remains underemphasized in Balthasar's work, as I think it does . . . it will not be promoted *for systematics* unless a move can be made from description to explanation" (see Randall Stephen Rosenberg, "Theory and Drama in Balthasar's and Lonergan's Theology of Christ's Consciousness and Knowledge: An Essay in Dialectics," [PhD diss., Boston College, 2008], 48). Doran, thus, attempts to integrate the dramatic-metaphorical approach (or "symbolic mentality") of Balthasar into a larger Lonerganian framework of theology, which I cannot address here (see Robert M. Doran, *What Is Systematic Theology?* [Toronto: University of Toronto Press], 2005).

perienced such hellish pain without actually losing the intellectual vision of God that accompanies the grace of union He necessarily enjoyed as the Incarnate Word.

In Chapters Four and Five, I will focus on the dimension of Balthasar's theology of Christ's suffering that touches on divine impassibility itself. In the former, I will present what Balthasar in dialogue with a variety of thinkers concludes from the Christological economy concerning God's own immanent life and argue for a Maritainian reappropriation of such theology of divine impassibility in contrast to the directions taken by other recent scholars influenced by Balthasar, Barth, and Maritain. In the latter, building on the correctives for his own conception of how suffering touches the divine life that I suggest may be found in both Maritain and Barth, I will highlight the detrimental effect of kenoticist thought (which is influenced by Hegel and often hyperbolic in expression) on Balthasar's discourse on God, even while granting a certain legitimacy to his fundamental intuition concerning divine receptivity. In Chapter Six, elaborating upon themes broached in the previous chapter, I will address in more detail the most difficult but significant aspect of Balthasar's theology of divine suffering, namely, its Trinitarian dimension and its relationship to the analogy of being as personified in Christ, the Incarnate Word, and conclude that the Trinity cannot be said to undergird sin itself in any meaningful sense. Thus, towards the end of the final chapter and in the Conclusion, I hope to clarify how Balthasar's manner of doing theology, at least with regard to the question of suffering in the divine life, can serve as an obstacle to precise theological discourse and to point the way toward a more philosophically rigorous way of formulating the divine truths that are manifest in the work of creation and salvation.

ABBREVIATIONS

CCC	Catechism of the Catholic Church
Denz.	*Compendium of Creeds, Defini tions, and Declarations on Matters of Faith and Morals*
SCG	Aquinas, Thomas. *Summa contra Gentiles*
ST	*Summa Theologiae*
Dare	Balthasar, Hans Urs von. *Dare We Hope "That All Men be Saved"? With A Short Discourse on Hell*
ET I	*Explorations in Theology*, Vol. 1, *The Word Made Flesh*
ET II	*Explorations in Theology*, Vol. 2, *Spouse of the Word*
ET III	*Explorations in Theology*, Vol. 3, *Creator Spirit*
ET IV	*Explorations in Theology*, Vol. 4, *Spirit and Institution*
GL I	*Glory of the Lord: A Theological Aesthetics*, Vol. 1, *Seeing the Form*
GL VII	*The Glory of the Lord: A Theological Aesthetics*, Vol. 7, *The ology: The New Covenant*
Jesus I	Ratzinger, Joseph. *Jesus of Naza- reth*, Vol. 1, *From the Baptism in the Jordan to the Transfiguration*
Jesus II	*Jesus of Nazareth*, Vol. 2, *Holy Week: From the Entrance into Jerusalem to the Resurrection*
Jesus III	*Jesus of Nazareth*, Vol. 3, *The Infancy Narratives*
John I	Speyr, Adrienne von. *John*, Vol. 1, *The Word Becomes Flesh*

John II	*John*, Vol. 2, *The Discourses of Controversy*
John III	*John*, Vol. 3, *The Farewell Discourses*
John IV	*John*, Vol. 4, *The Birth of the Church*
MP	Balthasar, Hans Urs von. *Mysterium Paschale: The Mystery of Easter*
TD II	*Theo-Drama: Theological Dramatic Theory*, Vol. 2, *The Dramatis Personae: Man in God*
TD III	*Theo-Drama: Theological Dramatic Theory*, Vol. 3, *The Dramatis Personae: The Person in Christ*
TD IV	*Theo-Drama: Theological Dramatic Theory*, Vol. 4, *The Action*
TD V	*Theo-Drama: Theological Dramatic Theory*, Vol. 5, *The Final Act*
TL II	*Theo-Logic: Theological Logical Theory*, Vol. 2, *Truth of God*
TL III	*Theo-Logic: Theological Logical Theory*, Vol. 3, *The Spirit of Truth*

Part I
THE DESCENT-SUFFERING OF CHRIST

CHAPTER ONE

The Infinite Solidarity of Divine Love
Balthasar on the Redemptive Descent

IN THIS CHAPTER, I will present a sympathetic and nuanced, even if cursory, account of Balthasar's theology of Christ's descent into hell, in effect setting the stage for a qualified defense of this theology in the next chapter. After a brief methodological note, I will begin by situating Balthasar's soteriology in the context of the development in modern theology of diverse approaches to the mystery of Christ's redemptive work, which he attempts to synthesize with emphasis on the *admirabile commercium*. Then, I will trace the steps in Balthasar's development of such a synthesis in dialogue with various figures (especially Barth and Moltmann), mentioning contentious elements along the way. Finally, I will highlight the element of atemporality Balthasar attributes to Christ's passion, particularly its culmination in His descent into godforsakenness on the Cross, which will have implications for the significance of "Holy Saturday."

METHODOLOGICAL NOTE

Much has been made recently of the lack of historical antecedents in the unanimous tradition of the Church's theological reflections on the datum of the redemptive Incarnation for Balthasar's so-called "theology of Holy Saturday."[1] Rather, I will focus here on the systematic aspects of the problem of Balthasar's soteriology at large. But systematic reflection on the nature of the death and descent of Christ in relation both to the triune God and sinful humanity is far from insignificant for determining

---

[1] See especially Alyssa L. Pitstick, *Light in Darkness: Hans Urs von Balthasar and the Catholic Doctrine of Christ's Descent into Hell* (Grand Rapids, MI: Eerdmans, 2007).

the precise ways in which Balthasar's proposals may be true to the data of divine revelation. The problem with privileging historical data, despite the historicity of revelation, is that claims to unanimity often overtake actual unanimity and dominant theological opinion is easily mistaken for definitive magisterium. Consider, for instance, the historic debates concerning the existence of a limbo for unbaptized infants or the dogmatic status of Mary's bodily assumption.[2] What seem to be most determinative of developments in ecclesial doctrine are conceptual antecedents more than historical antecedents. It is a task of speculative theology to explore the as-yet unknown (or lesser known) implications of already known articulations of revealed truth. The obscurity of the implications—that is, the difficulty of obtaining them due to their complexity—is precisely the arena of theological disputation, which must be undertaken systematically for any hope of success to be justified.

All of the patristic, medieval, and modern theologians base themselves ultimately on Sacred Scripture as the primary channel of divine revelation (or, at least, they purport to do so). But since Scripture itself is part and parcel of apostolic tradition, which is then received and appropriated diversely throughout the history of the Church's development, it is perhaps not very helpful to rely primarily on scriptural texts for justification of one's theological positions on particularly contentious questions. Each succeeding generation of scholars attempts to build on what came before it—even if that means first breaking down facades constructed in a faulty manner. Balthasar, for instance, writes theology in a manner that attempts to be comprehensive and thus systematic, even if he wants to avoid arid structures, and this means he builds on previous interpretive traditions, seeking to synthesize diverse schools of thought that have developed out of long-standing reflections on Sacred Scripture and its reception in Sacred Tradition.[3]

With all this in mind, I will limit myself to a systematic inquiry into the most accurate manner in which to understand the truths of our re-

---

[2] Concerning the former, for instance, see George J. Dyer, *Limbo: Unsettled Question* (New York: Sheed and Ward, 1964). Concerning the latter, see the brief but incisive comments of Joseph Ratzinger, *Milestones: Memoirs 1927–1977*, trans. Erasmo Leiva-Merikakis (San Francisco: Ignatius Press, 1998), 58–59.

[3] None of this is, of course, meant to undermine the central role of Sacred Scripture in theology. Concerning the relationship between Scripture and philosophical insight in systematic theology, see the masterful work of Matthew Levering, *Scripture and Metaphysics: Aquinas and the Renewal of Trinitarian Theology* (Malden, MA: Blackwell, 2004).

demption with a primary focus on contemporary authors as interlocutors with patristic and especially medieval figures.[4] Balthasar is, of course, the primary interlocutor here, but by engaging Balthasar in a contemporary context I will fittingly incorporate various recent attempts both to interpret Balthasar and to challenge him, particularly with regard to the question that seems to be at the center of all his work (and rightfully so), namely, the problem of evil. Thus, I will attempt to plumb the depths of the issues contemplated by Balthasar in dialogue with a tradition rich in philosophico-theological considerations.

SITUATING BALTHASAR IN THE SOTERIOLOGICAL LANDSCAPE

The complexity of theological opinion on the precise nature of the redemption and, particularly, of the descent into hell (confessed in the Apostles' Creed) is overwhelming. It is unclear how much weight is to be granted which figures since there is not necessarily an ever-decreasing degree of purity in faith as time marches on. St. Cyril of Alexandria speaks of Christ freeing all the damned in His descent.[5] St. Augustine thought that Christ descended to the deepest regions of hell, rescued the just and some unjust (who were elect), but did not suffer there.[6] Thomas Aquinas understood the descent partially in terms of Christ's solidarity with sinners and taking upon Himself the consequences of sin, but Aquinas did not speak of any sort of suffering in the descent on Saturday.[7] He likewise spoke of Christ descending "in effect" to all regions of hell, confounding the damned, giving hope to those being purged, and bringing glory to the holy, but Aquinas held that "in essence" He only descended to the realm of the just.[8] In accord with his development of substitutionary atonement, Luther sometimes places hell in Christ's agony and Crucifixion,[9] but he also at times

---

[4] I will not engage the patristic figures directly, however. For this, e.g., see Paul L. Gavrilyuk, *The Suffering of the Impassible God: The Dialectics of Patristic Thought* (Oxford: Oxford University Press, 2006).

[5] *7th Paschal Homily* 2 (*PG* 77, 552 A).

[6] See his final letter to Bishop Evodius on the topic, "Letter 164," in *The Nicene and Post-Nicene Fathers of the Christian Church*, vol. 1, *The Confessions and Letters of St. Augustine*, ed. Philip Schaff (Reprint, Grand Rapids, MI: Eerdmans, 1988).

[7] *ST* III, q. 52, a. 1.

[8] *ST* III, q. 52, a. 2.

[9] See *Luther's Works*, vol. 7, *Lectures on Genesis, Chapters 38–44*, ed. Jaroslav Pelikan and trans. Paul D. Pahl (St. Louis: Concordia Publishing House, 1965), 302–303.

seems to view the descent on Saturday as a triumphant harrowing of hell, which he says involves both Christ's soul and (postmortem) body.[10] In contrast, Calvin rejects any mythological image of Christ's harrowing descent on Saturday, locating His vicarious suffering for the elect in His passion.[11]

In the soteriological attempt to articulate God's own solution to the problem of evil, there are generally two antipathetic streams of thought, namely: (1) those who see redemption primarily as satisfaction (à la Anselm) and consequently define the descent merely as a triumphant advent to the dead, and (2) those who define the redemptive work primarily as vicarious substitution and consequently envision the descent in terms of damnation.[12] Since Balthasar adopts damnation language in regard to the sufferings of Christ, his interpretation of the meaning of Christ's kenotic love for sinful mankind is often accused of not being continuous with tradition. The typical Catholic position, at least since the time of the Catechism of Trent, has been to define Christ's descent into hell as simply the triumphal rescue of the dead awaiting the Messiah's advent, resulting in an enumeration of different hells, where the "hell of the damned" is that designated for those without faith in Christ (as either coming or having come).[13] On the opposite side of the spectrum are those who, basing them-

---

[10] See his Easter sermon on April 13, 1533, "Descent into Hades," in Eugene Klug, ed., *Sermons of Martin Luther: The House Postils*, vol. 2 (Ada, MI: Baker, 1996), 15ff.

[11] See his *Institutio Christianae Religionis* II, 16, 10; ET, *Institutes of the Christian Religion*, trans. Henry Beveridge (Grand Rapids, MI: Christian Classics Ethereal Library, 2002), 318.

[12] Perhaps striking a middle ground, Bernard Lonergan speaks of "vicarious satisfaction," defined as "voluntarily assuming punishment so that pardon for Rosenberg another's offenses, not one's own, may fittingly be asked and granted" (*De Verbo Incarnato*, 3rd ed. [Rome: Gregorian University, 1964], 509, cited by Rosenberg, "Theory and Drama," 230). He also maintains that "Aquinas has advanced far beyond Anselm, inasmuch as he explained vicarious satisfaction through the union of love that exists between Christ the Head and his members" (*De Verbo Incarnato*, 525).

At the same time, Lonergan allocates the notions of "substitution" and "satispassion" to the "symbolic mentality," which he contrasts with an explanatory, systematic mentality that has roots in "the logic developed by the Greeks and diffused through Hellenistic culture" (*De Verbo Incarnato*, 534; Rosenberg, 231, cf. 300). For another account of Lonergan on the redemptive work of Christ, see Charles Hefling, "A Perhaps Permanently Valid Achievement: Lonergan on Christ's Satisfaction," *Method: Journal of Lonergan Studies* 10 (1992): 51–76.

[13] In his "'He descended into hell': The Depths of God's Self-Emptying Love on Holy Saturday in the Thought of Hans Urs von Balthasar," in *Exploring Kenotic Christology: The Self-Emptying of God*, ed. C. Stephen Evans (New York: Oxford University Press, 2006): 218–245, at 227–229, Edward T. Oakes blames Augustine's *Letter to Evodius*

selves upon Reformation exegesis, insist that the culminating point of the redemptive work was the damnation Christ was deigned to suffer in place of the sinner.[14]

I think it is a mistake to relegate Balthasar's position to either side of the spectrum.[15] Rather, in a uniquely successful manner, he manages to combine the more traditional understanding of redemptive satisfaction with the more modern substitutionary approach to the redemption,[16] which seems to be demanded at least by a few of the great patristic authors (such as Origen, Athanasius, Cyril of Alexandria, and Cyprian).[17] Stephen Wigley sums up Balthasar's comprehensive approach, quoting from *TD* IV:

Balthasar's account of the atonement itself is governed by five themes which he finds to be central to the New Testament wit-

---

for initiating this development and points to some passages in which Thomas Aquinas elaborates the same type of doctrine (see *ST* III, q. 52). In another place, however, he points to Augustine holding the opposite position (see "*Descensus* and Development: A Response to Recent Rejoinders," *International Journal of Systematic Theology* 13, no. 1 [January 2011]: 3–24, at 9).

[14] See, for example, Martin Luther's 1535 commentary on Galatians 3:13: *Luther's Works*, vol. 26, *Lectures on Galatians 1535: Chapters 1–4*, ed. Jaroslav Pelikan and Walter A. Hansen (St. Louis: Concordia Publishing House, 1964), 277ff.; Jean Calvin, *Institutes of the Christian Religion* II, ch. 16, sects. 10–12, available on the Christian Classics Ethereal Library at http://www.ccel.org/ccel/calvin/institutes.iv.xvii.html (accessed on 11/4/2014).
Despite the common "substitution" model here, see the slightly different accounts of the two Reformers and their relationship to Balthasar in Oakes, "He descended into hell," 221–222, *Infinity Dwindled to Infancy*, 388; Alyssa L. Pitstick, "Development of Doctrine, or Denial? Balthasar's Holy Saturday and Newman's *Essay*," *International Journal of Systematic Theology* 11 (2009): 131–145, at 140. See also Balthasar's brief comparisons of Calvin and Luther in *TD* IV, 292 [G 270–271] and *MP*, 169–170 [G 245–246].

[15] For Balthasar's relationship to the Reformers, see Rodney A. Howsare, *Hans Urs von Balthasar and Protestantism: The Ecumenical Implications of His Theological Style* (New York: T&T Clarke International, 2005).

[16] Karen Kilby, in her *Balthasar: A (Very) Critical Introduction* (Grand Rapids, MI: Eerdmans, 2012), alludes to this point and a few others made here concerning his soteriology on 102.

[17] One must not presume that there is no historical antecedent for the positions elaborated by the Reformers. See his citations on *TD* IV, 254 [G 234]. See also Athanasius, *De Incarnatione*, ch. 4, 20, ET available at https://www.ccel.org/ccel/athanasius/incarnation.v.html. Nonetheless, in his "historical outline" of soteriology, Balthasar gives credit to a number of medieval and modern Catholic thinkers for explaining the ancient theme of solidarity in terms of representative substitution: *TD* IV, 297 [G 275–276].

ness: namely that (1) God's "only Son" has *"given himself up* for us all," (2) "to the extent of *exchanging places with us,"* thus (3) (negatively) *freeing* us from sin and death, (4) (positively) *drawing* us into *"the divine trinitarian life"* and (5) in all of which "the entire reconciliation process is attributed to God's merciful *love."*
. . . In the patristic period, von Balthasar observes that it is the second of these themes, that of the *exchange* which dominates, largely because of the need, following the christological heresies, to affirm both the full divinity and humanity of Christ (*TD 4:* 244–54). However, turning to the medieval period, particularly under the influence of Anselm, it is the third of the motifs, that of *ransom* or *satisfaction,* which emerges as most influential (*TD 4:* 255–66). Coming to the modern period, von Balthasar identifies the two dominant themes as being those of *solidarity* and *substitution.* What von Balthasar is concerned to show is that only a theodramatic theory of the atonement will suffice to allow all five themes to play their proper role.[18]

Thus, in attempting to balance out the hard leaning of the post-Tridentine Church to one side of the spectrum, his doctrine of the descent yields a highly developed understanding of the atonement not typically found in Catholic and Protestant thinkers alike.

Balthasar both defends Anselm against popular critiques[19] and treats Luther's innovative approach very sympathetically,[20] even though he critiques aspects of both as well.[21] In *Cordula oder der Erstfall,*[22] Balthasar criticizes Karl Rahner in the same breath both for not understanding the

---

[18] *Balthasar's Trilogy: A Reader's Guide* (New York: T&T Clark, 2010), 107–108.

[19] See, e.g., *TD* IV, 255ff. [G 235ff.]. For Balthasar's defense of Anselm's theory, see especially *Theo-Drama: Theological Dramatic Theory,* vol. 3, *The Dramatis Personae: The Person in Christ,* trans. Graham Harrison (San Francisco: Ignatius Press, 1993), 240ff.; *Theodramatik,* Band II: *Die Personen des Spiels,* Teil II: *Die Personen in Christus* (Einsiedeln: Johannes Verlag, 1978), 220ff.

[20] See *TD* IV, 284ff. [G 263ff.]. For Balthasar's appropriation of Luther, see Rodney Howsare, *Balthasar and Protestantism,* 42–76.

[21] For instance, Balthasar blames Aquinas's "attachment to Anselm" for "preventing him from taking account of the patristic theme of the 'exchange of places'" (*TD* IV, 263 [G 243]). John O'Donnell, SJ, sums up well Balthasar's posture toward Anselm and especially Luther (see *Hans Urs von Balthasar* [Collegeville, MN: Liturgical Press, 1992], 102–104).

[22] Balthasar, *Cordula oder der Erstfall* (Einsiedeln: Johannes Verlag, 1966), ET, *The Moment of Christian Witness,* trans. Richard Beckley (San Francisco: Ignatius Press, 1994).

redemption in substitutionary terms and for harping on the legalistic dimension of Anselm's satisfaction theory.[23] Despite his well-known esteem for the redemption as *Stellvertretung*,[24] he wishes to go beyond it to include aspects of other theories of redemption, not to mention adding "a trinitarian element."[25] Ben Quash notes:

> Balthasar's introduction to his main discussion of soteriology in volume iv deliberately eschews any facile reduction of Christ's saving work to one explanatory theory or metaphoric image. Here, in this pursuit of the meaning of the Cross into the dark space of Holy Saturday, we see him articulating a doctrine of salvation that has both substitutionary (or representative), and participatory aspects.[26]

Gerard O'Hanlon notes "Balthasar's discriminating acceptance of the original theological contribution by Luther to this issue [of the Pauline *pro nobis*],"[27] and that "Balthasar's concern is to bring the notions of solidarity and substitution together."[28]

---

[23] See Louth, "The Place of *Heart of the World* in the Theology of Hans Urs von Balthasar," in *The Analogy of Beauty*, ed. John Riches.

[24] Concerning this model, see Karl-Heinz Menke, *Stellvertretung* (Einsiedeln: Johannes Verlag, 1991); Joseph Ratzinger, "Stellvertretung," in Heinrich Fries, ed., *Handbuch theologischer Grundbegriffe*, vol. 2 (Munich: Kosel Verlag, 1963), 566–575, ET, "Vicarious Representation," trans. Jared Wicks, *Letter & Spirit* 7 (2011): 209–220.

[25] *Theo-Drama: Theological Dramatic Theory*, vol. 5, *The Final Act*, trans. Graham Harrison (San Francisco: Ignatius, 1998), 272; *Theodramatik*, Band IV: *Das Endspiel* (Einsiedeln: Johannes Verlag, 1983), 246.

[26] Quash, "The theo-drama," in *The Cambridge Companion to Hans Urs von Balthasar*, eds. Edward T. Oakes and David Moss (Cambridge: Cambridge University Press, 2004), 143–157, at 154.
   For a Protestant treatment of how representative (or vicarious) substitution as a model of redemption need not exclude participation in its outworking on the part of the redeemed (i.e., the distinction between inclusive versus exclusive representation), see Albrecht Ritschl, *The Christian Doctrine of Justification and Reconciliation: The Positive Development of the Doctrine*, trans. H. R. Mackintosh, ed. A. B. Macaulay, 546ff. (Clifton, NJ: Reference Book Publishers, 1966); German original in 1874.
   For a more recent discussion of these categories, see Wolfhart Pannenberg, *Systematic Theology*, vol. 2, trans. Geoffrey W. Bromiley (Grand Rapids, MI: Eerdmans, 1994), 429ff.

[27] See O'Hanlon, *The Immutability of God*, 185n73; *TD* III, 221–225, 295f.

[28] See *TD*, III, 245–246. O'Hanlon adds: "For one-sided treatments of solidarity, see *TD* III, 247–62, and of substitution, *TD III*, 263–91" (*The Immutability of God*, 185n76). Balthasar explicitly links solidarity and representation in *TD* III, 239n35 [G 220n12].

I will not enter into the historical developments in the various doctrines on the descent of Christ, but I will argue that there is at least a basis in Balthasar's later writings for understanding Holy Saturday as a metaphorical day that extends liturgically the sufferings historically undergone before and in the event of death on Friday, a position more evidently held by his friend and collaborator, Joseph Ratzinger (Benedict XVI).[29] Then, in the next Chapter, I take issue with a few Catholic thinkers who have placed Balthasar in the so-called Calvinistic camp,[30] acknowledging that sometimes Balthasar's language may include rhetorical excess (erring on the side of art or existential feeling in contradistinction to sapiential science),[31] but emphasizing the potential for legitimate advantage in a more balanced approach to the question. With a little careful exegesis of certain Balthasarian texts and a more rigorous analysis of the reflections therein, the coherence of his doctrine on the descent becomes evident and its continuity with tradition becomes less questionable.

BRIEF EXPOSITION OF BALTHASAR'S THEOLOGY OF CHRIST'S DESCENT

Balthasar's approach to the Holy Saturday doctrine is more nuanced than many would like to admit. His first step is to undermine the "traditional" division of hell into distinct spheres, noting, for example, that before Christ, "Sheol is more and more equated with Gehenna, the preliminary place of punishment."[32] This is not always clear when, for instance, he says that with the ushering in of the New Covenant, "we now find that the 'eternal fire' of Gehenna has opened up below Sheol (Matt 5:22, 29f.; 10:28; 18:9; 23:33; 25:41), balancing, as it were, the heaven that is now

---

[29] See, e.g., Ratzinger, *Introduction to Christianity*, trans. J. R. Foster (San Francisco: Ignatius Press, 2004), 290–301; *Einführung in das Christentum* (München: Deutscher Taschenbuch, 1971), 212–221.

[30] I mean Calvinistic with respect to the "penal" dimension of redemption theory, but concerning another facet of the problem, what T. J. White points out remains true: "Barth reinterprets Calvin's theology of penal substitution, affirming the descent into hell on the cross as the reprobation unique to Christ so that all might be elect. The idea is central to Balthasar's theology" ("Kenoticism and the Divinity of Christ Crucified," *The Thomist* 75 [2011]: 1–41, at 12n35). Indeed, I will argue in favor of a crucicentric interpretation of the doctrine of the descent.

[31] See O. H. Pesch, "Existential and Sapiential Theology—The Theological Confrontation between Luther and Thomas Aquinas," in J. Wicks, ed., *Catholic Scholars in Dialogue with Luther* (Chicago: Loyola University Press, 1970), 59–81.

[32] *TD* V, 354 [G 323]

open to all."[33] Again, "in the era after Christ 'Gehenna' is sometimes given a purifying function";[34] he then elaborates on the purificatory dimension of judgment. Nonetheless, his conflation of Old Testament *Sheol* and *Gehenna* allows him to affirm that although Christ cannot be said to have suffered the New Testament hell proper, his hell encompasses the eschatological no and the deepest possible suffering.[35] In other words, he wants to indicate simply that everyone was consigned to the same realm of perdition before Christ and that everyone is destined for hell antecedent to Christ's redemptive descent. Hence, he also states: "both 'paradise' and 'Gehenna' remain polyvalent and receive their theological unequivocalness only through the event of Holy Saturday."[36] *Gehenna* is an Old Covenant anticipation of the New Covenant hell, the "second death" or "lake of fire" (see Rev 20–21). Even if the spiritual states of men prior to redemption differ in degree, all stand in judgment before His grace due to original sin and thus share a common fate without Christ's redemptive work to differentiate them.[37]

---

[33] *TD* IV, 178 [G 164].

[34] *TD* V, 361–362 [G 330].

[35] See *The Mystery of Easter*, trans. Aidan Nichols, O.P. (San Francisco: Ignatius, 1990); "Mysterium Paschale," in *Mysterium Salutis: Grundriss heilsgeschichtlicher Dogmatik, Band III: Das Christusereignis, Teil 2*, ed. Johannes Feiner and Magnus Lohrer (Einsiedeln: Benziger Verlag, 1969): 133–326;, 172–173 [G 246–247] and TD V, 199 and 354 [G 323].

[36] *The Glory of the Lord: A Theological Aesthetics*, vol. 7, *Theology: The New Covenant*, trans. Brian McNeil, ed. John Riches (San Francisco: Ignatius Press, 1989), 229n3; *Herrlichkeit: Eine Theologische Ästhetik*, Band III, 2: *Theologie*, Teil 2: *Neuzeit* (Einsiedeln: Johannes Verlag, 1969), 212n3.

For a somewhat different analysis of this move, see Brian Doyle, OP, "'He descended into hell': The Theology of Hans Urs von Balthasar and Catholic Doctrine," *Nova et Vetera* (English Edition) 14, no. 3 (2016): 845–878, at 852ff. I think the two accounts merge where Doyle recalls:

> Balthasar also believes that the concept of Hades should be understood as being more "spiritual than local" and favors the interpretation of the *chaos magnum* [a great chasm between the NT hell and Sheol (Hades)] as something signifying a difference between the inner spiritual states of the "evil rich man" and Lazarus, rather than a localized division. This interpretation, Balthasar suggests, "opens up the way to a psychic solidarity between the dead Christ and those who dwell in the Hades of the spirit." (854)

[37] The timelessness of Christ's saving will may, therefore, affect men temporally existent prior to His historical Incarnation just as it does those temporally posterior. Doyle is therefore misguided to infer from Balthasar's theology of the descent that, for him, those who lived before Jesus were not afforded efficacious grace. See "Theology of Balthasar," 859.

The next step is to emphasize that the sufferings of Christ must in fact exceed (in some sense) all the pains associated with the judgment of justice and the pain of loss.[38] Joseph Ratzinger supports such innovation on both accounts, identifying the Judeo-Christian concept of hell primarily with death and the land of the dead (Sheol or Hades) and teaching that the descent of Christ into such a "state of being" must involve tremendous suffering.[39] It is perhaps less clear in Balthasar's case where the continuity lies between a kenotic approach to the descent and the trajectory of early Christian teaching.[40] It may help to ask: If, according to St. Paul, Christ assumed in His own flesh the very sinfulness of mankind,[41] would not the "hell" into which He descended in His passion encompass even the hell consequent to unbelief? In this case, God became a vicarious victim not merely of the past but perhaps, most of all, of the future rejection of His own messianic message. Although the more troubling point for those who

---

[38] See *TD* V, 256 [G 323].

[39] See Joseph Ratzinger, *Introduction to Christianity*, 300–301 [G 220–221]. In the context of the Kierkegaardian concept of *angst* and Sartre's development of it, Ratzinger notes that the scholarly consensus that *Sheol* referred both to death and hell only furthers the argument that the hell preceding redemption is precisely the utter loneliness Christ came to transform by descending into its depths, which nevertheless is consequently distinguished from the hell of those who finally reject such redemption.

Contrary to Oakes ("*Descensus* and Development," 20–21), Ratzinger is generally clearer regarding the distinction of abodes after Christ's death as well as allocating Christ's hellish sufferings, historically, to the experience of death on Friday, even though Saturday constitutes a distinct liturgical reality focusing on the significance of his being-dead.

See, e.g., Joseph Ratzinger and William Congdon, ed., *The Sabbath of History* (Washington, DC: The William G. Congdon Foundation, 2000), 21–22; see also Pope Benedict XVI, Angelus Address, November 5, 2006, available at https://w2.vatican.va/content/benedict-xvi/en/angelus/2006/documents/hf_ben-xvi_ang_20061105.html.

[40] Jacques Servais, in a postscript to translated conferences of Balthasar, says:

In an extreme position justified by none of the scriptural witnesses, Luther went so far as to declare Christ "damned." Careful not to cross such a line himself, von Balthasar nevertheless tries to transcend the extrinsicism of the traditional Thomist solution, in which the offense and reparation for the offense remain exterior to each other . . . demanding that [Christ] freely assume the inner condition of the sinner. In order to join the latter in his own freedom, the undertaking in his favor must in fact take place, according to [Balthasar], there in the very place where the refusal and curse took place. (*To the Heart of the Mystery of Redemption*, trans. Anne Englund Nash [San Francisco: Ignatius Press, 2010], 100–101; originally published, *Au coeur du mystère rédempteur* [Paris: Chambray-Tours, 1980])

[41] See, for example, Romans 8:3, 2 Corinthians 5:21, and Galatians 3:13.

truly believe in the Incarnation may be what consequences such suffering must have in the economy of salvation, I will leave aside the eschatological implications of an eminently kenotic understanding of the descent in order to approach the most common problem theologians have with Balthasar on the descent, namely, how it may be possible for Christ to suffer the hell of those who finally reject divine *caritas*.[42]

One aspect of the problem is precisely how divine grace can be said to remain in a soul (or better, a person) that plumbs the depths of condemnation, and another aspect of the same problem is precisely how the sufferings celebrated on Good Friday and Holy Saturday, respectively, are to be related to one another in the redemptive work of Christ as a whole. It is important, though, to begin with how Balthasar conceives the divine motive necessitating such a profound "descent" into the sufferings of sinful man. He takes from Barth (against Moltmann) the notion that all the suffering attributed to God is not in the end caused by any creature but ultimately derives from God's own infinite freedom.[43] But he offers a corrective to Barth (as he understands him) in saying that the condemnation

---

[42] I do not mean here to imply that Christ becomes damned (that is, literally suffers "the second death"); the new *Catechism of the Catholic Church* explicitly condemns such a view, which logically involves a form of universalism (CCC 633). Margaret Turek defends Balthasar's position on the descent as orthodox with the following "clarification" of current Church teaching:

> [W]hen the new *Catechism* echoes the Council of Rome in teaching that Christ, by his descent into Sheol, frees "the just who had gone before him" (CCC 633; see DS 587), it must be kept in mind that "the just" have been rendered so precisely by virtue of the grace issuing from the Son's death, descent, and resurrection, which grace is extended to every human being of every time and place (see CCC 634). What is ruled out, however, is conceiving that Christ descended into Sheol "to deliver the damned, or to destroy the hell of damnation" (CCC 633)—which means . . . that we cannot interpret the redemptive effects of Christ's descent as extending to the "fallen" angels, nor (concerning *human* freedom to which the grace of the redemption *does* extend) as making it impossible for human beings to refuse to correspond to God's saving love unto their own perdition, nor as providing the possibility of conversion after death ("Dare We Hope 'That All Men Be Saved' (1 Tim 2:4)?: On von Balthasar's Trinitarian Grounds for Christian Hope," *Logos* 1 (1997): 92–121, 121n69).

I am merely arguing here that the "hell" Christ suffers is worse than the hell suffered by any creature, even though he did not historically suffer the "second death" for which those who definitively refuse salvation are destined, because the endurance of His soul in divine grace (by virtue of the hypostatic union) does not mitigate but intensifies His suffering.

[43] See *TD* V, 237 [G 214].

assumed by Christ is not simply a vicarious substitution for the sinner—rather, it is a reflection of the infinite love that is God Himself and it in fact goes beyond any pain that is due sin.[44] Thus, the root and ground for the redemptive descent is the *ur-kenosis* constituting the Trinitarian processions themselves; the love of God is conceived by Balthasar as Trinitarian because of the nature of self-surrender, and the descent is a reflection of such love.

Distinguishing between the economic and immanent dimensions of the Trinity, Balthasar asserts (also against Moltmann): "the sinner's alienation from God was taken into the Godhead, into the 'economic' distance between Father and Son."[45] Steffen Lösel notes that Balthasar "adopts Adrienne von Speyr's term 'pre-sacrifice' (*Voropfer*) to describe the mutu-

---

[44] See *TD* V, 277 [G 251]. Still, Balthasar does not always clearly distance himself from crude expressions of penal substitution. Hence, Thomas G. Weinandy states:

> Jesus' experience of the wrath of God should not then be interpreted in what is commonly, though unfairly, understood as the classic Reformation (Lutheran) view, that is, that God took out his wrath on Jesus rather than on us. . . . I am thus not comfortable when von Balthasar states that "God unloaded his wrath upon the Man" (*Theo-Drama IV: The Action*, 345). Nonetheless, I would agree with von Balthasar when he argues for Jesus's "Holy Saturday" experience, which forms a major theme within his own Christology: "Jesus does not only accept the (to be sure, accursed) mortal destiny of Adam. He also, quite expressly, carries the sin of the human race and, with those sins, the 'second death' of God-abandonment." *Mysterium Paschale*, p. 90. . . . Pope John Paul II states: "Together with this horrible weight, *encompassing* the 'entire' evil *of the turning away from God* which is contained in sin, Christ, through the divine depth of his filial union with the Father, perceives in a humanly inexpressible way *this suffering which is the separation*, the rejection *by the Father*, the estrangement from God. *Salvifici Doloris*, n. 18." (*Does God Suffer?* [Edinburgh: University of Notre Dame Press, 2000], 219n8)

It should be clarified, though, that John Paul did not accept the view that, temporally speaking, Christ's soul suffered after the moment of death (see his General Audience, "He Descended into Hell," January 11, 1989, in *A Catechesis on the Creed*, vol. 2: *Jesus: Son and Savior* [Reprint, Boston: Pauline Books & Media, 1996], 483–488).

John Yocum also notes that "In John Paul's description [of Christ's suffering in *Salvifici Doloris*, no. 17], the suffering of the Son fills up the space between God and humanity, while for Balthasar the crucial 'space' is that between Father and Son. One might also ask how much Balthasar's theology is determined by a spatial imagination that is inadequate for speaking of the Triune being" ("A Cry of Dereliction? Reconsidering a Recent Theological Commonplace," *International Journal of Systematic Theology* 7, no. 1 [2005]: 72–80, 74n12).

[45] *TD* IV, 381 [G 355]. See also Antoine Birot, "'God in Christ, Reconciled the World to Himself': Redemption in Balthasar," *Communio* 24, no. 2 (1997): 259–285, at 285.

al self-giving relationship of Father, Son, and Holy Spirit."[46] Pointing to Balthasar's claim to go beyond Barth, White quotes the following passage from *Das Endspiel*:

> In fact we can go a step further than Barth; for he conceives ("double") predestination in such a way that Christ is the One chosen to be solely condemned on behalf of all the condemned. This comprehensive formula is too close, however, to the view that the sufferings of the Cross were a punishment. . . . The Crucified Son does not simply suffer the hell deserved by sinners; he suffers something below and beyond this, namely, being forsaken by God in the pure obedience of love. Only he, as Son, is capable of this, and it is qualitatively deeper than any possible hell. This signifies an even more radical abandonment.[47]

Thus, his theology reaches for the "heart" of God as revealed in and expressed by the Incarnation of the Word, culminating in the "consuming fire" (Heb 12:29) of the Cross.[48]

While the influence of Hegelian logic is discerned by some in

---

[46] Steffen Lösel, "A Plain Account of Christian Salvation? Balthasar on Sacrifice, Solidarity, and Substitution," *Pro Ecclesia* 13, no. 2 (2004): 141–171, at 163. Lösel speaks in another place of this concept in Balthasar:

> Although the Son suffers indeed at a particular point in history, his suffering is in fact "atemporal," "transtemporal and pretemporal." And yet, the cross as the ultimate sign of the Son's eternal "pre-sacrifice" does add a new dimension into the divine life. Balthasar daringly formulates with Adrienne von Speyr that the mutual abandonment of Father and Son, which is expressed at the cross, "lets the Father experience the measure of his love for the Son" ("Murder in the Cathedral: Hans Urs von Balthasar's New Dramatization of the Doctrine of the Trinity," *Pro Ecclesia* 5, no. 4 [1996]: 427–439, at 435).

[47] White, "Von Balthasar and Journet," 656n56, citing *TD* V, 277. Regarding differentiation of Barth from Balthasar on the topic, John Yocum points to a book by Alan Lewis (presumably, *Between Cross and Resurrection: A Theology of Holy Saturday* [Grand Rapids, MI: Eerdmans, 2001]):

> Barth is sometimes placed in this category [of theologians who speak of the "cry of dereliction" in terms of the Son's separation from the Father], but as a recent work by Alan Lewis rightly claims, his approach is more nuanced than most. In particular, Barth avoids the notion that the judgment that falls on the Son in his death is the judgment of the Father, reserving the association of judgment with the Father's vindication of the Son. ("A Cry of Dereliction?," 73n2)

[48] See, for example, *TD* V, 215 [G 193]. See also *TD* IV, 174 [G 159–160].

Balthasar's dialectic,[49] even though he explicitly repudiates the former (in conjunction with Moltmann's radical "death of God" theology),[50] he actually intends to base his descent-centered understanding of the passion upon a more literal interpretation of Galatians 3:13–14, Philippians 2:6–8, and 2 Corinthians 5:21 than is customary.[51] Balthasar insists, "It is not possible to dismiss the Pauline texts quoted, or other similar passages, as witnesses of a *later* New Testament soteriology, one that could conse-

---

[49] See, e.g., Bruce Marshall, "The Absolute and the Trinity," *Pro Ecclesia* 23, no. 2 (Spring 2014): 147–164; Ben Quash, "Drama and the Ends of Modernity," in Gardner, Moss, Quash, and Ward, *Balthasar at the End of Modernity* (Edinburgh: T&T Clark, 1999), 139–171; and "Between the Brutely Given, and the Brutally, Banally Free: Von Balthasar's Theology of Drama in Dialogue with Hegel," *Modern Theology* 13, no. 3 (1997): 293–318.

Oddly enough, Quash argues that the atemporality of Balthasar's theology of Holy Saturday bespeaks Hegelian epic and as a result is too mythological (see "Drama and the Ends of Modernity," 167). I am not sure what would render atemporality mythological unless one presupposes the impossibilty of transcending temporality.

On the opposite side, see Cyril O'Regan, *The Anatomy of Misremembering: Von Balthasar's Response to Philosophical Modernity*, vol. 1, *Hegel* (New York: Herder & Herder, 2014); Vincent Holzer, "La kénose christologique dans la pensée de Hans Urs Von Balthasar: Une kénose christologique étendue à l'être de Dieu," *Theophilyon* 9, no. 1 (2004): 207–236.

[50] See, for example, *TD* V, 243 [G 219]. He implicitly resists accusations of Hegelian influence when he states late in his career (without much further clarification), "the term dialectic has a unique, theological sense that must not be confused with any of the many meanings that philosophy has given it" (*Theological Logical Theory:* vol. 2, *Truth of God*, trans. Adrian J. Walker [San Francisco: Ignatius Press, 2004], 238 [*Theologik*, Band II, *Wahrheit Gottes* (Einsiedeln: Johannes Verlag, 1985), 216]).

He adds: "Among these we can mention the Platonic art of conversation, Kant's 'dialectical appearance,' and Hegel's dialectical logic, in which thought and reality share a common, unity movement" (238n44 [G 216n44]). Also, in the same volume, he overtly opposes Hegelian dialectic: *TL* II, 317 and 336n32 [G 289 and 306n5].

[51] Some of his other favorite passages follow: "I have the keys of death and hell" (Rev 1:18); "If I ascend to heaven, you are there. If I make my bed in hell, you are there" (Ps 139:8); "[A] hardening has come upon part of Israel, until the full number of the Gentiles come in, and so Israel will be saved. . . . For God has consigned all men to disobedience, that he may have mercy upon all" (Rom. 11:25–26, 32).

He also makes much of Ephesians 4:1–10; Ben Quash comments: "it is a dramatic presentation of just the 'oneness' referred to. . . . The one God from whom nothing is ultimately alien or separable is the same God who, fully present in Christ, can ascend and descend to the furthest reaches of the created order. Nothing is outside his reach; nothing is 'beyond' him" ("The theo-drama," in *Cambridge Companion to Hans Urs von Balthasar*, 143–157, at 153).

quently be relativized."[52] He is thinking of passages such as Romans 8:3: "Sending his own Son in the likeness of sinful flesh and for sin, [God] condemned sin in the flesh." Therefore, from Scripture he derives his emphasis on the condemnation of sin in the very flesh assumed by the Word.[53]

Balthasar, though, is sometimes charged with neglecting the Church Fathers when he reflects upon the soteriological implications of such passages.[54] He frequently quotes Origen, but support is also found, for example, in Athanasius, who says: "Here, then, is the second reason why the Word dwelt among us, namely that . . . He might offer the sacrifice on behalf of all, surrendering His own temple to death *in place of all*."[55] With respect to the satisfaction theory of Anselm, Balthasar says, "We can avoid the medieval side of his theory, that is, the reparation of God's injured honor, but we must substitute for it the idea of a divine love scorned by sin."[56] Ultimately drawing his inspiration from Paul, he distinguishes his

---

[52] *Mystery of Redemption*, 28 [F 28].

[53] The same motif is found throughout the mystical experience of Adrienne von Speyr: see, for instance, her *John*, vol. 2, *The Discourses of Controversy: Meditations on John 6–12* (San Francisco: Ignatius Press, 1993), 137–138; *John*, vol. 3, *The Farewell Discourses: Meditations on John 13–17* (San Francisco: Ignatius Press, 1987), 18, 346. See also William Schmidt, *The Sacrament of Confession as "Sequela Christi" in the Writings of A. von Speyr* (PhD diss., Pontifical Lateran University, Rome, 1999). Available from Dissertation.com.

[54] Attempting to balance the various dimensions of redemption theory, he does make the following generic reference to the aspect of substitution in patristic times: "the Fathers stressed that it was through the 'exchange of places' (2) that man was initiated into 'divinization' (4); in this context, it was quite possible to see man's liberation from the 'powers' as a work of God's love (5)" (*TD* IV, 317 [G 295]).

He also briefly addresses early patristic thoughts on the *admirabile commercium* in conjunction with later patristic "limitations" imposed upon the theme (see *TD* IV, 246ff. [G 226ff.]), which he then traces further through Anselm and Thomas until Luther returns to an emphasis upon (and exaggeration of) the former.

For a more sympathetic treatment of Balthasar's assimilation of Nyssa, see Anthony Cirelli, "Reassessing the Meaning of Thought: Hans Urs von Balthasar's Retrieval of Gregory of Nyssa," *The Heythrop Journal* 50 (2009): 416–424. For a broader and more sympathetic understanding of Balthasar's interpretation of the Church Fathers, see Deirdre Carabine, "The Father's: The Church's Intimate, Youthful Diary," in *The Beauty of Christ: An Introduction to the Theology of Hans Urs von Balthasar*, ed. Bede McGregor, OP, and Thomas Norris (New York: T&T Clark, 1994), 73–91. For another assessment, see Werner Löser, *Im Geiste des Origenes: Hans Urs von Balthasar als Interpret der Theologie des Kirchenvater* (Frankfurt: Josef Knecht Verlag, 1976).

[55] *On the Incarnation*, ch. 4, n. 20 (emphasis added).

[56] *Mystery of Redemption*, 35 [F 37]. He says elsewhere regarding Anselm's understanding of redemption: "Although Anselm's thought is by no means as 'medieval' as his oppo-

own interpretation from that typically attributed to Luther and Calvin, saying "it is not a question of the punishment of an innocent in place of the guilty; that notion does not appear anywhere [in Scripture]. . . . It is much rather the idea of substitution (I am dropping the adjective 'penal') that is at the center, the apostolic *pro nobis*, with all that it contains of the mysterious."[57]

Balthasar certainly holds that judgment upon sin is assumed in Christ's flesh, and he emphasizes the consequent separation of sin from sinner:[58]

> Now the Cross of Christ is judgment [John 12:31, 16:10–11]. . . . This inexorable judgment falls on the anti-divine reality of the world, on sin, but it is Christ who, according to Paul, "was made sin." . . . The experience of abandonment by God is undoubtedly situated at the center of the event of the Cross. This experience is that of sin given over to the hands of divine justice, to the fire of God's holiness.[59]

---

nents today assume . . . the word 'representation,' which many Catholics prefer to avoid, is used without hesitation by Protestants. This indispensable concept introduces into theology something that Anselm had pondered deeply but had formulated in a rather narrow way" (*TD* III, 117–120n50 [G 106–109n1]).

David Edward Lauber wrote a dissertation on the "modified Anselmian understanding of the atonement" in Balthasar (and Barth)'s soteriology (see Lauber, "Towards a Theology of Holy Saturday: Karl Barth and Hans Urs von Balthasar on the *descensus ad inferna*" [PhD diss., Princeton Theological Seminary, 1999], 4).

[57] *Mystery of Redemption*, 34 [F 35]. Dropping the adjective "penal" may suffice to meet the common objection mentioned in passing by Celia Deane-Drummond that "the concept of penal substitution [is] highly problematic as a model of the atonement" ("The Breadth of Glory: A Trinitarian Eschatology for the Earth through Critical Engagement with Hans Urs von Balthasar," *International Journal of Systematic Theology* 12, no. 1 [2010]: 46–64, at 50).

[58] Thus, Jacques Servais also says:

> [A] human-divine love that impels him to allow universal sin to be concentrated in his person so that the separation between sin and sinner might be effected in it and, through it, in us, in conformity with the mysterious assertion of Saint Paul: "For our sake he made him to be sin [not sinner!] who knew no sin, so that in him we might become the [salvific] righteousness of God" (2 Cor. 5:21). For sin, the object of divine wrath (1 Thess. 2:16), came to dwell in the beloved man, and in order to extirpate it from his heart, Christ accomplished a gesture of substitution that is much more than a purely juridical transfer. (*Mystery of Redemption*, 119)

[59] *Mystery of Redemption*, 34–35 [F 35–36].

Taking the latter aspect as the goal of the former, it is easy to see how the former is always understood as an expression of the kenotic love of God. Thus, he says:

> In God, wrath is not a passion; it is the total reprobation of sin, which contradicts the divine goodness; and it can be said that God, in loving sinful man, hates the sin and condemns it. But that detested sin is found precisely in the beloved man: it is he who has committed it. *It was thus necessary to be able to find a method* to separate the sin from the sinner—and it is of this that the Pauline texts speak to us. . . . [I]t is a question of a gathering together, a concentration of universal sin in Christ.[60]

Therefore, his "theory" of redemption is a synthesis of Anselmic and Reformed notions of satisfaction, leaving aside the excessive penal or juridical emphasis of the latter.[61] John O'Donnell recapitulates Balthasar's logic:

> Although some theologians have taught that the Father punishes the Son on the cross, Balthasar never teaches this doctrine. What he does say is that the whole biblical tradition affirms the wrath of

---

[60] *Mystery of Redemption*, 24 [F 22–23] (emphasis added).

[61] Matthew Levering, aligning Balthasar with Anselm as opposed to Abelard (represented principally by Karl Rahner), nonetheless demonstrates the value of juridical language in Aquinas's satisfaction model, understood in the context of creation, even if his take on Balthasar is negative overall.

Levering may have a point when he says, "Balthasar's insistence upon substitution, rather than satisfaction, does not convey the centrality of Christ's active love. Humankind is healed by sharing in Christ's work of love, not by sharing in the passive degradation (imagined by substitution theory) in which the Father pours out his wrath upon the incarnate Son" ("Juridical Language in Soteriology: Aquinas's Approach," *Angelicum* 80 [2003]: 309–326, at 315).

The classic critique of Anselm's theory is Gustaf Aulen, *Christus Victor: A Historical Study of the Three Main Types of the Idea of the Atonement*, trans. A. G. Hebert (New York: Macmillan, 1951). Jacques Servais points to Balthasar's intention:

> With the intention of better expressing the intrinsic character of the exchange between the Innocent one and sinners, von Balthasar proposes the notion of substitution (*Stellvertretung*), which to him signifies a true exchange of place (*Platztausch*), in accordance with the thought of Saint Paul: "Christ . . . though he was rich, yet for your sake he became poor, so that by his poverty you might become rich" (2 Cor. 8:9). The term suggests the gesture of someone who takes something upon himself in order to be able to remove it from the other. (*Mystery of Redemption*, 127–128)

God, and, indeed, that Jesus on the cross experiences this wrath. How should we understand this concept of the wrath of God? God's wrath is linked to his holiness. Moreover, God's wrath cannot be separated from his love. Since God is love, he must reject sin. Sin, which is hatred, cannot be incorporated into the divine life. Hence when God encounters lovelessness, he can only react with wrath. But, as Balthasar insists, God pours out his wrath on the sinner for the sake of his mercy. God manifests his wrath so that the sinner will be converted and so will be saved. On the cross, Jesus so identifies with sinners that the Father sees in him the "no" of humanity. To that "no" the Father can only react with wrath. Hence Jesus dies in absolute obedience to the Father. He remains the pure yes of obedience. Thus the Father also sees in him a radical "yes." As we have seen before, the death of Jesus is pure love in the midst of contradiction. He is separated from the Father insofar as he is made sin. He is in union with the Father insofar as his death represents his loving obedience.[62]

White notes the most distinctive feature of Balthasar's theory: "Most notably, Balthasar claims that the biblical concept of 'hell' takes on a new definition *in light of* Christ's separation from God on the Cross: All finite separations of sinful human beings must now be understood as encompassed by the 'ever-greater' separation of Christ from the Father in his descent into hell."[63] The Cross for Balthasar goes beyond mere solidarity with sinners to the point of separating sin itself from each person in whom it may reside (at any point in time), and his passion is therefore beyond any other, as *the* manifestation of Trinitarian love. It is true, "he achieves redemption for humanity by making the sinner's death of godlessness his own and by taking up God's wrath against the sinner into the disarming inner-divine communion of love where that wrath is transformed into love."[64] But since it is above all a work of the Trinity, an economic reflection of His immanent self-surrender, He is bound to suffer an eminently unique hell, in some ways incomparable to any other.[65] Lösel notes the following:

---

[62] O'Donnell, *Hans Urs von Balthasar*, 109.

[63] White, "Von Balthasar and Journet," 656 (emphasis original).

[64] Lösel, "A Plain Account," 166–167.

[65] See, for example, *TD* V, 256 [G 231].

[Balthasar] maintains that the dead must enter the *infernum* only as *if* it were their eternal place of damnation. Because of Christ's descent, however, sheol has only a conditional character for the dead. To account for this soteriological paradox, Balthasar speaks of the "paradoxical and self-annulling concept of a 'provisional *poena damni.*'" If the *poena damni* of those awaiting redemption in sheol is only limited and conditional, Jesus alone experiences hell to the fullest extreme. In fact, for Balthasar, hell is an exclusive experience of the divine Savior. Jesus' solidarity with the dead in sheol thus turns into Jesus' substitution for the dead in hell.[66]

In this way, sin itself becomes "severed" from mankind[67] and suffering itself is redeemed.[68] Birot says, "[T]he concept [of substitution] as applied to Christ contains a moment of the Trinitarian order which raises it beyond a simply physical or juridical representation. He who bears the sin of the world, Balthasar will say, does not simply suffer 'hell' in our place, but much more: something unique, something that transcends the notion of a simple changing of place."[69]

Birot also notes that Balthasar recalls Bulgakov's theology of the "lamb slain before the foundation of the world," according to which Christ suffers "something incomparable with and even contrary to the suffering of sinners," and yet it does encompass in its own way the tor-

---

[66] "A Plain Account," 151.

[67] See, for example, *Mysterium Paschale: The Mystery of Easter*, trans. Aidan Nichols (San Francisco: Ignatius, 1990), 173; "Mysterium Paschale," in *Mysterium Salutis: Grundriss heilsgeschichtlicher Dogmatik*, Band III: *Das Christusereignis*, Teil 2, ed. Johannes Feiner and Magnus Lohrer (Einsiedeln: Benziger Verlag, 1969): 133–326, at 246–247. See also Lösel, "A Plain Account," 151, citing *Theologik* II, 317.

[68] Balthasar says:

> I think that the proclamation of the Cross can help men accept sufferings that often seem intolerable, to accept them, not because a God suffers in solidarity with them—how would that relieve them?—but because a divine suffering encompasses all these sufferings in order to transform them into prayer, into a dialogue in the midst of abandonment, thereby conferring on all human tragedies a meaning they would not have in themselves, a meaning that is in the end redemptive for the salvation of the world." (*Mystery of Redemption*, 39 [F 41–42])

[69] Birot, "Redemption in Balthasar," 275. Also, "when the Son becomes incarnate and penetrates into the darkness of the world, he is able to 'take the place' of darkness and 'substitute' (*Stell-vertretung*) himself for it by virtue of his very position in the Trinity" (Birot, 282).

ments of hell.[70] For Balthasar, the hell that Christ suffers is that of God's infinite wrath towards sin itself because of God's "zeal" for His covenant, as revealed in the Old and New Testaments.[71] The radicality and uniqueness of Balthasar's take on the descent is evident perhaps above all in the following outline of its atemporality:

> Jesus does experience the darkness of the sinful state, not in the same way as the (God-hating) sinner experiences it (unless the sinner is spared such experience), but nonetheless in a deeper and darker experience. This is because it takes place in the profound depths of the relations between the divine Hypostases—which are inaccessible to any creature. Thus it is just as possible to maintain that Jesus' being forsaken by God was the opposite of hell as to say that it *was* hell (Luther, Calvin) or even the ultimate heightening of hell (Quenstedt). . . . [H]is experience of being abandoned on the Cross is timeless. Here too it is analogous to hell. This is why its actuality persists through all ages of the world. Jesus' agony lasts until the end of the world (Pascal); in fact, it goes back to the world's beginning. His mortal wounds are eternally open (Berulle). This timelessness is confirmed, in some precision, by those

---

[70] See Birot, "Redemption in Balthasar," 279–280, citing *TD* IV, 313ff. Indeed, it appears that Balthasar has borrowed much from this Russian Orthodox theologian's Trinitarian theory of redemption: see, e.g., *TD* IV, 313–314 [G 291–292].

[71] See Balthasar, *TD* IV, 338ff. [G 315ff.] He cites the following Old Testament passages for the notion of divine wrath: Isa 51:17, 22; Jer 13:13, 25:15–17, 27ff., 48:26, 49:12, 51:7; Ezek 23:32–34; Hab 2:15–16; Obad 16; Zech 12:2; Ps 79:9; Lam 4:21; Isa 53:1–6; Rev 19:15; Gen 49:9–12; Jer 25:30; Isa 63:1–6; Joel 4:13.

Birot states,

> [A]ny interpretation which views the suffering of the Cross as a *punishment* must be rejected: the Crucified one does not (simply) suffer the hell merited by sinners, he suffers something much more profound: an abandonment by God (Mk. 15:34), such as he alone is able to know it, a separation from his Father that surpasses all of the distances which separate God from sinners; in short, a suffering that no creature will ever be able to measure, and which alone is capable, *through a miracle of love*, of a qualitative "undergirding" (*Unterfassung*) of the sin of the world, in order to transform its alienation. Moreover, the suffering endured by Christ must be defined, also following scripture, as the experience of *the wrath of God* (338ff.), the cup of which Jesus accepted at Gethsemani [sic]. The Old and New Testaments attest to the reality of this wrath so forcefully (as much as love and mercy) that it is impossible to dismiss. Wrath consists (in the prophets) in God's "zeal" for his covenant. ("Redemption in Balthasar," 283 [emphasis original])

Christian mystics who are privileged to experience something of the dark night of the Cross.[72]

THE TIMELESSNESS OF CHRIST'S DESCENT

The cry of dereliction or abandonment, which comes to represent the depths of suffering into which the God-man descends in that timeless event celebrated on Holy Saturday, plays the most pivotal role in salvation history for Balthasar.[73] The descent of Christ into the hell that is His death (Sheol and Gehenna are understood to be the same)[74] is the most

---

[72] *TD* IV, 336–337 [G 313] (emphasis original). See also his peculiar treatment of time and "super-time" with respect to Jesus's death and Resurrection in *TD* V, 29–32 [G 24–26]. In *Das Ganze im Fragment*, a much earlier work, he states:

> True, the Son no longer hangs bleeding on the cross. But since the three hours of agony between heaven and earth were already the breakthrough of time into the eternal, as of eternity into the temporal—hours which cannot be measured by any chronological time, by any psychological feeling of time ("Jesus is in agony until the end of the world"—Pascal)—so the divine-human suffering is the most precious relic that the resurrected Christ, now free of pain, takes with him from his earthly pilgrimage into his heavenly glory. . . . It is true that Christ in heaven no longer suffers, but it is also true that the phenomena of his suffering are real, and not fictitious, expressions of his heavenly being. This being is not a quantitative intensification of the joy he knew on earth with all the sufferings excluded. It is not related to his earthly life at all in this partial and antithetical manner—with the same proportions of joy and suffering—but, rather, in the form of a total transfiguration and making eternal." (*A Theological Anthropology*, trans. Benziger Verlag [New York: Sheed and Ward, 1967], 247–248; *Das Ganze im Fragment* (Einsiedeln: Benziger Verlag, 1963), 272–273])

[73] In his earlier work, Balthasar seems to draw a sharper distinction between the events of Good Friday and Holy Saturday, but he seems to transition more and more in his later works, perhaps under the influence of Joseph Ratzinger, toward the view that the article of the descent is fulfilled by Christ's *kenosis* on the Cross, culminating in His death. For example, compare *Explorations* IV, 406 [G 392], to *MP*, 164 [G 240]. Ratzinger throughout his writings collapses the suffering aspect of the descent event into Christ's passion and death on Friday, even though the descent proper is celebrated on Holy Saturday; this will be elaborated upon in chapter four below.

[74] According to Balthasar, the Jewish tradition leading up to the time of Christ saw "Sheol [as] more and more equated with Gehenna, the preliminary place of punishment leading to ultimate damnation" (*TD* V, 354 [G 323]), which would indicate that everyone was consigned to the same realm of perdition before Christ—this position seems to function as an interpretation of the texts as constitutive of a mythological signification of the fact that everyone is destined to hell prior to Christ's redemptive descent.
It is, nevertheless, thanks to His transformative passion that, perhaps, His timeless

perfect reflection of the self-surrender that constitutes the infinite love of the Trinity itself. In fact, the Cross is the revelation of the Trinity:

> "The Son has been offering his sacrifice to the Father from the very beginning." There is a certain quality of "renunciation" in the eternal Trinitarian life: it is seen in the very fact that "the Father, renouncing his uniqueness, generates the Son out of his own substance," which can be designated a "pre-sacrifice." Once sin emerges, this "pre-sacrifice" turns into "actual renunciation," "just as, as on the basis of the 'pre-sacrifice' of the Son's eternal generation, God will unfold the Son's redemptive experience of forsakenness on the Cross." The Cross, and the Incarnation that envisages it, remain present reality within time "because they themselves are not the first thing: they are grounded in an eternal, heavenly will on the part of the Son to surrender and sacrifice himself, inseparably linked to the love of the triune God. The meaning of the Cross is only complete in God; it is in God that the Son's eternal self-surrender, which integrates his sacrificial death in time . . . in eternity the Son's will to give himself goes to these extreme lengths . . . it keeps this fulfillment [of the Cross] alive until the end of time and for all eternity." Thus there is nothing hypothetical about the "pre-sacrifice" of the Son (and hence of the Trinity): it is something utterly real, which includes the absolute and total exhaustion of the Cross. "All this is implicit from all eternity in the Son's decision, even if it is only completed historically on the Cross. . . . [S]acrifice, suffering, the Cross and death are only the reflection of tremendous realities in the Father, in heaven, in eternal life"; indeed, "they are nothing other than manifestations of what heaven is, namely, the love of God that goes to the ultimate."[75]

---

love encounters the freedom of every man in the mysterious "moment" of His death (which is thus understood in personalistic terms as an existential event). Again, "in the era after Christ 'Gehenna' is sometimes given a purifying function" (*TD* V, 361–362 [G 330]); thereafter he elaborates upon the judgment as purifying.

[75] *TD* V, 510–511 [G 466–467].

> [T]he infinite distinction of Persons within the one Being. In virtue of this distinction, which entails relations within the Trinity and hence facilitates that "laying up" of which we have spoken, the *Cross* can become "the revelation of the innermost being of God." It reveals both the distinction of the Persons (clearest in the dereliction) and the unity of their Being, which becomes visible

His heavy dependence here on Adrienne von Speyr's mystical visions lends itself to the ready critique of a need for a demythologization of the inherited language in order to distinguish adequately between the economic and immanent orders, which Balthasar attempts at times but with only partial success.[76]

It is with Adrienne's help that Balthasar conceives of time and eternity as mutually interpenetrating, thanks to the Incarnation: "'The Father is in eternal life, and the time of his heaven is eternal time; in seeking this eternal time we are joining the Son in seeking the kingdom in the super-time of eternal life.' . . . If, in Jesus Christ, eternal life has genuinely penetrated the world's temporal sphere, this temporal sphere does not unfold 'outside' eternity but within it."[77] Therefore, even His suffering takes on a timeless dimension—again he quotes von Speyr: "His mission is not temporal . . . there is a moment in history in which he suffers. But it is preceded by the timelessness in the bosom of God. . . . What is timeless is the real; the temporal is only a shadow of it."[78] Thus, just as "we can inscribe the temporal upon the eternal,"[79] so the temporal is in a sense eternalized. But the timelessness of heaven is different from the timelessness of hell. Heaven's time is a super-temporality, whereas hell is akin to being frozen in time. Christ embraced both realities, plumbing the depths of nonbeing first in order to bridge the chasm between it and *ipsum amor*.[80] Hence, Balthasar says:

[H]e can only punish men out of love, and in doing so he can take everything from them, timelessly, and return it to them, also timelessly. For the latter to be true, we must consider a third form of timelessness that coincides neither with the first (the bliss of

---

in the unity of the plan of redemption. Only a God-man, through his distinction-in-relation vis-à-vis the Father, can expiate and banish that alienation from God that characterizes the world's sin, both in totality for all and in totality for each individual. (*TD* V, 259–260 [G 234–235])

[76] I am thinking, for instance, of his continuous attempt to distinguish but adequately relate the economic and immanent dimension of the Trinity, rather than assuming simple identification. Speyr's passion experiences can be found in her journals, *Kreuz und Hölle* (Einsiedeln: Johannes Verlag, 1966); see also the much briefer account in Adrienne von Speyr and Hans Urs von Balthasar, "L'expérience du Samedi Saint," *Communio: Revue Catholique Internationale* 6 (Janvier–Fevrier 1981): 63–68.

[77] *TD* V, 250 [G 226].

[78] *TD* V, 251–252 [G 227].

[79] *TD* V, 264 [G 239].

[80] Drawing again on von Speyr, he seems to say the descent transforms hell into purgatory: see *TD* V, 363 [G 331].

God and of those in God) nor with the second (hell) . . . it is the condition of timelessness undergone by the Son on the Cross. . . . We have already said that it is possible for the Son to take upon himself the sinners' forfeiture of God only on the basis of a communion [*Unterfassung*] that renders the Son's state even more timeless than the timelessness of hell, since he alone, by taking into himself the sinners' God-forsakenness, can fully know what the loss of the Father means. Those Christians who are found worthy to experience something of the dark night of Christ's Cross have a faint idea of what this forsakenness is.[81]

Finally, in his *Theo-Logic*, although Balthasar is sometimes reticent to elaborate on the precise meaning of Adrienne's own statements, which he nevertheless quotes profusely without criticism,[82] there we find his latest account of the relationship between temporality and hell. He states:

"Hell is timeless": von Speyr hammers home this principle over and over again in many variations. The Cross itself was atemporal, because all the sins of past and future were gathered in the Son who had been "made sin." Hell is atemporal in another way, because it is definitive and affords no prospect of escape on any side. Thus, "hell is the extreme opposite to heaven, where all time is fulfilled in God's eternity." The absolute solitude of hell also makes this apparent. Since its "substance" is the sin of the world, become (or becoming) anonymous, there is no community in hell; one simply goes "missing" there without a trace. Everything that looks like love is now deposited; nor is there any hope. Consequently, one can at most guess at the footsteps of the Lord who has passed through hell, but because there is no path in hell,

---

[81] *TD* V, 307–308 [G 280–281]. He seems to contradict the point about the timelessness of Christ's Cross a few pages later, quoting von Speyr: see *TD* V, 310 [G 282].

[82] On the intended union of heart and mind between the two, see Johann Roten, SM, "The Two Halves of the Moon: Marian Anthropological Dimensions in the Common Mission of Adrienne von Speyr and Hans Urs von Balthasar," in *Hans Urs von Balthasar: His Life and Work*, ed. David Schindler (San Francisco: Ignatius Press, 2011). See also L. M. Miles, "An Introduction to Adrienne von Speyr," *First Things* (November 7, 2013), available at https://www.firstthings.com/web-exclusives/2013/11/an-introduction-to-adrienne-von-speyr, and the recent book on Speyr by Matthew Lewis Sutton, *Heaven Opens: The Trinitarian Mysticism of Adrienne von Speyr* (Minneapolis, MN: Fortress Press, 2014).

there is no following him, either, and his footsteps cannot really be located. There is only the purely objective stock-taking of the abomination that is the sin of the world.[83]

Then, in a footnote to this text, he quotes more of Speyr on the atemporality of "the Cross":

"On the Cross a total destruction of time occurs . . . ; now the hour in the true sense has come, but it has no direction." "The atemporality on the Cross is wholly relative to the suffering Lord. In hell, on the other hand, it is a property of the place" (ibid [*Kreuze und Hölle*], 240, 260). On the Cross "the whole of eternal time leads into the eternity of the Cross," because the Cross has always already been decided upon and must bear fruit for every past and coming eternity (ibid., 284). But this "totally destroys time" (ibid., 285). "The experience of agony that is had here stretches over the totality of time" (ibid., 362). In hell, however, time as such is "lost"; the attempt "to express it presupposes that one lives under the law of time and not in the timelessness that is neither eternity nor past time; it is not even the moment."[84]

There appears to be a contrast here between the timelessness of the Cross and the timelessness of hell proper,[85] but whether one extrapolates from such mystical reflections that the timelessness of Christ's sufferings are to be allocated to "Friday" or extended also into "Saturday,"[86] one thing is clear—that His hellish sufferings, although endured in time, transcend the ordinary time of earth not only in efficacy, but also psychologically (i.e., not merely objectively, but subjectively as well).[87] Without claiming

---

[83] *TL* II, 348–350 [G 318–319].

[84] *TL* II, 349n100 [G 318n26].

[85] On the other hand, Balthasar also reports Speyr stating: "Cross and hell are inseparable, like a single coin with two sides" (*TL* II, 232). This gives rise to "the question whether hell, which is the eternal night of sin, is so included in the mystery of the Trinity that the sin vanquished on the Cross is ultimately used to solidify what (at the Cross) still remains of the world's shaken structure (KH 1, 207–8)" (*TL* II, 346n79 [G 316n5]).

[86] Perhaps his clearest statement on the matter appears in his *Engagement with God: The Drama of Christian Discipleship*, trans. R. John Halliburton (San Francisco: Ignatius Press, 2008): "He arrives in the realm where time and space are nonexistent, whereas for us (on Holy Saturday), chronological or surface time continues. Then from the timeless, spaceless darkness of hell . . ." (36).

[87] To better understand this point, it may be instructive to consult Ratzinger's under-

definitively that Balthasar, at one point in his career or another, locates the atemporality of Christ's sufferings on Friday (that is, the historical dimension of the Cross), I would like to defend a more modest form of this "untraditional" approach to the descent, inspired by Joseph Ratzinger.

---

standing of purgatorial time in terms of the "existential moment" (*memoria* time); See *Eschatology: Death and Eternal Life*, trans. Michael Waldstein (Washington, DC: The Catholic University of America, 1988), 183–184, 230ff.; *Eschatologie: Tod und ewiges Leben*, (Regensburg: Friedrich Pustet, 1977), 151–152, 187ff.

CHAPTER TWO

A Response to Critiques of Balthasar's Theology of Descent-Suffering

IN THIS WORK, I do not intend to shy away from legitimate criticisms of Balthasar's theology. But, in this chapter, I will seek to defend a charitable interpretation of some of the points on which it seems he has not been evaluated in an entirely fair manner. I think primarily of Alyssa L. Pitstick's *Light in Darkness*, and thus will engage her debate with Edward T. Oakes in the context of her concern about the testimony of tradition. But I will dedicate most of my attention to more sagacious scholars, focusing on the critique of the eminent Dominican theologian, Thomas Joseph White, whose criticisms are worthy of consideration but nonetheless sometimes miss the points at which Balthasar may be driving. After presenting the chief points of critique proffered, I will attempt to clarify the meaning of Balthasar's doctrine of Christ's descent-suffering by means of a particular interpretation with these points in mind, before finally addressing the common theological concern that Balthasar's theology of the descent has no precedent in the (Catholic) Christian intellectual tradition. Hopefully, it becomes clear that while some of Balthasar's language may involve rhetorical excess, he offers legitimate soteriological insight into the profundity of Christ's suffering.

CHIEF CRITICISMS OF BALTHASAR ON THE DESCENT

White contests Balthasar's interpretation of the descent in his article, "Jesus' Cry on the Cross and His Beatific Vision," on the grounds of a Thomistic interpretation of the Catholic doctrine of Christ's *visio immediata*

Dei.[1] While White concedes with Thomas that Christ's beatific vision must have increased the acuity with which He suffered the sinfulness of man,[2] he argues against Balthasar that Christ's consciousness could not have suffered anything akin to damnation. He cites the authority of Thomas on the ability of Christ both to suffer "in the entirety of His soul" and to be consoled by "the Father's presence in the 'entirety of his soul.' . . . In this way, the happiness of being united in will with the Father could coexist with extreme agony in Christ, such that the two experiences were objectively distinct but subjectively (and therefore experientially) inseparable."[3] He also recalls the following:

> Following Damascene (*De Fide Orth.*, bk. III, ch. 19), Aquinas insists that the divine will suspended some of the experiences of consolation in the soul of Christ which would normally be present even in the suffering of a virtuous man. The point of such unique suffering is to manifest more profoundly the gravity of

---

[1] White, "Jesus' Cry on the Cross and His Beatific Vision," *Nova et Vetera* (English Edition) 5, no. 3 (2007): 555–582. A particular understanding of this doctrine and its relationship to the passion of Christ will be explored more in the next chapter.

[2] Drawing upon Matthew Levering's reading of Thomas (see *Sacrifice and Community: Jewish Offering and Christian Eucharist* [Oxford: Blackwell Publishing, 2005], 80), White says:

> The immediate vision in the soul of Christ, then, gave him a profound spiritual and psychological awareness of his confrontation with moral evil, and of his rejection by sinners. The conclusion I wish to draw here is that this knowledge necessarily *augmented* desire for our salvation *even as it simultaneously augmented his agony.* The two are inseparable, and both result from the presence in the soul of Christ of the beatific vision. ("Jesus' Cry on the Cross," 579, emphasis original; cf. 575)

See Thomas, *ST* III, q. 46, a. 6. I will elaborate upon this dimension of the issue in the next chapter.

[3] White, "Jesus' Cry on the Cross," 575; cf. 574. Thomas says,

> It is evident that Christ's whole soul suffered. . . . Christ's "higher reason" did not suffer thereby *on the part of its object,* which is God, who was the cause, not of grief, but rather of delight and joy, to the soul of Christ. Nevertheless, all the powers of Christ's soul did suffer according as any faculty is said to be affected *as regarded its subject,* because all the faculties of Christ's soul were rooted in its *essence, to which suffering extended* while the body, whose act it is, suffered. (*ST* III, q. 46, a. 7, emphasis added by White in n. 54)

This position is not subject to Balthasar's criticism in *Theo-Logic*; see *TL* II, 286–287 [G 261].

human sin as well as the unique love of Christ for human beings.[4]

But he proceeds to draw the conclusion that this concomitant joy excludes the possibility of Christ enduring those pains most fundamental to damnation, namely, definitive deprivation of grace and a personal aversion to the will of God.[5]

The reason White gives for Christ's inability to empty Himself to the point of suffering "damnation" is that despair, hatred of God, and the habitual state of sin characterizing the damned are not congruent with the blessedness of a soul hypostatically united to the Word. White certainly has a point in cautioning against "damnation language" as incongruent with the persistent *caritas* of Christ's soul.[6] Perhaps neglecting 2 Corinthians 5:

---

[4] White, "Jesus' Cry on the Cross," 576n57; see Thomas, *ST* III, q. 46, a. 3; q. 46, a. 6, co. and ad 2.

[5] See White, 559.

[6] White argues, "Because of this radical difference of causalities [love and its refusal], the two states that derive from them can rightfully be said to be essentially dissimilar. If this is the case, then they cannot be compared 'analogically' and the attribution of a 'state of damnation' to the sufferings of Christ implies a pure equivocation" ("Jesus' Cry on the Cross," 562n23).

Concerning the language of hell and damnation in regard to Christ's suffering, Balthasar at points speaks of Christ suffering even the "second death," as is peppered throughout *Mysterium Paschale*, which he nonetheless eschews as "a quickly written work" (*TL* II, 345n75 [G 315n1]), but at another point, he states the opposite in a less formal setting (a radio broadcast): "it makes no sense to call this suffering Hell, for in Jesus there is no kind of hatred of God" (*Du kronst das Jahr mit deiner Huld: Radio-predigten* [Einsiedeln: 1982], 75f., cited by John Saward, *The Mysteries of March: Hans Urs von Balthasar on the Incarnation and Easter* [London: Collins Religious Publishing, 1990], 44).

Balthasar defends his use of the word "hell" to describe Christ's sufferings thus: "The 'God-hostile flesh' (Rom 8:7), insofar as it is anti-divine, is incompatible with God; it is cast out of the cosmos that belongs to him 'into the outer darkness.' This darkness is, not death, but that which we can only term 'hell.' . . . The experience he undergoes is without analogies and stands apart from all other experiences" (*TL* II, 326 [G 297]).

Sachs also quotes from *The Von Balthasar Reader* the following excerpt from "Abstieg zur Hölle" (found also in *Explorations* IV): "[the abandoned Christ] disturbs the absolute loneliness striven for by the sinner: the sinner, who wants to be 'damned' apart from God, finds God again in his loneliness, but God in the absolute weakness of love who unfathomably in the period of noontime enters into solidarity with those damning themselves. The words of the Psalm, 'If I make my bed in the netherworld, thou art there' (Ps 139:8), thereby take on a totally new meaning" (see John R. Sachs, S.J., "Current Eschatology: Universal Salvation and the Problem of Hell," *Theological Studies* 52 [1991]: 227–254).

In this way, hell becomes a "gift of divine grace" (*Theodramatik* IV, 287f. and 293,

21 and Galatians 3:13, he emphasizes satisfaction in a non-substitutionary manner, pointing to St. Thomas:

> Aquinas, meanwhile, holds that Christ did subject himself to our fallen state for our sake and, in this sense, took our punishments upon himself for our redemption. But he also notes that it is impossible for an innocent man to submit to a penal substitution for the guilt due to another, as if he were to assume the sins of the other (*ST* I-II, q. 87, aa. 7-8). Instead, Christ "substitutes" his obedience for our disobedience so as to repair in our human nature the injustice done to God's loving wisdom by human sin.[7]

Apparently identifying any substitutionary approach as penal,[8] he adds the following:

> In discussing Paul's claim that "For our sake [God] made him to be sin who knew no sin, so that in him we might become the righteousness of God" (2 Cor 5:21), Aquinas (*In II Cor.* V, lec. 5, no. 201 [Marietti]) purposefully excludes any idea of a penal substitution (in which Christ would be himself representative of the sinner and suffer a vicarious punishment for guilt on our behalf). Instead, he refers this verse to Christ's assumption out

---

cited by Sachs, 244n76). These comments, however, are surrounded by rhetorical (or rather, mystical) excess, bordering on the mythological, which is not necessarily to stipulate that the excess derives from Speyr, as Balthasar himself may be at fault. Hence, Lois M. Miles notes the differences as follows:

> With regard to the abandonment, von Speyr emphasizes the constant presence and unity of the Father and the Spirit throughout the Son's experience, while von Balthasar seems (especially in *Mysterium Paschale*) to emphasize the extreme distance to which the Trinitarian unity can be stretched in order to include the Son's passage through the depths of the underworld. However, he follows von Speyr directly concerning the unity of the Triune God in *Theo-Drama V*. ("Obedience of a Corpse: The Key to the Holy Saturday Writings of Adrienne von Speyr" [PhD diss., University of Aberdeen, 2013], 177)

7 White, "Jesus' Cry on the Cross," 564n29.
8 Gérard Rémy tends to do the same in his two articles critical of Balthasar's soteriology, "La substitution: Pertinence ou non-pertinence d'un concept théologique," *Revue Thomiste* 94 (1994): 559–600 (see especially 562–564). See also Rémy's "La déréliction du Christ: Terme d'une contradiction ou mystère de communion?," *Revue Thomiste* 98 (1998): 39–94, which treats the occasionally excessive language in Balthasar as regulative, similar to White's analysis.

of love for us of a human nature capable of death and suffering (states that are consequences of sin).[9]

Finding substitution and satisfaction competitive, White therefore comments with regard to the pains proper to hell:

> Calvin suggests that the "pains of hell" experienced by Christ consist *principally* in his dread, sorrow, and fear of being forsaken by God as well as his experience of the wrath of God against human sin. Here what defines the state at essence is the judgment and wrath of God. I am suggesting, by contrast, that the pains of damnation stem, instead, from the voluntary refusal to embrace God's loving will, and the deprivation of the vision of God that results.[10]

Although he admits the presence of hope in the human soul of Christ,[11] he

---

9   White, "Jesus' Cry on the Cross," 576n58. Compare to Balthasar's excavation of scriptural and ecclesial sources for conceiving redemption in terms of vicarious representation (*Stellvertretung*) in *TD* III, 82–85, 113–114, 244 [G 74–77, 103–104, 224]; *GL* VII, 149 [G 137].

10   White, "Jesus' Cry on the Cross," 564 (emphasis original).

11   White seems to assert under the authority of Thomas Aquinas that Christ had theological hope (although Thomas is notorious for denying theological faith to Christ) in the following:

> Yet, hope is a complex virtue, according to Aquinas, precisely because within it expectation/desire can and do coexist with the non-possession of that which is hoped for. This means that in hope, desire and sadness, deprivation, and agony can and often do coexist. Pushing the question one step further we can ask if this desire *was itself* the "cause" of an increased suffering and agony? If so, then this inner tension of desire (as both hope and suffering) is a possible explanation for the inner meaning of the death cry of the crucified Christ." ("Jesus' Cry on the Cross," 565)

Again, he says:

> As Justin Martyr first noted, therefore, it suggests on Christ's part the *purposeful* invocation of a psalm, denoting an act of prayer and implying a claim to prophetic fulfillment. This line of reasoning raises the question of whether the invocation of the psalm by the historical Jesus implies that he was expressing a messianic hope even during his crucifixion. . . . In this case, the hope of vindication by God (such as that which occurs at the end of the psalm) could well be intended even in citing its opening line. ("Jesus' Cry on the Cross," 560–561)

He proceeds to argue there that in such a case there could not have been an "experience

cannot acknowledge the possibility of the coexistence of hope and a profound experience of separation (akin to the dark feelings of hellish despair experienced even by the mystics).[12]

Having similar concerns, Alyssa Pitstick transmutes her concern over deficiencies in Balthasar's Trinitarian theology into an indictment of Balthasar's apparent allocation of the deepest sufferings of Christ to Holy Saturday instead of Good Friday, a move impugned as Calvinistic and heretical.[13] It is certainly a valid question whether for Balthasar the key moment of redemption ought to be located in the passion or the descent.[14] Although it usually appears that Balthasar's view of Holy Saturday is atemporal, there are some texts that suggest he does hold the error ascribed to him by Pitstick. For example, in his *Explorations in Theology*, he says: "the descent into hell between Christ's death and resurrection is a necessary expression of the event of the redemption—not, indeed (as on Good Friday), within the history actually in progress, but (on Holy Saturday) in the history already accomplished of the old aeon, in the sheol of the Old Testament."[15] More clearly, he says in another work: "And here we encounter the well-known view of Luther, and above all of Calvin, according to which Jesus experienced on the Cross Hell's tortures in place of sinners, thus rendering superfluous a similar experience of Hell on Holy Saturday."[16] From

---

of radical disillusionment, despair, or accusation underlying Christ's last words."

[12] See White, 564–565. Balthasar not only admits the copresence of hope and an experience of total despair (on behalf of the lost), but he also seems to argue at points for a coexistence of beatific vision and theological faith in Christ. See *TL* II, 286–288 [G 261–263].

[13] See Alyssa L. Pitstick, *Light in Darkness* (Grand Rapids, MI: Eerdmans, 2007).

[14] It will become clear that Balthasar often subsumes both descent and passion under the keyword "Cross," which apparently for him serves to indicate the entirety of the passion, which culminates in the descent; the question is how precisely to understand the latter (in relation to His death).

[15] *Explorations in Theology*, vol. 1, *The Word Made Flesh*, trans. A. V. Littledale and Alexander Dru (San Francisco: Ignatius, 1989), 263; *Verbum Caro: Skizzen zur theologie*, Band I (Einsiedeln: Johannes Verlag, 1960), 286. Balthasar and Speyr may differ slightly on the Sheol-hell relationship:

> Von Balthasar analyses Old Testament death in Sheol and the creation of hell by the Son's descent. Von Speyr does not specifically explain differences between a pre-Christ Sheol and a post-Christ hell. She describes a partitioning of the underworld into hell proper and purgatory as well as opening the gates to heaven by the Son's passage through the abyss, but leaves the analysis to von Balthasar. He not only analyzes the content of von Speyr's writings but extends them along his particular lines of interest. (Miles, "Obedience of a Corpse," 184)

[16] *MP*, 169 [G 244].

these texts, it could be concluded that he is in error on this point and inconsistent with the existential approach to time and suffering.[17]

EVALUATION

While most scholars agree that for Balthasar there was always some consciousness in Jesus of His divine identity and yet real ignorance assumed (miraculously) for the sake of solidarity with sinners in His missionary descent into the dark depths of the human condition,[18] I have already quoted Balthasar to the effect that there is a greater separation between Christ on the Cross and the Father than there ever could be between damned souls and God. Critics are right to ask how this may be possible if Christ never lost the virtue of charity in His soul and damned souls (if there be any) are condemned precisely in their lack of *caritas*. The answer can be found, among other places, in the final volume of the *Theo-Drama*.[19]

The "separation" between God and Christ crucified is only phenom-

---

[17] It may be worth noting, however, that Pitstick does not quote such necessary proof texts.

[18] Lösel incorrectly asserts that for Balthasar, "Jesus does not know about his own divine identity" because of His absolute solidarity with sinners (see "A Plain Account," 144n15). Ben Quash correctly states:

> Balthasar believes that in his incarnate state Jesus knows (though initially only in a latent way) of his identity as the Son of God, but holds that he does not know the details of what the Father through the Spirit will set before him from moment to moment for the fulfillment of his mission. Jesus is aware of the formal scope of his mission, but uncertain of its content. Instead, he utterly abandons himself to the Father who guides him by the Spirit and in whom he has complete trust. He acts in a certain "economic ignorance" [he cites *TD* IV, 234].... For just this reason we can ascribe obedience and faith to him, and the perfection of his obedience (dependent as it is to some extent upon "not-knowing") is, paradoxically, one of the best demonstrations of his divine character as the "One Sent." ("The theo-drama" in *Cambridge Companion to Hans Urs von Balthasar*, 143–157, at 150–151)

[19] In the previous volume, there is the distinction between the godlessness of this world and divine godlessness or the godlessness of love (see *TD* IV, 323–324 [G 300–302]). Balathasar also says in reference to Christ's experience of abandonment on the Cross, "this is where Christ 'represents' us, takes our place: what is 'experienced' is the opposite of what the facts indicate" (*TD* IV, 335–336 [G 312]); there follows a footnote in which he quotes V. Taylor stating, "[J]esus felt the horror of sin so deeply that for a time the closeness of his communion with the Father was obscured. Glover writes: 'I have sometimes thought there never was an utterance that reveals more amazingly the distance between feeling and fact'" (*TD* IV, 336n8 [G 312n8]).

enal—it is a profound subjective experience, a psychological separation, not a metaphysical one (i.e., not the objective separation that exists where *caritas* does not).[20] But this subjective psychological experience of phenomenal rupture reflects, manifests, expresses, and reveals the "infinite distance" between the divine persons as self-subsisting relations of opposition.[21] Condemned souls exist in objective separation from the love of God. What they suffer is a subjective experience of separation or condemnation. In assuming the cursedness of sin itself by means of His descent into the being-dead of man, God suffers such *subjective* separation, and consequently the Son Himself encompasses the separation from God endured by the sinful subject.[22] If God is to empty Himself in becoming

---

[20] Pace Juan M. Sara, "*Descensus ad Inferos*, Dawn of Hope. Aspects of the Theology of Holy Saturday in the Trilogy of Hans Urs von Balthasar," *Communio: International Catholic Review* 32 (Fall 2005): 541–572, at 552, the "separation from the Father" of which Balthasar speaks is a psychological, not a metaphysical, separation (see, e.g., *TD* V, 263–264 [G 238]). Hence, even in an early work, Balthasar reflects:

> No one could utter this cry [of forsakenness] more intensely than he whose life it is to be everlastingly generated by the Father and, in this generation, to see the Father. Now he, too, *experiences what it means* to lose God, to know him only as the far-away Judge. The relationship by which Father and Son turn towards each other in an eternal dialogue *seems* to be turned into estrangement and indescribable loss, while, in the hour of darkness on the Cross, there is no light of hope and return at his disposal. Even for the most just of the just there is the iron law that in "the hour of God," "the day of God," which is the day of judgment and wrath, the good things of the Father, the faith *that is experienced and felt*, love and hope, are *deposited* with God so as to remain inaccessible. (*The God Question and Modern Man*, trans. Hilda Graef [New York: Seabury Press, 1967], 133, emphasis added)

[21] Balthasar distinguishes between the "infinite distance" that is constituted by the self-subsisting mutual *relations of opposition* in the immanent Trinity, on the one hand, and the apparent separation between Father and Son in the economic Trinity manifest in the Cross, on the other hand. Thus, he quotes von Speyr saying, "'what seems to us to be the sign of separation . . . [is] the separation that is perceptible to us'" (*TD* V, 262 [G 237]). Karen Kilby nearly draws from the Balthasarian texts the distinction I have made between the objective and subjective dimensions of His redemptive suffering (see *Balthasar*, 102n26), but her attempt to understand Balthasar's "infinite distance" language (see 107ff.) is severely lacking.

[22] See, e.g., *TD* V, 257, 260, 264 [G 232, 235, 238]. It "begins in the Incarnation and is completed on the Cross" "experienced not only in the body and the senses but also spiritually" even though "'the Father does not leave the Son for a moment'" (*TD* V, 263 [G 237–238]). Sin itself is absorbed by His human nature (without blemish), that it may be condemned in the flesh, resulting in a sort of separation of sin from sinner (see *TD* V, 266–267 [G 241–242]).

man, it seems fitting for His self-emptying to result in a more abysmal experience in Christ than can engulf a mere human being in relation to God, regardless of whether one accepts this abyss between the human consciousness of Christ and the bliss of the triune life as a reflection or revelation of an *ur-kenosis* in the Trinity itself. Hence, drawing upon Adrienne von Speyr, Balthasar reflects: "his experience of the abyss is at the same time entirely within him (inasmuch as he assumes in himself the full measure of the mortal sinners' estrangement with respect to God) and also entirely outside himself, for this experience is for him (insofar as eternal Son of the Father) something entirely foreign: he is on Holy Saturday in perfect alienation to himself."[23]

The crux of the matter is whether it is fitting or proper to the kenotic love of God to assume pains ordinarily consequent to human sinfulness.[24] White is right to insist that the God-man cannot fall into despair or hatred of God.[25] But let there not be a lacuna in making distinctions—must Christ succumb to the sin of despair in order to experience what it is like to be abandoned by God? Is it incongruent with the Incarnate Word to suffer all the consequences due to sin in His own flesh or was that precisely

---

Thus, Pitstick misses the mark when she claims that in order to "save us from a real state of alienation," not "only from feeling really bad about ourselves," Christ must be objectively and metaphysically abandoned by the Father (see "Response to Webster and Lauber," *Scottish Journal of Theology* 62, no. 2 [2009]: 211–216, at 214).

[23] Balthasar, "Descente aux enfers," in *Axes* (1970), 8; cf. *Explorations* IV, 411 [G 397]. He sees the Spirit as the unity that is always there; see, e.g., *TD* V, 262 [G 237], and *Epilogue*, 85–86 [G 66].

[24] For exploration of this theme, see Thomas G. Weinandy, OFM, *In the Likeness of Sinful Flesh: An Essay on the Humanity of Christ* (Edinburgh: T&T Clark, 1993). It is a misunderstanding to suggest with Randall Rosenberg that Balthasar seems to think Jesus assumes a fallen human nature (see "Theory and Drama," 116), as Balthasar holds only that Christ assumed the penalty of sin in His flesh, not that He committed or could have committed sin; thus, it is also incorrect to say Christ "takes on our *guilt*," which Rosenberg ascribes to Balthasar (180), if by this one means he becomes personally guilty of sin, but not if this phrase means to indicate that Christ takes away our guilt by His substitutionary self-offering.

Rosenberg notes that Balthasar approvingly quotes Jean Galot's words (see 189): "There is solidarity, it is true, but it extends as far as substitution: Christ's solidarity with us goes as far as taking our place and allowing the whole weight of human guilt to fall on him" (*La Rédemption: mystère d'alliance* [Paris: Bruges, 1965], 268, cited in *TD* IV, 297 [G 276]). But he emphasizes the words "guilt" rather than "weight of"—human guilt is assumed insofar as the suffering inherent in it is included in Christ's comprehensive suffering of sin itself (2 Cor 5:21; cf. Rom 8:3).

[25] For a corroborative account, see Jean-Pierre Torrell, *Pour nous les hommes et pour notre salut: Jesus notre rédemption* (Paris : Les Éditions du Cerf, 2014), 249.

the purpose for which God became man? One option is a straightforward reading of the New Testament texts frequently invoked by Balthasar, yielding the latter result. The other option is the odd formulation that "Christ suffers in the entirety of His soul, but His higher spiritual faculties are immune to deprivation because of the divine consolation also present in the entirety of His soul," apparently driven by a particular understanding of hylemorphic theory as it applies to Christ's human nature.[26]

---

[26] John Yocum argues against the now-popular interpretation of Jesus' words, "Father, why have you abandoned me?" as a cry of dereliction, struggling to make an exegetical argument against the notion: see "A Cry of Dereliction?," 76–77.

    While it may be true that Balthasar, among others, extrapolates too much regarding the Trinitarian relations from this enigmatic text, I would not go so far as to say that he makes too much of the cry because not only does he utilize many Pauline and Johannine texts in interpreting it, but it is also true that what he says regarding the profundity of Christ's spiritual agony (begun in the Garden of Gethsemane) does not contradict any of the contingent factors Yocum enumerates as contributing to his human experience of abandonment.

    Balthasar states in *Das Ganze im Fragment*: "Each one of the seven last words from the cross is a kind of totality of the gospel" (*A Theological Anthropology*, 280 [G 303]). When one approaches contingent events from the divine perspective of predestination, it is easier to see how Balthasar may jump from all these earthly circumstances to more of a God's-eye view of the events as experienced by the incarnate Son, an approach that is indeed criticized by Karen Kilby (see *Balthasar*, 65).

    In order to avoid attributing any godforsaken experience to Christ, Bruce Marshall takes up Augustine's approach:

> Whether the logic of ecumenical Christological dogma further allows divine rejection and Godforsakenness to be attributed to the Person of the incarnate Son is another matter. If so, it could only be in something like the sense in which sin is attributable to him, and not the sense in which suffering and death are attributable to him. So Augustine, for example, draws on the distinction between what is true of Christ *in propria persona* and what is true of him *in persona nostra* to understand his utterance from the cross of the opening words of Ps 22. Here it is crucial, Augustine suggests, to distinguish what Christ says on our behalf (*ex persona sui corporis*) from what he says about himself as an individual, what he says in the voice of the church from what he says in his own voice. (Marshall, "The Absolute and the Trinity," 154)

But this undue separation of Christ's "own person" (*persona propria*) from the "our person," the "person of his body" (*persona nostra, persona sui corporis*), is unbefitting and reflects a mistaken view either of sin or of the "godforsakenness" in question—the latter experience of utter sinfulness does not mandate personal sin!

    While I completely agree with Marshall's insistence that we keep in mind the distinction *secundum quod homo* and *secundum quod Deus*, the conclusion he draws does not follow: "a subject of the divine nature could not actually undergo divine abandonment. In virtue of his humanity a subject of this nature could suffer and die, but even in virtue of his humanity he could not undergo divine abandonment because he could not

Certainly, permanent objective separation from God is the consequence for irrevocably refusing God's love, but nothing precludes God from causing a grace-filled soul to experience solidarity with the hopeless.[27] Just as God can become a creature without losing His divinity, nothing prohibits Him from freely subjecting Himself to the deepest darkness of divine wrath and judgment upon sin. If, as White says, "[John and Mark] attribute to Christ . . . the expectation of salvation from God and the actual non-possession of that salvation (accompanied by actual suffering),"[28] then why cannot we say with Paul that God suffered the cursedness of sin itself in His own body and soul? If, as Thomas says, "to atone for the sins of all men, Christ accepted sadness, the greatest in absolute quantity,"[29] why can we not speak of such suffering as a "hell" unique to

---

cease to be divine" (156).

I believe there are some missing premises here. In fact, Paul D. Molnar, citing the same passage, makes the following critical inquiry:

> Let us suppose that forsakenness or abandonment should be understood in the restricted sense that he experiences our guilt and death in which we as sinners are abandoned by God who restores our humanity in Christ to proper union with God. Then we may reasonably ask: why must it be the case that if Jesus undergoes divine abandonment (assuming that this is what forsakenness means), he must "cease to be divine?" ("A Response: Beyond Hegel with Karl Barth and T. F. Torrance," *Pro Ecclesia* 23, no. 2: 165–173)

[27] Entering into the hell of human hopelessness does not necessarily involve succumbing internally to such hopelessness; in fact, hope can be restored to the place of human despair only if the suffering Redeemer maintains union with God in the life of grace. It is with this caveat that one ought to refine Balthasar's words concerning the hopelessness of the hell into which Christ descends, as early as his 1945 *Heart of the World*, trans. Erasmo S. Leiva (San Francisco: Ignatius Press, 1979), 109.

Some of the rhetoric in this work does, indeed, seem excessive—perhaps we may call it mystical hyperbole—for instance, when he says:

> It would be too easy to suffer if one could still love. Love has been taken from you. The only thing you still feel is the burning void, the hollow which it has left behind. It would be a joy for you if, from the depths of hell, you could still, and for all eternity, love the Father who rejected you. But love has been taken away from you. . . . You lived on love; you had no other thought but love; you were love. Now it has been taken away. (115–116)

It should be revised to clarify that the *feeling* of love was taken away, not love as an act itself, which pertains to the intellective will.

[28] White, "Jesus' Cry on the Cross," 570.

[29] *ST* III, q. 46, a. 6, co. It is telling and paradoxical that the very next phrase is the following qualifying subordinate clause (inspired by St. John Damascene): "yet not exceeding the rule of reason."

the Son's destiny to which the Father condemned Him (prefigured by the sacrifice of Isaac)? White's response is to set up an opposition between the substitutionary and satisfactory aspects of redemption by implying an equivalence between any theory of substitution and the "penal substitution" derived from the writings of Luther and Calvin, even using the word "substitutes" reluctantly and effectively reducing its meaning to that of satisfaction in Thomas.[30] His neglect of the substitutionary dimension of redemption clearly results in complacency with the satisfactory dimension. Balthasar, on the contrary, while shying away from the language of punishment, nonetheless affirms:

> It is essential to maintain, however, that the Crucified does not bear the burden as something external: he in no way distances himself from those who by rights should have to bear it. (Indeed, he is *in* them eucharistically!) Subjectively, therefore, he can experience it as "punishment," although objectively speaking, in his case, it cannot be such.[31]

---

[30] Nonetheless, in a recent book, White concedes:

> The idea that Christ suffered the pains of damnation on the cross for the sake of sinners is not an idea unique to Protestant thinkers, such as Luther and Calvin. It was taught by many Catholic thinkers of the late medieval period and was a theme in popular preaching in Catholic Europe throughout the seventeenth, eighteenth, and nineteenth centuries—for example, in the writings of Louis Chardon, OP (1595–1651), and Jacques-Bénigne Bossuet (1627–1704). If this idea never became the preferred theory for church doctrine, nevertheless it was never officially banned from use in theological speculation or from public expression in the pulpit. John Calvin, therefore, is not unique (or exclusively "Protestant") in holding to a form of penal substitution theory that posits Christ's experience of hell on the cross. (*The Incarnate Lord: A Thomistic Study in Christology* [Washington, DC: Catholic University of America Press, 2015], 388–389)

He later adds: "Aquinas's notion of the penalties of sin, or the pains of sin that Christ took upon himself for our sake, without any compromise of his own moral innocence, provides some point of real contact with the substitutionary atonement theories that are favored within the Lutheran and Reformed traditions" (436), but nonetheless concludes immediately: "We have no real reason, then, to abandon for ecumenical purposes the classical western account of the descent of Christ into hell as it is portrayed within medieval scholastic theology" (436). I have not been arguing for such abandonment, but for reconciliation or harmonization between diverse traditions.

[31] *TD* IV, 337–338 [G 314] (emphasis original).

According to Pitstick's radical interpretation of Balthasar, the *kenosis* of Christ is such that God literally becomes sin itself, even to the point that His divinity is cut off from His humanity in His death/descent.[32] On the opposite end of the spectrum, Oakes argues that since, as the ancient axiom goes, "what has not been assumed has not been redeemed," "when he died he took all earthly truths with him into hell, so that they could be raised with him into the presence of his Father."[33] To which one must ask: if Christ descended into the hell of the damned literally to "become sin," would not hell and sin themselves be redeemed? Given that the Trinitarian *ek-stasis* "undergirds" everything,[34] even the sin against the Holy Spirit, that is, godlessness itself,[35] contra the testimony of Christ (since everything He says is relativized by the kenotic heuristic), the effigies of all sinners are incinerated in the amorphous sin-entity that Christ somehow "assumes" in hell.[36]

Taking a more modest tack than Pitstick, regarding the manner in which Christ "assumes" the amorphous truth-being of sin itself, Matthew Levering interprets Balthasar thus: "Sin is the 'refuse' or 'chaff' that is con-

---

[32] See, e.g., Pitstick's *Light in Darkness*, 97, and "Development of Doctrine, or Denial? Balthasar's Holy Saturday and Newman's *Essay*," *International Journal of Systematic Theology* 11 (2009): 131–145, at 133. Martin Bieler, quoting Balthasar, responds to this particular charge:

> Balthasar interprets the *descensus* precisely as the "being dead of the Son of God." He even speaks of the borderline thought of a "suspension of the Incarnation." Holy Saturday is "so to speak, a suspension of the Incarnation," because Christ reaches a dimension which, humanly speaking, is not possible: the substitutionary atonement for all human beings. But it is only "so to speak" a suspension of the Incarnation because exactly in the being dead, the humanity of Jesus—and with it the kenosis of the eternal Son—is played out, as Balthasar emphasizes. . . . [H]e does not want to say that the Son has given up his divine attributes, as Pitstick claims. He only wants to hint at the fact that these attributes take on a different mode in the incarnate Son. Balthasar calls this a "change of modality" (*Modalitatswechsel*). ("God and the Cross: The Doctrine of God in the Work of Hans Urs von Balthasar," *Communio* 42 [Spring 2015]: 61–88, at 76–77, 81)

For response to various criticisms of Pitstick, see also Miles, "Obedience of a Corpse," 101–106, 121–126.

[33] Oakes, "*Envoi*: the future of Balthasarian theology," in *Cambridge Companion to Hans Urs von Balthasar*, 269–274, at 273.

[34] See *TD* V, 395 [G 361].

[35] See *TD* IV, 323–324, 362 [G 301, 337].

[36] See *Theo-Logik* II, 324, translated in Stefen Lösel's "Murder in the Cathedral," 434, much more adequately than Adrian J. Walker in *TL* II, 355–356. For an understanding of the notion of effigy here, see John Saward, *Mysteries of March*, 121, 131–132.

signed by Jesus to hell. It follows that the incarnate Son can truly bear all sin—in its hypostasized form, stripped of its association with particular disobedient persons—without perverting his own will."[37] Richard Barry, while admitting with Levering that Balthasar's mystical rhetoric is sometimes excessive, poignantly displays the biblical origins of Balthasar's metaphorical speech concerning sin, particularly, burden-load-thing and the goat of Azazel in Leviticus 16.[38] Pace Pitstick's interpretation, Balthasar's late *Theo-Logic*: *Truth of God* itself contains a statement of Speyr's that is contrary to Pitstick's interpretation of the same section, "Hell and Trinity": "'The horror is in sin and in the sinner and is borne by the Lord *without his being it himself.*'"[39] His controversial (and perhaps easily misinterpreted) comments in the same volume are anticipated already in the section on "Hell" in his earlier *Glory of the Lord: The New Covenant*. Although he speaks of the "absolute passivity of being dead,"[40] a notion he later abandons as insufficiently Speyrian,[41] it sounds there like he might

---

[37] Levering, "Balthasar on the Consciousness of Christ," 579. Speyr also speaks of this refuse or chaff as "objective sin," about which Matthew Sutton makes the following clarification:

> Von Speyr, of course, is not a theological or philosophical metaphysician. When she uses the phrase "objective sin," she means sin as it is separated from a particular subject or person; thus, "objective sin" means sin not attached to a subject. When someone sins and then confesses that sin, von Speyr thinks the sin is separated from subject and is thrust into hell. Augustine is correct when he says sin and evil have no objectivity. What I think von Speyr is driving at is that the "objective weight of sin" that Christ experiences on the cross and descent into hell is the full weight of the privation of the good, which means God's presence. He feels the full weight of being separated from God by his becoming sin for us. (*Heaven Opens*, Kindle Locations 4237–4241)

[38] See "Retrieving the Goat of Azazel: Balthasar's Biblical Soteriology," *Nova et Vetera* 15, no. 1 (2017): 13–35, at 22ff., especially 29 and 33.

[39] *TL* II, 350–351 [G 320], emphasis added. See also *TD* IV, 337–38 [G 314], cited even by his strong critic, Guy Mansini: "Balthasar himself, when pressed, confines the Son's 'becoming sin' to taking on the effects of sin" ("Balthasar and the Theodramatic Enrichment of the Trinity," *The Thomist* 64 [2000]: 499–519, at 508).

[40] *GL* VII, 230 [G 213].

[41] In *TL* II, 345n75 [G 315n1], Balthasar asks scholars to look no more to *Mysterium Paschale* for his theology since it was "a quickly written work" that did not fully appropriate the mystical insights of Adrienne von Speyr in this regard. The earlier emphasis may have been due to Karl Barth's influence, for better or for worse (see Lauber, "Towards a Theology of Holy Saturday," 75), and yet elsewhere he seems to preserve the balance better between Christ's passivity and activity in the descent, even earlier in his career (see *The God Question*, 130, 134).

Juan Sara is apparently unaware of this retraction when he emphasizes the passivity

be saying that Christ's divinity is separated from his humanity in the descent,[42] for all his hyperbole (a Rabbinic scriptural practice), it is clear in other passages that he does not mean to imply that Christ's *kenosis* involves an actual divesting of His divinity and metaphysical identification with sin itself in the descent.[43] It is, rather, a metaphorical divesting of His divinity in order to take on "the state of existence of this sin,"[44] incinerating the sin He assumes in the flesh by His infinite self-surrender.

Perhaps most pivotal, though, to Balthasar's understanding of the descent is its atemporality, the implications of which seem lost on Pitstick.[45] Conceding apparent inconsistencies in Balthasar, I would argue that one should appeal to the *Theo-Drama* for his definitive (or more developed) statement on the matter.[46] On the atemporality of Christ's suffering, quoting Speyr, he says:

---

of Christ in the descent (see *"Descensus ad Inferos,"* especially 547–548). Mark McIntosh also appears unaware of it (see *Christology From Within: Spirituality and the Incarnation in Hans Urs von Balthasar* [Notre Dame: University of Notre Dame Press, 2000], 110). T. J. White is also apparently unaware:

> The traditional position of the church understands Christ to be the active agent of salvation, with the power of God working through the instrumental medium of the human soul of Christ. By virtue of the inversion introduced in Balthasar's theory, Christ is himself passive before the Father and becomes himself the recipient of divine intervention. . . . Christ descends into hell not so much to illumine those in hell with the victory of redemption, as to become one with them in solidarity out of love, even in the midst of their distance from God." (*Incarnate Lord*, 429)

This is an exaggeration of Balthasar's motif of receptivity as constitutive of the Son, particularly exhibited in the passion of the Incarnate Word.

[42] See *GL* VII, 231 [G 214].

[43] See *GL* VII, 211 and 233 [G 195–196 and 216]).

[44] *GL* VII, 233 [G 216]. The timelessness of such an endeavor is also a theme of this volume (see *GL* VII, 225, 232 [G 209, 215]), even if, at the same time, he seems to emphasize the historicity of the descent on Saturday in the same work (see, e.g., *GL* VII, 230–232 [G 213–215]).

[45] Karen Kilby briefly mentions the "timeless" dimension of Christ's hellish experience (ascribed to Holy Saturday), according to Balthasar, and simply adds that it "raises some questions about whether one can describe the event of the Cross as historical," in *Balthasar* (108n39).

The simple answer to this critical query would be that the event of Christ's suffering is both historical and transhistorical, the latter being primarily represented by his being-dead on Saturday. She also references Pitstick's book a number of times both sympathetically and ambivalently (see especially *Balthasar*, 11n18, 121n68).

[46] A number of Balthasar scholars have pointed out the central importance of the final volumes of the *Theodramatik* to Balthasar's Trilogy and his work overall: see, e.g., Edward T. Oakes, SJ, *Pattern of Redemption: The Theology of Hans Urs von Balthasar* (New

"On the Cross he will feel lonesome unto death, unto a limitless, eternal death in which every temporal moment and viewpoint will completely disappear. What will be a short while for mankind [Jn 14:19] will be an eternal while to him." ... We see in this the timelessness of his suffering, the timelessness of the redemption. ... Nonetheless the timelessness of the Cross is not the mere negation of time that characterizes hell, but a "super-time."[47]

Pitstick rather pictures the suffering of His "descent" as a temporal event occurring after death and before Resurrection, whereas it should be seen as an experience of His soul in the abandonment of His passion. In fact, at the same time He suffered the Crucifixion on Friday, His soul also suffered the hell signified by Holy Saturday; in the passion, His soul entered another dimension of time in which the threshold between death and new life was met by the divine Person of the Son in the flesh of the One who suffered no longer after death on Friday. The "descent" and the Cross are one reality for Balthasar, His passion being the "time" in which He entered the world of the dead (Sheol) in the most profound sense. He suffered the pains of "being dead" while still alive in the "god-forsakenness" of His passion, with the "descent" of His soul begun in His obedience on Mount Gethsemane and culminating in the "cry of dereliction."[48] Pitstick unwittingly quotes the following passage from the final volume of the *Theo-Drama* illustrating the atemporal union of His passion on Friday and the suffering of the descent signified by Holy Saturday:[49] "The condition of timelessness undergone by the Son on the Cross ... must have sufficient 'space' for the (infernal) experience of sinners abandoned by God,

---

York: Continuum Publishing Co., 1997); Ben Quash, "The theo-drama," in *Cambridge Companion to Hans Urs von Balthasar*, 143–157, at 156; cf. Balthasar, "Noch ein Jahrzehnt," in *Mein Werk—Durchblicke* (Einsiedeln: Johannes Verlag, 1990), 77.

[47] *TD* V, 310 [G 282–283]; internal quote from Speyr's *John* III, 124. Regis Martin also reflects on Balthasar's conception of the descent as timeless suffering in quasi-poetic fashion, pointing to other texts as well (see his *Suffering of Love: Christ's Descent into the Hell of Human Hopelessness* [San Francisco: Ignatius Press, 2006]). He appeals for support to an intriguing sermon of Cardinal John Henry Newman's in *Discourses Addressed to Mixed Congregations* (London: Longman, 1891), 334–335 (see Martin, 90). Lauber points to the Barthian origin of characterizing the descent-suffering on the Cross as "eternal death" (see "Towards a Theology of Holy Saturday," 112).

[48] For the significance of obedience in Balthasar's soteriology, see Michel Beaudin, *Obéissance et solidarité: Essai sur la christologie de Hans Urs von Balthasar* (Québec: Corporation des Éditions Fides, 1989).

[49] See Pitstick, *Light in Darkness*, 111.

in two aspects: the intensity of the Son's forsakenness on the Cross and its worldwide extension."[50]

Pitstick knows full well that Balthasar does not accept the idea that Sheol is a place where souls were imprisoned after purgatory[51] until the "day" on which Christ "descended" so much as a spiritual condition suffered by those who died before Him.[52] Regarding the descent's transformation of the netherworld into the purgatorial fire, Balthasar asserts:

> Properly speaking, therefore, purgatory comes into existence on Holy Saturday, when the Son walks through "hell," introducing the element of mercy into the condition of those who are justly lost. Purgatory "has its origin in the Cross. The Father makes use of the fruit of the Cross in order to temper divine justice, which held the sinners captive, with new mercifulness. From the Cross, hope is brought down to the netherworld; from the Cross, a fire is unleashed in which justice and mercifulness are intermixed. Through the Lord's arrival there, the powers of the netherworld, of death and of evil, are driven, as it were, into the backmost recesses of hell, and the devil's chain is made shorter. Purgatory arises as if under the Lord's striding feet; he brings comfort to this place of hopelessness, fire to this place of iciness."[53]

Gehenna (identical to Sheol, as the common place of suffering for all who die before Christ) was not visited by the soul of Christ on earth's "Saturday" while His body rested in the tomb. Any word for the dark place

---

[50] *TD* V, 308 [G 281]; cited in *Light in Darkness*, 111.

[51] See Pitstick, *Light in Darkness*, 47–51, for example, for the argument that it is traditional (that is, in accord with the biblical exegesis of Church Doctors) to hold that there were some before Christ who entered Abraham's bosom without need of purgation, others who remained in purgatory until His descent to Abraham's bosom, and others already consigned to Gehenna (the hell of the damned, upon whom the descent could have no positive effect). She invokes earlier (on 18) the authority of St. Thomas for this position, citing *ST* III, q. 52, a. 2.

[52] Just as the word "descent" connotes change of location to a lower region but in proper theology does not denote such a physical meaning, the "day" of Holy Saturday is not so much a temporal phase for Christ, but it rather signifies an existential reality that is liturgically commemorated between passion and Resurrection and that indicates the purgatorial function of judgment for those who die in communion with God (hence the fires of purgation are not time-measured but experienced in subjective "moments" of existential import).

[53] *TD* V, 363 [G 331].

in which the dead reign takes on a new meaning in the New Covenant, namely, the spiritual condition of abandonment assumed by Christ (and those in profoundest communion with Him) in solidarity with sinners.

DEVELOPMENT IN TRADITION?

In support of all the aforementioned dimensions of locating the descent of Christ in the passion (the Cross), a close collaborator of Balthasar's, Pope Emeritus Benedict XVI, opines:

> The true Boddhisattva [sic], Christ, *descends into Hell and suffers it in all its emptiness.* . . . It is a seriousness which takes on tangible form in the Cross of Christ. . . . God overcomes evil . . . *on a Good Friday.* . . . He himself entered into the distinctive freedom of sinners but went beyond it in that freedom of his own love which *descended willingly into the Abyss.* . . . The answer lies hidden in Jesus' *descent into Sheol, in the night of the soul which he suffered*, a night which no one can observe except by entering this darkness in suffering faith. Thus, in the history of holiness . . . in John of the Cross, in Carmelite piety in general, and in that of Therese of Lisieux in particular, "Hell" has taken on a completely new meaning and form. For the saints, *"Hell" is* . . . a challenge to suffer in the dark night of faith, *to experience communion with Christ in solidarity with his descent into the Night.* One draws near to the Lord's radiance by sharing his darkness. One serves the salvation of the world by leaving one's own salvation behind for the sake of others. In such piety, nothing of the dreadful reality of Hell is denied. Hell is so real that it reaches into the existence of the saints. *Hope can take it on, only if one shares in the suffering of Hell's night* by the side of the One who came to transform our night by his suffering. Here hope . . . derives from the surrender of all claims to innocence and to reality's perduringness, a surrender *which takes place by the Cross of the Redeemer.*[54]

Unlike Ratzinger, Pitstick refuses to consider the depths of Christ's suffering in light of the quasi-atemporal "dark night" suffered by many great saints, let alone their self-described experiences of (subjective) condemnation. In a conference called *L'inferno e' solitudine: ecco l'abisso del uomo,*

---

[54] Joseph Ratzinger, *Eschatology*, 216–218 [G 219–220] (emphasis added).

Ratzinger reaffirms his own references in *Eschatology* to Christ as the fulfillment of the myth of Bodhisattva.[55] While certainly avoiding the errors attributed to Balthasar by theologians like Pitstick, he proceeds to offer existentialistic reflections on the anthropological meaning of death and the descent, linking Christ's experience to the dark night of the mystics.[56] Thus, following the train of thought he establishes in both *Eschatology* and *Introduction to Christianity*, he specifies that Christ suffered the hell or abandonment proper to the pains of death itself, the hell that precedes redemption, not the hell yet to exist that cannot be penetrated by the "word of love."[57] In the latter mentioned work, he explains:

> If there were such a thing as a loneliness that could no longer be
> penetrated and transformed by the word of another; if a state of
> abandonment were to arise that was so deep that no "You" could
> reach into it any more, then we should have real, total loneliness
> and dreadfulness, what theology calls "hell." We can now define
> exactly what this word means: it denotes a loneliness that the
> word love can no longer penetrate and that therefore indicates the
> exposed nature of existence in itself. . . . In truth—one thing is
> certain: there exists a night into whose solitude no voice reaches;

---

[55] See *Perche' siamo ancora nella chiesa* (Collana: Rizzoli, 2008).

[56] Pitstick also objects to speaking of Christ suffering anything like a dark night because she holds that Christ possessed the beatific vision, which I will address in the next chapter, and Christ's hypostatic union "surpasses the union of vision, which in turn surpasses the union of the 'dark night'" (*Light in Darkness*, 186), a criticism Rosenberg repeats (see "Theory and Drama," 303–304).

While this is true, she misses the point: obviously Christ did not *need* to endure the dark night in order to attain the union of vision, as do all other human beings (at least, according to Carmelite spirituality), any more than He needed to become human or suffer at all or eat or sleep, but nonetheless there is no reason why He could not endure something akin to the dark night, even if infinitely worse both by virtue of His perfect union with God and His most intimate (unpersonal) knowledge of sin.

Regarding St. John of the Cross's spiritual doctrine of the dark night, see Karol Wojtyla's first dissertation, *Faith in St. John of the Cross* (San Francisco: Ignatius Press, 1981).

[57] Pitstick criticizes as untraditional Balthasar's position that the hell of the damned did not exist until after Christ, arguing that before Christ some were condemned, some were destined to the limbo of children, some suffered purgatory before entering "Abraham's bosom," and everyone justified by grace waited in the "limbo of the Fathers" until the coming of Christ (*Light in Darkness*, 18, 47, 334). Ratzinger, then, would fall under this same indictment (for disagreeing with Thomas on this point, or at least Pitstick's interpretation thereof).

there is a door through which we can only walk alone—the door of death. In the last analysis all the fear in the world is fear of this loneliness. From this point of view, it is possible to understand why the Old Testament has only one word for hell *and* death, the word *sheol*; it regards them as ultimately identical. Death is absolute loneliness. But the loneliness into which love can no longer advance is—hell. . . . This article [of the Creed] thus asserts that Christ strode through the gate of our final loneliness, that in his Passion he went down into the abyss of our abandonment. Where no voice can reach us any longer, there is he. Hell is thereby overcome, or, to be more accurate, death, which was previously hell, is hell no longer. Neither is the same any longer because there is life in the midst of death, because love dwells in it. Now only deliberate self-enclosure is hell or, as the Bible calls it, the second death (Rev 20:14, for example). But death is no longer the path into icy solitude; the gates of *sheol* have been opened.[58]

It seems only logical to say that Christ suffered infinitely more than those saintly mystics who clearly participated in the pains of hell without losing the life of grace and that such hell did not necessitate the objective loss of the beatific vision consequent upon the hypostatic union.[59] In other words, He subjectively experienced complete and timeless abandonment, and because He still objectively possessed the beatific vision, His suffering was intensified in proportion to His perfect unity with the infinite love of the Trinity. This is no more contradictory than is the In-

---

[58] Ratzinger, *Introduction to Christianity*, 300–301 [G 220–221] (emphasis original).

[59] Pitstick uses texts of Balthasar suggesting that Christ's *"visio immediata Dei"* was not beatific as warrant to dismiss anthropological reflections on death as the darkest human suffering with reference to the descent. She also supposes without argumentation that it is impossible for Christ to have the beatific vision and suffer a worse hell than any of the mystic-saints. Making note of deficiencies in Balthasar's Trinitarian theology, she refuses to consider the depths of Christ's suffering in light of the dark night of many great saints, let alone the subjective experiences of damnation found, for example, in St. Teresa of Avila.

In fact, the descent presents a paradox similar to that involved in the reality of Christ lacking human awareness of His own divinity until a certain age, that is, the time when a human being normally becomes aware of His own identity as a person. According to a certain Thomist perspective at least, His human intellect must have possessed beatific and infused knowledge and yet, in accord with the psychical domain of acquired knowledge, He would not have been "experimentally" conscious of such knowledge until His human brain reached the development necessary for such.

carnation itself—it is the very essence of the Incarnation.

Those who claim Balthasar's notion of the descent is incongruous with tradition ought to remember and reflect upon the early patristic image of Christ as the fish on the hook swallowed up by the devil.[60] Furthermore, understanding the Pauline passages (not to mention Isaiah's Suffering Servant psalm)[61] concerning redemption in terms of total solidarity or *Stellvertretung* is not a modern invention,[62] and it implies Christ would have had to experience precisely what every human being (or at least, those who lived before His "hour") experiences in death. Balthasar, particularly in *Mysterium Paschale* (the limits of which he noted and I have emphasized), draws on this tradition to argue with the support of late medieval figures that in descending to the "lower regions of hell," as even Augustine and Aquinas teach, he must have suffered the fate of unredeemed mankind precisely so that they could be redeemed. Brian Doyle, OP, relying heavily on this text, points to difficulties in this understanding of Holy Saturday. He sums up Aquinas's arguments in his *Commentary on the Sentences*, which is replicated in the *Supplementum* of the *Tertia Pars* of the *Summa Theologiae* and recapped in the *Compendium Theologiae*:

---

[60] See, for instance, Gregory of Nyssa's *Catechetical Orations*, ch. 24. In addition to the comments of Augustine exposited by Oakes, Turek invokes aspects of medieval reflection that Balthasar and Ratzinger develop:

> Von Balthasar suggests that we consider the very source of redemptive grace as entailing Christ's descent into Hades/Sheol in representative assumption of the situation of all humankind who, under judgment as the progeny of the "First Adam," is tending (in absence of the Christ event) toward the realm of death in deprivation of the vision of God. Since, moreover, Christ's mission recapitulates the *concrete entirety* of human history (including whatever resistance to Christological grace I exhibit in my life), we may also consider St. Thomas' argument that the necessity for Christ's descent into Hades "lies in the fact that Christ has assumed all the *defectus* of sinners." (*In Libros Sententiarum* III, d 22, q. 2, a. 1, qla. 3). In the view of von Balthasar and Ratzinger, Christ's assumption of all the *defectus* of sinners as an act of supreme love involves his sharing (in an analogous manner) the alienation from the divine Father to which sin inevitably leads (CCC 603). ("Dare We Hope," 120–121n69)

[61] John Paul II refers to the prophet as "the fifth evangelist" (*Salvifici Doloris*, §17), who contributes to what he calls "the gospel of suffering" (see §6).

[62] In addition to the sources already cited, see, e.g., Simon Gathercole, *Defending Substitution: An Essay on Atonement in Paul* (Grand Rapids, MI: Baker Academic, 2015). Also, for a general history of redemption theories, see Laurence William Grensted, *A Short History of the Doctrine of the Atonement* (New York: Longmans, Green & Co., 1920).

Aquinas's conviction that the opportunity to merit ceases with death leads him to argue that, while it was fitting for Christ to descend into hell to free others from suffering, it is impossible that he should have suffered there. . . . [U]nlike Balthasar . . . Aquinas holds that it was unnecessary for Christ to suffer in hell because he had already made full satisfaction for mankind's sins by his death on the Cross. . . . Aquinas reasons that the fate of Christ's body must reflect the fate of his soul. He naturally concludes that, if Christ's body did not experience the effects of sin but remained incorrupt in the grave, then his soul also did not suffer the effects of sin in the form of punishment after death. In contrast, Balthasar teaches that Christ's *greatest* act of redemption is performed in Sheol in the *absence* of his body, which means that Christ merits the salvation of all of mankind as a disembodied soul.[63]

But despite Balthasar's shifting rhetoric on the issue, I think Doyle's assertion that Balthasar unequivocally attributes suffering to Christ's soul on Holy Saturday to be almost as misleading as his assertion that Balthasar envisioned the possibility of postmortem conversion.[64] Surely, a literal-temporal mentality would take some of Balthasar's more rhetorically excessive comments to mean that Christ goes to the hell of the damned to suffer condemnation in place of each unjust soul, thus redeeming them after their own deaths.[65] But this is a simplistic rendering of Balthasar's

---

[63] Doyle, "'He descended into hell': The Theology of Hans Urs von Balthasar and Catholic Doctrine," 848–849, 850–851. There is still that enigmatic passage from Aquinas's *Exposition of the Apostles' Creed* that Oakes invokes (see *The Sermon-Conferences of St. Thomas Aquinas on the Apostles' Creed*, trans. Nicholas Ayo, CSC [Notre Dame: University of Notre Dame Press, 1988], cited in *Infinity Dwindled to Infancy*, 214).

[64] See Doyle, "The Theology of Balthasar," 862, 876. Oakes and Ralph Martin (relying on Oakes) share this mistaken interpretation (see *Pattern of Redemption*, 318n35; *Will Many Be Saved? What Vatican II Actually Teaches and Its Implications for the New Evangelization* [Grand Rapids, MI: Eerdmans, 2012], 155, 162, 180, 275n123). Compare to Balthasar, *TD* V, 297 [G 270]; *Dare We Hope "That All Men be Saved"? With A Short Discourse on Hell*, trans. David Kipp and Lothar Krauth (San Francisco: Ignatius, 1988), 182 [G 29].

[65] Balthasar rejects any such kind of "cosmologization of hell," such as what is seen in Dante, in favor of "an anthropological, that is to say, interior, experimental understanding of what it means to be lost. As soon as this happened, the cry of forlornness on the Cross and the descent of the Redeemer, as well as the soteriological meaning of Christian com-passion became again, and more deeply, accessible" (*The God Question*, 139).

Hence, "the reality of the *poena damni* is spiritual and can be experienced only spiritually" (*The God Question*, 133). Contrary to those who want to blame Speyr for

Speyrian reflections on the mystical profundity of Christ's passion and death. If Christ were to have suffered the "second death" on Holy Saturday in a literal-temporal manner, he would have had to descend into the fire both in spirit and in body, yet His body lay in the tomb, as Doyle points out.[66]

To understand what Balthasar intends to convey, one must grapple with the notion of timelessness that pervades his account of Christ's ultimate redemptive work, as I have alluded to here.[67] In a very recent book, White makes the following argument:

> Balthasar is ambivalent about the very idea of such an interim state of the human soul separated from the body, either for Christ or for all the other members of the human race. . . . [I]t is in no way clear *how there can be an integral mystery of Holy Saturday for Balthasar*, at least as it is understood in the traditional sense. Why? Because one of the necessary conditions for the possibility of this mystery is that human immaterial souls *exist in the interim state* between death and bodily resurrection. Otherwise, there is no one to be redeemed on Holy Saturday as such, and that mystery merely becomes the symbol of something else (the Lord's solidarity with us in death and life after death). In some real sense, the descent for Balthasar does entail an "atemporal" sphere of existence that comes in or after physical death. But it does not entail the life of the subsistent immaterial soul separated from

---

Balthasar's conception of hell, Miles notes: "Balthasar adapts and extends von Speyr's notions of the depths of the Son's extreme obedience and his journey through hell, even though she does not appear to discuss questions such as the *poena damni*" ("Obedience of a Corpse," 185).

[66] See "The Theology of Balthasar," 851n19. He provides other reasons for why a different interpretation is needed without accepting them as such (see 870), and, as I have done elsewhere (especially in "Damnation and the Trinity in Ratzinger and Balthasar," *Logos* 18, no. 3 [Summer 2015]: 123–150), he points out that Ratzinger, whose reflections on Christ's passion generally support Balthasar's, "has never stated explicitly that Christ suffered the 'second death' in Sheol on Holy Saturday" (871).

In fact, Ratzinger explicitly indicates reservations with regard to this aspect of Balthasar's theology of the descent. See his 1956 review of Balthasar's *Die Gottesfrage des heutigen menschen*, cited by then-Cardinal Ratzinger in his 1997 reflections on his 1969 meditations on the Holy Triduum, *Meditationen zur Karwoche* (Freising: Kyrios Verlag, 1969), and *The Sabbath of History*.

[67] I have attempted to do this more fully in my "The Possibility of Universal Conversion in Death: Temporality, Annihilation, and Grace," *Modern Theology* 32, no. 3 (Summer 2016): 307–324.

the body. Consequently, it has more in common with the doctrine of Calvin and Barth, ultimately, than it does with either the classical eastern or western patristic and medieval accounts of the descent into hell as a real event that transpired on Holy Saturday. Furthermore, in the absence of a doctrine of the immaterial soul, it would seem that Christ himself must enter in some way into the resurrected state *immediately* after his human annihilation in death. And yet such an idea stands in contradiction to the teaching of the scriptures and the Apostles' Creed.[68]

Leaving aside for now the accusation of heresy on Balthasar's part, White here bolsters my case for a metaphorical interpretation of Balthasar's understanding of Holy Saturday. Although Balthasar sympathized with Rahner's notion of "resurrection in death,"[69] which is not synonymous with denying the immortality of the soul (but rather makes the latter radically conditioned by God's absolute will),[70] there is more basis in Balthasar for understanding the possibility of universal conversion in terms of a relative temporality structure peculiar to the existential event of human death.

---

[68] White, *Incarnate Lord*, 422. Here and in other places (see especially 387, 391, 426, 432, 434, 436), White is clearly thinking in dialogue with my previous work (see, e.g., my dissertation, for which he was an official reader in 2014). Elsewhere in the same chapter (on Balthasar), White states:

> Christ takes upon himself the burden of suffering that sinful humanity has incurred in order to deliver human beings into a life of righteousness with God. The descent into hell, then, [in this view] takes place in the soul of Christ even on Good Friday, as he bears within his human spirit the burden of spiritual separation from God in order to deliver us from that burden in a definitive way. . . . [Aquinas] maintains select aspects of [this] third view, albeit in ways very different from the perspectives of either Luther or Calvin. Likewise, Balthasar seeks unquestionably to interact with these distinct traditions in profound ways. . . . Balthasar rereads the diverse strands of tradition in innovative ways. Christ experiences the night of hell on Good Friday, as we see also in Calvin and Barth, but in differentiation from this, he also experiences this night on the day of Holy Saturday in the mystery of the descent among the dead. (434–435)

The last assertion seems to contradict what he says on 422.

[69] See *TD* V, 357 [G 326]; Karl Rahner, "The Intermediate State," in *Theological Investigations*, vol. 17: *Jesus, Man, and the Church*, trans. Margaret Kohl (London: Darton, Longman & Todd, 1981), 114–124, at 115.

[70] For a critique of this theory and argumentation in favor of the natural immortality of the soul from a modern perspective in continuity with the medieval, see Ratzinger, *Eschatology*, especially chs. 5–6 and Appendices I-II.

Rather than spin some odd theory of how Christ could have suffered bodily in Sheol even while His blessed corpse lay in the tomb,[71] it makes interpretive sense to broaden the meaning of the "moment" of death. Perhaps, then, Christ suffered the descent precisely in the existential moment of death itself before His soul departed His body to transport the good thief and the predestined of the old covenants to Paradise.[72]

Moreover, those who claim tradition dictates that Christ only descended to the limbo of the Fathers in glorious triumph cannot explain why throughout history the Holy Saturday liturgy has maintained an element of sorrow; that is, why it does not simply celebrate the glory of Christ releasing the just souls into full beatitude. Nor can they claim a monopoly on Tradition and assert this opinion as dogmatic—the Church in fact notes the following precaution (most relevant for disputed questions): "The Tradition here in question comes from the apostles and hands on what they received from Jesus' teaching. . . . Tradition is to be distinguished from the various theological, disciplinary, liturgical or devotional traditions. . . . In the light of Tradition, these traditions can be retained, modified, or even abandoned under the guidance of the Church's magisterium."[73] Balthasar merely attempts to return to the apostolic tradition made known in Paul's epistles (and preserved, albeit in minority, among the Fathers) that the human nature of Christ was engulfed by the fire of

---

[71] It is difficult to make sense of Speyr's statement, "In hell the Lord's bodily state becomes very different from what it was in life" (*Die Passion von Innen* [Einsiedeln: Johannes Verlag, 1981]), 141, translated by Sutton, *Heaven Opens*, location 4259). Of course, Augustine is notorious for holding that the souls in hell (and purgatory) suffered bodily in some sense even prior to the Resurrection. Perhaps there is a spiritual "copy," as it were, of the body with which the person maintains inextricable unity in death before reuniting in the general resurrection with the material component correspondent with such a "spiritual body" (see 1 Cor 15:44). For instance, Herbert Vorgrimler, utilizing Rahner, argues for this to make sense of Denzinger 385 (see "Christ's Descent into Hell—Is It Important?," *Concilium: An International Review of Theology* 1, no. 2 [1966]: 75–81, at 77–78).

[72] This is the best way to interpret the following words of Adrienne von Speyr: "in death he does not look into eternal life. . . . [N]ot as the living one of Easter, but as the dead one of Holy Saturday must he accomplish this journey. Not in the light of victory does he now want to observe sin, but in the darkness that characterizes it in itself" (*John*, vol. 4, *The Birth of the Church*, trans. David Kipp [San Francisco: Ignatius Press, 1991], 143).

This makes more sense, theologically, as soon as one realizes that this mystic does not speak in a linear mode, but rather reflects in non-systematic fashion on the concepts involved in redemption, utilizing symbols at her disposal (see Miles, "Obedience of a Corpse," 130, 142, 160).

[73] CCC 83.

God's jealous love for the sinner. Balthasar evidently realized that many of St. Paul's very clear comments about Christ's redemptive suffering for sinners were not taken seriously by this "traditional" doctrine of the descent; hence, the latter cannot be considered a part of Tradition as conduit of divine revelation, and the diversity of opinions among the Fathers allows for legitimate developments of doctrine to be proposed on this matter.

John Yocum, an opponent of Balthasar's exegesis of the "cry of dereliction," thinks something altogether foreign to scriptural exegesis is at work here:

> There is at least a hint here [Balthasar's reference to John of the Cross, Bernard, Therese, and others] of the privileging of interior experience as both a hermeneutical tool and the gauge of human life. Yet, if this is the case, why does the Bible tell us so little about it? Is the true significance of the cross and resurrection so enigmatically enclosed in one verse? It is at least worth asking whether this approach does not take us down paths that lead us not further in, but further away from the heart of the work of Christ as presented in the New Testament. We ought to be wary when Balthasar tells us that in dealing with the Passion, we have to go beyond exegesis.[74]

It is, indeed, true that *theologia* involves more than exegesis of text. Although Balthasar certainly utilizes more than one scriptural text in his interpretation of the doctrine, the centrality and significance of a doctrine is not determined by the number of texts that address it, but by its functionality in the *analogia fidei*. Tradition is not recourse to the inner experience of individuals, but to the living *memoria* of the Church comprised by saints, whose lives interpret for us the heart of the gospel message.[75]

Still, Jared Wicks complains that "[i]n the discussion [between Pitstick and Oakes], however, the 'voice of the Fathers' was not heard."[76] He concludes:

---

[74] "A Cry of Dereliction?," 80. For a contrary view of the cry, see Holly J. Carey, *Jesus' Cry from the Cross: Towards a First-Century Understanding of the Intertextual Relationship between Psalm 22 and the Narrative of Mark's Gospel* (London: T&T Clark, 2009).

[75] For a development of this kind of theology of tradition and scripture, see my "Revisiting the *Sola Scriptura* Debate: Yves Congar and Joseph Ratzinger on Tradition," *Pro Ecclesia* 24, no. 1 (Winter 2015): 85–114. For an account of Balthasar's implicit theology of revelation in accord with the Tubingen school, see Cyril O'Regan, "Balthasar: Between Tubingen and Postmodernity," *Modern Theology* 14, no. 3 (1998): 325–353.

[76] Jared Wicks, SJ, "Christ's Saving Descent to the Dead: Early Witnesses from Ignatius of

Regarding the debate over Hans Urs von Balthasar's theology of redemption, these early testimonies give strong support to his critics. They offer no indication at all of the descent being Christ's extreme experience of Godforsakenness in the netherworld. Christ does not go there because of human sin for expiatory suffering in a phase beyond his earthly Passion. He is not passive and suffering in going to the dead, but active soteriologically to bring light, release, and passage to heaven.[77]

The catena of texts he cites from the early second century to the year 300 (some of which are quasi-gnostic), nevertheless, neither exhausts the Catholic tradition nor excludes the possibility of the developments explicated by Balthasar and Ratzinger, among others, who treat the question in terms of diverse strands of tradition that are organically related in the course of time. Hence, the argument has been made here that the descent is a non-temporal extension of the mysterious depths of Christ's salvific suffering as *Stellvertretung*.[78] It may, in fact, be true that most (if not all) of the Fathers saw the descent primarily (if not exclusively) in terms of victory, but they do not (and certainly not unanimously) repudiate the idea that the descent also involved suffering. I have argued for the view that the descent-suffering actually occurred during the historical passion (on Friday), although I am not persuaded that the other view (i.e., that it continued on Saturday) is necessarily *contra fide*.

Paul Griffiths expertly displays how Pitstick overshoots the mark when she claims the "traditional doctrine" on the descent as binding magisterial teaching, without entering into questions of exegesis or the merits of each theory. As Griffiths aptly notes:

It is, I should say, teaching *de fide tenendum* that Christ's descent was as the divine-human person he is, and that its principal purpose was to liberate the righteous from the unpleasant condition in which they would otherwise have remained. There is plentiful conciliar and magisterial teaching on those matters, and it is, as Pitstick's thorough review amply shows,

---

Antioch to Origen," *Pro Ecclesia* 17, no. 3 (2008): 281–309, at 281.

[77] Wicks, "Christ's Saving Descent," 308.

[78] For a complementary study of Balthasar on *Stellvertretung* from a primarily scriptural standpoint, see the recent excellent essay by Richard Barry, "Retrieving the Goat," *Nova et Vetera* 15, no. 1 (Winter 2017): 13–35.

consistent in its emphasis on these points. It is also pretty clear, I think (and von Balthasar and Pitstick have no disagreement here), that it is at least doctrinal in the third degree that the victory wrought by the cross is not limited to this world, and that among the points of saying so is that the grammar of Christian doctrine requires some way of affirming that the burden of original sin under which (among others) the patriarchs of the Jews labor was lifted by Christ. But there is, so far as I can tell, nothing more on the descent that is properly doctrinal—whether *de fide* in either kind or to be received *religioso voluntatis et intellectus obsequio*. Everything else is, at the moment, matter for theological speculation.[79]

Comprehension of this assessment requires a robust understanding of the Catholic theology of the magisterium.[80] Building on Griffiths, Lois M. Miles points out the following in defense of the orthodoxy of Adrienne von Speyr's treatment of the descent:

> With regard to the pre-Christian dead, the Catechism states that "Scripture calls the abode of the dead, to which the dead Christ went down, 'hell'—*Sheol* in Hebrew or *Hades* in Greek—because those who are there are deprived of the vision of God." . . . [T]he Son experiences the same death as humans experience. . . . The Redeemer then delivers the righteous: [CCC 633]. . . . This fairly brief explanation of the Son's intent with regard to the righteous dead does not limit how far into hell the Son did or did not descend. Neither does the Catechism determine at what point the holy souls were released from the abode of the dead, whether at the beginning or end of his descent. Furthermore, it does not even mention a multi-tiered hell or the limbo of the Fathers as some traditions claim. While "Limbo" is mentioned in the Index of the Catechism, the text refers only to "children who have died without baptism" and not to a so-called "Limbo of the Fathers." So it appears that although a popular tradition may adhere to a multi-level hell that includes a limbo of the Fathers and a limbo

---

79 See Paul Griffiths, "Is There a Doctrine of the Descent into Hell?," *Pro Ecclesia* 17, no. 3 (2008): 257–268, at 265.

80 I am not able to enter into this here, but see, e.g., Avery Dulles, *Magisterium: Teacher and Guardian of the Faith* (Ave Maria, FL: Sapientia Press, 2010).

of the unbaptized, the official Catechism of the Roman Catholic Church does not require belief in these tenets as matters of faith.[81]

Of course, Pitstick replies to Griffiths, but in a somewhat enigmatic manner, resulting in nothing but an impasse.[82] Through tortured logic she argues that because the magisterium cannot clarify all terms involved in the debate and thus need not attempt to do so, what remains is her interpretation—the correct interpretation, that is—of what "the tradition" holds concerning the descent. She correctly concludes: "the key question is whether a new theological proposal is 'not contradictory of what has gone before,'" which she asserts to have shown elsewhere.[83] But she purports to have shown this simply by contrasting Balthasar's conception of Holy Saturday with the art, liturgy, and writings of a certain time period in the Church's history. The problem is not the contrast or even the time periods in question, but the *non sequitur* that Balthasar's fundamental approach to the descent cannot be integrated into the larger tradition, as if they are mutually exclusive (i.e., contradictory). For example, Pitstick thinks that conceiving the descent in terms of passivity, like that of a corpse, contradicts the notion of Christ descending as victorious savior. But there is nothing to prevent the possibility of the obedience of Christ being characterized as utterly receptive to the will of the Father and yet also manifest itself as actively victorious.[84] Similarly, assuming Pitstick is correct that

---

[81] Miles, "Obedience of a Corpse," 204. Sutton also develops this point:

> The distinction, which Pitstick misses, is that the Catholic Church's dogmas can be affirmed while also accommodating many different theological interpretations, especially if the interpretations of them have not received definitive magisterial dogmatic or doctrinal declaration.... The Catechism even acknowledges that the triumphant image is just a "first" interpretation that was given in the ancient church. [208] It currently dominates theological interpretation, but a theological interpretation of a dogma is not itself dogma. So there is clearly disagreement about the best interpretation of the dogma of the descent, but there is no disagreement between von Balthasar (von Speyr) and official church teaching about the dogma itself. The interpretations of dogmas can experience development. (*Heaven Opens: The Trinitarian Mysticism of Adrienne von Speyr*, Kindle Locations 4195–4197, 4200–4205)

[82] I have not seen her respond anywhere to Miles.

[83] See Pitstick, "Response to Webster and Lauber," 216.

[84] Speyr emphasizes the *Geschehenlassen* (or "letting happen") of the Son in death and descent (see Miles, 171; Speyr, *Subjektive Mystik*, [Einsiedeln: Johannesverlag, 1970], 116), but this does not mean He is entirely passive—rather, His "blind obedience" (*Ka-*

there is no pre-Reformation precedent for understanding the glory of the descent more in terms of the Cross than in terms of the Resurrection, that does not mean it is contradictory to do so.

If the Fathers understood the descent simply in terms of Resurrection (a dubious claim, certainly), it is not therefore forbidden to add to this conception the element of glory that existed on the Cross. Perhaps the glory of the descent is not simply that of the Cross or of the Resurrection but possesses its own peculiar significance.[85] Balthasar does not seem to utilize a hard distinction between passion and descent,[86] utilizing the metaphorical term "Cross" to refer to a cross-section of events, not simply the historical Crucifixion, and the reason may lie in his existential understanding of death itself (i.e., its relative temporality structure). More to the point, Pitstick simply misunderstands the concept of doctrinal development when she states: "the tradition's silence in applying the cross's 'glory' to the descent is indeed significant: if Balthasar is going to *develop* the doctrine along those lines, there must be something there to begin with. . . . [T]here is no such 'tradition' in that vein prior to the Reformation."[87]

---

davergehorsam) is entirely receptive of the Father's active love and thus emblematic of it. Hence, she says, "yet in another sense, his journey into the netherworld is the journey of a victor. Like a triumphant field marshal, he musters the defeated troops and the spoils of victory: the fettered powers of evil and conquered sin" (*John* IV, 143).

Miles adds: "His triumph lies not in his activity as a heroic god of mythological proportions but rather in his *Suscipe*, his perfect indifference and availability to the Father through the obedience of a corpse" ("Obedience of a Corpse," 182). Moreover, she responds to Pitstick by outlining the steps in Speyr's (not Balthasar's) treatment of the descent of Christ compared to the "popular tradition" (see "Obedience of a Corpse," 201–203).

[85] Lauber enumerates how, according to Barth (whom Balthasar followed on this score), the descent belongs in different respects to both the *status humiliationis* and *status exaltationis* (see "Towards a Theology of Holy Saturday," 127–128).

[86] Lauber argues that Balthasar differs from Barth in emphasizing a distinction between the sufferings of Friday and Saturday (see "Towards a Theology of Holy Saturday," ch. 3), but Lauber's reading of Balthasar is almost entirely limited to *Mysterium Paschale* (and earlier works), and Lauber admits even Barth sometimes appears to waver (see "Towards a Theology of Holy Saturday," 226).

[87] Pitstick, "Response to Webster and Lauber," 213. Balthasar also may have had an inadequate grasp of the theology of tradition as revelation; see his quick dismissal of the Tubingen school in *Explorations* I, 18. Balthasar leaves some clues to his own understanding of tradition in *Razing the Bastions*, trans. Brian McNeil (San Francisco: Ignatius Press, 1993), 36–37 [*Schliefung der Bastionen: Von der Kirche in Dieser Zeit* Einsiedeln: Johannes Verlag, 1952), 24–25].

He clearly does not conceive of tradition as one of the "sources" of revelation, comprised by the "consensus of the Fathers," a medieval conceptualization of the phenom-

There are certainly conceptual antecedents to Balthasar's articulation of the descent, which he quotes thoroughly, but they need not be so linearly related as Pitstick assumes.[88] Hopefully, she would admit that theologians are free to disagree on what passes for doctrinal developments in line with the deposit of faith until the magisterium authoritatively clarifies what is orthodox.

It is not clear how the majority tradition on the descent as simply triumphant encompasses an adequate reading of Scripture or whether it can withstand the theological scrutiny necessary for the Church to demand adherence to such a position.[89] In fact, Balthasar shows that the Jewish people traditionally understood Sheol in a much darker light than do the "traditional" theologians, and thus the descent was directed towards this dark abode of death, not to some state of natural happiness after a pre-Christian purgatory (a creative invention). Without returning to the biblical texts already cited in favor of Balthasar's position, it suffices to point to the suffering prophet Job as perhaps his favorite Old Testament figure of Christ. Unfortunately, the much-esteemed Cardinal Avery Dulles appears to side entirely with Pitstick rather than mediate a *tertia via*,[90] to which Oakes's only necessary response is to quote yet another scriptural text on the side of Balthasar: "In saying 'He ascended,' what does [Scrip-

---

enon. Rather, he understands tradition in terms of the Spirit exploiting in time the riches that lie inchoate in Christ Himself, whose revealing deeds and words were nevertheless publicly witnessed in full by the time of John's death. His monograph on Gregory of Nyssa displays an even more liberal understanding of tradition (see *Presence and Thought: An Essay on the Religious Philosophy of Gregory of Nyssa*, trans. Mark Sebanc [San Francisco: Ignatius Press, 1995], 12).

[88] For initial acquaintance with the theology of doctrinal development after Newman, see my "Development(s) in the Theology of Revelation: From Francisco Marín-Sola to Joseph Ratzinger," *New Blackfriars* 97, no. 1072 (2016): 661–676. See also Aidan Nichols, OP, *From Newman to Congar: The Idea of Doctrinal Development from the Victorians to the Second Vatican Council* (Edinburgh: T&T Clark, 1990).

[89] Even Kevin L. Flannery, SJ, a Balthasar critic, notes: "Surprisingly, Augustine held that Christ descended not to the limbo of the just but to the lowest regions of hell: *De Genesi ad litteram libri XII*, 33, 63 (see also *De civ. Dei* 17.11). Whom did he save from there? 'Whom he willed,' he says at *Ep.* 164.5.14. I argue against this notion." ("How to Think about Hell," *New Blackfriars* 72, no. 854 [1991]: 469–481, at 481n21)

Augustine's view on the intrinsic efficacy of grace coheres well with his approach to the descent; the difference from Balthasar consists in his restriction of election to "the few." For further development of this "minor" tradition on the descent, see David Lauber, "Towards a Theology of Holy Saturday."

[90] See Dulles, "Responses to Balthasar, Hell, and Heresy," *First Things* (March 2007), which includes Oakes's response and a reply to Oakes from Pitstick.

ture] mean but that he had also descended into the lower regions of the earth? He who descended is he who also ascended far above all the heavens in order that he might fill all things" (Eph. 4:9–10). The Jewish understanding of the "lower regions of the earth" certainly involved the notion of suffering, but, as if that were not enough, Oakes also calls to mind the image of Jonah's three days in the belly of a whale as a prefiguration of His suffering in the descent.[91]

Nonetheless, I have attempted here to point the way toward a *tertia via* between the dichotomy set up by Pitstick and Oakes. I agree with Pitstick that Christ's last words indicate that His suffering did not continue after death and with John Paul the Great that His soul enjoyed nothing but bliss immediately upon death.[92] Pitstick asserts the same position in her dissertation,[93] which Oakes notes is omitted from the later Eerdmans edition and ridicules.[94] Oakes argues:

> This invocation of Christ's beatific vision to avoid the implications of an expiatory Holy Saturday is deeply problematic, for it would also have to imply that Christ never left heaven in the first place (since according to Aquinas he enjoyed the beatific vision from the moment of his conception). . . . [T]here is absolutely *nothing* in the beatific vision that implies it serves as a kind of celestial anesthetic inuring the human soul of Jesus from pain.[95]

While I agree with the last statement, his reasoning here is confused. Why cannot Jesus's human soul simultaneously enjoy the beatific vision and be present in the depths of hell through some other modality besides that of

---

[91] See Edward T. Oakes and Alyssa L. Pitstick, "Balthasar, Hell, and Heresy: An Exchange," *First Things* (December 2006); Edward T. Oakes and Alyssa L. Pitstick, "More on Balthasar, Hell, and Heresy," *First Things* (January 2007). For exegesis of additional texts concerning the descent of Christ into hell, see Wilhelm Maas, *Gott und die Holle: Studien zum Descensus Christi* (Einsiedeln: Johannes Verlag, 1979), ch. 2.

[92] See his General Audience, "He Descended into Hell." John Paul is, of course, not alone in this position, which derives in part from the literal sense of Christ's words to the good thief on the cross (see, e.g., Philip Schaff, *The Creeds of Christendom, with a History and Critical Notes*, vol. 2, *The Greek and Latin Creeds* [New York: Harper and Brothers, 1877], 46n2).

[93] "*Lux in Tenebris*: The Traditional Catholic Doctrine of Christ's Descent into Hell and the Theological Opinion of Hans Urs von Balthasar" [PhD diss., Angelicum University, Rome, 2005], 84–85.

[94] See Oakes, "*Descensus* and Development," 16–17.

[95] Oakes, "*Descensus* and Development," 16.

consciousness (i.e., his salvific action)? Whether or not Christ could have both enjoyed the beatific vision and suffered the torments of the damned at once, the crux of the matter is precisely whether the *fruitio beata* began on Saturday or Sunday; that is, whether the descent-suffering took place historically on Friday in the midst of His passion and death or on Saturday proper. It seems more sensible for Christ to endure the pains of hell while still alive, being deprived of the *fruitio beata* even while possessing by His divinity the *visio beata*, rather than to undergo a real split of consciousness in which he both enjoys the vision and suffers its absence (which is not the position advocated by Oakes, but the only other alternative to it and the position defended here).[96]

I think Oakes is correct to dismiss Pitstick's "insistence that Christ descended only to limbo . . . that Christ only went to visit *the already redeemed*."[97] But Oakes also overshoots the mark when he proclaims: "the church clearly teaches that Christ continued and completed his work of redemption, indeed made it definitive, in his descent among the dead."[98] He cites the *Catechism of the Catholic Church*, paragraph 634, which speaks only of the descent "bring[ing] the Gospel message of salvation to complete fulfillment," thereafter articulating its universal significance (i.e., not its particular historicity). One can hear Pitstick already (rightly) distinguishing between the communication of the message of salvation and the element of (historical) suffering that comprises Christ's redemptive work. Balthasar, in fact, does the same.[99]

Matthew Levering compares what John Paul II says in *Novo Millennio Ineunte* (§§26–27) to what Balthasar says in his Trilogy.[100] He points out that although Balthasar speaks of Christ experiencing the hopelessness of human sinfulness on the level of "conscious not-knowing," he does not attribute "a perversion of will" to Christ and he maintains that Christ remains at least conscious of His divine identity and mission.[101] In other words, "there resides an implicit 'hope'" where the ecstatic distance between Father and Son is merely intellectual, not volitional. John Paul, on the contrary, "drawing upon Catherine of Siena and Therese of Lisieux, insists upon 'the paradoxical blending of bliss and pain,' without

---

[96] I will elaborate upon this thesis in the next chapter.
[97] Oakes, "*Descensus* and Development," 17.
[98] Oakes, 18.
[99] See *MP*, 150–151, 159 [G 226–227, 235].
[100] Particularly *TD* IV, 349, and *TL* II, 294.
[101] Levering, "Balthasar on Christ's Consciousness on the Cross," *The Thomist* 65 (2001): 567–581, at 578.

suggesting that the bliss is no longer experienced (§27)."[102] The full para-doxical reflection of John Paul follows:

> At the very moment when he identifies with our sin, "abandoned" by the Father, he "abandons" himself into the hands of the Father. His eyes remain fixed on the Father. Precisely because of the knowledge and experience of the Father which he alone has, even at this moment of darkness he sees clearly the gravity of sin and suffers because of it. He alone, who sees the Father and rejoices fully in him, can understand completely what it means to resist the Father's love by sin. More than an experience of physical pain, his passion is an agonizing suffering of the soul. Theological tra-dition has not failed to ask how Jesus could possibly experience at one and the same time his profound unity with the Father, by its very nature a source of joy and happiness, and an agony that goes all the way to his final cry of abandonment. The simultaneous presence of these two seemingly irreconcilable aspects is rooted in the fathomless depths of the hypostatic union.[103]

Hence, the most balanced understanding of the descent is gained by com-bining John Paul II's Wednesday audience (of January 11, 1989) address-ing the topic and his reflections in the apostolic letters *Salvifici Doloris* (§§17–18) and *Novo Millenio Ineunte* (§§26–27). While Balthasar himself may not be entirely clear about whether or not Christ historically suffered in hell *after* His death,[104] two successive theologian-Pontiffs could not be clearer.[105]

---

[102] Levering, 578n41. Levering also notes that, for Balthasar, "[t]he question of how Christ's human knowledge corresponds with his divine knowledge is thus placed to the side. Rephrasing the question in terms of consciousness, rather than of knowledge . . ." ("Balthasar on Christ's Consciousness," 576n32).

[103] *Novo Millenio Ineunte*, §26, available on the Vatican Website at https://w2.vatican.va/content/john-paul-ii/en/apost_letters/2001/documents/hf_jp-ii_apl_20010106_novo-millennio-ineunte.html [accessed 12/8/17])

[104] See especially *GL* VII, 230–232 [G 213–215]; *Explorations* IV, 408; *TL* II, 348 [G 317].

[105] For a critical assessment of Pitstick's latest book, *Christ's Descent into Hell: John Paul II, Joseph Ratzinger, and Hans Urs von Balthasar on the Theology of Holy Saturday* (Grand Rapids, MI: Eerdmans, 2016), see my book review in *Nova et Vetera* 16, no. 2 (2018): 665–669. Of course, those who hold the Tridentine position are also prone to pit Au-gustine and Aquinas against any present-day authority, but matters are not so simple. See, e.g., *In Symbolum Apostolorum Expositio*, a. 5, 926, in *Opuscula Theologica*, vol. 2, ed. Raimund Spiazzi, OP (Rome: Marietti, 1954), 204; ET, *The Sermon-Conferences of*

CONCLUSIONS

While Ratzinger (with relative clarity) limits Christ's sufferings temporally to Friday, allocating the sufferings celebrated on Holy Saturday to the historical time culminating in the "moment" of His death, Balthasar is less precise on the question.[106] Balthasar's latest statement relevant to the question seems to be the following quasi-poetical (mystical?) reflections:

> [P]assing through this place [where the Father is not], he is at once who he is (the sinless son of the Father) and who he is not, insofar as he is the bearer of all the sins of the world. Fundamentally, he goes in two opposite directions: (with the thief on his right) toward paradise and (with the one on his left, in order to fetch him) into deep hell. The contradiction, then, is that he is at once the farthest from hell and, as sin-bearer, the closest to it; that, being this dead man, he has lost his Word-character (hence the silence) and yet, at the same time, is also the Father's loudest and clearest message to the world.[107]

Just prior to this, though, he seems to place the descent into hell after Christ's return to the Father in spirit, relying on Speyr:

> After his death, into which he is flung as into the abyss, but before he goes through hell, there is indeed something like a pause,

---

St. Thomas Aquinas, 79.

Even the Dominican Thomist, Thomas Joseph White, grants:

Aquinas follows Augustine's interpretation of 1 Peter as proposed in his famous letter to Evodius. In fact, Augustine interprets the passage in such a way that it has something in common with what Calvin, Barth, and Balthasar wish to convey in speaking of a descent into hell. . . . They do wish to underscore, however, a kind of solidarity established in Christ between God and all human beings in the night of this world, including those who experience the deepest sense of spiritual suffering, alienation from God, or ignorance of divine things. On this precise point, it is interesting to read Aquinas's Augustinian interpretation of the passage from 1 Peter, which does offer some limited similarity to the thinking of Balthasar. (*Incarnate Lord*, 411; see *ST* III, q. 52, a. 2, ad 3)

[106] Furthermore, while Ratzinger appears to be silent on when Jesus enjoyed the beatific vision, John Paul II exclaims that Jesus enjoyed His communion with the Father immediately upon death (see "He Descended into Hell," *A Catechesis on the Creed* II, 483–488) and possesses the *visio* all along (*Novo Millenio Ineunte*, §§25–27). For more on the slight but significant differences between Balthasar and Ratzinger, see the Appendix.

[107] *TL* II, 351–352 [G 320–321].

in which he deposits the Good Thief in the promised paradise. But this signals the beginning of an indescribable paradox. He is the dead "sin-bearer" of all sins. As such, he passes through what, looked at objectively, is his victory, the sin separated from man on the Cross, which God eternally damns as the second—man-created—chaos.[108]

Perhaps this return "through hell" is the victorious reaping of the redemption sown in His descent-suffering on the Cross (i.e., His death itself).

In any case, the "descent into hell" signifies both the triumphal application of redemption to the souls who preceded Christ and the culmination of His glorious suffering in death itself,[109] containing all possible spiritual and moral pain (qualitatively speaking), temporally suffered while He hung upon the tree. The moment of His (and consequently everyone's) death cannot be entirely limited to a quantitative segment of time because it is an "existential moment" in which time and eternity come together in the soul suffering departure from its own body. Thus, Holy Saturday is not a mini-Easter, according to which the soul of Christ is triumphing over the wickedness of the dead—rather, it signifies the *hidden* power of His passion and future Resurrection.[110] As Christmas is the celebration of both Nativity and Incarnation (since His incarnation was made fully manifest to men in the Nativity), Holy Saturday represents liturgically the threshold between His suffering and His glorious triumph (not the latter

---

[108] *TL* II, 348 [G 317]. Elsewhere, Balthasar speaks of hell as chaos: "hell is the world's 'second chaos' (the Creator brought order to the first), which arose through sin and henceforth can be separated from sinner through the Cross of Christ. In this respect, Christ contemplates his own work of redemption in the darkness of hell: depersonalizing sin dissolves into the chaos" ("General Introduction to the Posthumous Works," in Adrienne von Speyr, *Book of All Saints*, trans. D. C. Schindler [San Francisco: Ignatius Press, 2008], 1–19, at 14).

[109] Even in his earlier writing, Balthasar does not see Holy Saturday as exclusively kenotic or pre-victorious: "The mystery of Holy Saturday is two things simultaneously: the utmost extremity of the *exinanitio* [self-emptying] and the beginning of the *Gloria* even before the resurrection" (*Explorations* I, 264 [G 286]). He also says: "It is precisely at this point [the cry of dereliction] that the soteriological *descensus* occurs. Out of this timeless hiatus of Holy Saturday." (*Convergences: To the Source of Christian Mystery*, trans. E. A. Nelson [San Francisco: Ignatius Press, 1983], 98).

[110] "[T]he silence of the Church on Holy Saturday ... ought to bear within itself an inkling of what tremendous, ineffable things are happening between heaven and hell" (*TL* II, 359 [G 327]). Concerning this silence, see the "Second Reading on Holy Saturday," in *The Liturgy of the Hours*, vol. 2 (New York: Catholic Books Publishing, 1976), 496.

alone nor the former alone),[111] as well as the day of Mary's suffering (that is, Christ within her!) and the mysterious "day" in which the Church now lives ("completing what is lacking in the sufferings of Christ"). Holy Saturday is both a sorrowful and happy occasion because it was through the descent into the utter abandonment of the Cross that the prisoner souls who preceded Him in time were redeemed (in that symbolic moment),[112] allowing Him to enter the Father's glory at death, having endured with impenetrable hope the judgment of wrath upon sin itself. All for the glory of the kenotic love of the triune God![113]

---

[111] See also Balthasar's *The Way of the Cross*, trans. Rodelinde Albrecht and Maureen Sullivan (New York: Herder and Herder, 1969), 30.

[112] Hence, early in his career, Balthasar comments on the liturgical practice of the Triduum: "On Holy Saturday there is no reason to sing Alleluia. The descent of Jesus into the reality of death that preceded Redemption is part of his humiliations, even though this ultimate humiliation, beyond which no other is possible, is already shot through with the light of Easter night, as for St John even the Cross itself. For this journey through Hades carries Redemption into it. This track through the trackless way makes an opening where before all had been completely closed" (*The God Question*, 133–134).

[113] It is not yet clear how God's love may be called "kenotic." In a later chapter, I will take issue with Balthasar's *ur*-kenotic theory of the processions, but that is not to deny the divine identity of the One who suffered as Son of Man (and the communion of life between the divine persons).

CHAPTER THREE

The Mystery of Christ's Beatific Suffering
Whether Christ Lost the Beatific Vision in His Descent-Suffering

INVOLVED IN BALTHASAR'S controversial theology of Christ's descent into hell are many complex questions intricately intertwined with one another, and thus it constitutes the flashpoint of his theology, where the two most significant influences on his thought converge, Karl Barth and Adrienne von Speyr.[1] One book cannot possibly treat every aspect of the issue adequately. Therefore, in this chapter, I will be concerned primarily with what comprises the experience of Christ's descent into godforsakenness, as far as speculative theology can address such a question, particularly in terms of the traditional doctrine that He possessed in His human intellect direct vision of the divine essence (*visio beata/beatifica* or *visio immedi-*

---

[1] Concerning the former influence, see D. Stephen Long, *Saving Karl Barth: Hans Urs von Balthasar's Preoccupation* (Minneapolis, MN: Fortress Press, 2014); John Webster, "Balthasar and Karl Barth," in *Cambridge Companion to Hans Urs von Balthasar*, 241–255; Stephen Wigley, *Karl Barth and Hans Urs von Balthasar: A Critical Engagement* (New York: T&T Clark, 2007).

Concerning the latter influence, see Johann Roten, "The Two Halves of the Moon"; Michele M. Schumacher, *A Trinitarian Anthropology: Adrienne von Speyr and Hans Urs von Balthasar in Dialogue with Thomas Aquinas* (Washington, DC: Catholic University of America Press, 2014); Matthew Lewis Sutton, *Heaven Opens*, Kindle Edition, locations 185ff. Balthasar himself wrote a volume specifically concerning each, *The Theology of Karl Barth*, trans. Edward T. Oakes, SJ (San Francisco: Ignatius Press, 1992), and *First Glance at Adrienne von Speyr*, trans. Antje Lawry and Sergia Englund, OCD (San Francisco: Ignatius Press, 1981).

ata). Certainly, the subjectivity of the Savior cannot be psychoanalyzed, and yet revelation contains some nuggets that allow not only for contemplative pondering, but also for rational reflection. Balthasar draws on both the "private revelation" granted the mystic, Adrienne von Speyr, as well as the history of theological reflection on the datum of the redemptive Incarnation, with the latter informing his reception of the former as far as it is possible to translate mystical experience into rational speculative discourse.[2] Presuming the genuineness of her experiences and acknowledging the fallibility of his (as well as her own!) understanding of such phenomena, it is the task of the theologian to evaluate critically the coherence of the insights proposed.[3]

Balthasar's (and Speyr's) theology of the descent has been critically assessed from various angles, but rarely from the perspective of the thorny problem of whether Christ enjoyed the beatific vision in His earthly life. While it is pertinent to engage the critiques of this theology already offered, perhaps the greatest light is shed on this issue of Holy Saturday when the question of Jesus's human consciousness is brought to the fore. My chosen task here is not so much to demonstrate the fittingness of the concomitance of the beatific vision to the hypostatic union, as others have done,[4] but to explore the possibility and fittingness of Christ enduring the

---

[2] I presume that Balthasar's intent is such, but arguably he ends up importing theological constructs foreign not merely to dogmatic theology, but even the very mystical experience he purports to communicate. See Blankenhorn's review of Pitstick's *Light in Darkness*, *Nova et Vetera* 6, no. 4 (2008): 951–955.

[3] On the contrary, after asserting that "[Barth's] influence on von Balthasar, however, has been greatly overestimated," Kevin Mongrain casually dismisses even the influence of Speyr:

> The assumption guiding my reading of von Balthasar is that von Speyr's influence on his theology was deforming rather than constructive, derived rather than original; von Speyr is essential for psychologically understanding von Balthasar but completely dispensable for theologically understanding him. Defending the scholarly validity of this assertion is beyond the scope of the present study. My hope is that the interpretation I am putting forward here will give scholars tools for refuting von Balthasar's misleading claims about her role in shaping his theology. (*The Systematic Thought of Hans Urs von Balthasar: An Irenaean Retrieval* [New York: Crossroad, 2002], 11–12)

> Rosenberg compliments Mongrain's study, but rightly contests this unjustified assertion: "Even keeping in mind his 'Irenaean retrieval,' one must consider von Speyr's influence on his theological project. Our investigation suggests that her influence, while indispensable to Balthasar, is also problematic" ("Theory and Drama," 302).

[4] See especially the recent work by Simon Francis Gaine, OP, *Did the Saviour See the*

greatest possible suffering, namely, loss (albeit objectively temporary) of the infinite joy that is naturally consequent to the beatific vision already possessed.

I wish here to engage secondary literature on Balthasar's theology of the descent of Christ's into hell on Holy Saturday, but only insofar as it aids in answering the following question: Did Christ lose the beatific vision for a time during His passion? In other words, if He had the beatific vision during His earthly life, is it possible for Him to lose it temporarily, and would it be fitting for him to suffer the loss of the vision (or perhaps only the *fruitio beata*)? Of course, if he did not already have the vision, then he could not suffer its loss. Hence, the nature of faith, the nature of the beatific vision, the possibility of the two coexisting in Christ's consciousness, and whether it would be fitting for one or both to exist in His soul before His resurrection must first be addressed, even if briefly. Despite the Thomistic-Scotistic difference concerning the intellectual versus volitional nature of supernatural beatitude,[5] it seems fitting (and not incongruent with Thomistic reasoning) for Christ both to possess the *visio immediata* (or *visio beatifica*)[6] during His entire earthly life (including death) and to suffer temporary loss of the *fruitio beata* that is naturally concomitant to such vision during His passion, at least, according to Balthasarian-Speyrian reasoning.

But before obtaining in dialogue with Balthasar-Speyr a nuanced conclusion concerning this aspect of the problem of Christ's descent-suffering, I will explore briefly how this particular aspect of the question (i.e., the Christological problem of Christ's human knowledge) arises out of Balthasar's soteriological reflections. I will then present a panoramic overview of the debate concerning the nature of Christ's human knowledge in contemporary

---

Father? Christ, Salvation, and the Vision of God (New York: Bloomsbury T&T Clark, 2015). See also Guy Mansini, "Understanding St. Thomas on Christ's Immediate Knowledge of God," *Thomist* 59 (1995): 91–124; Matthew Levering, *Christ's Fulfillment of Torah and Temple: Salvation according to Thomas Aquinas* (Notre Dame, IN: University of Notre Dame Press, 2002), 59–61, 74–75; Thomas Joseph White, OP, "The Voluntary Action of the Earthly Christ and the Necessity of the Beatific Vision," *The Thomist* 69, no. 4 (2005): 497–534; and Bruce D. Marshall's talk for the Thomistic Institute on October 2, 2015, entitled "Jesus' Human Knowledge: A Test for Theological Exegesis," available at https://soundcloud.com/thomisticinstitute/dr-bruce-d-marshall-jesus-human-knowledge-a-test-for-theological-exegesis-1022015.

5   See Zachary Hayes, "Heaven," in *The Modern Catholic Encyclopedia*, ed. Michael Glazier and Monika K. Hellwig (Collegeville, MN: Liturgical Press, 2004), 352.

6   Balthasar thinks the latter term was "all too abruptly" adopted in the history of theology (*TD* V, 470 [G 431]).

Catholic (Thomistic) theology.[7] Finally, I will bring Balthasar into the debate by presenting an interpretation of his understanding of the *fides Christi* and the notion of "laying up" items of knowledge not immediately pertinent to His mission. I will also provide a convenient recapitulating summary of the findings of this encounter between Balthasar-Speyr and the doctrine of Christ's *visio immediata*.

FROM SOTERIOLOGY TO CHRISTOLOGY[8]

I have already argued that the descent of Christ into hell, celebrated on Holy Saturday, ought not to be identified simply with either the hellish suffering of Christ in His passion and death or the communication of His redemptive grace to the dead because it encompasses both realities, as the hiatus between Good Friday and Easter Sunday. Hence, the descent is not most properly understood as one historical event, but signifies the complex and, in some sense, timeless redemptive transition from suffering to Resurrection.[9] But the deeper question is how precisely to understand

---

[7] Nicholas J. Healy, Jr., a Balthasarian, treats this question in a manner not quite Thomistic but in line with the classical position, but he conspicuously omits all reference to Balthasar: see "*Simul viator et comprehensor:* The Filial Mode of Christ's Knowledge," *Nova et Vetera* (English Edition) 11, no. 2 (2013): 341–355.

[8] Ordinarily, a systematic theology would treat Christology before soteriology, but since Balthasar's soteriology is both more controversial and more central to his project, I have begun with the latter and now transition toward Christological concerns, as the two fields are nonetheless interrelated (irrespective of pedagogical ordering).

   Also, Balthasar explicitly resists this ordering of treatises, preferring to address the person and work of Christ at once (see *TD* III, 149 [G 136]). Furthermore, Randall S. Rosenberg notes: "In his theology of Christ, Balthasar proceeds from a 'Christology of Consciousness' to a 'Christology of Being'" ("Christ's Human Knowledge: A Conversation with Lonergan and Balthasar," *Theological Studies* 71 [2010]: 817–845, at 822).

[9] Miles sums up Speyr's perspective on time:

> [N]o relationship exists between time in hell and either earthly or eternal time. Since hell expends "non-time" in a "non-place," there is no method of measuring space or time. It is a "way-less" and "time-less" "non-place." Von Speyr explains that if one outside of hell were to observe one going through hell—such as a mystic experiencing the descent into hell—that outside observer could measure the time such a one had been gone, just as the disciples could measure the days that the Son spent in the tomb. But "whoever goes through it, feels the non-passage of time; everything stops and remains the same or develops itself more and more into non-time. . . . Going through hell takes either all time or no time. The way is way-less as the time is time-less." For von Speyr, the expression "time stands still" aptly describes the experience of hell. ("Obedience of a Corpse," 78)

Christ's hellish suffering in relation to His identity as Son of God and what that entails for His human nature. The following observation of T. J. White may be a key to responding to his own conventional objections to Balthasar's understanding of Christ's *kenosis*:

> [A]ccording to Aquinas, the "economic mode" or "dispensation" of Christ's vision during his earthly life is understood to be very different from that of his vision in the exalted state of glory. In the latter state, his body and emotional psychology participate each in their own way directly in the glory of his resurrected life. . . . In the former state, however, this vision is not the source of any such experience. It does assure his soul of a continual knowledge of his own divine identity and will as the Son of God, but it *in no way* alleviates his "ordinary" states of human consciousness and sensation.[10]

Can we not conclude from this that the divine will could at least suspend experience of the joy ordinarily consequent to immediate vision of God's essence? The question of the nature of Christ's knowledge has to do with the doctrine of the descent insofar as ignorance is said to be assumed for the sake of our salvation and as a necessary condition for the possibility of Christ experiencing something akin to the "pain of loss" (which is the most significant *poena damni*).[11]

The question of what kind of ignorance is proper to Christ's human consciousness need not be determined prior to asserting that it may be fitting that He not experience the joy of being conscious (on a human operative level) of the immediate vision that follows from the logic of the hypostatic union.[12] If Christ's *kenosis* does not involve divesting enjoyment

---

[10] White, "Jesus' Cry on the Cross," 573–574. In a footnote at the end of this text, White says: "*ST* III, q. 14, a. 1, ad 2: 'From the natural relationship which is between the soul and the body, glory flows into the body from the soul's glory. Yet this natural relationship in Christ was subject to the will of his Godhead, and thereby it came to pass that the beatitude remained in the soul and did not flow into the body; but the flesh suffered what belongs to a passible nature.' *ST* III, q. 15, aa. 4–6, make clear that Aquinas understands 'the body' or 'the flesh' of Christ to include the passions and human psychology of the man Jesus" (574n52).

For a more elaborate exploration of Christ's human psychology, see Paul Gondreau, *The Passions of Christ's Soul in the Theology of St. Thomas Aquinas* (Scranton, PA: University of Scranton Press, 2009).

[11] I am here accepting the traditional position that it is at least supremely fitting for an intellectual being hypostatically united to the divine essence to possess the beatific vision.

[12] The nescience passages would, at least, suggest that despite Jesus's vision of the Father,

of being humanly conscious (at least in an immediate manner) of the divine essence, then it is natural to accept the triumphalist interpretation of the descent as merely *parousia* to the just who preceded Christ, awaiting His revelation in "Abraham's bosom." If, on the contrary, the descent is understood in terms of *kenosis*, and if the biblical attestations of ignorance in Christ are taken seriously (not in a merely metaphorical or rhetorical sense), then there is work to be done in squaring the *visio immediata Dei* attributed to Christ and the depths of spiritual agony evidently present in the passion.[13]

Both White and Thomas grant the point that the "immediate vision" would have augmented the intensity and sensitivity with which Christ suffered psychologically from human sinfulness, but neither considers the possibility that the divine knowledge of Christ and the experience of absolute "alienation" may not be incompatible in the descent. In other words, certainly Christ did not suffer actual loss of the state of grace or succumb to the sins of despair or hatred of God,[14] but does the infinite knowledge of

---

his earthly mind was not cognizant of all that would naturally be known of created things by the mind that is given understanding of the divine essence via the *lumen gloriae* (i.e., the blessed in heaven). Hence, Balthasar speaks a number of times of Christ "laying up" with the Father knowledge that is unnecessary to His mission (see *TD* III, 192 [G 176]; *TD* V, 259, 302, 389, 514 [G 234, 275, 356, 470]), even going so far as to say: "since all is obedience, he *is* moving toward the Father through this utter estrangement, but for the present he must not be allowed to know this" (*TD* IV, 356 [G 332]). Concerning his mission-consciousness, see also *TD* III, 166 [G 152].

[13] Balthasar's willingness to admit ignorance in Christ's human mind does not derive so much from a rational attempt to square His vision of God with His experience of abandonment, but to take certain scriptural texts seriously, and thus Christ's *kenosis* is said to involve not merely suffering, but a "depositing" of what would naturally belong to Him as Son into the Father's hands.

Against the scholastic consensus, Balthasar seeks to bolster a Johannine perspective, which "emphasizes Jesus' obedience as strongly as his supramundane knowledge. . . . [T]he greater good of this obedience required that the Son's intrinsically 'fitting' and 'direct knowledge' should be 'laid up' with the Father for reasons of 'economy'" (*TD* III, 192 [G 176]).

[14] Thomas Weinandy, after acknowledging his agreement with Balthasar's Holy Saturday doctrine and quoting John Paul II's *Salvifici Doloris*, states unequivocally:

It should be noted that while the Son, as man, experienced the full weight of our condemnation, he did not have the mind of a condemned sinner. The damned find God to be utterly loathsome and detestable, for he embodies all that is abhorrent to the condemned sinner—goodness, holiness and love. Jesus, in the midst of his abandonment, maintained a firm love of his Father and trusted that his Father would restore his loving presence. While Jesus, through Psalm 22,

His divine nature actually preclude the possibility of a divine suspension of the fruition which would ordinarily be consequent to the hypostatic union? Balthasar need only deny the *fruitio beata*: "the Trinity does not hover 'unmoved' above the events of the Cross (the view that Christ is somehow 'above' his abandonment by God and continues to *enjoy* the beatific vision), nor does it get entangled in sin as in a process theology à la Moltmann or Hegel, becoming part of a mythology or cosmic tragedy."[15]

Notwithstanding White's intention to defend the beatific vision in Christ and his attempt to interpret the cry of dereliction in that vein,[16] God's impotence to suspend at least the joy consequent to such vision (or human consciousness of any of its content) cannot be demonstrated.[17] If it is demonstrative to say that whenever an infinite good is known, it must be loved, and that both knowing and loving the infinite good bears the joy of such knowledge and love, then one would have to have recourse to a

---

gave voice to this abandonment, yet this same psalm expressed his trust and confidence in God's merciful power to rescue him. Though his experience was that of one of [sic] being abandoned, yet, in faith and trust, he was assured, despite all appearances, of his Father's unimpaired love. His "*Abba*" prayer in Gethsemane ... also manifested this trust in his loving Father (*Abba*), despite the seeming evidence and real emotions to the contrary. This too is the same point made in the Letter to the Hebrews [5:7]. (*Does God Suffer?*, 219n8)

[15] *TD* IV, 333 [G 310] (emphasis added). In *TD* V, Balthasar obliquely expresses essential agreement with Moltmann and distances him from "pure Hegelianism or a radical process theology," but he seems hesitant to accept the full thrust of Moltmann's Trinitarian theory, most likely due to the latter's lack of nuance regarding the economic-immanent relationship (see *TD* V, 172–173 [G 152–153]).

At the same time, it is evident that he wants to go beyond both Moltmann and Rahner, incorporating their insights into his theory of Trinitarian *ur-kenosis* (see, e.g., *TD* IV, 322–323 [G 300]); in the process of such synthesis, though he seems to appropriate too much of Bulgakov (see especially *TD* IV, 323–324 [G 300–301]).

[16] He utilizes the exegesis of R. Brown, C. K. Barrett, and R. Schnackenburg to contextualize the cry historically and to slight its profundity indirectly, apparently reducing it to a mere recitation of Psalm 22 (see White, "Jesus' Cry on the Cross," 571–572, 575).

[17] It is, of course, possible that "immediate vision of God" may have been present in the human soul of Christ without Him being conscious on an operative/functional level of such an objective vision (present in a higher state of consciousness suspended *in actu* by the divine will). For the descent doctrine here espoused it is only necessary to admit divine suspension of the *fruitio* ordinarily consequent to beatific *visio*, but contemporary Christology would like also to come to terms with the biblical passages concerning ignorance in Christ and one may argue that suspension of such *fruitio* makes sense only if there is a precedent suspension of human consciousness (of some kind) of the immediate vision derivative of the divine essence hypostatically one with the human nature of Christ. I will argue to the contrary here.

different view of Christ's vision. I am not convinced that it is intrinsically impossible for the joy naturally consequent upon such knowledge and love to be suspended, even though I do think it is demonstratively true to say perfect knowledge of an infinite good necessarily results in perfect love of said good. But Balthasar did not explicitly engage such argumentation and, perhaps, that is why at points he seems content merely to indicate that Jesus was always aware of His divine mission and, therefore, His divine identity. Hence, it is necessary in the course of treating Christ's passion (in the context of Balthasar's kenoticism) to establish the requisite view of the nature of Christ's knowledge of God during His earthly life.

THE CURRENT THOMISTIC DEBATE CONCERNING CHRIST'S "VISIO IMMEDIATA DEI"

The traditional view of Christ's fullness of knowledge in the flesh dates back to the patristic era.[18] But in the wake of the development of modern historical-critical methods of exegesis applied to the sacred page, even Thomist scholars began to distance themselves from the notion that Christ's human understanding of God, His natural (consubstantial) Father, is best described in terms of the *visio immediata* accorded the blessed upon glorification. Until relatively recently all Thomists agreed on this doctrine of their master,[19] endorsed by the magisterium numerous times.[20]

---

[18] See St. Fulgentius of Ruspe, *Letter* 14, cited by Bruce D. Marshall, "Jesus' Human Knowledge: A Test for Theological Exegesis," minute 14. Still, Thomas G. Weinandy, an opponent of the view, states: "The first known author to state explicitly that Jesus possessed the beatific vision was the author, Candide, in the ninth century" ("Jesus' Filial Vision of the Father," *Pro Ecclesia* 13, no. 2 [2004]: 189–201, at 189n1).

[19] See, for instance, H.-M. Diepen, "La psychologie humaine du Christ," *Revue Thomiste* 50 (1950): 515–562, where the Scotist Christology of Paul Galtier is refuted. See also Bernard Lonergan's textbook for the Gregorian University in the 1950's, *De constitutione Christi ontologica et psychologica*, particularly, Part 6, Section 2, recently published as *Collected Works of Bernard Lonergan*, vol. 7, *The Ontological and Psychological Constitution of Christ* (Toronto: University of Toronto Press, 2002), 204ff.

[20] See Pius X, *Lamentabili*, §§32–35 (Denz. 3432–3435); Decree of the Holy Office of June 5, 1918 (Denz. 3645); Pius XII, *Mystici Corporis*, §75 (Denz. 3812); Pius XII, *Haurietis Aquas*, §56 (Denz. 3924), which cites *ST* III, q. 9, aa. 1-3. Compare to the International Theological Commission, "The Consciousness of Christ Concerning Himself and His Mission," *Communio* 14, no. 3 (1987): 316–325. See also Jean Galot's analysis of the authority of the previous magisterial statements in his *Who is Christ? A Theology of the Incarnation,* trans. M. A. Bouchard (Rome: Gregorian University Press, 1980), 357n33. The latest magisterial statements are found in CCC 473, and John Paul II, *Novo Millenio Ineunte*, §§25–27.

Two principal representatives of the turned tide are Jean Galot, SJ,[21] from whom Balthasar draws on a semi-regular basis, and one of the most eminent living Thomists, Jean-Pierre Torrell, OP.[22] I cannot possibly enter into all the details of the debate that has since ensued, but I will indicate wherein I think lies the truth by engaging a few more interlocutors.

Advocating for a doctrine of "mystical filial knowledge" in Christ's soul in place of the beatific vision, Jean Galot argues that Christ need only have such perfect understanding in the Resurrection to be fit to communicate glory to the mankind He redeems. In order to live a life like the men with whom He has chosen total solidarity (excluding commission of sin), His mission requires nothing more than infused knowledge. In other words, it does not accord with the meaning and purpose of Incarnation for Christ's earthly life to be suffused with the vision proper to consummate glory.[23] Furthermore, he rejects as incommensurate the argument from analogy with mystical experiences that Christ could have uttered the cry of abandonment even while experiencing "the beatifying sentiment of the most complete union with the Father."[24] He dismisses out of hand the view he finds in Melchor Cano and others that Christ suspends the *delectatio* proper to the beatific vision during His passion, asserting that they must have forgotten that the joy of the vision necessarily accompanies the hypostatic union.[25] He also passes over Bertrand de Margerie's proposal that Christ's earthly beatitude "was perfect but incomplete,"[26] and he critiques Maritain's distinction between supraconscious and infra-conscious to ex-

---

[21] See Jean Galot, "Le Christ terrestre et la vision," *Gregorianum* 67, no. 3 (1986): 429–450.

[22] See Jean-Pierre Torrell, OP, "Le mystère du Christ chez saint Thomas d'Aquin," in Textes choisis et présentés (Paris: Cerf, 1999), 198-213. Paul Gondreau also, in his study of Christ's passions, indicates agreement with Torrell, who wrote the preface for his book.

[23] See Galot, "Christ terrestre," 434.

[24] Galot, 435 (my translation).

[25] See Galot, 435. On the contrary, even the traditional Dominican Thomist Reginald Garrigou-Lagrange allows for the possibility of God withdrawing the joy that is concomitant to the beatific vision without causing a cessation to the vision itself (see *Beatitude: A Commentary on Thomas' Theologica Summa, IaIIae, qq. 1–54*, trans. Patrick Cummins, OSB [Ex Fontibus Co., 2015], 89), going so far as to state that the vision would not cease even if God refused concurrence with the act of love that would naturally accompany it (see 94), while at the same time demonstrating the impossibility of the vision itself ceasing or being withdrawn once possessed (see 122). Gaine speaks of Cano's position at greater length (see *Did the Saviour*, Kindle Edition, locations 4938ff).

[26] Galot, "De la science du Christ. Science, préscience et conscience, même prépascales du Christ Rédempteur," *Doctor Communis* 36 (1983): 123–158, at 141 (my translation).

plain the coexistence of beatific vision and acquired knowledge in Christ's human soul as introducing an unbridgeable division into the human psychology of Jesus.[27] His solution, instead, is to appeal to *kenosis*, a profound reality indeed and very near to the heart of Balthasar. But the medieval solutions, particularly, are given short shrift.[28]

Galot rightly points out that the divine essence is not known by the Incarnate Son as an object, but as subject. Since "vision" implies subject-object duality, it is an inadequate analogy for Christ's own consciousness, which is entirely unique. Echoing Lonergan here (without citing him), Galot nonetheless draws the mistaken conclusion that while Christ cannot be said to possess faith, His knowledge of His own divine essence must be infused (not beatific).[29] But how could faith be lacking for a soul in the state of grace and possessing imperfect knowledge of God? Furthermore, he speaks of this infused knowledge, by which Christ has human consciousness of His divine identity, developing "according to the normal conditions of human growth."[30] But what could it mean for infused knowledge to develop in such a manner, given that humans do not naturally possess such? The attempt to render Christ an ordinary human, albeit concurrently divine, is misbegotten.[31]

---

[27] See Galot, "Christ terrestre," 436. William G. Most makes a similar criticism of Maritain's proposal, concluding that Maritain's treatment "makes him [Christ] almost schizoid" (see *The Consciousness of Christ* [Front Royal, VA: Christendom College Press, 1980], 160). A bit more will be said about Maritain's theory later.

   In the end, I think something like Maritain's articulation is necessary, although the language of psychoanalytic theory might not be the most helpful. In other words, Christ as *viator* must be distinguished adequately from Christ as *comprehensor* without dividing the person, a task indeed very difficult and complex.

[28] For another brief critique of Galot's thesis, see Jose Antonio Riestra, "Experiencia Mistica y Vision Beatifica en Cristo, segun Santo Tomas," *Studi Tomistici* 44 (1991): 318–325.

[29] See Galot, "Christ terrestre," 439–440.

[30] Galot, "Christ terrestre," 440. See also his "Problèmes de la conscience du Christ," *Esprit et vie* 92 (1982): 145–152, and *La Conscience de Jesus* (Paris: Duculot, 1971).

[31] Jacques Maritain attempts to understand the quasi-natural development of Christ coming to self-awareness; see his *De la grace et de l'humanité de Jesus* (Bruges: Desclée de Brouwer, 1967); ET, *On the Grace and Humanity of Jesus*, trans. Joseph W. Evans (New York: Herder & Herder, 1969). White claims that while Christ's "[natural acquired knowledge] is understood [by Aquinas] to have undergone progressive natural development in his self-understanding throughout his life," nevertheless this does not apply to Christ's "knowledge of supernatural mysteries (including that of his own identity as the Son of God)" ("Kenoticism and the Divinity of Christ Crucified," 16).

   I will not attempt to address this question here, but the distinct types of knowl-

Guy Mansini points out, contrary to what Galot seems to assume, that Aquinas does not insist on the necessity of the beatific vision for Christ's human soul, but instead argues for its supreme fittingness (*convenientia*), due to the nature of the hypostatic union and, especially, the soteriological purpose of His incarnation.[32] Mansini argues that because Christ knows exactly who He is, He knows the mystery of the Trinity itself, and because He "taught them as one who has authority" (Mark 1:22), He does not have mere faith in the Trinity, as do we.[33] Rather, possessing an immediate knowledge of the Trinity itself, which is precisely what constitutes the beatific vision as such, He must "share in the infinite act of understanding by which God himself in his divine nature understands and knows all things"[34] or "[possess] an immediate knowledge of God as he is in himself, the finite mind's sharing in the infinite act of understanding the infinite intelligibility that God is."[35] Of course, what we know of the beatific vision is very limited, as its mere existence is known only by faith, the nature of which we merely know by *via remotionis* to be a knowledge "[not] by way of a created similitude; rather, the divine being itself is what is immediate-

---

edge belonging to Christ (e.g., acquired, infused, beatific) do not discriminate between natural and supernatural data. It remains mysterious, nonetheless, how to understand Christ's developmental human self-awareness. Rosenberg reports Lonergan's opinion, which seems feasible enough (and similar to Maritain's):

> Lonergan explains Christ's supernaturally and naturally elicited acts of meaning were different at different times in his development. Neither the dignity of the Son nor the ineffable knolwedge rooted in his dignity changed. But this knowledge is unmediated, unimaginable, inexpressible, etc. With his natural growth . . . Jesus' finite supernatural acts also developed, as they were gradually completed and perfected in different ways. So we can interpret more precisely Balthasar [sic] expression that Jesus' beatific knowledge was dormant, by saying that Jesus communicated his inexpressible, ineffable knowledge at different levels of depth commensurate with his corresponding level of development at a particular phase in his historical life. ("Theory and Drama," 287)

[32] See Mansini, "Understanding St. Thomas on Christ's Knowledge of God," *The Thomist* 59, no. 1 (Jan 1995): 91–124, at 94–96; *ST* III, q. 7, a. 1; q. 9, a. 2. Lonergan, at least according to Frederick E. Crowe, SJ's notes, instead argues on the basis of necessity: "But in the case of Christ, he who is a divine and infinite person; from him the beatific vision proceeds not as something unowed and gratuitous but, as indicated above, as consequent upon the infinite act of existence which he is" ("The Consciousness of Christ," in *Collected Works of Bernard Lonergan*, vol. 19, *Early Latin Theology* [Toronto: University of Toronto Press, 2011], 559).
[33] See Mansini, "Understanding St. Thomas," 114ff.
[34] Mansini, 117.
[35] Mansini, 116.

ly present to the created mind."[36] Christ as *comprehensor* must possess this vision, meanwhile Christ as *viator* acquires knowledge; indeed, Lonergan speaks of the two planes of knowledge as ineffable and effable,[37] respectively, such that the latter attempts to express with ever more clarity the salvific content of the former.[38]

Building on Lonergan's discourse on "beatific knowledge" in place of the more widely used "beatific vision," Mansini speaks of "immediate knowledge" without denying its beatific quality. He explains why: "to avoid the imputation that, as perfectly happy, he could not suffer anything. Still, the problem is not to be got rid of by a terminological device. The immediate knowledge of God is, one supposes, something that, as a super-perfection of our humanity, and of our intellectual desire, makes us happy."[39] He rejects the notion that it is impossible to be both happy and sad simultaneously. Still, consider the following thought-experiment: Could a soul in heaven endure hellish suffering? If so, surely only by divine omnipotence. But is it more intelligible for the latter to bring about such a situation by withdrawing from the soul the joy that naturally follows the vision or by

---

[36] *ST* I, q. 12, a. 2.

[37] See Lonergan, *De Verbo Incarnato*, 332.

[38] Rosenberg summarizes Lonergan's articulation thus: "Living on earth, Christ had both effable and ineffable human knowledge, besides his divine knowledge. As a beholder (*comprehensor*), he immediately knew God by that ineffable knowledge which is also called beatific, and in the same act, though mediately, he also knew everything else that would pertain to his work. As a pilgrim (*viator*), however, he elicited those natural and supernatural cognitional acts which constitute his human and historical life" ("Theory and Drama," 145–146).

He adds: "Just as the mystics have the problem of translating their momentary, ineffable experiences into to [sic] effable terms, so Christ had to translate, you might say, his permanent mystical vision into effable terms as his human and historical life progressed" ("Theory and Drama," 305).

Charles Hefling went so far as to say: "*Ineffable knowledge* is a technical, not a rhetorical phrase. It means what it says: such knowledge is inexpressible, *even to oneself*. It is neither perceptual nor discursive.... Attempting to imagine what exercising it would be is attempting the impossible" ("Another Perhaps Permanently Valid Achievement: Lonergan on Christ's (Self-) Knowledge," *Lonergan Workshop* 20 [2008]: 127–164, at 153).

[39] Mansini, "Understanding St. Thomas," 119. In a fashion complementary to his "immediate knowledge," I have utilized the language of "perfect understanding" to allow room for the suspension of access to the "secondary objects" of the vision or whatever might not be pertinent to His mission at hand, which seems to be allowed by Lonergan in *De Verbo Incarnato*, Thesis 15, sixth part, cited by Mansini on 111n49 along with *ST* III, q. 10, a. 1. "Knowledge" typically connotes data, whereas "understanding" connotes profundity, something more active than receptive.

piling on top of the *fruitio beata* a wholly contradictory experience of loss (i.e., dereliction)? Certainly, it is intrinsic to the beatific vision (perfect understanding and consequent union with God) to be eternal and, thus, it would be supremely imperfect for an omnipotent power to withdraw such vision itself (perhaps by annihilation). Apply this consideration to the soul of Christ, the Incarnate Word, during His earthly life.

Jean-Pierre Torrell thinks it is impossible for beatific joy and the experience of abandonment to coexist together and, therefore, rejects the traditional notion that Christ possessed the beatific vision in life (without considering the possibility entertained here). Emphasizing that Aquinas only argues for the fittingness of such vision,[40] based on the divine economy according to which the salvation towards which human beings are directed is communicated only through the Incarnate Word, Torrell points out that Aquinas never specifies at which point Christ received the vision, or "the moment at which Jesus became the Christ."[41] He also points out that when faced with "the Aristotelian doctrine of the impossibility of opposed intense passions [coexisting] in the same subject at the same time,"[42] Aquinas invokes the fact that Christ is entirely unique and thus exempt from such a principle, choosing John Damascene over Aristotle.[43] Torrell recognizes that, at least according to Thomistic logic, Christ must either have the beatific vision or the virtue of faith and Sacred Scripture never alludes to Christ possessing faith, but to Him as the perfect revelation of the Father.[44] Without disputing such logic, he concludes that Christ's knowledge of the Father must be a "perfect and total" form of prophetic knowledge, a supreme form of infused knowledge.[45]

Paul Gondreau seconds Torrell's principal objection to Christ's earthly possession of the beatific vision, namely, that mutually opposed passions cannot coexist with such intensity in the soul of Christ at one and the same time. Gondreau sums up Torrell's position in a manner very reminiscent of Galot's objections (without mentioning him):

---

[40] Galot, "La science du Christ," 200.

[41] Galot, "La science du Christ," 205. There is here, perhaps, a Schillebeeckxian undertone here. Hence, the underlying issue may be how seriously one takes the conclusions of modern historical-critical biblical exegesis.

[42] Galot, 204.

[43] Galot, 205.

[44] Galot, 207.

[45] Galot, 211–212.

After pointing out that the causal exigency of Christ's enjoyment of the *visio Dei*—whereby Christ must first enjoy the full vision of God before he can lead the human race to this vision—is satisfied by the *resurrected* state of Jesus rather than by his entire earthly state (there is no need, in other words, to attribute a glorified condition to Jesus' humanity during his entire earthly existence if what characterizes his glorified resurrected state meets this same soteriological requirement), Torrell looks to the revealed knowledge offered to the prophets as analogous to the kind of human knowledge one can suppose was possessed by Christ. To explain, the prophets, as Thomas insists, partake in a special "light" (*lumen propheticum*) which permits them to know the divinely revealed realities they are charged to impart in a way that is fully consonant with a human mode of knowing; by a similar yet vastly superior kind of prophetic "light," Jesus, one could say, is permitted to know (in a human way rather than in the angelic mode that characterizes infused knowledge) all things that concern his redemptive mission.[46]

One might argue, in answer to Mansini's article (which neither Torrell nor Gondreau engage), that such "Christic" vision is sufficient to have the certainty Jesus had about the mysteries He proclaimed. But if the knowledge infused is nonetheless finite (i.e., not the divine essence itself), is there not room still for doubt? Could not the angels with their infused knowledge before their respective beatifications and condemnations still doubt what God had revealed to them, which was in all likelihood cognitively superior to any human prophet (*quidquid recipitur ad modum recipientis recipitur*)? Finally, would it not be more fitting for Christ to possess perfect knowledge of the Godhead connaturally and not through some process akin to merit-reward; or better, is it not fitting that the Redeemer possess the beatitude He wishes to impart upon the redeemed while He redeems them (i.e., not simply in Resurrection, but also in death and even life, given that each one of His acts was sufficient by itself to redeem mankind)?

None of this is considered. But the main concern for both Torrell and Gondreau (who does a superb job of exploring Christ's passions in Aquinas's writings) is "Thomas' suspension of the natural laws governing human psychology, whereby the bridge linking the higher and lower powers of the soul is effectively severed in order to allow for simultaneous suffer-

---

[46] Gondreau, *The Passions of Christ's Soul*, 451–452.

ing and joy in Christ's soul."[47] While Mansini also expresses puzzlement at the coexistence of intense joy and suffering in Christ's soul during the passion, he must have realized that the marvelous works of God in Christ often suspend natural laws—"oh ye of little faith!" (Matt 8:26). The "natural law" here referenced is the medieval notion of *redundancia*, whereby what the higher powers of the soul enjoy naturally redound to the lower powers; yet it is universally accepted that Christ's body did not enjoy the perfection of His soul by divine decree so that He might share more profoundly in the human condition (without sin—and it might be added, without intellective defect).[48] Ultimately, Gondreau designates the doctrine of Christ as *viator et comprehensor* as "highly problematic,"[49] which he recognizes as, at least in part, an attempt to specify "the way in which Christ could undergo both affective suffering as a result of his passible soul and supreme joy or beatitude as a consequence of the direct *visio Dei* his soul enjoyed."[50] Again, no consideration is given the possibility that such suffering coexisted with the *visio* but not the *fruitio* or *delectatio*.

Underlying the entire issue, of course, is to what extent one accepts the purported findings of modern historical-critical (i.e., diachronic) methods of scriptural exegesis, which are perpetually in tension with dogmatic claims about Christ.[51] Hence, the reason he states for rejecting such a scholastic axiom:

---

[47] Gondreau, 449.

[48] It would not be an intellectual defect of Christ's human mind not to know calculus or Chinese, but it would be one not to understand perfectly the truths He uttered, not because humans ordinarily understand their own speech perfectly, but because He is more than simply human—He is the God-man, a divine person. Yes, he acquired knowledge of much in life, but as long as He possessed human self-consciousness, He could not have lacked perfect understanding of His own identity, which must involve nothing short of immediate knowledge of God's essence.

[49] Gondreau, *The Passions of Christ's Soul,* 450.

[50] Gondreau, 441.

[51] Concerning the relationship between dogma and historical-critical exegesis, see, e.g., Joseph Ratzinger's famous Erasmus lecture, "Schriftauslegung im Widerstreit: Zur Frage nach Grundlagen und Weg der Exegese heute," in *Wort Gottes: Schrift–Tradition–Amt,* ed. Peter Hünermann and Thomas Söding (Freiburg: Herder, 2005), 83–116; ET, "Biblical Interpretation in Conflict: On the Foundations and the Itinerary of Exegesis Today," in *Opening Up the Scriptures: Joseph Ratzinger and the Foundations of Biblical Interpretation,* ed. José Granados, Carlos Granados, and Luis Sánchez-Navarro, trans. Adrian Walker (Grand Rapids, MI: Eerdmans, 2008), 1–29; and his *Fundamentals of Catholic Theology: Building Stones for a Fundamental Theology,* trans. Mary Frances McCarthy, SND (San Francisco: Ignatius Press, 1987), 153ff.

On the potential reconciliation of the notion of Christ's earthly beatific vision with the concerns of historical-critical exegesis, see T. J. White, "The Infused Science of

The Evangelists, who, as J.-P. Torrell remarks, "describe Jesus' agony in quite strong terms that hardly leave one suspecting of the joy that could have felt the effects of his sufferings." This witness of the Gospels explains why modern Biblical exegesis favors an image of Jesus that is closer to the man who "learned obedience through what he suffered" (Heb 5:8) than to the Christ who experienced a beatified soul since the very moment of his conception.[52]

I am happy to see Torrell (and Gondreau) take seriously Christ's "cry of dereliction," but I am disappointed in Gondreau for implying that Aquinas's Christ cannot learn obedience—that is precisely the point of the acquired knowledge, which Gondreau so often points out distinguishes Aquinas's Christology from the other medievals. Finally, I think it is inaccurate to speak of Christ *experiencing* beatitude from the moment of conception, both because there is no reason to suppose his human psychology did not develop self-awareness in accord with the natural laws of human development and because possessing beatitude (objective) need not mean experiencing it (subjective).

Throughout this struggle to reconcile Christ as man (*qua homo*) with Christ as God (*qua Deus*) is, of course, the effort to avoid the Scylla and Charybdis of Monophysitism and Nestorianism. Thomas G. Weinandy is most explicit in his attempt to steer clear of such heresies, meanwhile adding his voice to the modern choir questioning the scholastic consensus on Christ's beatific knowledge. Weinandy claims that the question itself of whether Christ possessed the beatific vision is inspired by a Nestorian Christology rather than a Cyrillian-Chalcedonian one, since for the former "the Son of God and the man Jesus are not ontologically united within the Incarnation, and so stand over against one another."[53] For him, then, in the context of the latter Christology, the only proper and meaningful question is: "Did the Son of God as man, within his human consciousness and intellect, possess a vision of the Father such that he (the divine Son) was humanly aware of himself as Son and so knew himself to be the Son, and thus, as a consequence perceived all that the Father willed for him during his earthly life?"[54] But this is simply a convenient (and perhaps dis-

---

Christ," *Nova et Vetera* 16, no. 2 (2018): 617–641.

[52] Gondreau, *The Passions of Christ's Soul*, 450–451. The internal quote is from Torrell's *Le Christ en ses mystères*, vol. 2, *La vie et l'oeuvre de Jésus selon saint Thomas d'Aquin* (Paris: Desclée de Brouwer, 1999), 338.

[53] Weinandy, "Jesus' Filial Vision of the Father," 190.

[54] Weinandy, 190–191.

ingenuous) way out of the debate.[55] Why cannot one ask: Did the Son of God as man, in His human intellect, possess a vision of the Father (i.e., the Godhead by *circumincessio*) such that He (the divine Son) possessed in His human mind an immediate knowledge of His own identity and so of the divine essence itself, and thus, as a consequence, understood things that are proper only to the beatific vision granted mere humans upon glorification?

Referring also to Lonergan's work, Weinandy proposes in place of the beatific vision "a human 'hypostatic vision,'" whereby "the person (*hypostasis*) of the Son possessed, as man, a personal human vision of the Father by which he came to know the Father as the Father truly exists."[56] He acknowledges that "Lonergan insists that Christ must also possess beatific knowledge [not just human self-awareness] in order for him to have a full and objective knowledge that exceeds that of subjective conscious experience."[57] But he disagrees with Lonergan that in being humanly aware of *who he is*, Christ's human mind must be(come) "fully knowledgeable as to *what he is*—God."[58] Weinandy clarifies that while he holds in agreement with Lonergan, "that the Son's human conscious experience is the subjective experience of the Son and not the perceptive experience of an object apart from himself,"[59] he adds: "I have equally argued that he obtained his human conscious awareness of who [he] is as the Son in relation to his human objective vision of the Father."[60] But how can He have an objective vision of the Father and not of the divine essence of which He is the originating hypostasis? Furthermore, if "it was in becoming humanly aware

---

[55] White later responds to Weinandy's concern with Nestorianism, outlining the historical antecedents for his own instrumental language in regard to Christ's human faculties: see his "Dyotheletism and the Instrumental Human Consciousness of Jesus," *Pro Ecclesia* 17, no. 4 (2008): 396–422.

[56] Weinandy, "Jesus' Filial Vision," 193.

[57] Weinandy, 193n7.

[58] Weinandy, 194n7. He also notes there that Lonergan holds (and he expresses no disagreement with this) that, "no created intellect can know God in his essence save through the beatific vision" (*Ontological and Psychological Constitution*, 217). When did he become aware of his divine identity? "Such an awareness would have come much earlier [than the age of twelve]—at the normal age when a human person becomes aware of who he or she is. The difference being that a human person becomes aware of his or her human identity and the Son incarnate becomes humanly aware of his divine identity as Son" ("Jesus' Filial Vision of the Father," 198n14).

[59] For a fuller understanding of Lonergan's point here, see *The Ontological and Psychological Constitution of Christ*, 267.

[60] Weinandy, "Jesus' Filial Vision," 194n7.

of the Father as Father that he became self-consciously aware that he was truly the Son of the Father,"[61] was He not also humanly aware of the Holy Spirit? Moreover, is it fitting for the Son of God to have only imperfect human awareness not only of His own hypostasis, but also of those eternally consubstantial to Him?

His answer to the first and second questions is to distinguish between objective and subjective knowledge:

> Obviously, in having a filial vision of the Father, the Son as incarnate is aware of the whole Trinity for to know the Father necessarily entails knowing the Son and the Spirit. However, it must be stressed that the Son's incarnate knowledge of the Trinity was not an objective knowledge, that is, a knowledge of a being ontologically distinct from himself, but rather a subjective knowledge, that is, a knowledge of who he is—himself being a person of the Trinity.[62]

This distinction, of course, bespeaks a peculiarly modern cognitional theory. Certainly, it is valid to distinguish between an informational type of knowledge and a personal familiarity kind of knowledge, as most modern languages do. But why does it make sense to put limitations on Christ's "human objective vision of the Father?" (my third question in his words). Even Lonergan's peculiar cognitional theory does not prevent him from recognizing that in order to be totally self-aware, Christ must have possessed immediate knowledge of the divine essence:[63]

> For Christ as man to understand clearly and to judge with certainty himself to be the natural Son of God and himself true God, the following conditions are required and sufficient: (1) consciousness of himself; (2) in which the subject (that which is aware of itself through consciousness) is the natural Son of God and himself true God; (3) a clear understanding of the quiddity of the natural Son of God and of the true God; and (4) a grasp of the identity between the conscious subject and the object thus

---

[61] Weinandy, 194n7.

[62] Weinandy, 197n13.

[63] See Bernard J. F. Lonergan, SJ, *Insight: A Study of Human Understanding* (New York: Harper & Row, 1978), which he composed concurrently with his major Christological texts, *De Constitutione Christi* and *De Verbo Incarnato*.

quidditatively understood. But these necessary and sufficient conditions are fulfilled by Christ's human consciousness and his beatific knowledge. . . . [T]he third condition is required, since one who does not understand what the natural Son of God is cannot clearly understand himself to be the natural Son of God.[64]

None of this, of course, prevents Lonergan from admitting both an ontological and psychological *kenosis* in Christ as *Incarnate* Word.[65]

The modern instinct is to divest Christ's humanity of perfection in order not to fall into Monophysitism, that is, to strip away (kenosis!) the divine implications for His humanity in order to make room for the latter to appear in greater solidarity with the rest of us. The alternative, in this perspective, is Nestorianism—that is, *Christus viator et comprehensor* must be two hypostases ("persons"), not one, which simply does not follow. Therefore, echoing Galot,[66] Weinandy concludes: "the Son did not fully grasp, as man, the awesome glory and incomprehensible splendor of who he is until he was raised gloriously from the dead."[67] Thus, it is only in Resurrection that Christ graduates from *viator* to *comprehensor*.[68]

Thomas Joseph White takes issue with both Jean Galot and Thomas Weinandy's treatments. Utilizing Herman Diepen, Jacques Maritain, and Jean Miguel Garrigues,[69] White argues that holding the traditional view

---

[64] Lonergan, *Ontological and Psychological Constitution*, 215, 217 (Latin original available on 214, 216). He also argues that in order for Christ to have suffered all sin, He must have known all sins, past and future (see *De Verbo Incarnato*, 556).
But, as Rosenberg notes,

> While Christ knew that it was good for God to choose [the actual world-order], Christ the man, along with the blessed, did not know [the other possible world-orders] by his human knowledge, beatific or acquired. Therefore, with regard to the question of Christ's knowledge on the Cross, it can be argued that Christ had knowledge of what caused his inner detestation and sorrow. . . . He did not, however, know if there could be a better universe. Whether or not this "not-knowing" was painful, Lonergan did not wish to speculate. ("Theory and Drama," 269–270)

[65] See Lonergan *Ontological and Psychological Constitution*, 223.
[66] Weinandy does not, however, cite Torrell.
[67] Weinandy, "Jesus' Filial Vision," 198n14.
[68] For an alternative doctrine of Christ as *comprehensor et viator*, see, e.g., Rudolf M. Schmitz, "Christus Comprehensor: Die 'Visio Beatifica Christi Viatoris' bei M.J. Scheeben," *Doctor Communis* 36 (1983): 347–359.
[69] Diepen, "La psychologie humaine du Christ," and "La critique du basilisme selon saint Thomas d'Aquin," *Revue Thomiste* 50 (1950): 515–562; Maritain, *On the Grace and Humanity of Jesus*; Garrigues, "La conscience de soi telle qu'elle était exercée par le Fils

is "essential for maintaining the unity of [Christ's] person in and through the duality of his natures."[70] In short, in order for Christ's human nature to be the sacred *organon* ("instrument") of His divine hypostasis, all His thoughts, words, and deeds must express "his intra-Trinitarian, filial relationship with the Father."[71] This requires not only that all His actions reflect the divine will, but that He have immediate knowledge of the divine will.[72] Against Galot's capricious reluctance to grant that the absence of vision mandates the presence of faith in a soul united to God, White pits his ally, Torrell, against him:

> The presence of a prophetic, infused knowledge cannot act as a substitute for faith, in the way Galot proposes. The Jesuit theologian claims that there is no faith in Christ, nor vision, but only a higher knowledge attained by prophecy. Yet as Jean-Pierre Torrell has shown, prophetic or infused knowledge alone is only a mediate, *indirect* knowledge of God attained through the *effects* of God. Necessarily, outside of the vision, all knowledge of God is through effects, and *only faith* permits a quasi-immediate contact with God, through love. Therefore even in-fused knowledge requires faith in order to orient it toward God. This latter contact, however, is obscure (nonevidential). . . . [The intellect of Christ] would believe in his divinity and divine will through faith.[73]

---

de Dieu fait homme," *Nova et Vetera* (French Edition) 79, no. 1 (2004): 39–51; and "L'instrumentalité rédemptrice du libre arbitre du Christ chez saint Maxime le Confesseur," *Revue Thomiste* 104 (2004): 531–550.

70 White, "The Voluntary Action of the Earthly Christ," 498.

71 White, 499. Concerning the instrumentality of Christ's humanity (intellect and will), White refers the reader to Theophil Tschipke, *Die Menschheit Christi als Heilsorgan der Gottheit* (Freiburg im Breisgau, 1939), FT, *L'humanité du Christ comme instrument de salut de la divinité* (Fribourg: Academic Press Fribourg, 2003).

72 I have restated the argument somewhat here, as White usually tends to say that in order for all His actions to reflect the divine will, Jesus must have immediate knowledge of the divine will (citing *ST* I-II, q. 4, a. 4). But this is not necessarily true if the Blessed Virgin Mary is indeed sinless, as she certainly did not enjoy the beatific vision in life. God may predestine any created will to perform all good acts without granting perfect understanding of His will.

Nonetheless, one might develop an argument on the basis of the distinction in spiritual theology between sin and imperfection (see, e.g., Garrigou-Lagrange, *Christian Perfection and Contemplation: According to St. Thomas Aquinas and St. John of the Cross* [Charlotte, NC: TAN Books, 2010], 428ff.), which might allow one to conclude that while Mary did not commit any sins, the deeds of Christ alone were always perfect.

73 White, "The Voluntary Action," 517–518. In fact, Torrell states:

White adds the following argument:

> In the absence of the vision, the infused science of Christ would lack such immediate evidence, and would have to be accompanied by faith. In this case, the prophetic awareness Christ had of his own divinity and will would have to be continuously accompanied by an autonomous decision of faith in the human heart of Christ and a repeated choice to welcome in trust this revelation *from his own divine self.* This would create, in effect, a kind of psychological autonomy in the man Jesus distinct from the willing of his divine subject, resulting in a schism between the two operations of the Incarnate Word.[74]

Alternatively, the infinite distance between Christ's created intellect and uncreated being can be bridged only by an immediate vision, which effectively "safeguards the unity of activity in the person of Jesus."[75]

If the beatific vision does not corrupt but, rather, perfects the human being, then for Christ's humanity to possess the same from conception would not make him any less human than the rest of us, no more than being conceived without sin rendered Mary less human, but rather more perfectly human in accord with God's original designs. Thus, White concludes concerning the Scylla and Charybdis of opposite Christological heresies:

> [A]t least in one very important aspect (i.e., with regard to the divine will), Christ's human actions *must not* be characterized

---

With faith we are in the order of the supernatural *quoad essentiam*, while with prophetic knowledge we remain in the order of the supernatural *quoad modum (acquisitionis)*. The two orders do not exclude one another, certainly, but the second is ordered to the first, and because the two are different kinds of realities, they must not be confused or made to play the role of one another. . . . [I]f we accord to [Jesus] infused illuminations characteristic of the charismatic knowledge of revelation, he will be enabled for his role as a divine messenger, but he will still not have direct access to God, since these illuminations do not suffice as a replacement of faith. ("La Science du Christ," 404, translated by White, "Voluntary Action," 517n41)

Concerning prophecy, see Torrell's *Recherches sur la théorie de la prophétie au moyen âge, xiie–xive siécles: études et textes* (Fribourg: Éditions Universitaires Fribourg Suisse, 1992).

[74] White, "The Voluntary Action," 519.

[75] White, 521.

by ignorance, or defectibility. What is at stake is not a principle of ideal humanity, but the very unity of the operations of Christ in his practical actions. In order for Christ to be fully human, his psychological choices must be rational and natural (against Monophysitism), but for them to be the choices of his divine person, they must be unified with his divine will on the level of his personal action (against Nestorianism).[76]

White does not seem to find difficulty with the notion of Christ possessing the beatific vision in the "heights of the soul" even while suffering spiritual and physical agony, even calling the former "pacifying."[77]

Weinandy later responds to White's criticisms of this position that he had recently espoused. He does not respond in detail to White's arguments, but instead undermines the mentality he thinks pervades White's article as crypto-Nestorian. The Nestorian accusation seems to imply that coming to human awareness of His divine identity and possessing a (supraconscious) immediate vision of the Father are mutually exclusive notions. But they are not, given that what is known by *visio* may be learned experimentally due to the distinction between acquired, infused, and beatific planes of consciousness/knowledge in Christ's soul. Weinandy advocates in place of the beatific vision the existence of a "human hypostatic vision of the Father,"[78] which would necessarily be ontologically inferior to the beatific vision Christ purportedly achieves in resurrection.

He sums up his own argumentation in the previous article thus:

> I gave two reasons why Jesus did not possess the beatific vision. The first is that the beatific vision is traditionally understood as a heavenly vision and thus a vision that is resurrectional in nature. Such a vision would then be contrary to Jesus' being able to live an authentic earthly life. Moreover, because the beatific vision has traditionally been understood as an objective vision of God obtained by someone who is other than God, to say that Jesus

---

[76] White, "The Voluntary Action," 515. Balthasar might also be accused of sometimes tending toward a kind of reverse Monophysitism, where Christ's two intellects (human and divine) are conflated into divine consciousness that has emptied itself to the point of becoming a mere human consciousness (aware of His divine identity, nonetheless); see *TD* III, 227 [G 208], Rosenberg, "Theory and Drama," 117, 308.

[77] White, "The Voluntary Action," 531n68.

[78] Weinandy, "The Beatific Vision and the Incarnate Son: Furthering the Discussion," *The Thomist* 70, no. 4 (2006): 605–615, at 613–614.

possessed the beatific vision implies Nestorianism, as if the man Jesus, who possessed the beatific vision, were a different subject/ being from that of the Son.[79]

If Jesus having the beatific vision implies Nestorianism, then He must not possess it either in life or in Resurrection. I think that White successfully argues that it is actually Weinandy's position that requires Nestorianism, a thesis Weinandy never addresses. Even if Weinandy's view is not Nestorian (let us not gratuitously accuse each other of heresy!), does not speaking of the beatific vision as "resurrectional in nature" imply divergence from Benedict XII's solemn proclamation against the idea that the beatific vision is only granted at the general resurrection?[80]

Against White's purportedly ambiguous use of language in reference to Christ's subjectivity, Weinandy explains:

> Because the Son is the sole person or subject within the Incarna-tion, what he knows and wills as man is done by him and so, from the very ontology of Incarnation, the human intellect and will are never autonomous "things" in need of being "brought into line," whether by the beatific vision or by any other means.[81]

Thus, Weinandy characterizes White's view in the following manner:

> The Son's humanity is the personal instrument through which he acts, in a similar way as I personally act through the use of my hand. However, my hand does not act "instrumentally" and nei-ther does Christ's "human will." Moreover, a "will" does not act apart from the one whose will it is, nor does a "will," as if it were an acting subject, subordinate itself to another will. Only persons subordinate their will to another person. To say that one will sub-ordinates itself to another will implies two persons.[82]

But the last statement is patently false, as the Chalcedonian dogmas clari-fy: there are two wills in Christ, human and divine, but one divine person

---

[79] Weinandy, 613n4.
[80] *Benedictus Deus* (Denz. 1000) Of course, Weinandy might hold the Rahnerian notion of resurrection in death. For a critique of this theory, see my "The Possibility of Univer-sal Conversion in Death."
[81] Weinandy, "The Beatific Vision," 609.
[82] Weinandy, 611.

(the Son/Word). Is the human not subject to the divine? Granted, a will does not act on its own, and Christ's will is not most properly designated an "autonomous thing."[83] But, surely, if there are distinct natures in Christ (personally united), one can speak of distinct operations and reflect on their interrelatedness. Likewise, a hand is not an instrument of the human person in the same way that the human nature of Christ is the instrument of his divine personhood because nature and person are not related in the same manner as part of a body is to the person who possesses (or rather, lives!) it. Yet Christ is an entirely unique reality—nature, what a thing is with respect to its operations, is distinct from person, the subsistent subject of all (real) predications.

Adopting language similar to Galot, Diepen, and Lonergan (about the Son becoming humanly self-conscious),[84] Weinandy points to a few places where White's language is insufficiently precise with regard to the nature-person distinction. While the former language is indeed preferable (that is, until it denies the beatific vision), Weinandy seems to want to make it impossible to speak meaningfully of the distinct natures in Christ. Hence, Weinandy is mistaken when he speaks as if the beatific vision and hypostatic union are opposed rather than congruent: "For White, it is not the *hypostatic* union, the ontological union whereby the Son of God exists as man, that guarantees the unity, and so conformity, of the human intellect and will with the divine intellect and will, but the beatific vision."[85] Rather, the hypostatic union implies the beatific vision, even if it does not necessitate it, and thus it is through the beatific vision (as an instrument!) that the hypostatic union renders the human intellect and will of Christ completely conformed to His divine intellect and will.

---

[83] Still, as Diepen says,

> [It is] not only the sanctity and impeccability of Christ which demands that constant dependence of the human will in its relationship to the divine will, but also His personal unity. Every person is not only a metaphysical and substantial unity, but also a psychological unity. And there is no psychological unity if each of Christ's two psychological centers that comprise the intimate constitution of the God-man is autonomous in its activity." ("La psychologie humaine du Christ," 535)

He then quotes St. John Damascene for support (see *De Fide orthodoxa*, I, 3, ch. 18).

[84] The question about Christ's human consciousness of His divine identity is not understood in terms of "how a man becomes conscious that he is the Son of God, but how the Son of God becomes humanly conscious of himself" (Galot, *Who is Christ?*, 336–337). See Diepen, "La psychologie humaine du Christ," 531.

[85] Weinandy, "The Beatific Vision," 612.

Recently, Simon Francis Gaine, OP, authored a very detailed and thorough defense of the classical doctrine of Christ's earthly beatific vision, engaging much of the same secondary literature here discussed. But he takes some distance from Lonergan's articulation and especially from Maritain's attempt to reconcile the doctrine with modern sensitivities (e.g., the emphasis on Christ's complete solidarity with human nature as it actually exists).[86] I cannot possibly do justice to Gaine's treatment here. But since at least one reviewer interprets him to be questioning the necessity for infused knowledge (proper to angelic beings) in a soul that already sees God "face to face,"[87] Gaine issued a clarifying article. There he argues that while infused knowledge is not necessary in his view to "translate" beatific knowledge into human categories, as it is possible for Christ to derive finite *species* by will from beatific knowledge,[88] it still might be useful for His mission and soteriologically purposive as the exemplary cause of all infused knowledge in human beings.[89]

More pertinent, though, is his criticism of Nicholas Lombardo's brief treatment of whether the beatific vision would impede ordinary human affectivity in Christ. Lombardo seconds Torrell's and Gondreau's reservations with respect to the earthly beatific vision of Christ, and he adds a few more arguments, which Gaine does not find satisfying. Lombardo argues incisively:

---

[86] His main objection to Maritain's theory, which will be discussed more later, seems to be its utilization of Freudian notions as well as the risk of bifurcating Christ's human mind (see *Did the Saviour,* locations 3771–3776). Despite objecting to what he dubs "quasi-Nestorianism" (location 3787), he admits:

> Only Maritain's theory fares reasonably well in this respect because, while escaping Agnoetism by granting Christ knowledge of the last day in his human supraconsciousness, it takes his denial of knowledge to extend only to conscious knowledge. Since the disciples were presumably only concerned with Christ's conscious knowledge, being quite oblivious to the very existence of supraconscious knowledge, his denial can escape the charge of deception." (*Did the Saviour,* locations 3874–3875)

[87] See Andrew Ter Ern Loke, "A Kryptic Model of the Incarnation," *Journal of Theological Studies* 68, no. 1 (2017): 465–468, at 465, citing *Did the Savior,* 154–155.

[88] See especially Gaine's "Is There Still a Place for Christ's Infused Knowledge in Catholic Theology and Exegesis?," *Nova et Vetera* 16, no. 2 (2018): 601–615, at 607. This is the key defect he sees here in Maritain's account (see 611–612); for some reason he does not impugn Lonergan here for the same.

[89] See Gaine, 614–615. White explains the need for such in line with Lonergan and Maritain, a defense that Gaine criticizes: "As Aquinas and many Thomists after him have rightly insisted, then, the knowledge of Christ's vision is 'communicated' to his ordinary human consciousness through the medium of a so-called infused, prophetic science" ("The Voluntary Action of the Earthly Christ," 516).

The affirmation of this divine dispensation [of the *redundantia*] implies that Christ's affections do not operate according to their nature, insofar as the affections of the will do not fully engage the passions of the sense appetite. This disengagement is foreign to human experience. . . . Aquinas describes a kind of interpenetration of sense appetite and intellectual appetite. Although they are different faculties, they do not operate independently. In his discussion of Christ's passions, however, Aquinas isolates the operation of different appetites, something he does nowhere else in his account of human affectivity, in order to resolve the difficulties presented by Christ's beatific knowledge.[90]

Thus, Lombardo notes that Aquinas must relegate Christ's human experience of sorrow and joy to the lower appetite since His intellect enjoys the immediate vision of God. Gaine responds that beatific joy should not impede finite joys in Christ any more than it will in the saints when they reunite with their risen bodies,[91] and that it is not a problem that Christ did not experience emotions in the same manner as us.[92] But Gaine's primary rebuttal is that the evidence in favor of Christ's beatific vision simply outweighs any such concern with the exceptionality of His human nature, which is sinless after all.[93] It seems that the legitimate points on both sides of the debate are preserved if one considers Christ's human mind to have the perfect vision without the perfect joy that is ordinarily consequent: he can experience emotion in a fully human, earthly manner and, at the same time, live completely united to the divine mysteries. In any case, regardless of how one understands the precise relationship between Christ's mind and His affections or that between the beatific, infused, and acquired knowledge of His human intellect, Gaine does an excellent job of defending the fundamental point that Christ must have possessed the beatific vision during His earthly life, marshalling the evidence of both Scripture and tradition.[94]

Thus, it was most fitting for Jesus the Christ, the Word Incarnate, to be endowed with the immediate vision of God's essence, toward which the

---

[90] Nicholas E. Lombardo, OP, *The Logic of Desire: Aquinas on Emotion* (Washington, DC: Catholic University of America Press, 2011), 216–217.

[91] Gaine, *Did the Saviour*, locations 5302–5306.

[92] Gaine, locations 5368ff.

[93] Gaine, locations 5238ff.

[94] Unfortunately, Gaines's treatment of Balthasar relies primarily on Alyssa Pitstick's *Light in Darkness* (see *Did the Saviour*, locations 421, 2787, 2808, 3537, 5442, e.g.).

prophets of old strived to direct His people's gaze. As Pope Emeritus Benedict XVI points out, it is most proper for the "New Moses," the prophet of all prophets, to possess an immediate and perfect vision of God:[95]

> Although Moses' immediate relation to God makes him the great mediator of Revelation, the mediator of the Covenant, it has its limits. He does not behold God's face, even though he is permitted to enter into the cloud of God's presence and to speak with God as a friend. The promise of a "prophet like me" thus implicitly contains an even greater expectation: that the last prophet, the new Moses, will be granted what was refused to the first one—a real, immediate vision of the face of God, and thus the ability to speak entirely from seeing, not just from looking at God's back. This naturally entails the further expectation that the new Moses will be the mediator of a greater covenant than the one that Moses was able to bring down from Sinai (cf. Heb 9:11–24). This is the context in which we need to read the conclusion of the prologue to John's Gospel: "No one has ever seen God; it is the only Son, who is nearest to the Father's heart, who has made him known" (Jn 1:18). It is in Jesus that the promise of the new prophet is fulfilled. What was true of Moses only in fragmentary form has now been fully realized in the person of Jesus: He lives before the face of God, not just as a friend, but as a Son; he lives in the most intimate unity with the Father. We have to start here if we are truly to understand the figure of Jesus as it is presented to us in the New Testament; all that we are told about his words, deeds, sufferings, and glory is anchored here. This is the central point, and if we leave it out of account, we fail to grasp what the figure of Jesus is really all about, so that it becomes self-contradictory and, in the end, unintelligible.[96]

---

[95] This seems to be a revision of his early position articulated in "Bewusstsein und Wissen Christi: Zu E. Gutwengers gleichnamigen Buch," *Munchener theologische Zeitschrift* 12 (1961): 78–81.

[96] *Jesus of Nazareth*, vol. 1, *From the Baptism in the Jordan to the Transfiguration* (New York: Doubleday, 2007), 5–6 [*Jesus von Nazareth: von der Taufe im Jordan bis zur Verklarung* (Freiburg: Herder, 2007), 30–31]. I owe this reference to Bruce D. Marshall (see his "Jesus' Human Knowledge: A Test for Theological Exegesis," minute four), which he thinks operates as the hermeneutical key that pervades Benedict's entire "trilogy" (a word Benedict rejects as applicable to his Jesus series, as the third is "not a third volume, but a kind of small 'antechamber' to the earlier two volumes" [see *Jesus of Nazareth: The Infancy Narratives* (New York: Random House, 2012), xi]).

Although Ratzinger is clearer here than is Balthasar, it should become evident by the end of this chapter that the Balthasarian-Speyrian perspective accounts for the problem that preoccupies Galot, Weinandy, and Torrell without replacing the *visio immediata* with an infused super-prophetic species.[97] Furthermore, rather than designate Christ's human knowledge as simply a "filial vision," this approach sees the vision as properly Trinitarian in scope.[98] This view manages to take the nescient passages of Scripture seriously without sacrificing what the hypostatic union implies by maintaining that Jesus possessed in exemplary fashion the dimension of trust that pertains to the virtue of faith, the certainty of His mission by virtue of His vision, the power to "deposit" or "lay up" in the Father both the *fruitio beata* in His passion and until the Resurrection certain items of knowledge not pertinent to His mission at present (e.g., the precise timing of the eschaton).

---

[97] In fact, Balthasar, in the first volume of his trilogy, seems to oppose this kind of view and to anticipate what Ratzinger affirms above:

> It is impossible to speak of Jesus' experience of God as if it were located between the experience of the Prophets and that of the Apostles as "standing over all" (Jn 3.31). Jesus' experience furnishes the form that conditions all other experiences, both before and after it. To speak of it means to speak of the unutterable reality which is behind and above what is utterable and which is what gives the latter its utterability.... The Biblical statements on the subject, especially Saint John's affirmations, set Jesus' experience of God wholly apart from the God-experiences of all the others, even of grace-filled men who have received a mission. The fact that no one has ever seen God, except his only-begotten Son (Jn 1.18), is affirmed not without a certain irony towards Moses, who is mentioned in the previous verse and to whom is ascribed the highest of all God-experiences in the Old Testament. It is a question of origin.... [W]e must concentrate not so much on the word "sent," for missions had been given also to the Prophets ... rather, we must note the direction of Christ's "coming," his origin from God and from heaven. Unlike prophetic persons, Jesus does not encounter a divine form of revelation. Because he comes from the Father, he himself *is* the form of God's revelation. (*Glory of the Lord: A Theological Aesthetics*, vol. 1, *Seeing the Form*, ed. Joseph Fessio, SJ, and John Riches, trans. Erasmo Leiva-Merikakis, [San Francisco: Ignatius Press, 1982], 321–322 [G 310])

[98] Speyr appropriates knowing God to the Father as origin, loving God to the Son as beloved, and enjoying that knowledge and love to the Spirit as fruition, understanding the doctrine of appropriation: see, e.g., *John*, vol. 3, *The Farewell Discourses*, trans. E. A. Nelson (San Francisco: Ignatius Press, 1987), 214.

EVALUATING BALTHASAR ON CHRIST'S "VISIO BEATA" (IN THE PASSION)

John Saward's brief critical appraisal of Balthasar's treatment of Christ's experience of godforsakenness is the most persuasive argument in favor of the Thomistic view that Christ enjoyed His vision of the Father in the intellective appetite (i.e., human spiritual faculties) while suffering a kind of *visio mortis* in the concupiscent and irascible appetites (i.e., animal faculties). He utilizes John Paul the Great's words concerning the coexistence of His "clear vision of God and the certainty of [H]is union with the Father" and "the tragic experience of the most compete desolation": "In the sphere of feelings and affection this sense of the absence and abandonment by God was the most acute pain for the soul of Jesus, who drew his strength and joy from union with the Father. This pain rendered more intense all the other sufferings. That lack of interior consolation was his greatest agony."[99] While John Paul's adherence to the scholastic tradition may be assumed, his words might also be interpreted in line with the theory he proposed as a possibility. But Saward concludes: "It is at least arguable that the greatest possible spiritual suffering is not so much the Godforsakenness of One who *hitherto* has enjoyed the vision of the Father but rather the feeling of God's absence in a soul that still, at some level, rests in his presence. . . . A hint of what this coincidence of profound peace and acute anguish might mean is to be found in the great mystics."[100] Ordinarily in tune with Balthasar, Saward here interprets him to be at odds with the tradition without good reason.[101] While I tend to agree with Saward's assertion that "[Balthasar] seems to me to distinguish insufficiently between the *feeling* of abandonment and its *reality*," again admirably citing a catechetical address from Pope John Paul, I do not think it necessarily follows that Balthasar's view of Christ's passion "runs counter to the Scholastic view that from his conception, even during his Passion, Jesus as man was *simul viator et comprehensor . . .* enjoying the beatific vision of his Father, and yet feeling a sorrow surpassing all the suf-

---

[99] See his General Audience of November 30, 1988, available in *Jesus, Son and Savior* [Boston: Pauline Books & Media, 1996], 472), cited from the *L'Osservatore Romano* edition in Saward, *Mysteries of March*, 56.

[100] Saward, *Mysteries of March*, 58 (emphasis original).

[101] Saward quotes Balthasar's *Theologik* (see 166n49), where Balthasar asserts that the Thomistic position "seems quite incredible and cannot be salvaged by the arguments adduced" (*TL* II, 287 [G 261]), but he is simply dismissing contemporary Thomistic articulations, not necessarily the notion that Christ in some sense possessed full vision of the Father.

fering endured or endurable by men in this present life." [102]

In fact, Saward himself notes in passing that in place of the Scholastic depiction of Christ's dereliction, "[Balthasar] would prefer to develop Adrienne's intuitions about Christ having vision as 'beholder' and faith as 'pilgrim,'" a thesis he notes is *"apparently* at odds with the traditional view" that Christ possessed the beatific vision during His earthly life. But he adds: "Balthasar and Adrienne try to get beyond the opposition of faith to sight. The Son as man does not like us 'walk by faith,' but he does have on earth 'the form of vision most closely comparable to our faith'; (faith, in any case, as St. Thomas Aquinas perceived, is itself a kind of seeing, has its own light)."[103] He does not elaborate on this latter point, which is precisely where the key to dissolving the tension lies, not in maintaining that faith and knowledge may coexist *per se*, but in exploring one's understanding of what constitutes the *visio beata* and its distinction from the concomitant *fruitio beata*. In other words, Saward and John Paul do not envision the possibility that Christ's experience of abandonment is "all-consuming, enveloping and penetrating the whole of Our Lord's soul,"[104] excluding the perfect beatitude ordinarily consequent to perfect knowledge of God, but not the intellective solace of knowing by virtue of infused grace that God has not in fact abandoned Him and enjoying the profound (intellective) peace that accompanies all mystical participation in the dark night.[105]

Not only does Balthasar not affirm outright that Christ's soul suffered the pains of Sheol while His body lay in the tomb, as established in the first two chapters, but also nowhere does he state that the *"visio mortis"*

---

[102] Saward, *Mysteries of March*, 55–56 (emphasis original).

[103] Saward, 57 (emphasis added).

[104] Saward, 55. Saward continues this sentence characterizing Balthasar's understanding of such with the clause, "excluding, *at any level*, joy or beatitude," which is precisely what I dispute here by way of distinction and qualification.

[105] Hence, the charity that engulfs Christ's soul exemplified in eminent fashion the knowledge and consolation that is intrinsic to the infused virtues of faith and hope, enjoyed by everyone who suffers in union with the love of God. Yet Balthasar sometimes wants to go further than to deny Christ the *fruitio beata* on the cross, excluding all joy whatsoever from the latter: "Suffering that is consoled is not ultimate suffering, it is not the Cross" (*Truth is Symphonic: Aspects of Christian Pluralism*, trans. Graham Harrison [San Francisco: Ignatius Press, 1987], 166).

But he also says at the same time that "Jesus' suffering on the Cross, including his being forsaken by God, could be seen as a paradoxical expression of his joy" (154). Perhaps these statements are reconciled when he concludes this essay on "Joy and the Cross" thus: "only in virtue of his filial intimacy with the divine Father can he suffer total abandonment by the Father and taste that suffering to the last drop" (169).

involves utter loss of the *visio immediata Dei*.[106] In fact, in a footnote to Christ's descent as a "state of perdition" (not a place), Balthasar says: "Of course, this does not mean approval of Calvin's doctrine, for the reason that the continuous *visio immediata Dei in anima Christi* makes his experience of hell wholly incommensurate with any other, gives it an 'exemplary,' soteriological and trinitarian significance."[107] In other words, the immediate vision of God in Christ (whether it be located in His human consciousness at all times or not) is precisely what permits Him to suffer so incomparably with the sinners for whom He descends into the deepest regions of the earth. He experienced complete abandonment without actually losing the grace/charity connatural to His beatified soul, even if His psychological awareness of His own blessed state of grace was temporarily suspended in becoming the object of the infinity of His Father's righteous anger.[108] In this way, it was possible for Christ to suffer the worst hell possible, experiencing in His soul at the culminating point of His passion (i.e., death) what it means to "become accursed for us" (Gal 3:13), the solitary object of the Father's wrath.

However, one might argue that Balthasar's position later evolved into one in which the hermeneutic of *kenosis* takes absolute priority. In the third volume of his *Theodrama* (in German, II/2), for instance, Balthasar seems to

---

[106] Miles recounts a double aspect of this "vision" in the symbolic language of Speyr's competing metaphors:

> Speyr does not attempt to unify the ideas of shapes or husks of sin within what she sees as an amorphous mass of melted and unrecognizable sin. These are two different aspects of sin in hell. There is the sin without the redeemed soul on which the Son gazes, the sin which he has discarded in hell. There is also the sin that the unredeemed sinner confronts and recognizes that this is who he is: this is his eternal state since he refused to repent. The Son contemplates sin in hell as an amorphous mass of objective sin, stripped away from any relationship to people as if it were sin without containers. . . . These sins have a sensible reality to which the sinner has given something of his own form. One could recognize the sinner from the sin. Every person in hell must confront their own sin and recognize that this is now what they are. Because the Son has gathered together every sin of every sinner in the world, he confronts each sin as his own. This great amorphous mass of sin appears to von Speyr as if it were a river in hades that seems to include all "the sediment of the world, the sin, so heavy, that it wholly sinks until the bottom of everything." ("Obedience of a Corpse," 180–181)

[107] *Explorations* I, 264n20 [G 285–286n6].

[108] Speyr, *Das Wort und die Mystik*, Teil 1, *Subjektive Mystik* (Einsiedeln: Johannes Verlag, 1970), 109: "One cannot describe this Night of the Lord simply as an antithesis to Grace, because it is also Grace; it cannot be described as the negation of an abundance."

feel compelled to deny the *visio immediata* in order to make sense of Christ's mission of obedience in His earthly life, having assumed the *fomes peccati*:

> We can say that Jesus is aware of an element of the divine in his innermost, indivisible self-consciousness; it is intuitive insofar as it is inseparable from the intuition of his mission-consciousness, but it is defined and limited by this same mission-consciousness. It is of this, and of this alone, that he has a *visio immediata,* and we have no reason to suggest this *visio* of the divine is supplemented by another, as it were, purely theoretical content, over and above his mission. Of course, the particular shape of the mission (which draws its universality from its identity with the self-consciousness of *this particular* "I") can contain a wealth of content, successively revealed, but its source and measure remain the mission itself . . . *since Jesus does not see the Father in a "visio beatifica"* but is presented with the Father's commission by the Holy Spirit, that is, his awareness of his mission is only indirect, it is possible for him to be tempted.[109]

Balthasar rightly asserts that it is not *necessary* to conclude from the hypostatic union to a perfect vision of God's essence in Christ's human mind, which is traditionally thought to involve knowledge of all things as caused by God. But he seems to assume that this means Christ did not actually possess perfect knowledge of the divine essence, which had to be suspended for the sake of the mission of obedience in solidarity with sinful mankind.

Thus, David Stuart Yeago challenges the idea that Balthasar assumes the traditional position on Christ's possession of the beatific vision, arguing that for him Christ's self-consciousness is simply his mission-consciousness, which is simply not enough. On the basis of some texts from the third volume of the *Theodrama,* Yeago states:

> Thus for von Balthasar Jesus' knowledge that he is the Son of God is simply identical with his knowledge of his mission: to know oneself as primordially the bearer of <u>such</u> a mission—a mission of universal scope and unsurpassable significance—<u>is</u> to know oneself a

---

[109] *TD* III, 166, 200 [G 152, 183], emphasis added. He further explains his position on 172–173 [G 158]. In the last sentence, there is a mistranslation of *unmittelbar* as "indirect," when it should read "immediate" (or "direct"), as Rosenberg notes (see "Christ's Human Knowledge," 828n55). Earlier in his career, he also seemed to think the beatific vision would undermine Christ's humanity (see *GL* I, 328n141 [G 316n1]).

divine, even if one does not and could not form for oneself the sentence, "I am divine." And to know oneself to be related to the Father by this commission is to know oneself as the unique Son of the Father, even if one has no "theoretical" awareness of the meta-physical implications of this relationship. On this same basis, von Balthasar simply denies the traditional position (recently affirmed in a strong form by Karl Rahner) that this self-knowledge implies the possession by Jesus of the visio immediata of the divine nature in his earthly career. Jesus' knowledge of himself as Son and of God as his Father is contained within his knowledge of his task, mediated to him by the Holy Spirit, and this mode of conscious-ness of his identity "excludes" the beatific vision. As von Balthasar points out, "mission essentially presses forward" towards its ful-fillment, and therefore consciousness of mission is not compatible with the beatific vision. The "contemplative moments" within the mission "mean no interruption in the life of mission, but rather the ever-new enabling of perseverance in it."[110]

He adds the following note:

> Balthasar adds in parentheses "zumindest zeitweise" which, whether zeitweise is to be taken as "sometimes" or "for a time," seems to leave open the possibility that Jesus could have experi-enced the beatific vision as one experience within his life, though not as an abiding constituent of his life. The analogy to Christian mystical experience invoked on p. 180 may be the background to this; von Balthasar may have in mind episodes in the Gospels such as the Transfiguration and Jesus' ecstatic rejoicing in the Spirit (Lk 10:21–24).[111]

Thus, he thinks that, according to Balthasar's reasoning, not only does Christ's consciousness of his divine mission not entail perfect vision of the Godhead, but it is actually befitting of His *kenosis* that He not possess the beatific vision.[112] In fact, Balthasar seems not to be too concerned

---

[110] David Stuart Yeago, "The Drama of Nature and Grace: A Study in the Theology of Hans Urs von Balthasar," (PhD diss., Yale University, 1992), 149–151. Randall Rosen-berg argues that here Balthasar is essentially in agreement with Rahner (see "Theory and Drama," 80–81).

[111] Yeago, "Drama of Nature and Grace," 151n59.

[112] Yeago also notes that, while Balthasar "borrowed from Rahner several important con-

with the matter, at least when he states in the third volume: "If therefore we take Jesus' entire awareness that he belongs to God and refer it to his mission, we shall not need to agonize over the relationship of his human self-consciousness to his divine self-consciousness."[113]

Still, in volume four, Balthasar is clearly struggling with how best to do justice to Christ's experience of abandonment, suggesting that Thomas's insistence upon Christ's beatific vision hinders his ability to develop further conclusions regarding the immensity of Christ's suffering:

> When Thomas comes to speak of Christ's sufferings—which, in contrast to Anselm, he does regard as having a value as *satisfactio* (49, 1–5)—his portrayal is strangely flat, almost moralizing in tone, in spite of all the superlatives he employs. He goes through the Passion narratives (46, 5) and gives why Christ has endured "all human sufferings" (if not *secundum species*, then *secundum genus*); he suggests why his pains were greater than any that can be experienced in this life (explicitly excluding hell: 46, 6, cf. obj. 3); but all the time he is careful to insist that, during the Passion, Christ could not lose the blessed vision of God: "God was never a cause of grief to his soul": 46, 7. . . . Finally, it is strange that Thomas, who had given a thorough account of the sufferings of Christ's soul, should later prefer to describe the Passion as a bodily event in a way that almost recalls Athanasius. There is no emphasis whatsoever on Christ's abandonment by God as the center of the Passion.[114]

This despite the fact that Thomas, he says, holds that Jesus "possessed *similitudinem peccati in carne*" and mentions Christ's abandonment "once, in order to show that the Father did not hinder the Son from suffering."[115]

While the third volume of his *Theodrama* gets the most attention on this score, there are a number of other places in the great Trilogy where Balthasar grapples with the problem of Christ's "immediate vision of

---

ceptual moves, especially the notion that not-knowing can under some circumstances be a perfection of human agency . . . and the notion of an implicit self-knowledge that gradually becomes explicit in and through a personal history," Rahner presents [Jesus' *visio immediata* of God] "as a direct consequence of the hypostatic union," rather than arguing from fittingness (*convenientia*) ("Drama of Nature and Grace," 150n58).

[113] *TD* III, 172 [G 157].

[114] *TD* IV, 263–264 [G 243–244].

[115] *TD* IV, 263 and 264n12 [G 243, 244n12].

God."[116] Hence, as Matthew Levering points out, "It is worth noting that volume V was published five years after volume III. In the later volume, Balthasar is taking the opportunity to clarify some of the positions adopted in the earlier volume, and he goes over much of the same terrain again in volume II of the *Theologik*."[117] Nonetheless, it all occurs in the context of Christ's "mission-consciousness," which is fulfilled in absolute obedience to the Father's will that He suffer the cursedness of sin itself and conquer it in the Resurrection.

In the final volume of the *Theodrama* (*Das Endspiel*), he seems to have obtained greater clarity on the matter, without of course treating it with scholastic precision. He wants to deny Christ's human (conscious) mind full access to the beatific vision, which is connatural to Him by virtue of His union with the Father, *during the passion*.[118] Thus, relying on *TD* V, 123–125, Matthew Levering concludes:

> Balthasar's insistence that Jesus must enjoy the immediate vision of the Father is likewise qualified. He emphasizes that "in the Lord's Passion his sight is veiled, whereas his obedience remains intact." This veiling holds for Jesus' entire life, if not to the same degree as the ultimate not-knowing Jesus experiences on the Cross: his mission "presupposes (right from the Incarnation) a certain veiling of his sight of the Father: he must leave it in abeyance, refrain from using it; this is possible because of the distance between Father and Son in the Trinity.[119]

---

[116] In the seventh volume of the *Glory of the Lord* (original German published in 1969), Balthasar in passing merely allows for the possibility that Christ need not possess the *visio beatifica*, not asserting its absence (as Pitstick claims in her *Light in Darkness,* 166) or actually treating the question:

> [T]he deepest experience of abandonment by God, which is to be vicariously real in the Passion, presupposes an equally deep experience of being united to God and of life derived from the Father—an experience that the Son must have had, not only in Heaven, but also as a man, even if this does not mean that his spirit must already enjoy a perpetual *visio beatifica*. Only one who has known the genuine intimacy of love, can be genuinely abandoned (not merely lonely). (*GL* VII, 216 [G 200–201])

[117] Levering, *Scripture and Metaphysics*, 128n88.

[118] See *TD* V, 123–124 [G 107–108]. He also there attributes a sort of faith to Christ's obedience, which will be discussed shortly.

[119] Levering, "Balthasar on Christ's Consciousness," 577; *Scripture and Metaphysics*, 128. Hence, it is also true that, for Balthasar,

This kind of approach to Christ's knowledge is similar to that of Jacques Maritain in his last book, *De la grace et de l'humanité de Jesus*.[120] Distinguishing between the supraconscious and infra-conscious dimensions of the human mind discovered by modern psychology, Maritain holds that Christ's supraconscious enjoys perfect knowledge of God, while His infra-conscious mind grows in "wisdom and grace" (Luke 2:52).[121]

Independently concurring with Balthasar on the profundity of Christ's intellectual suffering, he goes so far as to say:

> [A]t the moment of the Agony and of the Passion He can no longer enter there [His nest of refuge in the Father], He is barred from it by uncrossable barriers, this is why He feels himself abandoned. That has been the supreme exemplar of the night of the spirit of the mystics, the absolutely complete night. The whole world of the Vision and of the divinized supraconscious was there, but He no longer experienced it at all through His infused contemplation. And likewise the radiance and the influx of this world on the entire soul were more powerful than ever, but were no longer

---

The Son's obedience on the Cross, in order to bear sin fully, must be characterized by two elements: absolute faithfulness, and absolute lack of grounding in knowledge. Jesus only moves to the pinnacle of obedience (the pinnacle of union with the Father's will) by simultaneously entering the abyss of not-knowing. The highest obedience—the highest charity—is that which obeys without (conscious knowledge or hope). (*Scripture and Metaphysics*, 131)

I take "lack of grounding in knowledge" to indicate Balthasar's notion of "laying up" or "depositing" with the Father the knowledge not necessary for His mission at present. This is a very Ignatian understanding of obedience, as Lois M. Miles elucidates throughout her dissertation, "Obedience of a Corpse."

[120] For interesting reflections on the distinct planes of consciousness in Christ, see Maritain, *On the Grace and Humanity of Jesus*, 48ff. [F 50ff.].

[121] See Maritain, *On the Grace and Humanity of Jesus*, especially 49, 55–58. Andrew V. Rosato recently contested Maritain's thesis that Christ's humanity grows in grace, defending Aquinas's position that Maritain attempts to revise (see "Aquinas and Maritain on Whether Christ's Habitual Grace Could Increase," *Nova et Vetera* 15, no. 2 [2017]: 527–546).

Essentially, the debate is about whether Christ's soul grew in habitual grace or simply *auxiliae*. Rosato does not get at the heart of the issue, which is the reality that habits are perfected through acts enabled by particular graces (*auxiliae*) and there must not be anything sinful in Christ's soul for the *habitus* of grace and charity to grow in this manner. Thus, it is not adequate to speak only of a growth in the *manifestations* of Christ's habitual grace, as if habitual grace is not perfected through particular works, operative grace brought to fruition by cooperative graces.

seized at all by the consciousness, nor experienced. Jesus was more than ever united with the Father, but in the terror and the sweat of blood, and in the experience of dereliction.[122]

Yet Maritain's treatment of Christ's consciousness also differs from Balthasar's, invoking a "partition" in Christ's soul, something Balthasar will oppose.[123] In an attempt to try to reconcile Christ's enduring vision of the Father with His suffering the loss of experiencing it, Maritain says concerning the passion:

> In one sense—in the sense that He had the Vision of the divine essence—He was indeed blessed (III, 9, 2 ad 2), and even during His Passion (46, 8), in that which St. Thomas calls the higher part of the soul and which we call the divinized supraconscious of the latter. But, St. Thomas teaches, there was no *derivation* or *redundantia*, there was no repercussion of the higher part on the lower part, this is why the Beatific Vision has not at all prevented the suffering of Christ, in His Passion, from being greater than all the sufferings (46, 6).—*Dum Christus erat viator, non fiebat redundantia gloriae a superiori parte (animae) in inferiorem, ne ab anima in corpus* (46, 8). In this assertion of St. Thomas one finds an indication, quite inchoative no doubt and merely sketched, but valuable, of the notion of "partition," in the soul of Christ, between the world of the Beatific Vision and that of the conscious faculties, which I introduce here, and to which I attach a particular importance.[124]

---

[122] Maritain, *On the Grace and Humanity of Jesus*, 61 [F 64]. Hence, Maritain may have accepted a Balthasarian view of the descent. See also his "Beginning with a Reverie," in *The Collected Works of Jacques Maritain*, vol. 20, *Untrammeled Approaches*, trans. Bernard Doering (South Bend, IN: University of Notre Dame, 1997), 3–26, at 11n13; *Approaches sans entraves* (Paris: Librairie Arthem Fayard, 1973), 15n12. But he, like Ratzinger, does not project Christ's sufferings into the Trinitarian processions.

[123] Although Maritain speaks of "partition" in Christ's consciousness between "the supraconscious of the spirit divinized by the beatific vision" (*On the Grace and Humanity of Jesus*, 55, cf. 50), which takes the place in Christ of man's "pre-conscious of the spirit" (49n2, cf. 56, 58), and the "infra-conscious" plane of experimental/acquired knowledge (that is, His ordinary human consciousness), Maritain strives to maintain Christ's psychological unity (see especially 68, 77), particularly by reflecting on the influence of the former upon the latter (see 101–108).

[124] Maritain, *On the Grace and Humanity*, 60n15.

Meanwhile, in the second volume of the *Theologik*, Balthasar very briefly criticizes similar Thomistic treatments of the issue:

> One can only regret here that Johannes Stohr ... rehashes the old Thomistic theses on this point, relying above all on the incorrigible school [of] Thomist B. de Margerie, SJ. The claim that on the Cross Jesus experiences the beatific vision in the "apex of the soul," whereas the "lower parts of his soul" experience Godforsakenness, is especially incredible today and cannot be rescued with the arguments these authors have advanced.[125]

Notice, however, that this criticism does not apply to what Thomas himself says:

> It is evident that Christ's whole soul suffered. . . . Christ's "higher reason" did not suffer thereby *on the part of its object*, which is God, who was the cause, not of grief, but rather of delight and joy, to the soul of Christ. Nevertheless, all the powers of Christ's soul did suffer according as any faculty is said to be affected *as regarded its subject*, because all the faculties of Christ's soul were rooted in its *essence, to which suffering extended* while the body, whose act it is, suffered.[126]

---

[125] *TL* II, 287 n. 9 [G 261n9]. The same applies to M.-J. Nicolas, whom Jacques Servais quotes in support of his very brief argument that Balthasar maintained the traditional position on Christ's beatific knowledge and merely intended to reject Thomas's doctrine of *fruitio beata* in the experience of Calvary (see *Mystery of Redemption*, 102ff.):

> It is one thing to say that the vision of the divine essence remained during the most profound throes of the Cross; it is something else to say that it was entirely beatific. It did not in fact affect the lower powers that Jesus fully abandoned to their natural objects and to all the causes of suffering. But . . . Saint Thomas clarifies that the soul itself, being by its essence the form of the body, was the subject of the Passion while it was also the subject of beatitude. It is the same being that at once suffers and enjoys. (*Somme théologique*, vol. 4 [Paris: Les Éditions du Cerf, 1986], 343)

Servais's main contention is that Balthasar does not go so far as to oppose the condemnation of the following proposition by the Holy Office in June 5, 1918: "It is not certain that there was in the soul of Christ, while he was living among men, the knowledge possessed by the blessed or those who have the beatific vision" (Denz. 3645).

[126] *ST* III, q. 46, a. 7, emphasis added by White in "Jesus' Cry on the Cross," 575n54.

More significantly, this parenthetical criticism appears in a footnote to the following main text:

> Von Speyr maintains almost always that on earth the Son possessed the vision of the Father. It is rare that she speaks of Christ's faith. But we also find her saying that Jesus' obedience existed despite this vision or that as *comprehensor* [comprehender] he had vision and as *viator* [wayfarer] faith or that vision could veil itself into obedience.[127]

After noting that Adrienne von Speyr attributes the vision of the Father to Christ as *comprehensor* and faith to Christ as *viator* exercising obedience to the Father, Balthasar argues that because "in his human nature he must experience how man comes to terms with God," "we can speak of a depositing, a dimming, a non-use of his divine vision; his prayer must spring from his having become man."[128] Applying this kind of reasoning to the contentious topic of Christ's hellish suffering, Balthasar speaks of an "absolute overtaxing of knowledge" involved in the descent, wherein, "because he is dead, he cannot know [his victory, the sin separated from man on the Cross] as what he has made it to be. He can only 'take cognizance' of it as the fearsome agglomeration of all sins that no longer has the slightest connection with the Father who is the good Creator."[129]

Somewhat similar to Maritain's distinction between supraconsciousness or pre-consciousness and infra-consciousness (or, simply, consciousness) is Lonergan's distinction between *conscientia-experientia* and *conscientia-perceptio*. The former is the "unstructured awareness of oneself and one's acts" or a "certain presence of oneself to oneself," whereas the latter is the reflexive knowledge of oneself as an object in a world of objects.[130] This distinction between one's original consciousness of oneself (and one's acts) and one's conceptualization of this experience, like Maritain's distinction between the pre-conscious mind and the conscious mind, does not directly translate into the distinc-

---

[127] *TL* II, 286–287 [G 261]. Speyr even says, "[Mary] knows somehow about his vision of the Father, about his beatific vision of the Father" (*Subjektive Mystik*, 86, translated by Sutton, *Heaven Opens*, location 1778). Balthasar also notes her commentary on 1 Corinthians: "On earth the Son has an immediate and absolute knowledge of the Father, which as such cannot grow and to which corresponds an absolute mission" (*TL* II, 290n17 [G 264n17]).

[128] *TL* II, 288 [G 262–263].

[129] *TL* II, 348 [G 317–318].

[130] See Lonergan, *Ontological and Psychological Constitution*, 165 and 187.

tion between Christ's *visio immediata* (or "divinized supraconscious of the spirit") and His acquired or experimental knowledge (i.e., ordinary human object-consciousness). Nonetheless, as Aaron Pidel, SJ, recounts:

> Applying *conscientia-experientia* to the case of Christ's human knowledge turns out to have several advantages. First and foremost, it eliminates a tendency to posit an exaggerated psychological dichotomy in Christ. If the "I" belongs to person and consciousness belongs to nature, then there is in Christ one divine "I" experiencing himself *ex parte subiecti* through both divine and human consciousness. If the Word were present to Christ's human consciousness only *ex parte obiecti*, on the other hand, this would introduce a sort of unbridgeable chasm between the humanity and divinity of Christ. The human nature of Christ, conceived in this case almost as an autonomous "I," would gaze at the Word from an infinite distance.[131]

In other words, Christ's *visio immediata*, unlike the case of every other blessed soul, exists in the form of self-consciousness. Hence, for Lonergan, Christ's immediate knowledge of the divine essence is implied in Christ's awareness (or understanding) of His own identity.

Pidel also alludes to the fact that Balthasar's difficulties with conceptualizing the doctrine concerning Christ's beatific vision in life may derive from his understanding of what precisely constitutes the *visio beata*:

> "Mission-consciousness" is sufficient to ground Christ's "suprahistorical radiance." Here Balthasar parts company with Lonergan, who sees *scientia beata* as the condition for the possibility of revelation. . . . [T]his ostensible disagreement owes much to Balthasar's hyper-literal understanding of the "beatific vision." What Balthasar actually affirms of Christ comes close to what Lonergan affirms in Christ's "ineffable knowledge." Despite his reservations about the beatific vision, Balthasar depicts Christ, in substance, as a qualitatively unique *comprehensor*. He acknowledges that the theological tradition that would ascribe to Christ "everything knowable to man" is "long," "serious," and "solidly based on a biblical theme."[132]

---

[131] Pidel, "The Consciousness and Human Knowledge of Christ according to Lonergan and Balthasar," *Lumen et Vita* (June 2011): 1–25, at 6.

[132] Pidel, 15–16. He relies here on *TD* III alone.

While diverging from Pius XII's characterization of Christ's *visio* in *Mystici Corporis* (Denz. 3812), Balthasar's main qualm seems to be the necessity of denying to Christ knowledge of certain contingent objects that would ordinarily pertain to the beatific vision, as perfect understanding of the *causa prima* entails perfect understanding of all the effects pre-existent therein. But there is nothing to prevent God from possibly withholding particular items of knowledge (in addition to the *possibilia* commonly thought to be inaccessible to creatures) from one who possesses the immediate vision of God, as Lonergan seems to admit.[133]

Thus, understanding Christ's vision in terms of "mission-consciousness," whereby Jesus knows whatever the Father chooses to reveal to Him in the moment, is Balthasar's way of avoiding both a naïve conception of it as well as an overly abstract understanding of it. The former would paint a "pious picture" of "the little Child playing with pieces of wood in the form of a cross," that is, of Jesus as an infant knowing the details of His future.[134] The latter creates a division between the "upper regions" and "lower regions" of Christ's soul, which he thinks undermines His humanity.[135] Thus, Pidel is right to characterize the notion of the *visio* rejected by Balthasar as "a sort of discursive omniscience."[136] While Pidel thinks that Balthasar's conception of beatific knowledge in Christ is limited by "the ocular metaphor,"[137] Randall Rosenberg notes

---

[133] This is implied, for instance, in Lonergan's definition of Christ's beatific knowledge: "to know the triune God through the divine essence and, *in proportion to the perfection of this knowledge,* to know all other things in God as secondary objects" (see *Ontological and Psychological Constitution*, 206–207, referencing *ST* I, q. 12 and *ST* III, q. 10). Charles Hefling, likewise, notes that for Lonergan Christ's *scientia ineffabilis* is stripped of anything "empirically residual" ("Another Perhaps Permanently Valid Achievement," 152).

Hence, Pidel asserts, based on Lonergan's distinction between effable and ineffable knowledge in Christ, that "Christ does not, therefore, 'see' a detailed trajectory of his life," as "both Christ's immediate knowledge of the Trinity and his knowledge mediated 'in the Word' are beyond conceptualization and verbalization" ("Consciousness and Human Knowledge," 10–11).

But this kind of approach would have to take into account the tradition of Christ's infused knowledge as the means by which the ineffable is rendered effable in some sense. Gaine contests such a "tradition": see especially "Christ's Infused Knowledge," 605–607.

[134] *TD* III, 173 [G 158]. Thus, in the same place, he criticizes Aquinas for teaching that Jesus could only learn from things, not persons, as the latter would be unbefitting to his dignity (see *ST* III, q. 12, a. 3).

[135] *TD* III, 196 [G 180].

[136] Pidel, "Consciousness and Human Knowledge," 19.

[137] Pidel, 18. I think, rather, that Balthasar's misgivings revolve around the question of the

that Balthasar's reticence to use the terminology of *visio* is due precisely to his judgment that "describing God's entrusting of himself to us as a *visio Dei* is always an inadequate and one-sided portrayal of this open encounter, since God can never be an object totally available to our sight."[138] He adds with Balthasar: "Only by conceiving this reality as a trinitarian *event* rather than as 'the abstract contemplation of essence' can we hold together the 'interplay of vision and nonvision.'"[139] Of course, all of this comes to a head in the question of Christ's consciousness in His passion and death, where His experience of abandonment seems to exclude the possibility of an enduring beatific bliss.

Thus, it is not enough to say that "the content of his *visio immediata* is his mission," as does Rosenberg,[140] because comprehension of His mission implies complete understanding of the divine essence since His *missio* and *processio* are identical, as Balthasar frequently asserts,[141] even if Christ kenotically suspends access to everything that would ordinarily be included in the *visio immediata Dei*.[142] Moreover, asserting along with Pitstick a distinction in Balthasar between *visio beatifica* and *visio imme-*

---

contingency of "secondary objects," perhaps unbeknownst to him. Lois M. Miles (as will be seen later) discerns in Balthasar the Scotistic view that the "vision" (i.e., supernatural beatitude) is constituted by perfect love rather than perfect understanding.

Miles notes that for Speyr, "The 'optical' loss can be construed as epistemological if one equates seeing with knowing and understanding with enlightenment. This distinction makes no difference in von Speyr's thought, however, since she also maintains that the Son surrenders his understanding to the Father in *Suscipean Bereitschaft*" ("Obedience of a Corpse," 165).

[138] *TD* V, 395–396, cited in Rosenberg, "Christ's Human Knowledge," 829. Here there is convergence with Lonergan, but his remedy to the inadequacy is more Speyrian than Thomistic. The predominant influence of the Eastern Fathers on Balthasar's conception of heaven is palpable in *TD* V, 395–408 [G 361–374].

Rosenberg thinks that Balthasar is following a synthesis of Benedict XII's declaration on the beatific vision with Gregory Palamas's theology of divine incomprehensibility established by Aquinas in *ST* I, q. 12 (see Rosenberg, "Theory and Drama," 109–110).

[139] Rosenberg, "Christ's Human Knowledge," 829, quoting *TD* V, 407.

[140] Rosenberg, 828.

[141] See, e.g., *TD* V, 80–81, 124 [G 70–71, 108]; *TD* III, 154, 173, 201 [G 142, 158, 184].

[142] Still, Rosenberg is right to assert: "Balthasar seems to waver in his Christology about whether or not Christ maintained the beatific vision. He claims that Jesus 'does not see the Father.' But it is interesting to note that, for Balthasar, Jesus has the Father's will in his mind's eye and that this knowledge is 'direct' or 'immediate'" ("Theory and Drama," 105).

Thus, Balthasar thinks: "In Adrienne von Speyr's work, perhaps no mystery of the faith appeared harder to her than an adequate formulation of the relation between vision and faith in the lived experience of the God-man" (*TL* II, 286 [G 261]).

diata, Rosenberg states: "Balthasar often denies Jesus the *beatific vision*, but grants him an *immediate vision*."[143] I maintain that this is not so much a technical distinction in Balthasar as it is a preference for different terminology, given that, in his view, Christ's suffering in the passion-descent must exclude beatific joy. Finally, Rosenberg notes that, in volume three of the *Theodrama*, Balthasar attributes faith as defined in Hebrews 11:1 to Christ in His economic assumption of ignorance concerning the details of His own future, contrary to what the Congregation for the Doctrine of the Faith will later teach in opposition to the work of Jon Sobrino, SJ, namely, that faith even in an exemplary form cannot be attributed to Christ's human soul.[144] Therefore, to complete the present Balthasarian-Speyrian consideration of the nature of Christ's enduring *visio*, it is necessary to examine an earlier explicit treatment of faith in Christ.

BALTHASAR AND SPEYR ON FAITH AND VISION IN CHRIST

One might be tempted to think that Balthasar did not accept the doctrine of Christ's *visio immediata* because he clearly held that Christ possessed the virtue of faith (albeit, in an exemplary manner), but this is to misunderstand in which sense he attributes faith to Jesus. In a relatively early essay, entitled "'Fides Christi': An Essay on the Consciousness of Christ," he tackles the issue.[145] Scripture scholars will immediately think here of the unending debate about the meaning of πίστις Χριστοῦ Ιησοῦ (see Gal 2:16, 20; Gal 3:22; Eph 3:12; Phil 3:9; Rom 3:22, 26).[146] Balthasar does not try to resolve the technical question concerning whether the genitive in question ("the faith *of* Christ Jesus") is objective or subjective, but he is

---

[143] Rosenberg, "Christ's Human Knowledge," 828.

[144] See *TD* III, 171 [G 157]; Congregation for the Doctrine of the Faith, *Notification on the Works of Father Jon Sobrino, SJ*, no. 8, available at the Vatican Website, http://www.vatican.va/roman_curia/congregations/cfaith/documents/rc_con_cfaith_doc_20061126_notification-sobrino_en.html (accessed 8/23/17); Rosenberg, "Christ's Human Knowledge," 826.

[145] See *Explorations in Theology*, vol. 2, *Spouse of the Word*, trans. A. V. Littledale and Alexander Dru (San Francisco: Ignatius Press, 1991), 43–79. Also, for his understanding of faith, see *GL* I, 131–425 [G 123–410]; "The Faith of the Simple Ones" and "Two Modes of Faith," in *Explorations in Theology*, vol. 3, *Creator Spirit*, trans. Brian McNeil, CRV (San Francisco: Ignatius Press, 1993), 57–83 and 85–102; John Riches, "Balthasar and the Analysis of Faith," in *The Analogy of Beauty*, 35–59.

[146] These are the passages Balthasar cites in *ET* II, 57n15.

happy to conclude that "it is a third term towering over both."[147] This conclusion reflects his understanding of how faith may be ascribed to Christ (during both His earthly life and heavenly glory).

His fundamental argument is that Jesus possessed (and possesses) faith as it is conceived in the Old Testament, not as it is conceived in the New. The former functions in a provisional manner, as Old Covenant gives way to New, but it essentially signifies God's own fidelity to His people. Thus, he opens his essay with the following argument:

> If it is true that the Bible as a whole increasingly uses the term *faith* (in growing measure up to the prophets, and especially Isaiah) as the adequate expression for the way the chosen people related to God; and thus, if within this framework, this term also truly reflects how the individual members of the people of God related to their God of the Covenant; if indeed the Biblical idea of faith includes even more so *God's* faithfulness toward his people and assumes that this fidelity is a presupposition and prototype to be imitated (recall that the Hebraic term encompasses more shades of meaning than the Greek); then, speaking a priori, it cannot be otherwise in the case of Jesus.[148]

He later adds, in response to Aquinas's objections to the notion that Christ could possess faith on the basis of Christ's possession of the beatific vision:[149]

> Now if we proceed only from the concept of faith based on the specific differences between the meaning of faith in the New Testament in its relation to the Old, then this conclusion is unavoidable. But if we keep in mind that the New Testament concept *completes* and *perfects* the Old Testament concept, fully displaying its crucial priority, then we will not automatically emphasize the moment of negativity (the nonseeing) and thus the provisionality of the attitude of faith. To do so would obscure the perfection already lurking in the very core of faith itself: faith's definitive nature, which expresses the complete correspondence between

---

[147] *ET* II, 57.

[148] *ET* II, 43.

[149] See ST III, q. 7, a. 3, cited on 64–65. He also notes without citation concerning the impossibility of faith in Christ: "Not only do the scholastic theologians speak this way, but we find even Augustine already saying this" (65).

God's fidelity and man's fidelity, would be overshadowed.[150]

He does not, therefore, reject the position of Aquinas, or, for that matter, the position of Augustine and Bonaventure,[151] that faith and vision are mutually exclusive, that is, when faith is conceived as provisional (in the New Testament manner). Hence, he also states:

> If one simply juxtaposes the Platonic-Aristotelian concept of in-tuitive or conceptual vision with the New Testament concept of faith, then of course Thomas is absolutely right: one cannot at the same time see *and* believe something. Faith by definition is an assent to something as true, based on what authority says rather than what the evidence of one's own senses attests. However, this answer to the limitations of Greek thought does not mean that the fullness of the act and attitude of faith of the Old Testament have thereby been exhaustively described, particularly in its cen-tral dynamism.[152]

In other words, if faith is conceived simply as a virtue of the intellect, then Christ has no need of it; but if it is conceived in a broader manner, similar to the sense in which hope can be attributed to Christ's soul,[153] then it may be ascribed to Him. Hence, while "the darkness and enigmatic

---

[150] *ET* II, 65 (emphasis original).

[151] See *ET* II, 69.

[152] *ET* II, 65–66. He also explains: "The man who is perfect before God, Jesus Christ, cannot possibly relate with indifference to this integration of the true attitude of man to God as it took shape in the course of the Old Testament. It is only if we look at the distinctive New Testament meaning in the Greek term *pistis* (which means holding the announced kerygma to be true as well as the individual statements either contained in it or implied by it) that we will of course have to admit that Christ, who is the essential content of this kerygma, has nothing to do with this kind of faith. In this sense he stands over faith" (51).

[153] *ET* II, 67:

> Christ's foreknowledge has not hindered his hope. Hope does not need to be uncertain. On the contrary: uncertainty is the worm in the fruit of hope and stands in contrast to its formal object. Thus infallible hope is the most perfect hope. The saints in heaven, however, hope in the sense of their earthly mission: Peter hopes for the visible Church; Christ, however, hopes for the salvation of the whole world.

Aquinas also says hope in some sense can exist in Christ, as Balthasar notes (see 67); see also *ST* III, q. 7, a. 4.

obscurity in the knowledge that faith provides, which seems to be an essential feature of it" because "the sight of the countenance of God makes the act of faith interiorly impossible,"[154] insofar as it is synonymous with trust or self-surrender, "he [Jesus] is the only one who possesses this attitude in all its fullness and who can impart it to those who have entrusted themselves to him."[155] Again, "precisely in this dimension of faith as struggle [see Rom 1:17] one is linked with what faith must have been for Jesus himself."[156] Thus, he thinks that there is some sense in which the blessed in heaven also possess faith. He cites Matthew of Aquasparta, who despite agreeing with the scholastic consensus "on the logical ground of a wholly intellectual definition of faith,"[157] nonetheless introduces a caveat, arguing that because the beatific vision does not "grasp God exhaustively" (as Aquinas teaches as well),[158] "they therefore come to appreciate God ever more as the One who is ever greater than what they see. . . . [I]n this sense it would not be inappropriate to say that the blessed believe something because they do not *know* everything."[159]

Balthasar does not fail to note that he is not in total agreement with Aquinas on the matter when he alludes to his preference for Durandus and Gerson, noting that while the latter "sought to have the *habitus fidei* continue on in the *visio* even without the act of faith," Aquinas "in contrast, felt that this held true only for certain features of faith: its certainty and steadfastness."[160] He does not seek to refute the latter, but he adds concerning the former that they returned to the "oldest interpretations" of 1 Corinthians 13:13 in Tertullian, Irenaeus, and Origen, according to Paul Henry's analysis. Therefore, he concludes: "the love that believes all and hopes all (1 Cor 13:7) will never die out, 'and so there remain (*nuni de menei*) these three: faith, hope and love.'"[161]

Henry Donneaud challenges this account of faith by pointing out

---

[154] *ET* II, 69.
[155] *ET* II, 54.
[156] *ET* II, 62.
[157] *ET* II, 69.
[158] See Aquinas's distinction between immediate vision of the divine essence and comprehension of it, which God alone possesses, in *SCG* III, chs. 51 and 55.
[159] *Quaestiones disputatae de fide*, q. 6 ad 3, cited in *ET* II, 69.
[160] *ET* II, 70. Note that even Durandus and Gerson (and, thus, also Balthasar) here remain in line with *Benedictus Deus*, where Benedict XII declares that "such a vision and enjoyment of the divine essence [in the blessed] do away with the *acts* of faith and hope in these souls, inasmuch as faith and hope are properly theological virtues" (Denz. 1001 [emphasis added]).
[161] *ET* II, 70.

that the material and formal objects of both faith and (beatific) vision are the same. Perhaps he is right to question the assertion that the dynamism of abandonment and surrender in the midst of obscurity continues into the blessed afterlife.[162] Nonetheless, there is a rich tradition of *epektasis* (roughly translated as "upward striving") in the East, particularly St. Gregory of Nyssa,[163] whose influence on Balthasar, alongside St. Gregory of Nazianzus and Origen, is easily discernible throughout his work.[164] Leaving aside the details of this ancient debate, it is also noteworthy that what Balthasar calls Old Testament faith is precisely the notion of faith that Martin Luther advances over the scholastic theology of the three infused virtues.[165] In any case, it is evident from what has been said that Balthasar's qualified attribution of faith to Christ does not stand against the doctrine of Christ's possession of the beatific vision during His earthly life.[166] Hence, in the first volume of the Trilogy, he affirms the coexistence of the two in Christ:

> In christological terms this universal Biblical structure at the very least means that the *visio immediata* which Christ has of the Father (that is, of God) may fluctuate between the mode of manifestness (which befits the Son as his "glory") and the mode of "concealment" (which befits the Servant of Yahweh in the hiddenness of his Passion). . . . [A] living faith is content to stand before the face of the God who sees, whether or not one sees him oneself. . . . [H]e, proclaiming the Word of the Father, is always coming *from* the vision of the Father, that he always has this vision "at his back," as it were,

---

[162] See Henry Donneaud, OP, "Hans Urs von Balthasar contre saint Thomas d'Aquin sur la foi du Christ," *Revue Thomiste* 97, no. 2 (1997): 335–354, at 353.

[163] Gregory of Nyssa, *De Vita Moysis*, PG 44, 465AC, quoted in Balthasar, *TD* V, 397 [G 363] (cf. 77n46 [G 67n46]); see also *Vita Moysis* 2, PG 44, 405C. For an English translation of Gregory's work, see *The Life of Moses*, trans. Abraham J. Malherbe and Everett Ferguson (New York: Paulist, 1978).

[164] The same kind of conception of divine life as "eternal increase" is present also in Adrienne von Speyr (see, e.g., *John* III, 251).

[165] For faith as trust or confidence [*Zuversicht*], see "Preface to the Epistle of St. Paul to the Romans," trans. E. Theodore Bachman, in *Luther's Works*, vol. 35, ed. E. Theodore Bachmann (Philadelphia: Fortress Press, 1960), 370–371. Pope Benedict XVI favors Aquinas to Luther in *Spe Salvi*; see Adam G. Cooper, "Hope, A Mode of Faith: Aquinas, Luther and Benedict XVI on Hebrews 11:1," *Heythrop Journal* 53 (2012): 182–190. I thank Michael Root for the Luther reference.

[166] For Speyrian reference to the coexistence of knowledge and faith (super-excellently) in God, see, e.g., *TD* V, 97, 124 [G 85, 108].

while he is in the process of accomplishing his mission; and it also means . . . that he is always on this way back to the Father.[167]

Based on this and other texts, in a dissertation on Adrienne von Speyr, Lois M. Miles opines that Speyr and Balthasar share a view of the beatific vision that is more Scotistic than Thomistic, that is, as primarily a union of love rather than of knowledge, even if Balthasar sometimes also seems to incorporate the Thomistic understanding.[168] This enables Miles to explain the apparent discrepancy between Balthasar's Speyrian admission that Christ possesses perfect vision of the Father (in the manner willed by the Father, according to the present moment of Christ's missionary purpose) and his reluctance at times to grant that Christ was endowed with the beatific vision during His earthly life. Thus, Miles implies that while Balthasar may deny presence of the beatific vision in Christ's earthly consciousness when he is confronted with the Thomist conceptualization of it,[169] he nonetheless preserves the doctrine in a Scotistic manner (i.e., emphasizing beatitude as a perfect union of love). If this is the case, then Balthasar would be arguing that while Christ's love never wavers, the beatific knowledge that would ordinarily precede such may be "laid up" or suspended from His human consciousness by the divine will in its paternal mode (that is, *via* the subsistent hypostasis of paternity).[170] But this says nothing of the joy that ordinarily follows perfect love, and perhaps there is a way to view Speyr's mystical insights, appropriated by

---

[167] *GL* I, 329, cited in Miles, "Obedience of a Corpse," 121. Speyr also says about Christ's consciousness, particularly during His passion: "the Lord comes out of the eternity of the Father, bringing his entire vision with him. Not until death does he attain the full poverty of being nothing but human, which a human person already has at birth. His death, fundamentally, is his birth. Here too he first lives through the experience of total forsakenness" (*John* III, 283).

Speyr is not here denying the hypostatic union (see Miles, 165), as a literalist interpretation (à la Pitstick) would insist, but rather reflecting on the profundity of humility exercised in the Incarnation. What Speyr conveys here is that each of the two apparently opposite truths, namely, Christ's immediate *scientia Dei* and His kenotic surrender in absolute trust (i.e., His total solidarity with sinful humanity in righteousness), are more perfectly fulfilled at different times in His mission, the former during His public ministry (before and after death), the latter during His nativity and passion.

[168] See Miles, 117ff.

[169] See Miles, 118–123, 165.

[170] Speyr recounts: "He [the Son] has asked him [the Father] to remove this knowledge [of 'the hour'] in order to be better and more fully human. He has 'pruned' himself, so to speak, in order to be a real human being" (Balthasar [ed.], *Die Nachlasswerke*, vol 11, *Ignatiana* [Einsiedeln: Johannes Verlag, 1974], 21).

Balthasar, in a way that is consonant with Thomistic thought.

Miles makes clear that Speyr's Ignatian vision of Christ's passion involved the God-man's willing suspension of everything that belonged to Him, except for His love, including all His understanding, memory, and knowledge.[171] Miles recounts: "the Son surrenders his understanding to the Father in *Suscipean Bereitschaft*. Once again, von Speyr understands the love of God to be the source of the Son's vision."[172] If Christ is said not to lose His *visio immediata* and yet to surrender His entire intellect to the Father in solidarity with sinful humanity, then perhaps the former is constituted more by perfect love than perfect knowledge or understanding, so reasons (or assumes) Speyr. In any case, whether supernatural beatitude is properly constituted by perfect knowledge or by perfect love or somehow by both simultaneously (as if neither intellect nor will possessed causal priority), the joy to which each gives rise in heaven could be "laid up" by Christ with the Father (more precisely, with the three divine persons in their hypostatically distinct manners), and this is precisely what would constitute the most profound suffering of Christ's passion in full solidarity with the death of sinful humanity.

Concerning the question of Christ's surrender of the beatific vision, Matthew Lewis Sutton sums up Speyr's perspective, based on the latter's posthumously published *Subjektive Mystik*:

> In descending to the dead, the Son gives up his vision of the Father, which is von Speyr's understanding of the Son's becoming sin for us (2 Cor. 5:21). There is nothing more for him than the stark blindness of his obedience. The blindness is complete. It is a cave with no light. The Son's renunciation of the vision of God substitutes for Adam and Eve's lost vision of heaven. The Son descends into the night of hell. In the formless, timeless night of hell, the Son loses all dialogue with and vision of the Father. He is blinded by the sin of the world and understands himself as completely abandoned: "the way is wayless as the time is timeless."[173]

---

[171] See *Das Buch vom Gehorsam* (Einsiedeln: Johannes Verlag, 1966), 46; *John* IV, 76, 100, 142; *The World of Prayer*, trans. Graham Harrison (San Francisco: Ignatius Press, 1985), 51; *Das Wort und die Mystik*, Teil II, *Objektive Mystik* (Einsiedeln: Johannes Verlag, 1970), 230.

[172] Miles, "Obedience of a Corpse," 165.

[173] Sutton, *Heaven Opens*, locations 1737–1742. The internal quote is from *Subjektive Mystik*, 13.

Again, "The Son took on Adam and Eve's nonvision. Through the resurrection of the Son by the Father, this night of nonvision has been changed into the light of the full vision of the Father."[174] Even prior to His passion, Christ chooses to live in solidarity with human ignorance, at least concerning "the hour" (Matt 24:36).[175] Speyr articulates Christ's nescience thus: "The triune, divine love is so great that if the Son as man would decide for himself the hour, the divine Father would certainly agree with him. But since the Son as man wants to be only the reflection of this divine love, he chooses uncompromisingly not to know. He wants what the Father wants."[176]

In another place, Speyr makes clear that this entails neither that He surrendered His own divinity nor that He lacked the beatific vision during His earthly life: "As God, Christ has the same knowledge as the Father and the Holy Spirit. As man, he possesses from the first instance of his existence the beatific vision of God."[177] But Sutton adds: "However, she understands the coming darkness of the passion as the Son letting his humanity take on human sin and all its grave effects, which include being robbed of the vision of God."[178] At the same time, referencing another work of hers, he asserts: "Von Speyr's account, I must emphasize, maintains that the Son even in the absolute night of forsakenness always has the essential beatific vision of the Father."[179] I assert that the best interpretation of such apparently conflicting statements is precisely the theses defended here: that God suspended the access of His human mind to at least some of the "secondary objects" pertinent to the beatific vision and, ultimately, suspended

---

[174] Sutton, location 1759–1760.
[175] Granting the beatific vision connatural to the hypostatic union of Christ, it is at least disputable whether a comprehensive knowledge of the future belongs ordinarily to the blessed vision, as God may will some events future to us (ever-present to Him, of course) to be dependent upon other futures yet to be determined; in other words, God may will that the time of "the hour" be conditional upon how much prayer and fasting is done by His people, for instance, in which case knowledge of such would not necessarily result from immediate vision of God's essence.
[176] *Das Buch vom Gehorsam*, 40, translated by Sutton, *Heaven Opens*, location 3684.
[177] *Die Magd des Herrn: Ein Marienbuch* (Einsiedeln: Johannes Verlag, 1969), 97n1; ET, *Handmaid of the Lord*, trans. E. A. Nelson (San Francisco: Ignatius Press, 1984).
[178] Sutton, *Heaven Opens*, location 3811, citing *Die Passion von Innen*, 54 (location 3812); ET, *The Passion from Within*, trans. Lucia Wiedenhover (San Francisco: Ignatius Press, 1998).
[179] Sutton, *Heaven Opens*, locations 4225–4226, citing *Der Grenzenlose Gott*, 2nd ed. (Einsiedeln: Johannes Verlag, 1981), 54; ET, *The Boundless God*, trans. Helena M. Tomko (San Francisco: Ignatius, 2004).

His experience of the *fruitio beata* during His passion, or at least, in the existential moment of His death-descent.

RECAP OF CHRIST'S "BEATIFIC SUFFERING"[180]

By engaging Balthasar and forcing him into dialogue with several contemporary Thomists, I have argued that it is fitting for Christ to possess the very (beatific) vision He wills to impart upon those for whom He suffers while He endures the very passion by means of which He desires to do so, but it seems unfitting that He enjoy the *fruitio beata* naturally concomitant to such vision (even in "the higher passions" of His rational soul) while He endures such pain. In fact, it seems most fitting that He suffer precisely the loss of that consequence of His hypostatic vision which constitutes the misery of the sinners for whom He so deigns to suffer (i.e., the *fruitio*), "becoming sin without knowing sin" (2 Cor 5:21), not by partaking in it but by co-assuming even its most profound (subjective) consequence (i.e., the ultimate consequence of sin for the sinner). What greater work of solidarity is there than solitarily undergoing the fate proper to sinful mankind in such a manner unnatural to a being most perfectly (i.e., hypostatically) united to the Word of Love Itself? Such a work of omnipotence is no less impossible than the economic prevention of the joy of the "higher parts" of Christ's soul from redounding to its "lower parts" and hylemorphically bound sacred body. Without denying the possibility of the latter proposal for how Christ could have possessed the beatific vision and yet experienced dereliction on the Cross, it is not necessary to divide Christ's human psychology in such a fashion if He, instead, forfeited the *fruitio beata* itself even while maintaining the intellective *visio immediata* fittingly integral to His incarnate status. There is no such incongruent partitioning of His human identity (or "personality," in contemporary psychological terms), if the vision alone is maintained during His passion. An analogous scenario occurs among the mystic-saints: the person suffers great spiritual attacks on all levels (e.g., via imagination, memory, perception, emotion/

---

[180] If one were to be particularly systematic about the issue, then the following sequence of questions would be in order: (1) whether Christ had faith and/or the beatific vision: (a) nature of faith, (b) nature of beatific vision, (c) whether faith and vision can coexist, (d) whether it is fitting for one or both to exist in the soul of Christ before the Resurrection; (2) whether Christ's suffering entailed temporary loss of the beatific vision: (a) if he did not already have the vision, then he could not suffer its loss, (2) if he had the vision, is it possible for him to lose it temporarily?; (3) if he had the vision, would it be fitting for him to suffer the loss of the vision (or of the *fruitio beata*)?

passion, even sensation), but none of the doubts or temptations that accost the saint penetrate the intellect itself as the harbinger of faith or the will itself steadfast in hope (which, of course, accompany the invisible infusion of divine charity constitutive of habitual grace). These may report possessing still a deep peace in knowing that they have not separated themselves from God, but the deepest and darkest of agonies are mere participations in Christ's own total loss of consolation, intellective and appetitive, which nonetheless left His immediate knowledge and love of God untouched.

Finally, there is no added theological benefit to the possible view that Christ maintained the *fruitio beata* and, at the same time, paradoxically suffered a most hellish passion, as if the *fruitio* itself would permit greater suffering or the concomitance of opposites would befit the redemptive work. But it is opportune before concluding this chapter to recap in more systematic fashion what has been discussed here in question and answer format for the sake of maximum clarity.

Whether Christ suffered in the descent?

Historically on Saturday, no; in some sense, on Friday and in death, yes.[181] The descent into hell bespeaks solidarity with humanity even in death, and thus His experience of death itself is the archetype of human death both insofar as it is an event of unnatural violence and insofar as His inextricable union with God is transmuted to all who participate in the mystery of redemption, each in his own peculiar measure.

Whether He suffered the pain of loss in His passion and death?

Yes, insofar as He could experience something akin to the loss of grace, namely, loss of the enjoyment of His beatific state (i.e., the *fruitio beata* due His perfect humanity).

Whether He possessed the beatific vision in His earthly life?

Yes, insofar as His kenotic mission required it. Not only is it fitting for the perfect humanity of Christ to be endowed with unmediated (i.e., perfect) knowledge of God, it is also appropriate to Christ's salvific mission of assuming sinful flesh without *malum culpae* for His soul to endure at the culmination of life the withdrawal of the joy that naturally follows such

---

[181] See the first three chapters.

unmediated vision and the perfect love of God that is necessarily concomitant. Even assuming the possibility of perfect vision/knowledge without perfect love, it certainly would not be fitting for Him to be stripped of such love. It might even be argued that Christ's human love of God must have been perfect and that, therefore, He must have possessed the perfect knowledge of God that would be necessary to possess such love. But there is no reason why Christ's soul could not be stripped of the perfect joy that naturally follows such knowledge and love.

Whether Christ possessed faith in His earthly life?

Just as it may be argued in some qualified sense that Christ possessed the theological virtue of hope, as does Thomas Joseph White (with reliance on Aquinas),[182] one must also clarify that insofar as faith is self-surrendering (i.e., radically obedient) trust, it is not incompatible with the hypostatic vision of Christ's soul, but it is incompatible insofar as the lack of immediate vision is presupposed.[183] For this reason, Christ is in some sense a prophet, even though he is beyond all prophets, as *viator* and *comprehensor*. Levering sums up Aquinas's reasoning on the matter:

> [A]n integral component of prophecy is lack of clear intellectual "vision," and Christ possesses from the moment of his conception the "beatific vision" of the Word. . . . [T]hose who possess such beatific vision (including the blessed in heaven) "cannot be called prophets" [ST II-II, q. 174, a. 5, *sed contra*]. How, then, is Christ a "prophet"? Aquinas gives a complex answer. He argues that as "comprehensor"—that is, as regards his beatific knowledge— Christ is not a prophet. But as "wayfarer"—that is, as regards his infused knowledge—Christ *is* a prophet. . . . Christ's office as prophet, in short, must stem from his infused knowledge, not his beatific or acquired knowledge. . . . Aquinas holds that Christ's prophecy draws particularly upon the species infused into his imagination, which explains his imaginative portrayals of spiritual realities such as heaven and hell. Like a prophet, then, Christ

---

[182] See White, "Jesus' Cry on the Cross," 575ff.; compare to *ST* III, q. 7, a. 4.

[183] It is not a problem, as Oakes suggests (*Infinity Dwindled to Infancy*, 219n96), that Thomas also says, "the soul of Christ did not comprehend the divine essence" (see *ST* III, q. 10, a. 1), since Thomas distinguishes between perfect understanding and comprehension, which alone the divine essence itself possesses as *prima causa* (see *SCG* III, chs. 51 and 55.).

ONE OF THE TRINITY HAS SUFFERED

receives infused knowledge about supernatural realities, and he communicates this knowledge (e.g., the mystery of the Trinity) to his fellow human beings. In Aquinas' view, however, Christ is at the same time far more than a prophet. This is so primarily because Christ does not receive infused knowledge in a transitory way but rather possesses it from the beginning as "habitual" knowledge.[184]

Whether the earthly Jesus possessed ignorance?

Insofar as he grew in "grace and wisdom" (Luke 2:52), He had to have lacked some supernatural knowledge. But, in order to be ignorant of things ordinarily known via immediate vision of God, He must have been capable of "laying up" (i.e., suspending the access of His human consciousness to) some of the knowledge that would naturally be entailed by an unmediated understanding of God's essence. It is, therefore, simplistic of Oakes to state: "For Jesus to have some kind of Thomistic, hypostatic 'gleaning' of the future by virtue of his status as the incarnate Logos of God would be to rob his theodramatic participation in God's drama of salvation of its specifically human dimension."[185]

Is it possible or fitting for God to withhold knowledge of certain things from Christ's human consciousness (e.g., the date of His second coming) as well as the joy ordinarily consequent to the "visio immediata" during His passion/death?

If it is not necessary for the soul of Christ always to have perfect human knowledge of God's essence and everything pre-contained in it, as Aquinas presupposes when he argues for the mere fittingness of the beatific vision in Christ,[186] then it is possible for Christ to be ignorant not only of

---

[184] Levering, *Torah and Temple*, 73–75. For a Thomistic account of the role of imagination in prophecy, see Serge-Thomas Bonino, OP, "Le role de l'image dans la connaissance prophétique d'après saint Thomas d'Aquin," *Revue Thomiste* 89, no. 4 (1989): 533–568.

[185] Edward T. Oakes, SJ, "Balthasar's Critique of the Historical-Critical Method," in *Glory, Grace, and Culture: The Works of Hans Urs von Balthasar*, ed. Ed Block, Jr. (Mahwah, NJ: Paulist, 2005), 161.

[186] Nonetheless, see Gilbert Narcisse, OP's treatment of the significance of argumentation from fittingness (*convenientia*), *Les raisons de Dieu: Argument de convenance et esthétique théologique selon saint Thomas d'Aquin et Hans Urs von Balthasar* (Fribourg:

132

things that may not pertain to the beatific vision (e.g., *possibilia*—do these include contingent futures?), but also of other things God might will to be excluded from His own human consciousness for the sake of some end (e.g., complete solidarity with the human condition, absent sin). Whether or not it is fitting for Christ's kenosis to be expressed in human ignorance of one thing or another (e.g., the details of His own earthly future), it seems fitting that at least the joy naturally concomitant to perfect knowledge and love of God be suspended during His passion. If His suffering is to be truly spiritual, the archetype of all subsequent (and previous) mystical participation in the *visio mortis* that only He can endure with perfect charity. This "suffering of love" exceeds in intensity and profundity even the pain of loss in which the damned languish. Finally, whether it is possible or not, it would seem less fitting for Christ to maintain the *fruitio beata* while enduring His passion, as He willed to "become sin without knowing sin" (2 Cor 5:21) and to "become accursed for us" (Gal 3:13), that is, to endure the harshest suffering imaginable due to the proportionality of punishment to the gravity of man's sins, which of course is infinite due to the infinite dignity of the good offended.[187]

Is it possible or fitting for God to have withdrawn the beatific vision itself from the soul of Christ during the passion?

It is certainly possible, given the fact that it is possible for Christ never to have possessed the vision during His earthly life. But since it was fitting that He possess the vision, it would seem unfitting that He lose the vision by extraordinary mandate, unless of course such were necessary for His redemptive mission. It does not seem necessary that the vision be withdrawn from Him for His soul to endure the loss of the joy ordinarily inherent to such. But if it is, in fact, impossible for the joy that follows the vision to be withdrawn without the vision itself being stripped away, then it would be fitting for the vision to be lost as well at the hands of the Father. Part of the complication, however, is how one conceives the nature of such vision. For instance, one might conceive the vision not primarily in terms of intellectual union, but in terms of love, in which case it could not be lost. But the question is

---

Éditions Universitaires Fribourg, 1997).

[187] Aquinas offers arguments in *ST* III, q. 46 regarding the intensity and type of suffering endured by Christ, but he fails to question whether or not it is fitting to possess the *fruitio beata* during His passion, even while he defends the possibility of His suffering coexisting with the *fruitio beata* in different regions of His human soul (a. 8), presupposing its fittingness.

whether it would be unfitting for Christ to lose His understanding of the Father, that is, to assume human ignorance, which Aquinas certainly deems unfitting, but which Speyr deems necessary according to her Ignatian vision of the passion in terms of the *Suscipe* prayer, as Miles articulates.

Is it possible or fitting that Christ would have rejoiced during His passion?

It seems to bifurcate the psychology of Christ to hold that Christ rejoiced in the upper regions of His soul and yet was without consolation in the lower regions, much like Maritain's proposal of a supraconsciousness and an infra-consciousness. It is true that the divine Word would have rejoiced at the love expressed in the suffering endured by Christ's humanity and that the divine person is the subsistent principle of unity for the two natures (divine and human), but it seems unlikely that the suffering humanity of Christ would have enjoyed His perceived (or subjective) abandonment by the Father. Thus, the great Thomist Jean-Pierre Torrell feels compelled to deny the presence of the beatific vision in Christ's earthly life not because of any purported conflict between beatific knowledge and ordinary human cognition, but because opposites cannot coexist in the appetitive realm (namely, beatific joy and spiritual agony). Torrell does not consider the possibility of the beatific joy and not the beatific vision itself being withdrawn. Perhaps he assumes that such is not a possibility. On the other hand, those who hold that Christ possessed beatific joy throughout His passion either minimize the spiritual nature of His agony or suppose that appetitive opposites may coexist in the same soul.[188] But even if the latter is a possibility, such a passion would seem to be less intense than a passion in which beatific joy is suspended because no loss could be more profound than the loss of the perfect fruition proper to the beatific (or better, hypostatic) vision of God. Therefore, if it is fitting that Christ suffer the full extent of punishment due to sin without Himself succumbing to sin, it is

---

[188] *ST* III, q. 46, a. 8, ad 1:

> The joy of fruition is not opposed directly to the grief of the Passion, because they have not the same object. Now nothing prevents contraries from being in the same subject, but not according to the same. And so the joy of fruition can appertain to the higher part of reason by its proper act; but grief of the Passion according to the subject. Grief of the Passion belongs to the essence of the soul by reason of the body, whose form the soul is; whereas the joy of fruition (belongs to the soul) by reason of the faculty in which it is subjected.

necessary that He suffer this pain of loss rather than the coexistence of beatific joy with the variety of human pains assumed (e.g., betrayal, contrition), and yet He must at the same time persevere in the life of grace, which itself is the condition *sine qua non* for the infinite redemptive gravity of Christ's passion.

CONCLUSION

Adrienne von Speyr is clearer than Balthasar in affirming that Christ did indeed possess an unmediated vision of the Father during His earthly life, that is, until His passion. Balthasar is apparently unsure of the matter, wavering between assuming something like Jacques Maritain's view of Christ's beatific vision—namely, that it exists in some supraconscious realm but not the infra-conscious (until the Resurrection)—and conceding to the view popular among modern exegetes, namely, that God in Christ assumed the ignorance of fallen humanity. What is consistent in his peripheral references to the problem is his confusing usage of the phrase "laying up" or "depositing," or more often "laid up" or "deposited" (in German, *hinterlegung* or *hinterlegt*),[189] which he derives from Speyr's speculations regarding Christ's kenotic surrender during His earthly life of divinely infused knowledge (not His perfect union with the Father that she thinks constitutes the *visio beata*).

If Balthasar truly were of one mind and mission with Speyr, he must have held that Christ's chief suffering in His passion, culminating in that mysterious event of death itself, is precisely the loss not of His perfect knowledge of God or of His perfect love of God, but the loss of the perfect joy that ordinarily follows perfect knowledge and love of God. I have argued that such a loss willed by God (the Father) is possible, but also that, according to Speyr-Balthasar, Christ's possession of the beatific vision in life is not ruptured by the suspension of His access to certain secondary objects of the vision (e.g., future contingents that need not be known for the fulfillment of His mission). Thus, the language of "depositing" concerns items that would ordinarily be known by a soul hypostatically united to the Word, but which the Father (in communion with the Son as well as the Spirit) wills to withdraw from His human consciousness without

---

[189] He utilizes this notion usually in reference to Christ's human intellect kenotically surrendering fullness of access to the divine, but also sometimes with respect to the constaints placed on finite freedom by its rootedness in infinite freedom (see, e.g., *TD* V, 259, 302, 389, 514 [G 234, 275, 356, 470]).

affecting His supernatural beatitude.[190] The descent of Christ into hell is, then, that paradigmatic, enigmatic, and exemplary instance of the Father's withdrawal of something ordinarily concomitant to the beatific vision, namely, the joy itself naturally (but perhaps not necessarily) consequent to the perfect vision that most fittingly belongs to the Word Incarnate. What could be more hellish a loss than this? Perhaps here is the key to the analogy between Christ's own suffering and the pain of loss undergone by those who are deprived of supernatural life: He does not lose grace or glory, but He experiences the loss of the *fruitio beata* even while remaining in perfect union of intellect and will with God.

Given that Christ's human awareness of His divine identity is infused as a result of the grace of hypostatic union, that it is possible and fitting for God to withhold knowledge of certain contingencies from His human consciousness so that He may better fulfill His mission in solidarity with sinful humanity, and that Christ's own union of intellect and will with God is unlike any other, perhaps it is more fitting to call His own vision of God a hypostatic vision (as Weinandy does), instead of imposing on Christ's intellect a category that properly applies to creatures elevated to the order of glory (i.e., beatific vision). In other words, Christ's hypostatic vision of God may not be most aptly understood in terms of the human intellect being gratuitously enlightened by the impression of the intelligible species of God's own essence by means of a perfect *lumen gloriae*,[191] but better understood in terms of Christ's own peculiar communion with the Father, whereby He was in some sense capable of growing in "age, wisdom, and grace" (Luke 2:52), yet without ever being humanly unaware of His own divinity or of what the Father willed (not to withdraw from His human intellect) in fulfillment of the Son's redemptive mission on earth. In this manner, in His passion and death, Christ was able to know with complete certainty the Father's infinite love for Him and all human beings in Him (since faith is never properly attributable even to His human intellect as such). At the same time, he was able to endure the greatest pain of being stripped of the infinite joy that naturally accompanied His hypostatic union with God for the sake of making friends out of His enemies (Col 1:21–22; Rom 5:10), that is, every human being as in need of redemption from sin.

---

[190] Hence, Balthasar states that "the greater good of [Jesus'] obedience required that the Son's intrinsically 'fitting' and 'direct' knowledge should be 'laid up' with the Father for reasons of the 'economy'" (*TD* III, 192 [G 176]).

[191] St. Thomas speaks of qualitative difference in regard to the *lumen gloriae* granted the blessed and to Christ in *ST* III, Suppl, q. 92, a. 3, ad 12; see also *ST* I, q. 12, aa. 6–8.

While Balthasar is at times unsure of whether any knowledge is necessary to Christ besides awareness of His own divine identity and filial mission, and while he speculates that out of kenotic love the Son humbly suspends access to His divine intellect in His human consciousness, if he follows Speyr, he must believe that the *fruitio beata* was taken from Him during the passion, expressed most fully in the cry of dereliction, which is the triumphant means by which He glorifies every person dead in sin, whom He meets in timeless solidarity. It is most fitting that the joy of the beatific vision (*fruitio beata*) be taken away from Christ's human soul during His passion and death, that is, for Him to suffer the loss of the infinite joy that is naturally consequent to the immediate knowledge (*visio immediata*) and the perfect love of God that are essential to supernatural beatitude, regardless of which logically follows the other. To suffer such a fate at the hands of His own Father, no less, is a greater hell (that is, pain of loss) than any hell/loss possibly suffered by a creature that never possessed such an immense grace. Surely, the timelessness proper to Christ's hell (i.e., His temporary loss of eternal bliss) would be incommensurable with that of the damned and that of the blessed, as even the time of earth is incommensurable with the time of purgatory (and yet the mystics are sometimes granted a participation in each).[192] Of course, this view of Christ's passion and death, wherein the element of subjective timelessness would enter most profoundly, requires the admission of the existence of a perfect union of intellect and will between Christ's human nature and divine nature.

---

[192] Perhaps Einstein's theory of general relativity provides an analogical (and thus imperfect) glimpse into the incommensurability that exists between all kinds of (super-)temporalities. Ratzinger alludes to this in *Eschatology*, 230ff. [G 187ff.].

Part II

TRINITARIAN UNDERGIRDING

Introduction to Part II

WHILE PART ONE of this work is largely concerned with the controversial question of how precisely to understand the doctrine and event of Christ's death and descent into *Sheol* from both an ontological and psychological perspective, in dialogue with the work of Hans Urs von Balthasar, Part Two concerns the problem of whether God may be said to suffer not merely in Christ's humanity (especially, His consciousness), but in Himself as Trinitarian Creator and Redeemer of a fallen world. Balthasar also has much to say concerning the latter question. Unfortunately, like Rahner, Balthasar eschews the distinction between *De Deo Uno* and *De Deo Trino*. As a result, when he speaks about divine suffering, he is thinking of it almost exclusively in terms of the Trinitarian relations and the ultimate intimacy that exists between them and Jesus Christ as Incarnate Word. He does not wish to bifurcate the suffering of Christ according to His natures, but rather to understand His suffering as proper to His divine personhood. I will argue, essentially, that there are better ways of ameliorating classical Catholic theology with respect to the question of the suffering of the God-man than his own mixture of Barthian, kenotic, and Speyrian metaphorical-analogical discourse. I will strive to maintain and defend what I think is genuinely insightful in his attempt at a Trinitarian theology of suffering, and at the same time, seek to purify it of excesses literary (dramatic), metaphorical, and mystical in nature.

In chapter four I begin to address Balthasar's theology of divine suffering *as divine*, that is, the question of divine impassibility. It is one thing to say that Christ's human suffering somehow relates to the divine hypostasis that animates His human nature, or that God by omnipotence condescends to the point of suffering *in the human nature* of the Incarnate Word. It is another thing to say that the suffering of Christ reveals an even deeper, aboriginal suffering mode of being that is intrinsic to the divine life as Trinity, or that Christ's temporal suffering is a mere reflection of the eternal expropriation that constitutes each divine person. I will confront the latter claim, particularly, by recourse to Jacques Maritain's Thomistic approach to this question in a modern context, on which Balthasar purports to build. I will propose that, perhaps, the reality Balthasar intended to capture in his misguided notion of Trinitarian *ur-kenosis* is the centrality of divine affectivity as constitutive of the self-diffusive love of God as *ipsum esse*. Howsoever much God may be said to suffer, in a qualified manner, from the sins of mankind, it cannot alter the very being of God or originate there.

In chapter five I seek to discern to what extent Balthasar's theology of divine suffering might be unduly influenced by post-Hegelian kenoticism, whether his theological discourse might be defended as essentially metaphorical in nature, and how one might properly speak of divine self-enrichment without succumbing to panentheism. In other words, without being able to resolve the larger question of the proper role of metaphor in theology, I will attempt to clarify how one might uphold in a qualified manner a Balthasarian perspective on the dynamic relationship between the Trinitarian God and a sin-laden world.

In chapter six I explore and critique particular metaphors and analogies employed by Balthasar, in close dialogue with the mystical experience of Adrienne von Speyr, for the Trinitarian life, the epistemic nature of which he does not clarify. I will argue that it is the systematic theologian's task to sift through the mystical mixtures of metaphorical analogy, rhetorical excess, and ecstatic expression for properly analogical discourse concerning the divine life and its relationship to the suffering and sinfulness of human beings, which God willed to take upon (within?) Himself in the person of the Word Incarnate. Balthasar did not succeed wholly in doing this, whether he intended to do so or not, and seems rather to confuse the orders of theological discourse, literary hyperbole, and mystical insight. For such demythologization to occur, Thomistic Trinitarian theology must take the place of Balthasar's attempt to establish an analogical relationship between the "different" relations that constitute the Trinitarian life and the infinite distance that exists between the good Creator and the moral evils initiated by free creatures.

Thus, through these three angles of entry into the complex theology of divine suffering in Balthasar, I offer a critical re-evaluation of Balthasar's soteriological Trinitarian theology, that is, of the Trinitarian "undergirding" of sin and salvation, in dialogue with contemporary Balthasar scholarship.

CHAPTER FOUR

Theodramatic Impassibility and Divine Affectivity after Balthasar

THE RAGING DEBATE over divine impassibility in contemporary theology among Christians of all stripes is so extensive that one can hardly keep a reign on it. One of the most notable and nuanced contributors is Hans Urs von Balthasar. While he takes a certain distance from the debate as such, his peculiar appropriation of kenotic theology has certainly moved it in a new direction. I am referring in particular to his thesis that the Trinitarian processions are constituted by what he calls *ur-kenosis*, or an original analogue to the love-filled suffering revealed in Christ, and his super-kenotic doctrine of Christ's descent as the perfect created reflection of the *ek-stasis* between the first and second divine persons of the Trinity. His treatment of the descent and his Trinitarian theory are very much interconnected, and therefore much of what he thinks about one has implications for the other.

In this chapter, I will focus on his kenotic approach to the divine life insofar as it is central to the debate on impassibility, that is, to explore the implications for God in Himself of Christ's suffering as a revelatory event for Balthasar.[1] First, I intend to present Balthasar's own articulation of the matter, which draws on a variety of authors from Maritain to Barth to Moltmann and Bulgakov. Then, I will zero in on Maritain's contribution in particular and briefly address comparisons to Rahner. Next, I will trace quickly how Balthasar and his influences have been received by more recent theologians who have sought to go beyond him. In the end, I will attempt to sift through the various claims with the logical rigor exhibited

---

[1] The relevance of his Trinitarian theory to the passibilist debate is apparent to any reader of Balthasar's *Theodramatik: Das Endspiel*.

by Thomists like Maritain and the insight proffered by theologians like Barth.

It is imperative to contrast how Balthasar treats the question of divine impassibility, which appears to be a hodgepodge of thoughts patched together without much of an underlying structure, with how Maritain, whose esteemed essay, "Quelques réflexions sur le savoir théologique," Balthasar cites as support (more, a launching pad for his own kenotic speculations), treats the question.[2] There is no reason to posit a divine analogue to human suffering *per se* because the "perfection of suffering" is not a notion mandating passibility in God.[3] I am therefore concerned with clearing the way for affectivity to stand out as the true ground in God for the suffering He permits men to experience, where the second person of the Trinity is the most direct correlate of such and therefore could be designated as, in a certain sense, the *"ur-kenosis"* of God.

Building on ancient and contemporary articulations of divine passibility, such as Origen and Jean Galot,[4] Balthasar goes beyond Jacques Maritain's (and Karl Barth's) qualified predication of passibility to God, rooted in the Son's eternal act of Incarnation, where divine receptivity to evil is willed in His creative act, rather than being intrinsic to the relationships that define the divine persons: "the event of the Incarnation of the second divine Person does not leave the inter-relationship of those Persons

---

[2] See Jacques Maritain, "Quelques réflexions sur le savoir théologique," *Revue Thomiste* 69 (1969): 5–27. Throughout the article, wherever Maritain reflects on the question of divine suffering, he refers back to his position on the problem of divine permission of moral evil (i.e., his theory of grace, predestination, and foreknowledge).

   But I am not able here to flesh out the relationship between the two issues in Maritain compared to Balthasar, as I do elsewhere (see my "God's Relation to Evil: Divine Impassibility in Balthasar and Maritain," *Irish Theological Quarterly* 80, no. 3 [August 2015]: 191–211).

[3] In order to make clear exactly why this is so, I will include parenthetical reference to three "middle positions" with respect to passibility, influenced potentially by both Maritain and Balthasar, to aid reflection on precisely how suffering ought to be conceived or where in God it ought to be located, so to speak.

[4] Thomas G. Weinandy, OFM, argues that Jean Galot (but not Maritain) goes too far in the direction of passibilism (see *Does God Suffer?*, 163n31). Balthasar thinks Galot does not go quite far enough (see *TD* V, 242 [G 218]).

   Nicholas J. Healy refers to Weinandy's book as "a rigorous and creative defence of this traditional understanding of immutability" (*Being as Communion*, 132n109), according to which "suffering and change [are] predicated of the human nature of Christ while . . . strict immutability and impassibility [are attributed to] his divine nature" (132).

unaffected."[5] Balthasar's posture on the issue has been deeply influential in Catholic circles, and thus not only will I trace his conceptual relationship with figures like Maritain, Rahner, and Barth, but also I will do so in part by briefly detailing how his unique synthesis of the first and the last thinkers has been received by a few contemporary theologians of divine impassibility. But first I must examine Balthasar's articulation of the matter in more direct fashion.

Jacques Maritain's cursory treatment of divine impassibility, which I treat elsewhere with respect to his understanding of the grace-freedom dynamic,[6] provides a philosophically attuned articulation that does not exclude the notion of receptivity in God and highlights the affectivity of God without projecting contingent categories into the divine life itself. I will seek to legitimate this kind of approach against those who assume the Balthasarian reading (or appropriation) of Maritain. Thus, I will argue that Balthasar's notion of *ur-kenosis* or self-surrender in God may be maintained in a modified form, that is, if it is appropriated to the Son and construed in consonance with the perennial doctrine of divine impassibility. In other words, in the place of Balthasar's theory of a primordial self-emptying constitutive of the Trinitarian life itself ought to obtain a more modest thesis in line with Maritain's understanding of God's relation to evil and suffering,[7] namely, that God's essence does encompass the "perfection of suffering," which is precisely divine affectivity and the root of His intentional *passio* with respect to creation.

BALTHASAR'S AMBIVALENT POSITION

Any attempt to contextualize Balthasar's thought on divine impassibility would be vast, and even the passages in the final volume of the second part of his trilogy that touch upon this topic are too numerous to analyze in full. Therefore, in addressing the specific question of intra-Trinitarian suffering, I will restrict myself primarily to a segment of *Das Endspiel*,

---

[5] *MP* 30 [G 152].
[6] See my "God's Relation to Evil: Divine Impassibility in Balthasar and Maritain."
[7] See "Quelques réflexions," Jacques and Raïssa Maritain, Œuvres complètes, vol. 14 (Fribourg: Éditions Universitaires; Paris: Editions St.-Paul, 1993), 791–792; Jacques Maritain, *Neuf leçons sur les notions premières de la philosophie morale* (Paris: P. Téqui, 1951). These sources are cited repeatedly by multiple authors in the volume of essays edited by James F. Keating and Thomas Joseph White, *Divine Impassibility and the Mystery of Human Suffering* (Grand Rapids, MI: Eerdmans, 2009).

namely, his survey of the so-called 'theologians of the pain of God'[8] and the subsequent sections in which further conclusions are drawn.[9]

Although he is usually careful to avoid intrinsic attribution of suffering to God's love,[10] at points he evidently wants to expand the way in which contingent predicates (i.e., anything involving nonbeing) are attributed to God beyond the *modus predicandi* of extrinsic analogy. For example, he says, "the 'suffering' with which the creature is familiar is something quite different from being 'receptive,'" and then he says "once God is drawn into the total process of being."[11] One may argue in light of other passages that he does not mean to predicate process of the very being of God, but is simply referring to the economy of the Incarnation (i.e., God as having entered a finite world).[12] He argues for a real "pathos" in God, which he says is evident in some of the Fathers, distinguishing various ways of understanding it.[13] Even though he maintains divine immutability,[14] he seems to opt for an extreme interpretation of "pathos," citing approvingly Origen's words: "If this is true of the Son, it must be true of the Father: Does not he, too, the long-suffering and merciful One, 'somehow suffer? In his Providence he must suffer on account of men's suffering, just as the Son suffers our *passiones*.'"[15] It will become clear, though, in light of other passages, that Balthasar is not here approving of the assertion that man's sinfulness

---

[8] Although this section is preceded by a disclaimer of sorts (on 212), his treatment mostly consists in agreements with the authors presented.

[9] Perhaps it is worth relaying, as noted earlier, that in *Theologik*, vol. 2, *Wahrheit Gottes* (Einsiedeln: Johannes Verlag, 1985), 315n1, Balthasar asks scholars to look no more to *Mysterium Paschale* for his theology since it was "a quickly written work" preceding full appropriation of the insights of his mystic friend, Adrienne von Speyr. Hence, as a late work, the *Theo-Drama* ought to be regarded as his definitive statement on the questions there treated.

[10] For example, he says, "the unchangeable God enters into a relationship with creaturely reality, and this relationship imparts a new look to his internal relations" (*TD* III, 523 [G 479]), and again, "something in God can develop into suffering" (*TD* IV, 328 [G 305]).

[11] *TD* V, 213 [G 192].

[12] For instance: "'But the Three-Person God has never ceased being One and Infinite.' So we cannot speak of a 'process' in God, as if he could attain fullness only through the world's sinful alienation" (*TD* V, 264 [G 239]).

[13] See, for example, *TD* V, 218–222 [G 197–200]. For example, pointing to an anticipation of "the solution proposed by Karl Barth," he says: "If God, says Gregory, wishes to save men by freely choosing suffering, He suffers impassibly; since He suffers freely, He is not subject to suffering but superior to it" (*TD* V, 219 [G 197]).

[14] See *TD* V, 222 [G 200].

[15] *TD* V, 221 [G 199].

affects God directly, although he does approve of the attribution of suffering to the Father as enjoying infinite communion with the Son. This answer forms part of his response to the following question, which lies at the heart of his concerns: How can we say with the Scythian monks that "One of the Trinity has suffered" and maintain the Athanasian rule?[16] His answer is to find an eternal analogue to the suffering of Christ's human nature in the Trinitarian processions of the Godhead itself.[17]

He wants to distinguish his own appropriation of the "theology of pain" from that which "sees God's *essence* coinvolved, in the Hegelian manner, in the world process."[18] He points out the tension in Moltmann between a Hegelian-inspired panentheism and a Christian doctrine of free divine passibility. Bound to the former, he says, is identification of "immanent *processio*" with "economic *missio*," apparently indicating divergence from his own theory.[19] Even the "Christian" side of Hegel's thought, according to which the "bifurcation" in God contains all of history and godforsakenness within itself, "needs some clarification."[20] He concludes that "Lutheran Hegelianism" cannot avoid mythology precisely because it identifies the world's suffering with that of God and thus confuses the divine and finite worlds.[21]

Karl Barth is certainly the most influential theologian in Balthasar's thought,[22] and Balthasar takes Barth's side against Moltmann in tracing all the pain endured by God to His own freedom, not to any creature, since the latter has no power to reach into the heart of the divine.[23] At the same time, he adds to Barth the notion that Christ's condemnation is in a way

---

16 For the history of this statement, "One of the Trinity has suffered," see Werner Elert, *Der Ausgang der altkirchlichen Christologie. Eine Untersuchung uber Theodor von Pharan und seine Zeit als Einfuhrung in die alte Dogmengeschichte* (Berlin: Lutherisches Verlagshaus, 1957), 71–132, cited by Martin Bieler, "God and the Cross," 77n68.

17 This chapter suggests a different answer, partially on the basis of Maritain's thought, which I also suggest was misappropriated by Balthasar.

18 *TD* V, 227 [G 205].

19 See *TD* V, 228 [G 206] and 234 [G 211].

20 See *TD* V, 229 [G 207]

21 See *TD* V, 231 [G 208]: "[Deliberately submerging the life of God in the world's coming to be] achieves a certain distance from Hegel, but formally his 'ambivalence' remains. In short, the model for seeing pain and death *in* God remains pain and death *outside* God in the world, and this cannot avoid the danger of mythology."

22 I consider the immensely influential figure of Adrienne von Speyr more a "mystic" than a theologian, not that the two are mutually exclusive or that a theologian should not "do theology on one's knees."

23 See *TD* V, 237 [G 214].

the consequence of love's own inner logic (that is, the Trinitarian life).[24] Balthasar seems to agree with Barth that the Cross is not a temporal repetition of an eternal reality within the Trinity and yet "the Father is no mere spectator of the Passion."[25] But he does not say whether he agrees or disagrees with Barth's stance against the notion that God "continues to suffer eternally after Christ's temporal sufferings."[26] Balthasar highlights Barth's "failure" to discern in the Trinitarian life an archetype of Christ's "obedience unto death on a cross."

When speaking of intra-Trinitarian self-surrender, by adding the German prefix "*ur-*" to the Greek term *kenosis*, Balthasar introduces a qualification, albeit ambiguous, into his attribution of suffering to God.[27] More radical than Barth on suffering in God, at least in the following attempt to distance himself from Moltmann, Balthasar takes care to introduce the distinction between the economic and immanent aspects of the Trinity: "the sinner's alienation from God was taken into the Godhead, into the 'economic' distance between Father and Son."[28] But, for Balthasar, the *ur-kenosis* that constitutes the inner life of God enables Him to suffer with love in Christ something much worse than (and yet encompassing) the torments of the damned; thus, his Trinitarian theology becomes a theology of the descent. For Balthasar, death, suffering, and hell take on meaning in the descent of Christ into hell only in the context of Trinitarian love: "The Judgment that takes place within the Trinity can be understood only in terms of the suffering love between Father and Son in the Spirit."[29]

Balthasar, therefore, asserts that neither Jean Galot nor Maritain, to whom the former was indebted, went far enough in their reflections on the reality of suffering in God.[30] They sought to preserve divine immutability and at the same time permit a free divine decision for "a world that can involve these Persons in pain." But while Maritain denominates suffering as a metaphor mysteriously applicable to God, Galot locates real suffer-

---

[24] See *TD* V, 277–278 [G 251–252]. It may be worth pointing out that although he most likely adopted the damnation language of Luther and Calvin in a spirit of ecumenism, it is evident that he differs from them in some significant respects on the vicarious nature of His suffering. See, for example, Antoine Birot, "God in Christ," 275n14.

[25] *TD* V, 238 [G 215].

[26] *TD* V, 239 [G 216].

[27] See Birot, "God in Christ," 281. Birot notes this move also in Bulgakov.

[28] *TD* IV, 381; see also Birot, "God in Christ," 285.

[29] *TD* V, 278 [G 252].

[30] See *TD* V, 242 [G 218].

ing in "the embrace of the divine joy."[31] Balthasar takes up this paradoxical union of suffering and joy in God along with the key notion that the "bond between love and pain" is founded "in the reciprocal 'ecstatic love' of the Persons, who 'bring forth one another through reciprocal surrender of self.'"[32] Galot adds, though, that the ecstasy is not painful in itself—it is a love which contains the primordial origin of the pain involved in love of humanity. So while Balthasar presumably wants to exclude with Galot the notion of pain from God's suffering, he borrows Galot's point (against Maritain) that suffering in God is not merely metaphorical in order to center his Trinitarian theology on the notion of *ur-kenosis*.

Professedly elaborating upon Galot's approach to the distinction of divine persons in *ek-stasis*, he says every theology of pain "is insufficient unless . . . we can identify, in the Trinity, the basis for attributing to God things like pain and death." Thus, he wants to "attribute to God, impassible in his essence, a possibility that he himself has willed."[33] Consequently, he ends up making God the primary analogate in the analogy of suffering, effectively subsuming the immanent dimension of the Trinity under the economic dimension of the Trinity in a manner differing little from Moltmann's theology.[34] An alternative position would be that the Son alone is

---

[31] Almost willing to recognize that Galot goes beyond Maritain, Balthasar states: "[Galot] deliberately and courageously opposes the long tradition of God's *apatheia*, though not without taking refuge behind J. Maritain's celebrated 1969 essay in which the Thomist adopts a position contrary to Thomas and the aforesaid tradition" (*TD* V, 239 [G 216]). The latter assertion is disputable, but interpretation of Thomas will not be undertaken here.

[32] All quotations in this paragraph are from *TD* V, 241 [G 217–218].

[33] *TD* V, 234 [G 211].

[34] See *TD* V, 242 [G 218]. Steffen Lösel does, however, point out that Balthasar's theodramatic approach to the Trinity lacks an apocalyptic dimension:

> I have found the claim that Balthasar's distinction between the economic and the immanent Trinity minimizes the impact of the cross of Christ on the eternal, triune God to be inaccurate. However, my detailed analysis of Balthasar's theology of history has shown that by concentrating on the theo-drama as an event between heaven and earth on the *cross* of Golgotha, Balthasar does minimize the impact of God's engagement in history. In this sense, Balthasar presents what I term an "unapocalyptic theology," that is, a theology that neither attributes any theological significance to God's ongoing engagement throughout the course of history nor to God's final and consumptive *adventus* in this world. ("Unapocalyptic Theology: History and Eschatology in Balthasar's Theo-Drama," *Modern Theology* 17, no. 2 [2001]: 201–225, at 219)

In support of the concern of an unapocalyptic eschatology in Balthasar, see, e.g., *TD* V, 48 [G 41].

characterized by a *kenosis* freely undergone such that the love that constitutes the union of the divine persons is supra-kenotic and the primary analogate in the analogous structure of *kenosis* is created being.[35]

Balthasar proposes instead an "interweaving of Christ's suffering and the suffering of the Trinity."[36] The Father in begetting the Son surrenders everything He is, the Godhead itself; and the persons are infinitely distinct, consisting in reciprocal relations (paternity and filiation). Accordingly, "the distance between the Persons, within the dynamic process of the divine essence, is infinite."[37] Balthasar continually returns to the theme of divine person as subsisting relation consisting in self-surrender.[38] For whatever can be criticized in such a theory, he does well to differentiate between the "infinite distance" that is constituted by the self-subsisting reciprocal relations in the immanent Trinity, on the one hand, and the apparent separation on the Cross between Father and Son in the economic Trinity. He refers to "what seems to us to be the sign of separation" as "the separation that is perceptible to us,"[39] adding that "the Father does not leave the Son for a moment."[40] Hence, there is no real "alienation of the Son from the Father," but only a psychological experience of separation (hence the cry of dereliction).[41] This "subjective" separation, as it were, "begins in the Incarnation and is completed on the Cross,"[42] and is "experienced not only in the body and the senses but also spiritually."[43] The Spirit provides the unity that is most profoundly present where the phenomena of a rupture between Father and Son appear.[44]

---

[35] This is part of the modest conclusion to which I will point in the end as being along the lines of Maritain's thinking.

[36] *TD* V, 245 [G 221]: "[T]he whole Trinity accomplishes the Incarnation, which is already a kenosis on the part of the Son; the Son's whole life, and his Passion most of all, is both a work of the Father and a revelation of him; the Father, the perfect Abraham, surrenders his Son (cf. the parable of the Vineyard)" (*TD* V, 240 [G 216–217]).

[37] *TD* V, 245 [G 221].

[38] See *TD* V, 255 [G 230–231].

[39] *TD* V, 262 [G 236–237].

[40] *TD* V, 263 [G 238].

[41] See, for example, *TD* V, 264 [G 238–239].

[42] *TD* V, 262 [G 237].

[43] *TD* V, 263 [G 237].

[44] See, for example, *TD* V, 262 [G 237]. Also, in the *Epilogue* to the Trilogy, he more clearly assigns the Spirit the role of unity transcending difference:

> Here "To Be," as perfect self-expression and as self-surrender within the identity, will be the personal difference of Father and Son, a difference that must, as love, have its *fruitfulness as Holy Spirit.* "Son" is therefore at the same time

Therefore, distinguishing economic and immanent dimensions of the Trinity, he says: "This 'economic' reality is only the expression of something 'immanent' in the Trinity."[45] Although he wants to locate suffering and death in the economic Trinity, not the immanent Trinity, he still seeks a "foundation" for such in the immanent Trinity, since the economic expresses the immanent.[46] However, in so doing, he at times blurs the line between the two dimensions.[47] Consult the following texts from volume four:

[T]he *Trinity does not hover "unmoved" above the events* of the Cross (the view that Christ is somehow "above" his abandonment by God and continues to enjoy the beatific vision), nor does it get entangled in sin as in a process theology à la Moltmann or Hegel, becoming part of a mythology or cosmic tragedy.[48]

His wounds are not mere reminders of some past experience. Since this drama is experienced by the *economic Trinity, which is one with the immanent Trinity*, it is constantly actual. . . .[49]

While this view is right to *locate the historical work of Jesus in the realm of the eternal, or*, as we have said, *the economic Trinity in the immanent Trinity*, we must ask whether it is sufficient.[50]

The next thing for consideration is the abiding actuality of the historical Passion, not primarily because it affects every human being who enters history at any time, but rather because—as we have already shown—*what takes place in the "economic" Trinity is cherished and embraced by the 'immanent' Trinity* and, in particular, by the Holy Spirit.[51]

"Word" (as self-expression). He is "expression" (as the One who shows himself). He is also, and equally, "child" (the One lovingly begotten). And this personal difference must be overtaken in the personal unity of the different Persons, a unity that does not abolish these differences but rather unites them in the *unity of the fruitfulness transcending the differences*. (*Epilogue*, 85–86 [G 66], emphasis added)

[45] *TD* V, 258 [G 233].
[46] See Birot, "God in Christ," 281–282.
[47] See, e.g., *TD* IV, 333, 363, 393, 390.
[48] *TD* IV, 333 [G 310] (emphasis added).
[49] *TD* IV, 363 [G 338] (emphasis added).
[50] *TD* IV, 393 [G 366] (emphasis added).
[51] *TD* IV, 390 [G 364–365] (emphasis added).

Consequently, in volume five, he states categorically: "'everything serves to reveal this eternal relationship' . . . *we can inscribe the temporal upon the eternal*—paradoxically and in a way that can be misunderstood in a Hegelian direction."[52] The foundation in God Himself for the mystery of the Cross is the "primordial *kenosis*" or self-surrender constituting the infinite distinction-in-union (to be distinguished from real "separation") between each mutually opposed subsisting relation.[53]

This dialogical-dialectical approach[54] clearly carries over into Balthasar's treatment of time, life, and joy in God. He refers to the "super-time of eternal life"[55] as well as the "timelessness in the bosom of God."[56] He says, "this temporal sphere does not unfold 'outside' eternity but within it."[57] Is this not analogy without negation/apophaticism? It certainly manifests a common inheritance of Barth to conceive eternity as in some way temporal because dynamic (where the Boethian formula *"totus simul"* is erroneously thought to imply staticity).[58] It remains unclear precisely how the "super-time" of the Trinitarian blessedness relates to the timelessness of the descent and hell.[59]

---

52 *TD* V, 264 [G 239], emphasis added. Repeating Balthasar's phrase, Birot says: "The Christological concept of mission, which Balthasar finds in Scripture, and which he interprets, with Thomas, as the economic figure of procession, ultimately requires that we *inscribe* economic modes *within the immanent modes of the trinitarian relations*" ("Redemption in Balthasar," 278 [emphasis original]).

53 *TD* V, 260 [G 235]. "[T]he *Cross* can become the 'revelation of the innermost being of God.' It reveals both the distinction of the Persons (clearest in the dereliction) and the unity of their Being, which becomes visible in the unity of the plan of redemption. Only a God-man, through his distinction-in-relation vis-à-vis the Father, can expiate."

54 *TL* II, 43ff. [G 40ff.].

55 See *TL* II, 250 [G 225].

56 *TD* V, 251–252 [G 227–228], emphasis added. "'[A]lready as Son in the Father he was the Lamb of God. . . . His mission is not temporal; it is already perfected before its beginning. Certainly there is a moment in history in which he suffers. But it is preceded by the *timelessness in the bosom of God'* . . . [H]is whole suffering—a suffering that goes to the utter limits—follows from and actually expresses his eternal triune joy."

57 *TD* V, 250 [G 226].

58 See, for example, Adrian Langdon, "Confessing Eternity: Karl Barth and the Western Tradition," *Pro Ecclesia* vol. 21, no. 2 (Spring 2012): 125–144; Gary Culpepper, "'One Suffering in Two Natures': An Analogical Inquiry into Divine and Human Suffering," in *Divine Impassibility and the Mystery of Human Suffering*, 97n44; Robert Jenson, "Ipse Pater Non Est Impassibilis," in *Divine Impassibility*, 117–126.

59 Nonetheless, Balthasar does try to specify this relation:

> On the Cross he will feel lonesome unto death, unto a limitless, eternal death in which every temporal moment and viewpoint will completely disappear. What will be a short while for mankind [Jn 14:19] will be an eternal while to him. . . .

Atemporality is certainly a key concept for Balthasar's understanding of the descent and consequently of our redemption.[60] "These two forms of time-lessness—the God-forsakenness of the damned and the God-forsakenness of the Son on the Cross—are not simply unrelated. The latter is because of the former."[61] Since his every mention of timelessness seems to be connected to godforsakenness and not to the immanent Trinity, God's eternity is not conceived by Balthasar as completely atemporal. It is rather "super-temporal," that is, transcending the distinction between the temporality of the world and the atemporality of hell.

Asserting that the eternal becomes temporal, Balthasar avoids the Hegelian trap of attempting to transcend the distinction via a superior "synthesis" of the two.[62] But at times it seems his poetic spirit overcomes his capacity for theological precision. For example, he strangely asserts that there is no pain without joy and no joy without pain.[63] Certainly there

---

We see in this the timelessness of his suffering, the timelessness of the redemption. . . . Nonetheless the timelessness of the Cross is not the mere negation of time that characterizes hell, but a "super-time." (*TD* V, 310 [G 282–283])

See the third chapter of Gerard O'Hanlon's *The Immutability of God* for an extensive discussion of Balthasar's understanding of eternity's relation to temporality.

[60] See *TD* IV, 336–337.

[61] *TD* V, 311 [G 283]. Pointing to the importance of this notion for his Christology and consequent soteriology, he also says in an earlier volume:

In order to illustrate this reciprocal causality [between Christ and the historical world], we could refer to Jesus Christ's "time." Insofar as he knows that he is the Only Son of the Eternal Father, he has his own particular time (even as man), measured by his acceptance of the Father's will concerning his particular, all-embracing mission. But insofar as he genuinely becomes man, his existence is subject not only to general human and historical time but also to that modality of time that is marked by universal sin ("subject to futility"). So the question arises—prior to all dramatic action—how, cleaving entirely to the Father's will, he can surrender himself to this modality of "*vanitas.*" From this point we can anticipate the difficulty of the entire doctrine of the divine-human person of Christ. It will have to combine the freedom of the "descent" with the unfreedom of the existence that results from it; the intuitive knowledge of the Father with the veiled nature of an exemplary "faith"; the unity of the divine and the human will in himself with the—"economically" necessary—clash between perfect obedience and instinctive horror in the face of the task of bearing sin. The dramatic essence and constitution that make Christ both Alpha and Omega infuse drama into every aspect of his being, his action and his conduct. (*TD* III, 15–16 [G 14–15])

[62] See *TD* V, 264 [G 239]].

[63] See *TD* V, 253 [G 228–229]. He argues similarly in his essay, "Joy and the Cross," but

are modifications or qualifications needed here in order to avoid the falsity of mere "paradoxism." He attempts to justify it with the comment, "On the cross, the lived reality of death, objectively, is life; so extreme suffering, objectively, is joy."[64] There is confusion here—Christ's death is a means to the end of our eternal life, from which one cannot conclude that joy, which is constitutively an experience (i.e., it pertains to a subject as such), always accompanies pain, another experience constitutively subjective (in the classical sense of the term). Again, "He is beyond life and death as known in the world."[65] While the Thomist would insist that life precedes death with respect to God, according to the structure of the analogy of being, it sometimes appears as if Balthasar wants to say God relates to both in equal or reciprocal manner. He is certainly correct to assert that joy is caused by God, coming from "heaven" rather than "earth,"[66] but he also wants to affirm the preexistence of its opposite in God.[67] Although one clearly perceives a dialectical logic at play in the following enumeration of opposites interpenetrating in God, one could argue that the "modes" are inferior to that in which they participate: separation is a mode of union, death a mode of life, suffering a mode of bliss, godforsakenness a mode of "profound bond with the Father in the Holy Spirit."[68]

Balthasar Meets Maritain

Going outside the *Theo-Drama* for a moment (but remaining with his later thought), Balthasar displays evidence of an attempted appropriation of Maritain also in the following statements made in a conference setting:

---

there he leaves room for suffering without joy (not joy without suffering!); see also *Truth is Symphonic*, 152–169; *Glory* VII, 532–540 [G 500–507].

[64] *TD* V, 254 [G 230]].

[65] *TD* V, 245 [G 221].

[66] See *TD* V, 256 [G 231].

[67] See *TD* V, 252–253 [G 228–229].

[68] *TD* V, 257 [G 232]:

Such distance [namely, alienation from God] is possible, however, only within the economic Trinity, which transposes the absolute distinction of the persons in the Godhead from one another into the dimensions of salvation history, involving man's sinful distance from God and its atonement. We have to show, therefore, that the God-forsakenness of the Son during his passion was just as much a mode of his profound bond with the Father in the Holy Spirit as his death was a mode of his life and his suffering a mode of his bliss.

[I]t seems to me that this proposition of the Son [namely, the Passion] touches the heart of the Father—humanly speaking—more profoundly even than the sin of the world will be able to affect it, that it works in God *a wound of love* already from the beginning of creation—if not to say that it is the sign and expression of this ever-open wound in the heart of the Trinitarian life, a *wound* identical to the procession and circumincession of the Divine Persons in their perfect beatitude. This *wound* is earlier than that which Saint Anselm had in mind, to wit, the offense made to the Father by sin and expiated by the Son.[69]

While Balthasar wants to preserve a form of divine impassability, he undermines it by obscuring the line between the economic and immanent dimensions of the Trinity, wishing precisely to utilize the aforementioned reflections of Maritain. Stating, "We need to trace this intuition of the philosopher Maritain [on the mysterious perfection of suffering in God] back to the life of the Trinity," he cites Francois Varillon and H. Schurmann with approval saying: "in God, becoming is a perfection of being, motion a perfection of rest, and change a perfection of immutability. . . . Can we consider life without movement to be life?' . . . The 'death of God' actually takes place in him in the *kenosis* and *tapeinosis* of the love of God."[70] It is one step to say the dynamism of self-motion necessarily implies any "change" or "passibility" and another to conclude from this that the Trinitarian processions must be constituted precisely by suffering in some original form (i.e., "*ur-kenosis*"). The "suffering" of God due to the existence of evil, or His being affected by the evil He wills to permit, Balthasar wants to trace back to a *primordial* "wound" of sorts that is to constitute the very being of God as triune.[71] Maritain clearly does not go this far and his understanding of moral evil does not necessitate it, even if his consequent understanding of divine foreknowledge arguably leaves room for such speculations on the basis of some kind of "super-temporality" in God.[72] The central

---

[69] *Mystery of Redemption*, 37–38 [F 39–40], emphasis mine.

[70] *TD* V, 243 [G 219], emphasis original. Balthasar there cites Maritain, *La souffrance de Dieu* (Paris: Le Centurion, 1975) and his "Réflexions."

[71] For Balthasar's use of the term "wound" in this context, see *Mystery of Redemption*, 37–38 [F 39–40].

[72] The topic of super-temporality in God, explicit in Balthasar and one might say implicit in Maritain, will not be a point of focus in this chapter, although the necessary groundwork according to which one would have to contextualize this question will be provided.

question to be addressed is how Maritain's thought, which is utilized not only by Balthasar but also many holding "middle positions" in the passibilist debate, relates to the thesis of some primordial form of "suffering" constitutive of God's essence. The contributions of Maritain to the question of predestination and divine foreknowledge form the background to his comments on the "wound" that free men are said to inflict on God.[73] Without any comment that would indicate acquaintance with the former, Balthasar purports to build upon the latter.

While Maritain may have accepted a Balthasarian view of the descent,[74] at the same time, he does not project Christ's sufferings into the Trinitarian processions themselves.[75] In the following excerpt from his exemplary essay on theological knowledge, Maritain establishes the philosophical foundation for his position on divine impassibility:

Each time that a creature sins (and in each case the creature takes the first initiative, the initiative of nothingness), God is deprived of a joy ("above and beyond" according to our way of looking at things) which was due to Him by another and which that other does not give Him, and something inadmissible to God is produced in the world. But even before triumphing over what is inadmissible by a greater good which will overcompensate for it later on, God Himself, far from being subject to it, raises it above everything by His consent: In accepting such a privation (which in no way affects His being but only the creature's relation to Him), He takes it in hand and raises it up like a trophy, attesting to the divinely pure grandeur of His victorious Acceptance (ours is never such except at the cost of some defeat); and this is something that adds absolutely nothing to the intrinsic perfection and glory of the divine *Esse*, and is eternally precontained in Its essential and super-eminent infinity. For this is an integral part of a mysterious divine perfection which, even though it has reference to the privation of what is due to God by creatures existing at some

---

73 See Charles Journet, *The Meaning of Evil*, trans. Michael Barry (New York: P. J. Kennedy & Sons, 1963), 183, citing Maritain, *Neuf leçons*.

74 See his *On the Grace and Humanity of Jesus*, 61 [F 64], and "Beginning with a Reverie" in *Untrammeled Approaches*, 3–26, at 11n13 [*Approches sans Entraves* (Paris: Librairie Arthème Fayard, 1973), 15n12].

75 It is worth noting that Joseph Ratzinger, commonly taken as a Balthasarian, also seems to follow Maritain's more cautious path here: see my "Damnation and the Trinity in Ratzinger and Balthasar," *Logos* 18, no. 3 (Summer 2015): 123–150.

particular point in time, is infinitely beyond the reach of these creatures. In fact, the creature, by his free nihilation, is indeed the cause of the privation in question in whatever concerns itself, in his relation to God, which is real only from his side, responsible for some privation or other of what is due to God. And such privations are presupposed from all eternity by that mysterious divine perfection I am speaking about. The divine perfection is eternally present in God and, by the infinite transcendence of the Divine Being, is the unnamed exemplar, incapable of being designated by any of our concepts . . . which corresponds in uncreated glory to what is suffering in us. . . . What sin "does" to God is something which reaches God in the deepest way, not by making Him subject to some effect brought about by the creature but by making the creature, in its relation to God, pass over to the side of the unnamed perfection, the eternal exemplar in Him of what suffering is in us.[76]

Thus, Maritain holds a merely receptive relationship to moral evil in the divine being. Practically every time Maritain refers to the suffering of God, he makes sure to clarify that he is speaking metaphorically in applying such a term to the divine. Hence, he states:

There are concepts whose object also implies limitation and imperfection in its very notion and so cannot be said of God except metaphorically, but which in the reality to which it refers as we experience it, does designate a perfection *emerging* above the sensible, as is the case with suffering in the human person. Suffering is an evil and an imperfection, but by the fact that the spirit approves of it and consents to it and seizes upon it, it is incomparably noble as well. . . . From this we can understand that the concept and the word *suffering* can be used only metaphorically with regard to God and that nevertheless we ought to seek in an *unnamed* divine perfection the eternal exemplar of what in us is suffering with all its noble dignity.[77]

Maritain reflects on something Balthasar addresses frequently through-

---

[76] "Quelques réflexions," 19–21; translation provided in *Untrammeled Approaches*, 257–258.
[77] Maritain, *Untrammeled Approaches*, 261 [F 23].

out his many works, stating that "[Christ] does keep for all eternity His five wounds which are glorious forever," which he says is metaphorically reflected in the sufferings reported by Our Lady of LaSalette; and just before this, he states: "this mysterious perfection which in God is the unnamed exemplar of suffering in us, *constitutes an integral part of the divine beatitude*—perfect peace at the same time infinitely exultant beyond what is humanly conceivable, burning in its flames what is apparently irreconcilable for us."[78]

Balthasar's own kenotic project lends itself in a particular way to the tendency to insist that the "intentional dependence" of God upon creation is truly analogous to human suffering.[79] If the divine act of creation is to be truly free, there must not be any dependence in God on His contingent effects, and therefore the fact that we must think of the Creator as in some way related to His creation (in a metaphysical sense) rather indicates the deficiency of discursive thinking about the "contingency" of the divine will with respect to creation. The "wound" in God of which Maritain speaks is neither an intra-Trinitarian reality nor a real *passio* in God as God, but it signifies the divine affectivity manifest in Christ, where the evil committed by free creatures is eternally accepted by the divine will, which expresses itself in the passion of Christ.

Balthasar reflects beautifully on the fire of God's love engulfing all the impurities assumed by the suffering Son, ultimately consuming Him *pro nobis*.[80] While the love of God is one in the three divine persons, it is fitting alone for the Son to take on human nature in order to bear such infinite fire on our behalf and for our sakes. Why does it not suffice to identify the Son as the hypostatic self-surrender of God as such? Is not the *kenosis* of God Christ Himself? "Suffering keeps us receptive to love."[81] But if the Son is divine receptivity, is He not the receptivity of love personified? Cannot these things be constitutive of filiation as a relation in mutual opposition to paternity and spiration?

The *kenosis* of Christ is indeed the perfect reflection and manifestation of God's eternal and unchanging love, as the eternal being-affected of God is infinitely concentrated in the *passio* of Christ—divine affectivity becomes temporalized in the Sacred Heart of Jesus. The divine subject

---

[78] Maritain, *Untrammeled Approaches*, 259 [F 21–22], emphasis original.

[79] Concerning the real distinction between real and intentional dependence, see W. Norris Clarke, SJ, *Explorations in Metaphysics: Being–God–Person* (Notre Dame: University of Notre Dame Press, 1994), 81n8, 87, 192–195, 205ff.

[80] See Clark, *Explorations*, 268 [G 243].

[81] Clark, 255–256 [G 231].

underlying the two natures of Christ really suffers all the evils of history because the infinite love of pure act has freely overflowed into the economy of salvation. This suffering is infinitely concentrated in the God-man, but it properly manifests the perfection of God's love. Hence, as Maritain affirms, the perfection of suffering is eminently contained in God without the defectibility of suffering itself (as it exists in the world). This perfection cannot be simply identified with divine *caritas* without qualification—there is a real identity between the two and even a notional proximity, but it is important to state that, conceptually speaking, the term "perfection of charity" does not necessarily include the note "perfection of suffering." I am proposing that the latter concept links to the former via the notion of affectivity and that the reality of God's charity therefore includes the particular perfection that is peculiar to suffering (with God). In other words, eternal divine affectivity suffices as the analogue of the suffering of the God-man in time, and it is not appropriated to any one of the divine persons, but the Son alone tends freely toward *kenosis* in the Incarnation (and therefore can be called in Himself *ur-kenosis*).[82]

Theodrama and Divine Impassibility: Beyond Maritain and Rahner

While almost all his talk of suffering in God appears in a Trinitarian context, Balthasar also exploits philosophical reasoning in support of his moderate passibilism, namely, that in God there must be some analogous ground for the reality of suffering experienced in the world. Thus, before attending to the specifically Trinitarian dimension of divine suffering for Balthasar, it is important to recognize that throughout the *Theodramatik* he does advocate a certain form of suffering or passibility in God, despite his affirmations of divine immutability.[83] Yet he manages to maintain

---

[82] Balthasar approaches this kind of perspective when he states: "If it is possible for one Person in God to accept suffering . . . it must be something profoundly appropriate to his divine Person [that is, the Son], for—to say it once again—his being sent (*missio*) by the Father is a modality of his proceeding (*processio*) from the Father" (*TD* III, 226 [G 208].

[83] For statements of Balthasar admitting immutability in principle, see *Theo-Drama: Theological Dramatic Theory*, vol. 2, *The Dramatis Personae: Man in God*, trans. Graham Harrison (San Francisco: Ignatius Press, 1990), 278 [*Theodramatik*, Band II: *Die Personen des Spiels*, Teil I: *Der Mensch in Gott* (Einsiedeln: Johannes Verlag, 1976), 253]; *Theo-Drama: Theological Dramatic Theory*, vol. 3, *The Dramatis Personae: The Person in Christ*, trans. Graham Harrison (San Francisco: Ignatius Press, 1993), 523 [G 479]; *TD* V, 222 [G 200]; and for reticence towards it, see *MP*, 34 [G 152]; *TD* II, 9,

such a philosophical claim only in the context of revelation:

> Christian theology has to hold unswervingly to the fact that the
> God who manifests himself in Jesus Christ exists in himself as an
> eternal essence (or Being), which is an equally eternal (that is, not
> temporal) "happening"; when we ponder God's being, we must
> not forget this fact for an instant. . . . [T]he divine "essence" and
> "being" . . . manifests itself, in the historical "happening" of Jesus
> himself, as an eternal "happening." . . . We must resolve to see
> these two apparently contradictory concepts as a unity: eternal
> or absolute Being—and "happening." This "happening" is not a
> becoming in the earthly sense: it is the coming-to-be, not of some-
> thing that was not (that would be Arianism), but, evidently, of
> something that grounds the idea, the inner possibility and reality
> of a becoming. All earthly becoming [is] a reflection of the eternal
> "happening" in God, which, we repeat, is per se identical with the
> eternal Being or essence.[84]

This is a key difference from Karl Rahner.[85] Gerard O'Hanlon argues that

---

280, 293 [G 9, 255, 266–267]; *TL II*, 352n131 [G 321n57].

　See especially, Gerard O'Hanlon, *The Immutability of God*, for extensive discussion
of how Balthasar both affirms and denies not only divine impassibility, but also divine
immutability; O'Hanlon seems to conceive the two as inextricably standing or falling
together, construing Balthasar's analogical argumentation in as persuasive a form as
possible.

[84] *TD* V, 67 [G 58–59]. Hence, Larry Chapp is able to claim:

> God's existence is pure act, not so much in the Aristotelian sense of an abso-
> lute actuality in contradistinction to the potentiality of the world (although
> Balthasar grants a certain legitimacy to the medieval reformation of Aristot-
> le's notion of God as Pure Act), but rather as absolute *event*. The theology of
> revelation becomes incoherent when revelation is conceived of as an attempt to
> capture something of the immutable God in a bottle, so as to provide us with
> an indisputable, supernaturally provided, universal concept that all can agree
> upon. This is not only impossible, but it betrays a fundamentally Hellenistic
> conception of divinity with its opposition between the temporal and the eter-
> nal. ("Revelation," in *Cambridge Companion to Hans Urs von Balthasar*, 11–23,
> at 19)

[85] Rahner's view on divine immutability can be seen in *Theological Investigations*, vol.
1, *God, Christ, Mary, and Grace* (Baltimore: Helicon, 1961), 330; see also J. Norman
King and Barry L. Whitney, "Rahner and Hartshorne on Divine Immutability," *International Philosophical Quarterly* 22, no. 3 (1982): 195–209. The dispute between the
two is perhaps most vivid in *Karl Rahner in Dialogue: Conversations and Interviews*,

Balthasar and Rahner differ on immutability more than Balthasar would like to admit.[86] In fact, Balthasar appears to align Rahner with Bulgakov on the immutability of the triune God,[87] only later (in the same volume) to express fundamental agreement with Bulgakov's Trinitarian "doctrine of redemption."[88] Nicholas J. Healy defends Balthasar against Rahner's view, stating: "Balthasar is, of course, committed to maintaining God's immutability, and thus a distinction between the economic and the immanent Trinity."[89] Meanwhile, Edward Oakes thinks that Balthasar adopts Rahner's famous Trinitarian axiom.[90] Steffen Lösel as well indicates that "Balthasar relativizes the ontological distinction between the economic and the immanent Trinity."[91] Finally, Antoine Birot thinks that, like Bulgakov (but with greater success), Balthasar is able to transcend the attempts of Rahner, Moltmann, and process theology to identify the economic and immanent dimensions of the Trinity.[92]

1965–1982, ed. Paul Imhof and Hubert Biallowons, trans. Harvey D. Egan (New York: Crossroad, 1986), 126–127. See also O'Hanlon's treatment of Rahner v. Balthasar in *The Immutability of God*, 31–32.

[86] On their differences, see *The Immutability of God*, 36–37. Guy Mansini offers some incisive comments on the same question: see his "Rahner and Balthasar on the Efficacy of the Cross," *Irish Theological Quarterly* 63 (1998): 232–49.

[87] See *TD* IV, 277–278 [G 256–257].

[88] *TD* IV, 313–14 [G 291–292].

[89] *Being as Communion*, 127. "The laws of the 'economic' Trinity arise from the 'immanent' Trinity. . . . But the economic Trinity cannot be regarded as simply identical with the immanent" (*TD* III, 157 [G 143]).

[90] See *Pattern of Redemption*, 279. See Karl Rahner, *The Trinity*, trans. Joseph Donceel (New York: Crossroad, 1970, 1997), 22 and 31 ["Der dreifaltige Gott als transzendeter Urgrund der Heilsgeschichte," in *Die Heilsgeschichte vor Christus*, vol. 2 of *Mysterium Salutis: Grundriss heilsgeschichtlicher Dogmatik* (Einsiedeln: Benziger Verlag, 1967), 328 and 336].

For an attempt to iron out the imprecision in Balthasar's treatment of the immanent-economic relationship as it pertains, particularly, to the Father's "self-disappropriation," see Margaret Turek, *Towards a Theology of God the Father: Hans Urs von Balthasar's Theodramatic Approach* (New York: Peter Lang, 2001).

[91] "Murder in the Cathedral," 436. Lösel adds that: "Balthasar writes: '(I)t seems, as if only this revelation of the "economic" Trinity brings out the whole seriousness of the "immanent" Trinity' (Balthasar, *Theo-Drama* IV, 320). In the English translation, the German *'erst'* has been translated with 'for the first time,' a translation which is in my view imprecise. Accordingly, I have translated it here with 'only'" ("Murder in the Cathedral," 436n53).

[92] Birot, "'God in Christ, Reconciled the World to Himself': Redemption in Balthasar," *Communio* 24, no. 2 (1997): 259–285, at 281–282 (emphasis original).

Balthasar's ultimate answer to the question of divine impassibility is the following:

[I]f we ask whether there is suffering in God, the answer is this: there is something in God that can develop into suffering. This suffering occurs when the recklessness with which the Father gives away himself (and *all* that is his) encounters a freedom that, instead of responding in kind to this magnanimity, changes it into a calculating, cautious self-preservation. This contrasts with the essentially divine recklessness of the Son, who allows himself to be squandered, and of the Spirit who accompanies him.[93]

Hence, for Balthasar, there is in the tri-hypostatic essence of God a primordial analogue to the suffering that follows contingently upon creation and sin—it is the "condition of possibility" (to use a Kantian phrase he frequently utilizes) for divine affectivity to exist in God's relationship to His creatures.[94] Balthasar takes Maritain's insight into the "wounds" that God suffers in relation to His creatures and moves beyond attributing suffering to God in a metaphorical manner to argue that the inner-Trinitarian relations are constituted by an original analogue to creaturely suffering, designated *ur*-kenosis. Maritain recognizes instead that evil is a privation, not an entity itself, and therefore has no original analogue in God. Thus, what God "suffers" is precisely His own willed receptivity to the evils initiated by created freedom, but His consequent will takes into account every proposed resistance to His antecedent will. Suffering is not a reality inherent to God's identity because evil is initiated by creatures, according to God's free decision to permit resistance to His own primordial desires, but it is a relative nonentity to which God subjects Himself in the Incarnation of the Word, consubstantial with the Father and Spirit but hypostatically united to the "flesh" in which sin is punished.

---

[93] *TD* IV, 327–328 [G 305], emphasis added.

[94] *TD* IV, 335 [G 312]: "Here the God-man drama reaches its acme: finite freedom casts all its guilt onto God, making him the sole accused, the scapegoat, while God allows himself to be thoroughly affected by this, not only in the humanity of Christ but also in Christ's trinitarian mission. The omnipotent powerlessness of God's love shines forth in the mystery of darkness and alienation between God and the sin-bearing Son."

Divine Impassibility after Balthasar and Maritain

I think that the way to get beyond the problems with Balthasar's doctrine of God is to go behind them; that is, to return to the philosophical analogical discourse that got sublimated by his Speyrian mystical discourse, which replaces precision with hyperbole. Jacques Maritain offers a Thomistic alternative to Balthasar's own articulation, although the latter sought to incorporate and transcend Maritain's formulation of the matter. Despite the differences between Balthasar's and Maritain's articulations of divine impassibility, many today have unwittingly taken the Balthasarian reading of Maritain as a point of departure for their own articulations, which suffer from the same sorts of problems as does Balthasar's own. Yet their utilization of other sources for Balthasar, such as Karl Barth, sometimes results in slightly more intelligible articulations of divine impassibility. To a greater or lesser degree, four influential thinkers on divine impassibility from relatively distinct schools of thought—Gary Culpepper, Robert Jenson, Bruce McCormack, and David Bentley Hart—are manifestly influenced by a Balthasarian reading of Maritain, each utilizing it in distinct manners. I certainly cannot do these complex thinkers justice here, but it might be illuminating to explore just a little bit how some Christian theologians today have received twentieth-century Catholic reflection on divine impassibility.

Of the four theologians I have designated as influenced apparently by the Balthasarian appropriation of Maritain (which also incorporates and transcends Barth's perspective), Culpepper seems to be the most indebted to Maritain himself (as Balthasar reads him).[95] For Culpepper, Christ's suffering (and Incarnation) shows us that our suffering can be a "participation in the eternity of the joyous suffering of the divine persons."[96] Human suffering finds its proper analogical basis ultimately in the distinction between divine persons and proximately in the distinction between the antecedent and consequent wills in God.[97] He borrows from Maritain the notion that the permissive will of God encompasses a divine "wound" caused by sin,[98] constituted by the Father's knowledge and permission of the sufferings imposed upon His incarnate Son. God Himself is said to

---

[95] See Culpepper's essay "'One Suffering in Two Natures': An Analogical Inquiry into Divine and Human Suffering," in *Divine Impassibility and the Mystery of Human Suffering*, 77–98.

[96] Culpepper, 98.

[97] See Culpepper, 78 and 96n42.

[98] See Culpepper, 87.

"suffer" in the secondary sense of the word, that is, in being an object of action.[99] Thus, the Father "suffers" the otherness of the Son, being "moved to love by the other," and the Son likewise suffers the Father. The person moving each to love is the Spirit.[100] This suffering is infinitely greater than that of His antecedent will from the moral evil initiated by His creatures.[101] But the "suffering" of God is simply a being-moved by another.[102] The human suffering of Christ, therefore, is merely a human form of the divine suffering intrinsic to the Trinitarian processions.[103] Hence, for Culpepper, there is an analogical basis in God for the reality creatures experience as suffering, revealed in the economic manifestation of God's eternal nature (i.e., Jesus Christ).[104]

There seems to be a fusion here of Maritain's and Balthasar's approach to divine impassibility, but it is a faulty synthesis. Such a position falls prey to a temptation to make the love of God admit the necessity of an object *ad extra*, an objection Culpepper inadequately counters.[105] Again, there is at work here a reluctance to distinguish between the economic and immanent dimensions of the Trinitarian God—to project onto the inner life of the Trinity an image (albeit exemplary) of the drama of suffering endured by Christ in the face of those who resist His grace is just too much kataphaticism. Divine self-movement, a Platonic notion employed to describe the dynamism interior to God,[106] need not entail being acted upon by another, whether this "other" exists *ad intra* or *ad extra*. It takes divine revelation to know that the "movements" of divine knowledge and love involve a multiplicity of subsistent relations in the one Supreme Being. To speak of these relations in terms of action and passion is to venture onto the terrain of affirming multiple yet truly distinct wills in the one God.

With Maritain's theory of nihilation in mind, Culpepper's development of his insight concerning affectivity in God appears misguided. Maritain merely admits that the antecedent will of God "suffers," so to speak, the nihilation of free initiatives to moral evil, yielding a consequent will that does not ensure the salvation of all and thus involves God in a kind of eternal disappointment that nevertheless cannot take away from

---

[99] See Culpepper, 81–82.
[100] See Culpepper, 89ff.
[101] See Culpepper, 86–88, 90.
[102] See Culpepper, 82, 88, 90, 92, 96–97.
[103] See Culpepper, especially 95ff.
[104] See Culpepper, 93.
[105] See Culpepper, 93.
[106] See Culpepper, 92.

the infinite joy that constitutes His essence. But Culpepper, like Balthasar (following Barth), wants to go a step further both to say that there is suffering, properly speaking, in God due to this rupture and that there is also a deeper ground for such a reality constitutive of the inner life of the Trinity. I think Maritain, as a good Thomist, would quickly rebut such an extrapolation on the grounds that suffering as such is an evil and therefore a privation; privations do not demand the existence of correlate realities in God, as the analogy of being is rather constituted by entities and only relates in a cognitional and relative manner to nonentities. Maritain's insight was rather to discern in love-filled suffering a relative perfection that is not notionally present in *caritas simpliciter*—hence the necessity for the notion of affectivity in God. It is a wholly distinct endeavor to see suffering itself as an entity worthy of analogous representation in the very constitution of the Trinitarian processions, for which no one has proffered proper metaphysical justification.

Although Culpepper draws most directly upon Maritain's line of thought to argue for a modified form of divine passibility,[107] he explicitly states essential agreement with Robert Jenson's analysis of (super-)temporality and also admits some agreement with the Barthian position of Bruce McCormack.[108] While there are certainly problems with Barth's Christology, and his concept of affectivity in God borders on the anthropomorphic, the positing of humility in God, the distinctive mode of being-God that is the Son,[109] who is most fittingly made Incarnate, anticipates in a way what I would like to revise in Balthasar à la Maritain.

Robert Jenson exhibits concerns similar to those of Maritain when he argues for a divine providence that takes into consideration time-bound prayerful petitions in an indeterminist manner. He wants both to maintain Thomas's causal view of providence (i.e., his answer to the problem of necessity in predestination) and to give the prayer of petition a determinative power in the divine execution of that providence.[110] He also argues

---

[107] See Culpepper, 86–88.

[108] See Culpepper, 97n44. For McCormack, see his essay, "Divine Impassibility or Simply Divine Constancy? Implications of Karl Barth's Later Christology for Debates over Impassibility," in *Divine Impassibility*, 150–186.

[109] See McCormack, "Divine Impassibility," 170ff. It is unclear what the link is between humility and affectivity for Barth, but it appears there is one.

[110] See Jenson's essay "Ipse Pater Non Est Impassibilis," in *Divine Impassibility*, 117–126, at 125–126. This is also not outside the realm of concern for Balthasar, although he does not capitalize on the issue: "We recall the doctrine of intercessory prayer as set forth by Thomas, concerned to preserve the freedom of the *causa secunda*: the immutable God

for something similar to Balthasar's "super-temporality," namely, that time and timelessness are together constitutive of eternity.

Jenson's novel approach to time sees an analogous relationship between narrative time and the immanent life of God.[111] He defines narrative time as "neither linear nor cyclical . . . the ordering of events by their mutual reference."[112] This "immanent narrative time" is neither a total negation of linear time, nor is it identical to linear time. The Trinitarian processions are, therefore, the archetype of all times.[113] The eternal for him cannot be the mere negation of time; it must both transcend and encompass the narrative time in which God reveals Himself. Hence, Jenson reframes the whole question of impassibility versus passibility in God in terms of his own conception of time, which he extrapolates from divine revelation. Like Balthasar, he too emphasizes that God's history with us is the economic revelation of something about the immanent Trinity. Nevertheless, he maintains that Moltmann's God is no more biblical than the impassible God invoked from Nicaea to Chalcedon.[114]

Jenson wants to transcend the language of paradox and reframe the question so as to deny both passibility and impassibility of God, since Scripture affirms He is in some way affected by human sinfulness.[115] For him there is "passio" in the Father and the Son, but only in a dynamic manner, since in the economic order, God is always "in narrative" with us. Taking a cue from Origen's apparent attribution of suffering to the Father, Jenson asserts that both impassibility and passibility must be only partially negated of God, and hence the two are not conceived as mutually exclusive (where one is the total negation of the other). Thus, God is not the total negation of both attributes—rather, a partial negation of passibility is most applicable to a God that transcends but lives within linear time. God is both within and without narrative time, thus indicating impassibility and passibility in different respects (an analogy for which he sees in Western music).[116] However, his faulty point of departure is the assertion that if we can say that "One of the Trinity has suffered," there is

---

is affected by the freedom of his creature insofar as, from eternity, he has included the latter's prayers in his providence as a contributory cause" (*TD* IV, 278 [G 257]).

[111] See Jensen, "Ipse Pater," 124.
[112] Jensen, 122.
[113] See Jensen, 124.
[114] See Jensen, 120.
[115] See Jensen, 120–121.
[116] See Jensen, 121ff.

no grammatically correct sense in which we can say, "God is impassible."[117] His argument is ultimately undermined from the beginning by the false claim that the Cyrillian formula inevitably undercuts the attribution of impassibility to God.

Bruce McCormack's Barthian approach attempts to sever divine impassibility from divine immutability, upholding the latter with no interest to preserve the former.[118] Yet the proposal that the subsistent relation of filiation inherently involves a primordial humility (whose created realization would be the obedience of Christ's human nature) comes closest to what I have proposed in reconciling Balthasar and Maritain.[119] In this model, divine suffering in time is understood as the "outworking" of the humility that is itself proper to God as Son (the originate or begotten Deity).

McCormack's Barth does better than Balthasar insofar as he appropriates humility to God the Son, and since humility here seems to be quasi-equivalent to Balthasar's *ur-kenosis*, the fittingness of suffering would be in such a way effectively limited to the Son.[120] Insofar as hu-

---

[117] Jensen, 119.

[118] See McCormack's essay, "Divine Impassibility or Simply Divine Constancy? Implications of Karl Barth's Later Christology for Debates over Impassibility," in *Divine Impassibility*, 150–186, at 173, 180

[119] See McCormack, 170ff.; see also my "God's Relation."

[120] While Nicholas Healy seems only to see in Balthasar an *ur-kenosis* attributed to the Father's act of begetting the Son, other Balthasarians, such as Gerard O'Hanlon (see *Immutability of God*, 14 and 20) and John Riches (see "Afterword," in *The Analogy of Beauty*, 193), refer to the inner-Trinitarian "kenosis" of the processions, for which there is much basis in the *Theodrama*. Ben Quash says,

> Balthasar has taken a theological model with a long pedigree—a kenotic interpretation of the second Person of the Trinity in the economy of salvation—and has extended it to apply to all three Persons of the Trinity in the differentiated unity of their immanent life. The total "kenosis" of each and the thankful ("eucharistic") return to each of himself by the others becomes the ground of Trinitarian unity, being, and love. ("The *theo-drama*," in *Cambridge Companion to Hans Urs von Balthasar*, 143–157, at 151)

For Balthasar's Trinitarian *(ur-)kenosis*, see, for instance, *TD* III, 188 [G 172]; *TD* IV, 323–331 [G 300–308]; *TD* V, 243–246 [G 219–222]. Concerning the "kenosis" of the Holy Spirit, see *TD* II, 256, 261 [G 232, 237]; *TD* III, 188 [G 172]; *TD* IV, 362 [337]; *A Theological Anthropology*, 73 [G 94]; see also Jeffrey A. Vogel, "The Unselfing Activity of the Holy Spirit in the Theology of Hans Urs von Balthasar," *Logos: A Journal of Catholic Thought and Culture* 10, no. 4 (Fall 2007): 16–34.

Steffen Lösel, however, correctly notes: "Although Balthasar refers at times to the Spirit's experience of suffering, he emphasizes that the Spirit only reflects the passion of the Son. He emphasizes that 'we cannot state a *kenosis* of the Spirit's freedom' (Hans

mility (and obedience) is a created moral virtue, it cannot be applied in one-to-one fashion to any divine person—a robust doctrine of analogy is needed for anyone who wishes to discern the sense in which such can be predicated of the transcendent. But even Barth, the self-declared enemy of *analogia entis*,[121] sees a problem with transposing onto the triune God the event-quality of the salvation economy.[122]

Without attributing a multiplicity of wills to the divine nature, something analogous to humility and obedience may be appropriated to the Son's distinctive mode of being-God insofar as He is most fittingly made Incarnate.[123] Christ's *kenosis* reflects the divine receptivity that is the second divine person, and, in this sense, whatever perfection belongs

---

Urs von Balthasar, *Theologik*, vol. III, *Der Geist der Wahrheit* [Einsiedeln: Johannes Verlag, 1987], 218). Cf. also *idem, Theologik* III, 188; idem, *Pneuma und Institution. Skizzen zur Theologie* IV (Einsiedeln: Johannes Verlag, 1974), 264ff." ("Murder in the Cathedral," 438n64).

Late in his career, Balthasar states: "we clearly see the Son's 'economic' death as the revelation, in terms of the world, of the *kenosis* (or selflessness) of the love of Father and Son at the heart of the Trinity. As we have shown, this is the precondition for the procession of God's absolute, non-kenotic Spirit of love" (*TL* III, 300 [G 276]).

[121] See his *Church Dogmatics* I/1, *The Doctrine of the Word of God: Part 1,* trans. G. W. Bromiley and T. F. Torrance (New York: Continuum, 2004), xiii.

[122] See, e.g., *Church Dogmatics* IV/2, *The Doctrine of Reconciliation: Part 2* (New York: Bloomsbury, 2004), 59. Nonetheless, he also expresses agreement with Patripassianism (see *Church Dogmatics* IV/2, 357). Balthasar sees a problem with Barth's reluctance to impose the events of the passion onto the internal life of God, in effect separating the processions from the missions (see *TD* V, 236–239, 243–246). I agree with David Lauber's assessment that Balthasar veers closer to Moltmann than he should in critiquing Barth, whose modesty should serve as a corrective for Balthasar (see "Towards a Theology of Holy Saturday," 344).

[123] See *Church Dogmatics* IV/1, *The Doctrine of Reconciliation: Part 1* (New York: T&T Clark, 1961), 193. For an appreciatively critical appropriation of Barth's Trinitarian theory, see Thomas Joseph White, OP, "Intra-Trinitarian Obedience and Nicene-Chalcedonian Christology," *Nova et Vetera* (English Edition) 6, no. 2 (2008): 377–402. For a refutation of the idea that humility may be properly applied to God, see also Guy Mansini, "Can Humility and Obedience be Trinitarian Realities?" in *Thomas Aquinas and Karl Barth: An Unofficial Catholic-Protestant Dialogue*, ed. Bruce L. McCormack and Thomas Joseph White, OP (Grand Rapids, MI: Eerdmans, 2013), 71–98.

Mansini, therefore, rightly criticizes Balthasar for "[imagining] the Son 'offering' to become incarnate and the Father being 'touched' at this offering" ("Humility and Obedience," 96). But he does not capitalize upon Thomas's words that "for the Son *to hear* the Father is to receive his essence from him" (97, citing *Super Evangelium S. Ioannis Lectura*, no. 2017). If to receive His essence from the Father can be called in some sense "hearing," then the divine receptivity of the Son must in some sense be the exemplar of created obedience.

to humility may be appropriated to the Son in an eminent way. In other words, since the divine being proper to the second hypostasis is filiation and therefore characterized by a free tendency toward Incarnation, supposing the free decision to create, the Son is the exemplar of all created obedience, even though He does not actually exercise obedience except by means of the human will of Christ. Thus, I think it warranted to predicate humility of God in an improper manner, at least by way of metaphorical analogy. Since "obedience" is a manifestation of humility and etymologically signifies "hearing" (*ob-audire*) in its deepest sense (i.e., listening) and listening is fundamentally a form of receptivity (even if it formally supposes a distinction of wills), the Incarnation of the Son points to the divine exemplar of such creaturely virtues, that is, the receptivity proper to the Son's self-surrender.[124]

Building on Augustine's analysis of *apatheia* (ἀπάθεια),[125] David Bentley Hart asks a question very pertinent to Balthasar's own reflections on divine impassibility and immediately answers it:

> For Gregory of Nyssa it is even possible to say that nothing that does not lead to sin is properly called a pathos [*Contra Eunomium* III.4.27, GNO II; 44]. But, one might ask, at this point has not the meaning of the term impassibility been so thoroughly altered as to have no real use? Is it not the case that once we have admitted love into our definition of the word we have thus rendered it unintelligible, inasmuch as love is a reaction evoked by what one suffers of another? To state the matter simply—No: love is not primordially a reaction, but the possibility of every action, the transcendent act that makes all else actual; it is purely positive, sufficient in itself, without the need of any galvanism of the negative to be fully active, vital, and creative.[126]

He adds:

> [A]t least according to the dominant tradition, love is not, in its essence, an emotion—a pathos—at all: it is life, being, truth, our

---

[124] White speaks of the Son's divine receptivity, invoking Thomas, in "Intra-Trinitarian Obedience," 398–399. Mansini speaks of obedience in terms of hearing in "Can Humility and Obedience be Trinitarian Realities?," 78.

[125] See *De Civitate Dei* XIV.ix.4 (CCL 48: 428), cited in David Bentley Hart, "No Shadow of Turning: On Divine Impassibility," *Pro Ecclesia* 11, no. 2 (2002): 184–206, at 195.

[126] Hart, "No Shadow of Turning," 195.

only true well-being, and the very ground of our nature and existence. Thus John of Damascus draws a very strict distinction between a pathos and an "energy" (or act): the former is a movement of the soul provoked by something alien and external to it; but the latter is a "drastic" movement, a positive power that is moved of itself in its own nature. Of such a nature, most certainly, is love. Or—to step briefly out of the patristic context—as Thomas Aquinas puts it, love, enjoyment, and delight are qualitatively different from anger and sadness, as the latter are privative states, passive and reactive, whereas the former are originally one act of freedom and intellect and subsist wholly in God as a purely "intellectual appetite."[127]

This is essentially what I have proposed, referencing Catholic phenomenologists on affectivity. Thus, he concludes: *"Apatheia,* defined as infinitely active love, 'feels' more than any affect could possibly impress upon a passive nature."[128]

However, clearly learning from Balthasar (but without citing him),[129] Hart goes beyond this articulation of divine impassibility by referring to "the eternal *event* that is God's being"[130] and asserting, "God's eternal being is, in some sense, kenosis."[131] Underlying this conviction is a concession that pervades his work—a concession to Heidegger's critique of onto-theology as encompassing much (if not all) of classical and scholastic metaphysics. Therefore, his penchant for the Platonic over the Aristotelian yields the notion that God is as much beyond being as He is beyond becoming, and yet both may be super-eminently predicated of His *energeia* (ἐνέργεια).[132] Hence, the Orthodox theologian prefers the Greek Fathers to

---

[127] Hart, 195.

[128] Hart, 200. It is also important to note: "To call this infinite act of love *apatheia,* then, is to affirm its plenitude and its transcendence of every evil, every interval of sin, every finite rupture, disappointment of longing, shadow of sadness, or failure of love—in short, every pathos" (Hart, 199).

[129] The clearest allusion is the final sentence of the body of his article, in which his reliance on Balthasar could not be more obvious: "the terrible distance of Christ's cry of human dereliction, despair, and utter godforsakenness—'My God, My God, why hast thou forsaken me?'—is enfolded within and overcome by the ever greater distance and always indissoluble unity of God's triune love: 'Father, into thy hands I commend my spirit'" (Hart, 205).

[130] Hart, 197.

[131] Hart, 202.

[132] Hart, 190:

the Latin Father and scholastics, even though he tries to incorporate the latter. Balthasar, however, enters more directly into dialogue with Western metaphysics, even if he also suffers from Heideggerian influence.

Despite intending to maintain a distinction between the immanent identity of God and His economic manifestations,[133] Hart fails to purify analogical theological discourse of the imperfection proper to the world of becoming. Hart and Balthasar seem to share a similar perspective on analogical predication, projecting categories of dynamism peculiar to the created world into the Trinitarian life itself. In other words, paradoxically, one who denies what I might call the "theorem of analogy"—borrowing Bernard Lonergan's phraseology[134]—ends up collapsing the economic and immanent dimensions of the Trinity, even if the express intent is precisely apophasis.

CONCLUDING EVALUATIONS

There is simply no need to ground human suffering in the Trinitarian processions. Despite Balthasar's attempt to transcend the debate on impassibility through an odd usage of paradox and analogy, the depth of his theology is undermined by his imposition of the mystery of *kenosis* upon the intra-Trinitarian life. Even though he attempts to distance himself from Rahner's (in)famous identification of the immanent and economic Trinities,[135] his doctrine of *ur-kenosis* constituting the very distinction of persons in God effectively involves a conflation of the two dimensions in the form of a forced unification (that is, he never distinguishes real vs. logical identity).

If God the Son suffers, albeit in the human nature of the Word *incarnate*, and whatever is said of one divine hypostasis must be said of the

---

The only way in which the distinction between being and becoming can be overcome (if this is at all possible or desirable) is by way of a complete collapse of the difference. Being must be identified with the totality of becoming as an "infinite" process. Otherwise one cannot avoid some version of Heidegger's onto-theological critique (and frankly, Heidegger's critique almost certainly holds against the complete system anyway).

[133] Hart, 191–192.

[134] Lonergan calls the development of the distinction between the natural and the supernatural "the theorem of the supernatural." See Bernard J. F. Lonergan, SJ, *Grace and Freedom: Operative Grace in the Thought of St. Thomas Aquinas: Collected Works of Bernard Lonergan*, vol. 1, ed. Frederick E. Crowe, SJ, and Robert M. Doran, SJ (Reprint, Toronto: University of Toronto, 2000), 18–20, 185–187, 210ff.

[135] See Karl Rahner, *The Trinity*, 22.

others, must we not conclude that the Father and the Spirit likewise suffer via the human nature of Christ? Certainly, the mode of union between the Father and the Spirit, on the one hand, and the human nature of the incarnate Son, on the other, differs from the mode of union between the second divine person and His human nature. However, if the divinity of Christ is in need of a human nature in order to suffer, could we not sustain the Athanasian rule by specifying that it belongs uniquely to the constitutive relation of filiation to be inclined to suffer by assuming passibility?[136] Moreover, the Father and the Spirit must be said to suffer economically, as whatever is said of one divine hypostasis must be said of the others (excepting the subsistent relations of opposition defining each), even if the distinction between the economic and immanent must be asserted so as to prevent equivocations that may infringe upon the absolute freedom of the transcendent God.

Perhaps realizing the danger of importing economic categories into the Trinitarian relations themselves, O'Hanlon effectively contrasts Maritain's take to Balthasar's:

> The question remains open as to whether this Trinitarian drama involves a "wound" in God which is identical to the Trinitarian processions themselves, or is merely "consequent" on the decision to create—the question already raised as to whether or not God is essentially kenotic. . . . [Balthasar] is asserting that while secondary, created causes cannot *per se* change God, they can, when taken into the Trinitarian life, become part of that eternal drama of love which allows opposites to exist and reconciles them.[137]

---

[136] With this one could agree with Balthasar's earlier articulation of the matter:

> [T]he conditions of mankind become transparent to the conditions of the Word in its divinity. And in the Passion (which here leads to the kenosis of the Incarnation in its greatest intensity and obviousness), through the sufferings of humanity, are revealed both the victory and the power of God and the will of the divine person of the Son (and in him the will of the whole Trinity) to let himself be affected by this suffering. The subject of the suffering is the person who is the Word (and the Son is the Word precisely as a divine person, not as a divine nature, which he shares with the Father and the Spirit), even if he requires human nature in order to suffer. (*A Theological Anthropology*, 275–276 [G 298])

[137] O'Hanlon, *The Immutability of God*, 34.

It is because God is the object of His own permission of evils initiated by creatures that He can be said to be "affected" by such evil,[138] albeit indirectly, such that the *sym*pathy (συμπαθεια) inherent to His infinite love for His creatures wills to become *em*pathy in the form of the Son's incarnation, who represents the free tendency of divine receptivity (in Son and Spirit as from the Father) to surrender itself (*kenosis*) in love.[139]

But if the expression "economic Trinity" is truly to denote a divine Trinity (albeit under the aspect of its free self-communication in salvation history), must we not affirm that it is a really identical even though logically distinct reflection of the "immanent Trinity"? It is immediately apparent that while Balthasar does not simply identify the immanent and economic dimensions of the Trinity, he does not sufficiently "*distinguish* in order to unite" them.[140] For example, further qualification is needed to add theological precision to what may be called "mystical excess" in Balthasar's

---

[138] There are typically two meanings given to "affectivity," namely, ontological and psychological. Ontologically, it simply means being the object of some act, whether internal or external to the subject. Psychologically, it indicates the capacity of the heart (or the person's core being) for value-laden experience. There is an analogous relationship, though, between these two meanings, which is glimpsed if one realizes that feelings are typically involuntary responses to stimuli, whether internal or external to the subject.

In other words, one can only be affected by something when one is the object of some value-laden act (i.e., experiencing oneself responding to an act presupposes the fact of being the object of some act). Moreover, affectivity is closely aligned with emotivity, and we can recognize in ourselves the existence of emotions or sentiments that are not tied up with animal appetites, but are spiritual in nature, even if still imperfect (see Dietrich von Hildebrand, *The Heart: An Analysis of Human and Divine Affectivity*, ed. John F. Crosby [South Bend, IN: St. Augustine's Press, 2007]). Hence, when affectivity is predicated of God, only the perfection belonging to spiritual feelings (e.g., compassion) is intended and attributed to the transcendent *per via eminentiae*.

[139] Hence, Maritain concludes toward the end of his article:

> To the problem of evil taken in all its dimensions, there is only one answer, the answer of faith in its integrity. And at the heart of our faith is the certitude that God, anyway Jesus said so, has for us the *feelings of a Father*. . . . [T]he great mystery of what, in an infinitely perfect and infinitely happy God, corresponds to what suffering is in us, not with regard to the frightening mark of imperfection it implies, but with regard to the incomparable grandeur that it also reveals. ("Reflections," in *Untrammeled Approaches*, 263 [F 26], emphasis original)

[140] This scholastic axiom, *distinguere per unire,* is of course the great theme of Maritain's monumental *Distinguer pour unir; ou, les degrés du savoir* (Paris: Desclée de Brouwer, 1946), ET, *The Degrees of Knowledge*, trans. Gerald B. Phelan (Notre Dame Press, IN: University of Notre Dame, 1995). But whether or not Balthasar accepts this principle or rather wishes to diverge in part from it on an operative level would be a question of research concerning, in fact, his unique approach to analogy.

"infinite-distance" or *ek-stasis* description of the Trinitarian processions. I propose that the following qualifying addenda are needed for the theory to be acceptable in any sense: (1) there is also an infinite union between the persons; (2) the distinction of mutual opposition between the persons is not a real "separation" or "rupture"; (3) the "self-surrender" attributed to the processions is not "temporal" or "free" in any sense ordinarily derivative of contingent experience; and (4) avoiding all subordinationism, paternity does not preexist filiation—rather, the two are relations that exist concomitantly. The first two points Balthasar concedes,[141] and the last two are deficiencies commonly observed in Balthasar's treatment. It does not seem that this idea of infinite distance between persons really necessitates the *ur*-kenotic theory of the Trinitarian processions, which is the foundation for all of Balthasar's speculations about the Trinity. But the transposition of Christ's suffering onto the Godhead as a whole is a subtle move made *ad initium* without thorough justification.

Thus, I have sought to create a *rapprochement* between Balthasar's Trinitarian *ur*-kenotic answer to the problem of divine impassibility (in the Christological economy) and Maritain's creative Thomistic view of an antecedent will that "suffers" metaphorically the infliction of human resistance to divine grace. Arguing that Balthasar does not truly build upon Maritain's approach, as he may appear to do, I propose that the proper route for doing so is that of divine affectivity: God freely empathizes with the human condition through the Incarnation, thanks to the divine affectivity by which He sympathizes with the creatures who create the evil they suffer. There is an analogous (rather than equivocal) relationship between the notion of affectivity as an ontological category that designates being an object of an action and the psychological notion of affectivity as feeling something in response to an internal or external stimulus. But not only are feelings psychological responses to being the object of some action (or "happenings"), affectivity as the quality of the heart whereby the person has value-laden experiences could apply in an analogical manner to God insofar as spiritual feelings (such as compassion) have a perfection that is not tied up with lower appetites.

In other words, borrowing from Catholic phenomenologists of love (i.e., Wojtyla and Hildebrand),[142] I want to attribute some kind of emo-

---

[141] See, respectively, *TD* V, 260, 263; 262–264 [G 235, 237–238; 237–238].

[142] See, for example, Karol Wojtyla, *Person and Community: Selected Essays*, trans. Theresa Sandok (New York: Peter Lang, 1993), 169–171, and Dietrich von Hildebrand, *The Heart*, Part 1.

tivity to the love of God, not as if His "feelings" are of the same quality as ours, but maintaining that there is some kind of affective element to His love. Yet, in order to maintain a Thomistic notion of divine impassibility, I want to argue that God is not directly affected by any creature; rather, He is affected by His own free decisions to permit every evil that actually occurs, which means He is receptive in an intentional manner (not in a "real" manner, in the scholastic sense) to the evils free creatures initiate. As God's love is not cold or abstract, the free tendency of His self-diffusive goodness is to surrender Himself to the will of His creatures; hence, His free self-surrender is personified in the Son, who could therefore be appropriately called the *ur-kenosis* of God.[143]

Thus, affirming the affectivity of divine love should suffice as a solution to the debate over the "passibility" of God. While it is not proper to say that God suffers in Himself eternally, it is possible to say that He is eternally affected by evil in an indirect manner.[144] He is "affected" by evil insofar as He wills eternally to permit evil and His decision to do so is constitutive of His essence since He is really identical to His own decisions (and thus all His actions are actions upon Himself). Therefore, He is called "affective," at least by virtue of the receptivity of His will and intellect to the "line of nonbeing," and in the Incarnation this eternal συμπαθεια (sym-pathy) becomes the Redeemer's personal experience of (relatively) infinite evil, descending into the darkness in order to raise mankind heavenward. In philosophical terms, as the actions of God are in some way determinative of His eternal and unchanging essence, the category "passio" of Aristotle can be said to be, in an analogous manner, as "primordial" to God (in the person of Christ) as are the predicates "ουσια" and "*relatio*."[145] Hence, Pope Benedict XVI went so far as to say that the God of Revelation is ερος as well as αγάπη (*caritas*).[146]

---

[143] Graham Ward notes that Balthasar associates this view with "Luther and the Lutheran kenoticists of the seventeenth and nineteenth centuries," labeling it "Christomonistic" (see Ward, *Balthasar at the End of Modernity*, 45). For Balthasar, instead, *kenosis* constitutes the essence of Trinitarian love. The problematic nature of this view will be addressed in different ways in the chapters that follow.

[144] John Paul II affirms the same in his Encyclical *Dominum et Vivificantem*, which seems to appropriate some of Balthasar's reflections on the Trinity, all the while sticking to the scriptural texts and avoiding mystical hyperbole (see §§39 and 41).

[145] See Ratzinger, *Introduction to Christianity*, 182–184, for this assertion concerning *relatio* as "an equally primordial form of being" as *substantia* (or *ousia*); see *Introduction to Christianity*, 145–148, for discussion of affect in the God of Revelation versus the God of philosophy.

[146] See *Deus Caritas Est* §§7–8, and especially §10. He indicates, particularly in note 7 of §9,

that he adopts the position of "Pseudo-Dionysius the Areopagite, who in his treatise *The Divine Names*, IV, 12–14 (PG 3, 709–713) calls God both *eros* and *agape*." Ratzinger, in fact, seems to come closer to Balthasar's position in *Behold, the Pierced One: An Approach to a Spiritual Christology* (San Francisco: Ignatius Press, 1986), 56ff., especially 57–58 [*Schauen auf den Durchbohrten* (Einsiedeln: Johannes Verlag, 1984), 48ff., especially 49–50], but it is difficult to judge precisely where he falls in the spectrum between Adrienne von Speyr's "mystical excess," as it were (adopted by Balthasar), and Maritain's moderately Thomistic approach. He is certainly more careful than Balthasar, but he does not say enough for one to draw out clearly a precise formulation of his position on the matter.

CHAPTER FIVE

Trinitarian Suffering and Divine Receptivity
Dialectic and Metaphor

IN HIS TREATMENT OF GOD'S RELATIONSHIP TO EVIL, Balthasar seeks to maintain a delicate balance between the kenoticist strain of contemporary theology and the traditional theology of divine immutability articulated by Augustine, Aquinas, and their disciples. Wishing to avoid both the "classical dogmatism" on divine impassibility and the mythological excesses of modern passibilist accounts, Balthasar strives to incorporate contingent realities into God's immutable identity via the intra-divine personal relations themselves as eternally enriching. Guy Mansini summarizes Balthasar's argument in the *Theodramatik* regarding the relationship between the Trinitarian God and the created world: "If creation is really to count and add something to God, if created freedom is to be in real dialogue with God, if the event of the Cross is really to matter to the interior life of God, then the reality of God must be such as to be an ever-more increasing event of Trinitarian exchanges."[1] Concurring with this straightforward interpretation, I will attempt to decipher whether there might still be legitimate insight in Balthasar's treatment of divine suffering, despite his engagement with kenoticism. Thus, while still generally appreciative of the dialogue Balthasar's articulation generates, this chapter will critically engage methodological dimensions of his soteriology in thorough dialogue with various interpreters of Balthasar.

Recall that one of the central Balthasarian theses is that the Trinitarian processions are constituted by what he calls *ur-kenosis*, or an original

---

[1]   Mansini, OSB, "Balthasar and the Theodramatic Enrichment of the Trinity," 508.

analogue to the love-filled suffering permeating Christ's redemptive work. Mark A. McIntosh comments on a passage from *Das Endspiel*:

> [T]he divine Persons have themselves, on the Cross and in the Resurrection, revisited the alienated distance between human and God, emplotting it once more with the "space" between the Father and the Son: "The extreme distance between Father and Son, which is endured as a result of the Son's taking on of sin, changes into the most profound intimacy. . . . The Son's eternal, holy distance from the Father, in the Spirit, forms the basis on which the unholy distance of the world's sin can be transposed into it, can be transcended and overcome by it." (*TD* 4, 361–2; see also *TH*)[2]

Hence, pointing to the Father as the origin of Trinitarian surrender, Balthasar reflects: "Inherent in the Father's love is an absolute renunciation: he will not be God for himself alone. He lets go of his divinity and, in this sense, manifests a (divine) God-lessness (of love, of course). The latter must not be confused with the godlessness that is found within the world, although it undergirds it, renders it possible and goes beyond it."[3]

It is statements like these and many others that lead some to believe Balthasar is unduly influenced by Hegel, albeit via Moltmann and Bulgakov.[4] But the matter is quite a bit more complicated. Not only does the

---

[2] McIntosh, "Christology," in *Cambridge Companion to Hans Urs von Balthasar*, 24–36, at 35. Levering keenly observes: "The problem nonetheless remains: how does a fundamentally 'intellectual' distance—it has to be such, since the divine Persons never hate each other—encompass a willful distance constituted by hatred of God?" (*Scripture and Metaphysics*, 130). He notes that Balthasar, in *Theologik* II, 321–322, thinks Speyr solves this problem but the text is enigmatic.

[3] *TD* IV, 323–324 [G 301]. This is the kind of approach Edward Oakes adopts in his essay, "He descended into hell," where what might be called the aesthetic excess of paradoxism is exhibited (see 218–219). By this term paradoxism I mean to indicate the tendency to view affirmation of apparent contradiction as a pathway to truth, born of the notion that truth at its profoundest consists in the (at least, apparent) truth of contradictories, the most radical *coincidentia oppositorum* (convergence of opposites).

[4] In *TD* V, Balthasar obliquely expresses essential agreement with Moltmann and distances him from "pure Hegelianism or a radical process theology," but he seems hesitant to accept the full thrust of Moltmann's Trinitarian theory, most likely due to the latter's lack of nuance regarding the economic-immanent identity (see *TD* V, 172–173 [G 152–153]).

At the same time, it is evident that he wants to go beyond both Moltmann and Rahner (on the opposite side of the debate), incorporating their insights into his theory

distinction between the so-called immanent and economic trinities play a significant role in the great debate concerning divine impassibility, but discourse on analogical versus metaphorical predication also ought to figure into this complex question. Kevin Duffy, on the basis of contemporary Thomistic analysis, critiques the notion that Balthasar's divine discourse is justifiable by recourse to metaphor, as Gerard O'Hanlon forcefully argues.[5]

---

of Trinitarian ur-kenosis (see, e.g., *TD* IV, 322–323 [G 300]); in the process of such synthesis, though, he utilizes Bulgakov, perhaps too much (see especially *TD* IV, 323–324 [G 300–301]).

[5] See Duffy, "Change, Suffering, and Surprise in God: Von Balthasar's Use of Metaphor," *Irish Theological Quarterly* 76, no. 4 (2011): 370–387; see also O'Hanlon's response: "A Response to Kevin Duffy on von Balthasar and the Immutability of God," *Irish Theological Quarterly* 78, no. 2 (2013): 179–184. Duffy mentions Balthasar's option for a neo-Chalcedonian Christology, problematic with respect to coherent theological discourse, according to Rahner, who opts instead for classical Chalcedonianism (see O'Hanlon, *Immutability of God*, 171, cited by Duffy, 382n61).

The deep-seated difference between Balthasar and Rahner has its roots in their very distinct appropriations of modern philosophy. Rahner's theology is fundamentally characterized by the "transcendental Thomism" of Joseph Maréchal, while Balthasar is more skeptical of the anthropocentric tendency born of the subjectivist epistemology inherent in Maréchal's purported synthesis of Thomas and Kant in *Le point de départ de la métaphysique: leçons sur le développement historique et théorique du problème de la connaissance*, 5 vols (Bruges-Louvain, 1922–1947).

Brian Daley, however, states that "Like Karl Rahner and other Catholic theologians of the mid-twentieth century, Balthasar's understanding of scholastic philosophy was heavily influenced by Maréchal's dynamic perspective" ("Balthasar's Reading of the Church Fathers," in *Cambridge Companion to Hans Urs von Balthasar*, 187–206, at 205n25). Surely, Balthasar's approach is "dynamic," but in the course of his critique of Rahner, he comes to repudiate his earlier call to engage Maréchal (see "On the Tasks of Catholic Philosophy in Our Time," in *Communio* 20, no. 1 [Spring 1993]: 147–187; Fergus Kerr, "Balthasar and Metaphysics," in *Cambridge Companion to Hans Urs von Balthasar*, 224–238).

Karen Kilby argues that Rahner's Kantianism is not as determinative of the weaknesses discerned in his theology as is commonly argued (see *Balthasar*, 7, referencing her argument in *Rahner: Theology and Philosophy* [London: Routledge, 2004], and her essay, "Balthasar and Karl Rahner," in *Cambridge Companion to Hans Urs von Balthasar*, 256–268). Meanwhile, Rowan Williams and John Riches concur that the respective theologies of Balthasar and Rahner are irreducibly at odds on certain key points precisely because of this fundamental philosophical difference (see John Riches, "Afterword," in *The Analogy of Beauty: The Theology of Hans Urs von Balthasar*, ed. John Riches [Edinburgh: T&T Clark Ltd., 1986], 186–188).

For a concise and precise summary of Rahner's development of Maréchal's attempted synthesis and Balthasar's critique of this project, both foundationally and in its theological implications, see Rowan Williams's essay, "Balthasar and Rahner," in *The Analogy of Beauty*, particularly, 15–21. See also Cyril O'Regan's comments on the difference

Therefore, I will engage Duffy's argument in dialogue with defenders of Balthasar on this point.

Before beginning to investigate whether or not Balthasar's analogical discourse on Trinitarian suffering is coherent, I must probe briefly the role of Hegelian dialectic in Balthasar's Christocentric approach, engaging the most relevant secondary literature throughout. Cyril O'Regan recently did a masterful job of exonerating Balthasar of the accusation that he is fundamentally Hegelian.[6] Still, I will argue that Balthasar borrows more from kenoticism with respect to the Trinitarian Being than is acceptable for the classical Christian theology of divine impassibility,[7] and yet in the process of engagement nonetheless reaps legitimate insight into the profundity of divine suffering and into the very identity of God, assuming his discourse is effectively demythologized through rigorous philosophical parsing. Therefore, once I have explored the influence of dialectic in Balthasar's Christology and assessed the metaphorical character of his theology of divine life, it is possible to clarify in what sense one might speak of divine self-enrichment through the salvation economy and in what ways Balthasar's discourse on God ought to be tempered by philosophical precision.

Hegelian Dialectic and Christocentric Analogy

Before turning ultimately to the question of divine receptivity, it is imperative to take a brief foray into the topics of dialectical-analogical discourse concerning the Incarnate God. According to what is sometimes called "the Athanasian rule," whatever is said of one divine person must be said of the others, except the mutually defining relations by which each subsists in

---

from a Christological perspective, "Von Balthasar and Thick Retrieval: Post-Chalcedonian Symphonic Theology," *Gregorianum* 77 (1996): 227–260, 256ff.

    For Balthasar's comments on Maréchal, Williams cites, in addition to *Karl Barth: Darstellung und Deutung seiner Theologie* (Reprint, Einsiedeln: Johannes Verlag, 1976), *Love Alone is Credible*, trans. D. C. Schindler (San Francisco: Ignatius Press, 2004), 34; *GL* I (149); and *Herrlichkeit: Eine Theologische Asthetik*, Band III: *Im Raum der Metaphysik*, Teil 1: *Altertum* (Einsiedeln: Johannes Verlag, 1965), 799, 881, 884, 904.

[6] O'Regan displays how Balthasar consistently undercuts Hegel's pseudo-Christian project in many respects, even though he maintains a dialogue with post-Hegelian theological concerns; see *The Anatomy of Misremembering*. Kevin Mongrain anticipates O'Regan's fundamental project of casting Balthasar as subverting the gnosticism of Hegel (see *The Systematic Thought of Hans Urs von Balthasar*, 133ff.). Adequate engagement with O'Regan's voluminous treatment would require much more space than is available here.

[7] I will not examine the patristic and medieval sources here.

distinction from the others. Christologically, the question revolves around the so-called *communicatio idiomatum*.[8] Gerard O'Hanlon displays the connection between the Christological and Trinitarian dimensions of the issue in Balthasar's attempt to resolve it:

> [Balthasar] arrives at the necessity of positing a real kenosis in God, and from his repeated emphasis on the ontological, personal identity of the Logos as the subject who unites the two distinct natures in Christ, he will refuse to limit the change and suffering which Christ experiences [to] his human nature alone. This is the advance on Chalcedon and its traditional interpretation which Balthasar proposes. The tendency to consider the human nature of Christ as an *instrumentum conjunctum* which does not affect the divine person he sees as Nestorian in character. And so he is anxious to insist on a more than merely logical *communicatio idiomatum*, to accept that the formula "one of the Trinity has suffered" does indeed mean that God has "suffered," albeit mysteriously. But why "mysteriously": why not say univocally that God suffers? Because—and here we find Balthasar's respect for Chalcedon—there *is* an enduring and incommensurable difference between God and the world, between the divine and human "unmixed" natures of Christ.[9]

In fact, Balthasar seeks to build on Jacques Maritain's reflections and go beyond them,[10] utilizing twentieth-century Hegelian-influenced Protestant sources from Moltmann to Barth.[11]

Thomas Weinandy offers the following reflection concerning Balthasar's posture on the question of divine impassibility in relation to Hegel and Moltmann:

---

[8] For explanation of this term, see J. F. Rigney, "Communication of Idioms," *New Catholic Encyclopedia*, vol. 4, 2nd ed. (Detroit: Gale, 2003), 25–27.

[9] O'Hanlon, *The Immutability of God*, 43, also cited by Oakes, "He descended into hell," 244n48.

[10] O'Hanlon comments: "with Varillon Balthasar believes one must go further [than Maritain] and at least begin to suspect that in God becoming is a perfection of being, movement a perfection of immobility and mutability a perfection of immutability" (*The Immutability of God*, 71).

[11] Celia Deane-Drummond points out several similarities between Balthasar and Moltmann's theology, particularly on the relationship between the Cross and the Trinity (see "The Breadth of Glory," 49 especially), but she also thoroughly exhibits disturbing signs of an evolutionist worldview.

[W]hile he wishes to uphold the immutability and impassibility of God in himself, he also argues that, because of God's free and loving engagement with the world, he can be said to be mutable and passible in his relationship to the created order. His perfect immutable love allows him to be affected by the created order and so respond to it. Von Balthasar wishes to steer a position between the mythological notion of God's action in the world as, he believes, is found in Hegel, Moltmann, process theologians and others, and that of the traditional position, as found in Aquinas, where God appears to be disengaged from the vicissitudes of human life.[12]

Whether the ghost of Hegel lurks in the background (à la Moltmann) remains a valid question, and Balthasar is cognizant of it.[13]

Perhaps incorporating Hegelian dialectics into his interpretation of key scriptural texts,[14] in dialogue with Moltmann's radical "death of God"

---

[12] *Does God Suffer?*, 13n38. Weinandy's own position is that "God in himself as God does not suffer. . . . However, it must be asserted as well that this does not mean, as we will see, that God does not grieve over sin and evil" (153). It seems, then, to be Maritain's position essentially, but he regrettably counsels against all speech of divine suffering (see 170).

　　The Balthasarian Martin Bieler is rightly confused by this, but he does not resolve such (as he thinks) by exalting instead David Bentley Hart's treatment (see "Causality and Freedom," *Communio* 32 [Fall 2005]: 407–434, at 430). Bieler rather adds to the confusion when he interprets Maximus the Confessor's dictum that "God in Christ experienced pain in a divine way because he experienced it voluntarily" ("God and the Creator," 80, citing *Ambiguum* 5) by transposing Aquinas's argument that, "the higher a nature is, the more intimate to the nature is that which flows from it" (*SCG* IV, ch. 11, no. 1), to "the ability to feel pain" (80).

[13] For instance, "If our reflection proceeds (as in the case of Moltmann) exclusively from the perspective of the Cross, the divine freedom to create the world becomes questionable (just as Moltmann questions it)" (*TD* V, 234 [G 211]). Brian J. Spence points out differences (as well as similarities) between Moltmann's and Balthasar's relationship to Hegel's philosophy of religion; see "The Hegelian Element in Von Balthasar's and Moltmann's Understanding of the Suffering of God," *Toronto Journal of Theology* 14, no. 1 (1998): 45–60.

　　Concerning Balthasar's intention to avoid Moltmannian conflation of immanent and economic Trinity, despite common "crucicentrism," see David Luy, "The Aesthetic Collision: Hans Urs von Balthasar on the Trinity and the Cross," *International Journal of Systematic Theology* 13, no. 2 (2011): 154–169, at 155.

[14] For example, he states: "What we see in Christ's forsakenness on the Cross, in ultimate creaturely negativity, is the revelation of the highest positivity of Trinitarian love" (*TD* V, 517 [G 473]).

theology,[15] Balthasar reflects on hell's relationship to the economic Trinity, intending to rescue the imagery of the Old Testament from the realm of the merely metaphorical.[16] Interpreting Philippians 2, especially, he states:

> The event by which he consents to be transferred from the form of God into the "form of a servant" and the "likeness of men" (Phil 2:6f.) affects him as the eternal Son. It does not matter whether we say that eternity enters into time "for a while" or that eternity takes a particular "time" and its decidedly temporal contents into itself: neither statement explains how such a process is possible. We can call it *kenosis*, as in Philippians 2, but this does not imply any mythological alteration in God; it *can* express one of the infinite possibilities available to free, eternal life: namely, that the Son, who has everything from the Father, "lays up" and commits to God's keeping the "form of God" he has received from him. He does this in order to concentrate, in all seriousness and realism, on the mission that is one mode of his procession from the Father. There is nothing "as if" about this: the outcome is that he is forsaken by God on the Cross. Yet this "infinite distance," which recapitulates the sinner's mode of alienation from God, will remain forever the highest revelation known to the world of the diastasis (within the eternal being of God) between Father and Son in the Holy Spirit.[17]

---

[15] See, for example, *TD* V, 243 [G 219]. Despite explicitly confessing an understanding of divine suffering essentially in agreement with Moltmann (see Balthasar and Speyr, *Mystery of Redemption*, 38 [F 40]), their differences on divine impassibility are outlined throughout *TD* V. See also Steffen Lösel, "Murder in the Cathedral," especially 428–429, and Thomas G. Dalzell, "The Enrichment of God in Balthasar's Trinitarian Eschatology," *Irish Theological Quarterly* 66 (2001): 3–18, at 4–5.

[16] See *TD* V, 214–215 [G 193].

[17] *TD* III, 228 [G 209]. Concerning this "infinite distance" within God, Karen Kilby enumerates "two routes by which he arrives at this point" and only considers the second, which itself is not formulated very well. The first route is, in fact, the fundamental one, and it is the notion that the divine persons as distinct hypostases are utterly other than one another, a notion she confesses not to understand (*Balthasar*, 109–110).

In other words, the divine hypostases are who they are precisely insofar as their identities must be irreducibly distinct from one another (i.e., the divine persons possess in an exemplary fashion the irreducible difference that distinguishes one personal subject from another); the Thomistic Trinitarian language of "mutual relations of opposition" help express this point, and she never has recourse to such a key expression. Since the "second route" (the Cross as revelation of Trinitarian relations) is really founded upon the first route, as the economic Trinity reflects but does not exhaust the immanent

Balthasar seems to endorse the trend in modern theology of professedly abandoning "a Greek theo-ontology of 'absolute Being'" in favor of "the Johannine definition that God is love," succumbing to the oft-repeated claim that a truly impassible God must be indifferent and uncaring toward His creation, instead of recognizing Greek metaphysics as providentially included in the notions themselves employed by the sacred writers.[18]

Furthermore, in the final volume of the *Theodramatik*, quoting Hegel with apparent approval, he states:

> "[T]he human, the finite, the frail, the weak, and the negative are all features of the divine. All this is in God himself; otherness, finitude, negativity are not outside God. . . . [T]hey are an element of the divine nature itself." . . . This is of course the idea of the Trinity, indissolubly bound to the Cross and death of Christ; yet we can still ask whether Christ is to be regarded, on the one hand, as the unique historical event or, on the other, as the necessary, the highest "representation" of the most general law of being.[19]

In the end, it remains unclear what his answer is to this question, if it is not "both." It is interesting to see Balthasar summarizing Hegel in a way that could very well apply to his own thought (particularly in *TD* II and IV):

Trinity (for Balthasar), a point on which she also is not keen, her comments about deriving a Trinitarian theory from questionable exegesis of the "cry of dereliction" (on 107–108) are misguided.

Hence, Gerard O'Hanlon says:

> We saw how realistically Balthasar described this death—to the point of Christ's experience of the "second death" of the sinner in hell. It is Balthasar's argument that the Trinitarian personal distinctions, based on the opposition of relations, are indeed sufficiently real and infinite to embrace, without loss of unity, the kind of opposition between Father and Son which is involved in their common plan to overcome sin. This is so because divine love has the power freely to unfold its richness in such different modalities that the Son's experience of opposition in a hostile sense remains always a function and an aspect of his loving relationship to the Father in the Holy Spirit. (*The Immutability of God*, 119 [emphasis added])

But Balthasar does also at times utilize quasi-Hegelian language to describe the Trinitarian distinctions (see, e.g., *TD* IV, 325 [G 302]).

[18] See, for example, *TD* V, 213, 217f., 235 [G 291, 195f., 212]. For theological application (particularly, Origen's) of the Greek philosophical notion of apatheia, see Gerard O'Hanlon, *The Immutability of God*, 69.

[19] *TD* V, 226 [G 204].

Hegel emphasizes that the absolute Idea's self-expropriation—and its adoption of the categories of nature and history—becomes visible in the destiny of one man, Jesus Christ. In the end, however, this is only the visible appearance of a basic spiritual law, namely, that if there is to be a uniting of the "infinite with the finite," the finite must not cling to itself: it must surrender to the infinite.[20]

But adopting some aspects of Hegelian logic is a far cry from embracing it in the full force of its metaphysical and epistemological consequences or the Hegelian project as such.[21] The question of consistency and coherence in such cautious appropriation is always valid, nonetheless. Balthasar has this to say about the Hegelian dialectic: "We are not saying that the eternal separation in God is, in itself, 'tragic' or that the Spirit's bridging of the distinction is the sublation of tragedy, that is, 'comedy.' Nor are we saying, in a Hegelian sense, that the trinitarian drama needs to pass through the contradictions of the world in order to go beyond the 'play', to go beyond the 'abstract, and become serious and concrete.'"[22]

The influence of the German dialectical mode of thinking on Balthasar's conceptualization of Trinitarian life is already discernible in the second volume of the *Theodramatik*: "The hypostatic modes of being constitute for each other the greatest opposition we could think of (and so are always inexhaustibly transcendent to each other), precisely so that the most intimate interpenetration we could think of becomes possible."[23] Balthasar subscribes to both dialectical and dialogical "methods" as complementary in the second volume of the *Theologik*.[24] "Dialectic," classically understood, is prominent in Plato and other ancient authors, even though

---

[20] *TD* IV, 128 [G 118]).

[21] See Cyril O'Regan's *The Anatomy of Misremembering* for a thorough examination of Balthasar's anti-gnostic posture toward Hegelianism. In the context of defending Balthasar's conviction that Christ's kenosis must reveal something about the immanent Trinity, even while the immanent-economic distinction must be maintained, Vincent Holzer tries also to distance Balthasar's "analogical dialectic" from Hegel's "dialectic of identity" (see "La kénose christologique, 210–211, 233ff.).

[22] *TD* IV, 327 [G 304].

[23] *TD* II, 258 [G 234], cited and translated by Rowan Williams (better than Graham Harrison), "Balthasar and the Trinity," in *Cambridge Companion to Hans Urs von Balthasar*, 37–50, at 41.

[24] See *TL* II, 43ff. [G 40ff.]. Some use the term "dialogical" to distinguish Balthasar's methodology from that of Hegelian dialectical logic (e.g., see Aidan Nichols, *Say It Is Pentecost*, 71–72), but "dialectical" need not have Hegelian overtones or implications.

it does not take the same shape or form as in Hegel.[25] While Balthasar may intend to adhere more to Kierkegaard's literary-dialectical style, it might be argued that Kierkegaard himself, although it was almost his sole purpose to oppose Hegel, evidently could not escape entirely the influence of Hegelian logic.[26] This is because, while Kierkegaard flips Hegel on his head in giving primacy to the individual over the universal, he shares with him an implicit rejection of Aristotelian syllogism in favor of a form of dialectical reasoning that, while not confounding the first logical principle of contradiction, exhibits a proclivity to replace distinction, division, and definition with pure paradox.[27] Although Balthasar certainly utilizes some Hegelian *terminology*, at least he strives admirably to avoid the pitfalls of attempting to synthesize Thomistic analogical discourse with ide-

---

[25] Implicitly resisting accusations of Hegelian influence, Balthasar himself states: "the term dialectic has a unique, theological sense that must not be confused with any of the many meanings that philosophy has given it" (*TL* II, 238 [G 216]), adding: "Among these we can mention the Platonic art of conversation, Kant's 'dialectical appearance,' and Hegel's dialectical logic, in which thought and reality share a common, unitary movement" (238n44 [G 216n44]).

Even while still utilizing Hegelian terminology (especially in the *Theo-Logic*), he overtly attacks Hegel's dialectic in theology:

From the theological, and especially the Johannine, point of view, dialectic can occur only in the form of the denial of the one and only truth—that God is love, as he proves in giving up his Son—and so in the form of sin. Sin has no place in a "dialectic" (such as Hegel's) that claims philosophical neutrality. Yet this dialectic is only a late form of a theological dialectic that imagined it could or had to sublate the principle of noncontradiction by declaring that man simultaneously yea-says and gainsays, believes and disbelieves, loves and hates, is *Justus et peccator* [righteous and sinner]. (*TL* II, 317 [G 289])

Balthasar also criticizes Hegelian logic applied to the Trinity and Its relationship to creation, arguing that Hegel and Buddhism are ignorant of both sin and the Holy Spirit (see *TL* II, 336n32 [G 306n5]).

At the same time, it is undeniable that when it comes to the Cross, borrowing from Luther, he indulges in a dialectic that cannot simply be attributed to St. John in place of any philosopher: "In the suffering Lord there exists an unconquerable dialectic between the infinite suffering by means of which he [Christ] exhibits the effect of sin on God and the equally infinite suffering that, having been 'made sin' (2 Cor 5:21) on account of his unity with all sinners who offend God's love, he causes in God" (*TL* II, 325 [G 296], see also 326 [G 297]).

[26] See, e.g., Jon Stewart, *Kierkegaard's Relations to Hegel Reconsidered* (New York: Cambridge University Press, 2003).

[27] Despite these similarities, Balthasar does not much like Kierkegaard's own critique of Hegel; see O'Regan, *Anatomy of Misremembering*, 275–276, 584n2.

alist dialectical discourse (i.e., Hegel's radicalization of Kant's antinomous approach). Nonetheless, whether or not he succeeds is debated.[28] Matthew Levering, hinting at Balthasar's conspicuous incorporation of German dialectic into Thomistic metaphysics, comments on Balthasar's mutation of analogical discourse: "Once 'analogy' ultimately overturns the principle of contradiction, one wonders whether the limits of human language about God have been overstepped."[29] The question, of course, is whether Balthasar stretches analogy beyond the principle of contradiction, and if so, how precisely.

Balthasar generally intends to transition from dialectic to dialogic to analogic; the last item Aidan Nichols characterizes as "enquiry into reflection of the Trinity in the truth and being of the world."[30] Fergus Kerr notes that "[Balthasar and Erich Przywara] would agree that Aquinas's notion of analogy is not a semantic theory, just about the use of words, as many interpreters would say. On the contrary, the 'analogy of being' (not that Aquinas ever used the phrase) refers to the creature's real participation in the divine life, anticipated here and now by faith."[31] Nicholas

---

[28] Primarily concerned with the unity of the Trinity and pointing to Balthasar as one example of the problem, Bruce Marshall begins his argument: "Trinitarian theology has generally assumed it could avoid the theologically unhappy consequences they had in Hegel's own hands. But the confidence of theologians that they could embrace Hegel's novel Trinitarian claims while avoiding his radical revision of central Christian teachings has been, I will suggest, misplaced" ("The Absolute and the Trinity," 148).

In other words, Marshall deems it naïve to suppose that parts of Hegel's thought, at least with respect to the divine, may be appropriated without assuming the logical consequences drawn out by Hegel himself. His fundamental argument is that adoption of Hegelian dialectic in regard to the Trinity inevitably involves restricting the divine freedom to create.

While I agree that a conflation of immanent and economic Trinity does succumb to Hegel's denial of divine transcendence, Balthasar makes valiant efforts to preserve the distinction, even if he resists the Augustinian-Thomistic mode of reflection on the immanent Trinity in favor of the salvation-historical view, which sees the immanent Trinity only through the prism of the salvation economy. Ben Quash argues that Balthasar is significantly influenced by Hegel concerning aesthetics and drama (see J. B. Quash, "Between the Brutely Given").

[29] Levering, *Scripture and Metaphysics*, 132, cited by John Yocum, "A Cry of Dereliction?" 74n8.

[30] Nichols, "The Theo-logic," in *Cambridge Companion to Hans Urs von Balthasar*, 158–174, at 164.

[31] Kerr, "Balthasar and Metaphysics," in *Cambridge Companion to Hans Urs von Balthasar*, 225–226. For more on the relationship between Erich Przywara's and Balthasar's metaphysics, see James Zeitz, "Przywara and von Balthasar on Analogy," *The Thomist* 52 (1988): 473–498; Giovanni Marchesi, *La Cristologia Trinitaria di Hans Urs von*

Healy reflects on the analogical relationship between the immanent and economic dimensions for Balthasar:

> The relation between the events of the economy and the eternal processions within the Godhead is one of analogy (difference-within-unity). The simple reason for this distinction is the ontological difference between God and the finite world. A God who does not radically transcend the process of world history is a mythological God unworthy of belief. However, this abiding difference does not mean that the immanent Trinity is merely formal or static, with the seriousness of love and death reserved for the economic Trinity. In fact, the economic Trinity reveals just the opposite to be the case: "The immanent Trinity must be understood to be that eternal, absolute self-surrender whereby God is seen to be, in himself, absolute love; this in turn explains his self-giving to the world as love, without suggesting that God 'needed' the world process and the Cross in order to become himself."[32]

This type of reasoning, more than being a product of Hegelian influence, results from his dialogue with Karl Barth, whose influence is indisputable and whose rapprochement with process thought is disputable.[33] But, as John Webster notes, he goes beyond Barth's Christocentrism:

> [B]oth [Balthasar and Barth] explore how God's saving works and God's immanent being are mutually interpretative, particularly through reflecting on the obedience of the Son as the form of the intratrinitarian relations. In both, this issues in a doctrine of God which registers the effects on trinitarian teaching of the Son's

---

Balthasar: Gesu Cristo pienezza della ivelazione e della salvezza. (Brescia, Italy: Queriniana, 2003), 224–226.

Marchesi notes that Balthasar later shifts away from his earlier assessment of Przywara in his "Die Metaphysik Erich Przywara," *Schweizer Rundschau* 33 (1933): 489–499, towards adopting Nicholas of Cusa's "non-other" in his *Herrlichkeit* III/1, 956.

[32] *Being as Communion*, 129. Balthasarians sometimes make too much of analogy as a heuristic for understanding the entirety of Balthasar's theology, stretching the proper notion beyond recognition; see, e.g., Georges de Schrijver, *Le merveilleux accord de l'homme et de Dieu: Étude de l'analogie de être chez Hans Urs von Balthasar* (Leuven: Leuven University Press, 1983).

[33] Barth's influence is well known, but for Balthasar's relationship to Barth, see especially D. Stephen Long, *Saving Karl Barth;* see also John Webster, "Balthasar and Karl Barth," in *Cambridge Companion to Hans Urs von Balthasar*, 241–255.

act of self-emptying, though without imperiling the aseity of God. Though Balthasar presses the logic of kenosis further than Barth, his core claim ("that the God-man can surrender himself to God-abandonment, without resigning his own reality as God"; *MP*, 81) is explicitly derived from Barth.[34]

Perhaps, then, Balthasar would have done better to emphasize his Barthian inheritance over and against his sympathy for Moltmann's intentions. Yet it is up to Barth scholars to determine to what extent process theology may have influenced even Barth.[35] Even though he is not fundamentally Hegelian (like Moltmann), Balthasar sometimes tends to capitulate too much to contemporary death of God theology, which nonetheless itself is sublated by the Trinitarian theology that he extracts from the mystical visions of Adrienne von Speyr, who certainly exerted the most profound influence.[36]

In any case, O'Hanlon offers a compelling defense of Balthasar's understanding of the divine being as "Trinitarian event," arguing that God's eternal being is both immutable and "super-mutable."[37] Central to this

---

[34] Webster, "Balthasar and Karl Barth," in *Cambridge Companion to Hans Urs von Balthasar*, 252.

[35] Balthasar himself considers Barth to be "unthinkable apart from Hegel" (*Theo-Logic: Theological Logical Theory*, vol. 3, *The Spirit of Truth*, trans. Graham Harrison [San Francisco: Ignatius Press, 2005], 40 [*Theologik*, Band III, *Der Geist der Wahrheit* (Einsiedeln: Johannes Verlag, 1987), 34]. In response to Bruce Marshall's article, "The Absolute and the Trinity," which targets the appropriation of Hegelian dialectic to Trinitarian theology in authors like Balthasar, Paul D. Molnar, although essentially in agreement with Marshall's critique, adds Barthian considerations distinct from what Balthasar seems to be advocating ("A Response: Beyond Hegel with Karl Barth and T. F. Torrance," 173).

While I sympathize with his reflections in terms of the Athanasian rule, I think the predication of pain to the divinity must be one of metaphorical analogy, even though the union of the Son's divinity to Christ's humanity is hypostatic, precisely because it is a question of how the divine suffers in the human.

[36] The notional link between Moltmann and Speyr seems to be Russian kenoticism, especially as seen in Bulgakov (see, e.g., *TD* IV, 314 [G 292]); but this is merely a peripheral observation of similarities, not a historical claim. To see how Adrienne von Speyr's thought factors into Balthasar's, see especially Michele M. Schumacher, *A Trinitarian Anthropology*.

[37] For this notion in Balthasar, see, e.g., the interesting footnote in *TD* III, 159n18 [G 145n18]; see also *TL* II, 352 [G 321]. Ben Quash notes the patristic origin of some of his more controversial points:

Maximus the Confessor had prepared the ground for Balthasar's elevation of

notion that there is an event-quality to the divine being is the idea that in God is the perfection of both being and becoming, as if the perfection of becoming is not simply *ipsum esse*.[38] It is argued that *ipsum esse* is not as "static" as it is commonly assumed to be, but rather contains within it both the staticity of being and the pure dynamism of becoming (hence the event-quality of the Trinitarian life).[39] O'Hanlon wants to clarify that

---

existence to the level of a special mode of being (perhaps even the most divine mode), in order to overcome the difficulties with the language of essence (see *CL*, 56–57). Gregory of Nyssa had argued for the suitability of dynamic categories for description of the immanent life of God (*TD* 5, 77). His galvanized ontology of the divine life can lead him to suggest that it is not only love which has a heavenly form that can tentatively (analogically) be attributed to the Trinitarian Persons, but that faith and hope have such a heavenly form too. Human experiences of faith and hope have their analogical counterparts in the way that the Persons of the Trinity are eternally oriented to one another in anticipation while eternally having this mutual anticipation met, rewarded, and exceeded in the response of the others. ("The theo-drama," in *Cambridge Companion to Hans Urs von Balthasar*, 151–152)

Regarding the influence of Maximus on Balthasar's thought, see Cyril O'Regan, "Von Balthasar and Thick Retrieval." Pitstick argues that Balthasar misinterprets Maximus: "Development of Doctrine or Denial," 141.

38 Hence, it strains the limits of language to justify Balthasar's use of the term "event" in reference to God's inner life as "analogous" (see Anne Hunt, *The Trinity and the Paschal Mystery* [Collegeville, MN: Liturgical Press, 1997], 63). On the merely metaphorical character of attributing mixed perfections (purified by the *via eminentiae*), see, e.g., *The Catholic Encyclopedia: An International Work of Reference on the Constitution, Doctrine, and History of the Catholic Church*, vol. 2, ed. Charles G. Herbermann et al. (New York: Robert Appleton Co., 1907), 63.

39 Guy Mansini argues that the Balthasarian "event" must exist in itself (as substance), if it is not to be process or becoming, and adds: "If one wants to think of such an 'in itself' as a pure event, as a pure liveliness, then what is wanted, it would seem, is a sort of pure act—a line of thought already well developed in the history of Western theology and metaphysics" ("Balthasar and the Theodramatic Enrichment of the Trinity," 518).

To the objection that such an argument unduly forces Balthasar's thought into Aristotelian categories, Mansini responds:

This is not a matter of a Thomistic and Aristotelian account of change versus some other possibility of thought. There is no other analysis of change besides that of Aristotle. There are denials of change, from Parmenides to (in his own way) Hume. There are assertions that some kinds of change are really other kinds of change, as with the reduction of qualitative to quantitative change in materialism. There are assertions of novelty with no ground or cause, with Nietzsche and Bergson. There are reversals of the priority of act to potency, with Hegel. But there is no analysis of change, a location of the principles of change, except that of Aristotle. It is hard to see how the invocation of a change in God

this is not a capitulation to process theology:

> Within this context [of trinitarian kenosis] there is no simple identification, as in Process Theology, between the world process (including the cross) and the eternal, timeless "process" of the divine hypostases. The economic does not constitute the immanent Trinity. Rather, we must tentatively approach the mystery of the inner-trinitarian event by means of a negative theology which rules out any inner-wordly experience and suffering in God, and yet which establishes that the conditions for the possibility of such realities outside God are in fact to be found within God. But these realities of pain outside God have Christological and trinitarian implications, so that one is then forced to conclude that the trinitarian event must also allow God to participate in suffering.[40]

While the God of the philosophers may be immutable being, the God of Christian revelation, it is thought, must be "something more," namely, infinitely dynamic—this seems to cohere better with the vision of God as Trinitarian life, the very life of *amor ipsum*.[41] Certainly, there is even more to the God of revelation than is discoverable in the realm of pure philosophy, but it is another question whether that "something more" is aptly expressed in the terminology of dynamism.

Evidently, speaking of God in terms of event involves more than simply affirming dynamism of the life of divine love. O'Hanlon states:

> This emptying [of cross and incarnation] is real even if throughout it God still remains God. This means that an historical event affects God. This is so even though the temporal cross is pres-

---

unlike that which we find in our earthly experience, therefore, can be anything more than words. Change requires passive potency; it requires composition in the subject of change. To speak of change that is not like this, that does not involve a passage from potency to act, is not to speak of anything at all. ("Balthasar and the Theodramatic Enrichment," 518)

[40] O'Hanlon, *The Immutability of God*, 38.

[41] After much ado about the intra-Trinitarian freedom of the divine processions (against Thomas), Antoine Birot states: "These things cannot be understood unless the mystery of God is seen to be, from the beginning, a mystery of love, and thus in a metaphysical sense as both being and event simultaneously" ("The Divine Drama, from the Father's Perspective: How the Father Lives Love in the Trinity," *Communio* 30 [Fall 2003]: 406–429, at 413n10 [emphasis original]).

ent eternally in God so that it is real in God "before," "during," and "after" its earthly occurrence and, in particular, even after the resurrection, the cross of Jesus is an abiding reality in heaven, the eternal God being capable of containing all these different modalities. There is a great mystery here, in the way a temporal event can be present to God eternally and can affect God albeit in a non-temporal way.[42]

Thus, Antonio Lopez, also arguing for the event-quality of being, states: "Beings, then, can be considered events inasmuch as they appear proceeding from being itself, the ever-greater ground that does not have 'beyond itself,'" and concludes that there is "a real identification between the being-given of every phenomenon and its ontological structure."[43] Yet he thinks it is Balthasar's "understanding of eternity that prevents Balthasar from confusing event with historical becoming," according to which "Being is Super-Becoming."[44] But there is a tendency here to conflate the self-manifestation of being with being itself (i.e., phenomenology and metaphysics) in an attempt to transcend the limits of ontological-analogical discourse, which ends up succumbing to the perils of onto-theology that it intends to avoid.[45] Hence, there is more at stake here than word choice.

---

[42] O'Hanlon, *The Immutability of God*, 28.

[43] Antonio Lopez, "Eternal Happening: God as an Event of Love," *Communio* 32 (Summer 2005): 214–245, at 218–219.

[44] Lopez, 233.

[45] In addition to the Heideggerian attempt to "transcend" classical ontology, there is the "transcendental" method, which tends to adopt a Kantian mentality according to which phenomena alone are available for analysis, relegating the "noumenon" to the realm of the unknown. Anne Hunt, for instance, in the process of saving the "psychological analogy" for the Trinitarian life from Balthasarian critique, utilizes Lonergan's later work to conclude:

> [A] (theo)logic that is based, not on refined philosophical notions of being and the logic of reason, but on the phenomenon of love tangibly disclosed in the paschal mystery . . . serves to deconstruct not systematics as such but the metaphysical in systematics. It challenges the philosophically fashioned notions of God we have come to accept and arouses the healthy suspicion that perhaps it is metaphysics rather than revelation that has led us to understand God as a being with these divine perfections. The result is a theology that is demonstrably better equipped to meet the contemporary demand for evidence of God and the very plausibility of Christian faith in that context. ("Psychological Analogy and Paschal Mystery in Trinitarian Theology," *Theological Studies* 59 [1998]: 197–218, at 217)

Despite my paraphrasing of the argument from the perspective of the analogy of being, the argument seems to be fundamentally Christological[46]—it is not an accident that Balthasar notoriously designates Christ as the Incarnation of such analogy, the "concrete *analogia entis*":[47]

> [T]here is the basis in God for what can become suffering. . . . It seems strange that the kind of influence which the earthly life of Jesus has on the *persons* of the Trinity should have no foundation at all in their own *nature*. . . . Christ's humanity is an appropriate expression of the divinity. . . . [T]he obedience of Christ [is] the supreme manifestation of the divine being. . . . [T]he whole being of the Son is there to express and represent the Father. . . . [Created realities] point to a mode of love that embraces a self-giving to the point of being freely affected by the other, and a divine enrichment that is neither necessary, nor temporal, nor caused by anything external to God.[48]

So does it make sense to speak of this Trinitarian life as an eternal event? One last comment from O'Hanlon is necessary to assess the meaning Balthasar evidently intends to convey:

> The relationship between God and Christ is one of *expression* and of *dialogue*. . . . By "expression," a term developed in some detail by Balthasar in his treatment of Bonaventure, he does not mean that Christ is a mere reduplication of the Father. Rather—and this takes us on to the second aspect of the relationship—Christ is personally other than the Father, so that God is revealed as a trinitarian event in which there is mutual interaction and dialogue between the personal poles. In being so clear about the tri-personal nature

---

46 Hence, Lopez adds: "There can be no speech about God apart from what the person of Christ reveals of God . . . the very person of Christ presents himself as an event" ("Eternal Happening," 221–222).

47 As Aidan Nichols, OP, notes: "After the writing of his Barth book, variant versions of this formula pullulate in Balthasar's work," citing *A Theology of History*, 74, and *Epilog*, 69 (see Nichols, *A Key to Balthasar*, 85n91). See also *TD* III, 221–222 [G 203]. Regarding Balthasar's Christocentric metaphysics, see Junius Johnson, *Christ and Analogy: The Christocentric Metaphysics of Hans Urs von Balthasar* (Minneapolis, MN: Fortress Press, 2013). For more on the significance of Christological debates in Balthasar's theology, see Cyril O'Regan, "Von Balthasar and Thick Retrieval."

48 O'Hanlon, *The Immutability of God*, 44–45.

of the mysteriously one, identical, absolute, divine being, Balthasar is affirming the reality of a real I/Thou exchange within God who is love.[49]

Granted, love is an interpersonal reality, but I fail to see exactly what dialogue has to do with event, process, becoming (that is, *change*)—eternal dialogue need not be mutable. Either God is eternally self-changing because of His interpersonal nature (and then there is little in the way of saying He can be changed by creatures, particularly since God became one) or there is no change, no process, no event-quality to the infinite love that constitutes His hypostatically interpersonal nature.[50]

The fact that God became man, that Christ reveals something (in fact, a great deal!) about God, and even that therefore God may be said to be affected (at least, in some sense) by the sins of men, none of this seems to

---

[49] O'Hanlon, 47.

[50] Confusion (i.e., the potential for equivocation) abounds when Lopez attempts to stretch the meaning of event to include both the mutable and immutable, citing Balthasar's dependence on Speyr's *World of Prayer*, 28–74:

> The relation of love between the Father, Christ, and the Holy Spirit just described compels us, Balthasar contends, to perceive God as a triune mystery of love, a love that is both an eternal being (*esse*) and an eternal *event* (*Geschehn, Ereignis*) of absolute donation. To qualify the divine essence in terms of event may seem a little too daring if we insist on including all the various connotations this term can have. . . . "[E]vent" refers to the unpredictable taking place of something, whose historical coming-to-be out of a transcendent ground that is different from itself first causes wonder and then sets in motion a process of expectation and fulfillment. Moreover, events appear and come to pass: this temporal finitude is yet another sign of the ontological difference that both separates them from and unites them to their source. The concept of event is broad enough to include also that which is not necessarily positive: in fact, since it appears legitimate to think of event from the point of view of real donation, it seems difficult to exclude the possibilities of risk, loss, and even rejection. As we have seen, on the one hand, one could describe creation, historical occurrences, and phenomena as such as events; on the other hand, one could rightly claim that Christianity itself is most adequately understood as an event (Jn 1:14). Can this term also refer to divine love itself? After a painstaking passage from the missions of the Son and the Holy Spirit to the immanent Trinity, Balthasar contends not only that it can, but, even more radically, that every other event is to be understood in light of the trinitarian event, i.e., the absolute mystery whose life is an agapic threefold donation in which each one wants the other to be, lets the other be, consents to its generation or inspiration, prays to the other and lives with the other an eternal conversation of expectation and fulfillment, unfathomable gratitude and surprise. ("Eternal Happening," 225–226)

warrant employing terms of mutability (like surprise, gratitude, risk, etc.).[51] There is simply no reason to import the mutability of Christ's human nature into the immutable being of *ipsum esse*. The inner life of the Trinitarian God need not be an amalgamation of being and becoming in order not to be static—being is not static insofar as this means inert, but dynamic insofar as such denotes activity (as opposed to passivity). Thus, if "event" implies temporality, then it cannot apply to the divine life, assuming one grants the status of the supreme being as *actus purus*. Hence, the language of "event" when speaking of the Trinitarian processions must be designated, at best, as metaphorical since it does not precisely indicate in what sense God might be receptive and tends to connote passivity ("happening").

THE "METAPHOR DEFENSE"

Kevin Duffy argues against what he calls "the metaphor defense" of Balthasar on divine impassibility, opposing as incoherent the argument of Gerard O'Hanlon (and Thomas Dalzell)[52] that Balthasar's predica-

---

[51] Lopez attempts to spin a definition of surprise in God that is not incongruent with immutability thus:

> [C]ontrary to what often happens among human beings, surprise in God does not mean that one of the persons unexpectedly discloses to the others what was previously, avariciously, kept secret. Rather, it has to do first of all with the fact that the hypostases are eternally other (person), and, second, with the mysterious nature of the reciprocal gift that the eternal happening of God is: the ever-greater, personal, gratuitous love that generates gratitude both for the gift that is eternally given and received and for the "expectation" that is always already "fulfilled." This gratitude, when seen from the point of view of the eternal over-fulfillment of the divine expectation, is a fundamental element of what Balthasar calls surprise. ("Eternal Happening," 241–242)

[52] In defense of Balthasar's thesis that the Trinity is in some ways enriched by its relationship to creation, Dalzell has recourse to the "metaphor defense" that Duffy in turn rebuts:

> When Balthasar talks about the Trinitarian event in terms of an eternal "I-thou" relationship, he is clearly speaking analogically. But when he starts to describe the dynamism of that "I-thou" in terms of suffering, surprise, and increase, he is using properly metaphorical language. He argues that concepts alone fail to tell us much about the mystery of God's love and must be combined with metaphor and image. To his mind, this way of paradox yields more knowledge than conceptual thought alone, and is closer to the approach of the Scriptures. Yet, if this use of metaphor means suspending the objections from negative (apophatic) theology, Balthasar does recognise that metaphorical language can be stretched too far and needs a corrective. Hence if he thinks "the metaphysical without

tion of change, suffering, and surprise to God is justifiable on the basis of Balthasar's unique blend of metaphor and analogy. Striving to clarify the difference between metaphor and analogy, Duffy responds to the Balthasarian claim that "God is metaphorically super-mutable, but in a non-creaturely way" by engaging contemporary philosophical discussions of metaphor, siding ultimately with Thomas's restriction of analogical predication (in the case of God) to created realities that do not involve intrinsic imperfection.[53] In Duffy's view, Balthasar so blurs the line between metaphorical and literal (analogical) predication that his predications of suffering to God cannot be merely metaphorical and the value of analogical predication in theological discourse is undermined.[54] The result is confusion: "For 'I-thou' discourse between the divine persons is analogous; divine surprise at the content of their dialogue is metaphorical. A statement that God is immutable is analogous; to say that he is super-mutable is metaphorical."[55] O'Hanlon's argument seems to be that mutability, in Balthasar, can be both affirmed and denied of God in different respects such that the *via eminentiae* takes precedence, and yet Duffy illustrates that only metaphor can be both affirmed and denied and still remain coherent. In the end, it is apparently unimportant to Balthasar to clarify when a predication is metaphorical and when it is properly analogical; thus, Duffy accuses him of a "qualified pan-metaphoricism," a perspective that Balthasar does not seek to justify.

Furthermore, Duffy claims that certain statements are by their very nature to be taken literally, not metaphorically, and that "I cannot make a statement such as 'there is super-change in God' metaphorical simply by saying that I am speaking metaphorically or that I am associating my statement with a metaphor."[56] He argues that metaphor and simile are generally equivalent and that where a real simile exists, the predication cannot be then denied, whereas when Balthasar says, "there is something like change in God," it would not make sense for him later to say that, literally speaking, there is nothing like change in God, and therefore his affirmation is

---

the metaphorical is empty," he does accept that "the metaphorical without the metaphysical is blind." ("The Enrichment of God," 8)

[53] Duffy, "Von Balthasar's Use of Metaphor," 375: "Some terms can only be used metaphorically [of God], because creatureliness is part of their meaning. Change, suffering, and surprise, like courage, sorrow and contrition, imply creaturely imperfection."

[54] See Duffy, 379, citing Blankenhorn, "Von Balthasar's Method of Divine Naming," *Nova et Vetera* [English Edition] 1, no. 2 (2003): 245–268, at 257.

[55] Duffy, 380.

[56] Duffy, 383–384.

a literal one.[57] After taking out such "hard distinctions," Duffy confesses:

> Von Balthasar's understanding of the divine nature stands or falls on whether or not new analogical senses of change, suffering, and surprise can pass muster in their own right. The nub of von Balthasar's project, as articulated in the metaphor defense, is to bring what is proper to poetry and symbolism into theological language by extracting what is most distinctive in metaphor and expressing it in literal, analogical terms. . . . [L]iteral statements containing expressions such as "super-change" or "something like change" would have to be vehicles for what, in metaphors, escapes paraphrase and is intimated rather than asserted.[58]

It remains unclear not only how something that is intimated may be asserted, but also whether there are any metaphorical statements about God that yield anything significant for our knowledge of God as such.

It seems from Balthasar's adamant use of such rhetorical excess that he wants to restore to metaphor an epistemic validity that equals that of literal predication (in this case, analogical), and this on the basis of the centrality of metaphor in Scripture's language about God (particularly in the Old Testament). And this does not necessitate collapsing all knowledge into the realm of the metaphorical.[59] But Duffy concludes his essay thus:

---

[57] Duffy, 384.

[58] Duffy, 386. Hence, O'Regan seems to argue that Balthasar's divine discourse is fundamentally symbolic (or "meta-symbolic") (see, e.g., *Anatomy of Misremembering*, 228). Anthony C. Sciglitano, Jr., with O'Regan's tacit approval, judges that O'Regan's Balthasar strives to go beyond not only equivocity and univocity, but even analogy itself, because of its "linear logic" or "the inability of conceptual and categorical terms," such as impassibility and immutability, to apply to divine dynamism (see Sciglitano, "Death in Cyril O'Regan's *The Anatomy of Misremembering*," *Nova et Vetera* [English Edition] 14, no. 3 [2016]: 1003–1014, at 1011; cf. O'Regan's reply in the same volume to Sciglitano's commentary on his book, "Response to Readers of *The Anatomy of Misremembering*, Volume 1 (*Hegel*)," 1015–1025, at 1016–1018).

[59] While Duffy briefly reports the views of George Lakoff and Nicholas Lash that theological discourse is universally metaphorical and cites radical statements of Anthony Kenny and Robert Butterworth (see "Von Balthasar's Use of Metaphor," 380–381), a veritable slippery slope argument against what he calls the "metaphor defense" of Balthasar's fluid usage of analogical and metaphorical predication, he neglects to mention that it is typical of transcendental Thomists, who frequently draw upon Paul Ricoeur as well, to speak of language as fundamentally metaphorical, particularly in the realm of theology, since what transcends ordinary experience is being approached. Despite his eventual misgivings with this school of thought, represented for him principally by Rahner,

Given the way in which human language works—its *modus signif-icandi* (mode of signifying)—von Balthasar is to be seen as trying to state what cannot be stated literally. Predicating change, suffering, and surprise of God, he tries to give literal expression to what in metaphors is essentially non-propositional, and to what is intimated or suggested rather than asserted. The result in a classical context is incoherence.[60]

Is human language really so restrictive? Certainly, poets daily attempt to put in words what cannot be expressed, at least in prose. But the point is that Balthasar is purportedly writing theology, not poetry. That is precisely the problem—to what degree ought mystical utterances be translated into rational discourse? Perhaps "kataphatic excess" is the inevitable result of such a project. Duffy's proposed remedy is to pay greater attention to the Chalcedonian distinction between the divine and human natures of Christ.[61]

If change, suffering, and surprise cannot be predicated of God either metaphorically or literally, then they are such imperfect realities that they cannot find any place in God, however one conceives these realities, which seems an unacceptable conclusion in light of the events of salvation history (particularly, the redemptive Incarnation). While I think it is necessary to emphasize the *communicatio idiomatum* and the lack of a precise understanding of the relationship between grace and nature contributes to Balthasar's shift toward a "neo-Chalcedonianism," it is also true that the horizon of grace has so perfected nature through Christ that we can learn something, even if it remains beyond the realm of propositional truth, about the love that is God through a modest phenomenological analysis of human love in its primordial innocence. Hence, O'Hanlon replies to Duffy:

> Qualities like increase ("ever-more"), receptivity, and surprise have not, of course, traditionally been seen as perfections, and this is where von Balthasar's claim will stand or fall. Arguing from the human experience of love, von Balthasar notes that love given is not perfected until received, that mystery increases rather than decreasing in proportion to greater intimacy, so that a knowledge that is "already in the picture" is symptomatic of a

---

Balthasar does not seem exempt from this "transcendentalist" error; see *TL* II, 273–275 [G 247–248].

[60] Duffy, "Von Balthasar's Use of Metaphor," 387.

[61] See Duffy, 387.

love grown cold. Again, where love is on the way to perfection, there exists a reserve and discretion that allow and want the other to be other in a way that preserves the freedom of self-giving and the creativity, wonder, and surprise which accompany that freedom. As Duffy notes, materiality and composition, including of course temporality, are intrinsically creaturely and so may not be predicated analogously of God. But, with careful modification, even "light" and "generation" may so be predicated, perhaps even "desire" (Rowan Williams in Duffy) and certainly liveliness.[62]

Of course, as beautiful as such expressions may be at first sight, it is incumbent upon the theologian to parse out with precision what exactly is being said and determine which claims can be justified.

Thus, Bernhard Blankenhorn, OP, while pointing to the role of Speyr's mysticism and dialogical philosophy as detrimental,[63] focuses precisely on Balthasar's peculiar employment of the doctinre of divine naming via the *analogia entis*, which he understands in dialogue with Karl Barth (imitating Erich Pzywara's example).[64] Blankenhorn argues effectively that Balthasar seems to distort the *via eminentiae* in particular by "operating on the premise that creaturely limitation must have its foundation in God,"[65] that is, by "his refusal to fully negate attributes found in creation that seem to be intrinsically tied to limitations."[66] Straining the limits of language, Balthasar wants to predicate death, surprise, becoming, potentiality, and other notions ruled out by Aquinas's threefold method of divine naming.[67] Balthasar's insufficiently apophatic approach to divine naming results in the projection onto the inner life of God notions that are peculiar to created reality, such as the fact that freedom needs time and space to respond to love with thanksgiving.[68]

Blankenhorn argues that contrary to the interpretation common to O'Hanlon and Dalzell, Balthasar does not speak of his theological pred-

---

[62] O'Hanlon, "A Response to Kevin Duffy," 182.
[63] See Blankenhorn, "Balthasar's Method of Divine Naming," 245–268, at 253, 256, 261, 263, 265.
[64] Joseph Palakeel explores this as well, without very convincing evaluative judgements, in *The Use of Analogy in Theological Discourse: An Investigation in Ecumenical Perspective* (Rome: Pontificia Universita Gregoriana, 1995), chs. 1–3.
[65] Blankenhorn, "Balthasar's Method," 255.
[66] Blankenhorn, 263.
[67] See Blankenhorn, 245.
[68] See Blankenhorn, 253.

ications in terms of metaphor because metaphor for him is an inadequate basis for real knowledge of God through revelation.[69] Perhaps Balthasar does not sufficiently appreciate metaphor as a unique form of analogical predication in theological discourse, but Blankenhorn hastily dismisses the possibility that receptivity may in a qualified sense be a simple perfection. Recognizing receptivity as a perfection does not require "posit[ing] the ability to be *negatively* affected by another as divine perfection,"[70] nor does it correspond to a failure to distinguish "the limited as limited and the limited as imperfect perfection,"[71] nor does it involve affirming "that potency as such is act as such, and becoming as such is being as such."[72] Still, Blankenhorn is right to assert:

> The understanding of the content of supernatural revelation, however, itself requires reason and philosophical analogies. We must bring a philosophical understanding of humanity to the revelation of Christ, and while this understanding must be perfected by grace, it must include true philosophical insights into human nature. We cannot say what is creaturely and what is divine if we refuse to distinguish the content of the revelation of Christ and the humanity of Christ. Without a philosophical *analogia entis* that plays a determining role in the interpretation of revelation, the image and the original would fuse into one, and we would have no way of distinguishing the two.[73]

It is for this reason that Speyr's mystical imagery, which Balthasar does not sufficiently appropriate for theological discourse, must be philosophically demythologized. In other words, the problem for Balthasar is that he attempts to fuse metaphorical discourse with analogical predication, thus leaving little room for philosophico-theological precision.

DIVINE SELF-ENRICHMENT

Having addressed in cursory fashion a few recent theologies of impassibility that seem to have received Balthasar's attempt both to incorporate and

---

[69] See Blankenhorn, 257–258, quoting *Theologik* II. He also notes that this is the interpretation common to Thomas Rudolf Krenski, Margaret Turek, and Anne Hunt (see 258).
[70] Blankenhorn, 264.
[71] Blankenhorn, 267.
[72] Blankenhorn, 267. See the previous chapter for a bit more on this question.
[73] Blankenhorn, 266.

transcend Maritain's and Barth's perspectives on the matter, I will continue to employ the Thomistic reasoning exemplified in Maritain to decipher
whether or not the ultimate result of Balthasar's reflections on divine receptivity to creation may be acceptable in a revised, qualified form. Without engaging in the debate concerning the ontology of receptivity and *relatio* with respect to the intra-Trinitarian relations, which is beyond the
scope of this work,[74] I will argue that it does seem there is a sense in which
it can be said that the triune God "enriches" Himself through His own
creative activity insofar as diffusing one's glory into participatory manifestations may be designated "self-enriching."

The concluding paragraph of the entire *Theodramatik* asks, "What
does God gain from the world?" and answers, "[a]n additional gift" given
by each divine person to the other, as the world is given "divine things"
"and return[s] them to God as a divine gift" by its participation in the
interior life of God.[75] Thomas Dalzell thinks this aspect of Balthasar's
theology is opposed to Aquinas's position:

> God freely allows himself out of love, it is suggested, to be affected
> by the freedom he has made and any increase implied is situated

---

[74] Balthasar seems to use the principle that there is greater dissimilitude between God and
creation than similitude to speculate about the event-quality of God's inner-Trinitarian
processions: see, for example, *TL* II, 82–83 [G 76–78]. But concerning the relational
ontology that would be indispensable for further discussion of receptivity in God as
Trinity, see Norris Clarke, *Person and Being* (Milwaukee: Marquette University Press,
1998), an extended version of his article, "Person, Being, and St. Thomas," *Communio*
19, no. 4 (1992): 601–618; "Response to David Schindler's Comments," *Communio* 20,
no. 3 (1993): 593–598; "Response to Long's Comments," *Communio* 21, no. 1 (1994):
165–169; "Response to Blair's Comments," *Communio* 21, no. 1 (1994): 170–171; Hans
Urs von Balthasar, "On the Concept of Person," *Communio* 13, no. 1 (1986): 18–26;
Joseph Ratzinger, "Concerning the Notion of Person in Theology," *Communio* 17, no. 3
(1990): 439–454; David L. Schindler, "Norris Clarke on Person, Being, and St. Thomas," *Communio* 20, no. 3 (1993): 580–592; "The Person: Philosophy, Theology, and
Receptivity," *Communio* 21, no. 1 (1994): 172–190; Kenneth L. Schmitz, "The Geogra-
phy of the Human Person," *Communio* 13, no. 1 (1986): 27–48; "Selves and Persons: A
Difference in Loves?" *Communio* 18, no. 2 (1991): 183–206. For the critiques addressed
by Clarke and Schindler, see Steven A. Long, "Divine and Creaturely 'Receptivity': The
Search for a Middle Term," *Communio* 21, no. 1 (1994): 151–161, and George A. Blair,
"On *Esse* and Relation," *Communio* 21, no. 1 (1994): 162–164.

[75] *TD* V, 521 [G 476]. Thus, Healy begins his book on Balthasar presenting the concluding
section of *Das Endspiel* as the fundamental philosophical contribution of Balthasar's
dramatic theory to the metaphysical synthesis of Thomas Aquinas. See Healy's *Being as
Communion*, 1–6.

in an eternal increase resulting from the ongoing exchange of love constituted by the divine processions. While Aquinas understood creation in terms of a real relationship of dependence between the creature and God, he safeguarded God's transcendence by ruling out the existence of a real relationship between God and creation. The fact that Balthasar understands the increase implied by created freedom's affecting God to be over and above an already realized perfection of divine love ensures that God's transcendence is not compromised and so it can be argued that he makes a good case for leaving Thomas' position behind.[76]

Perhaps offering a defense of Balthasar's nuanced posture with respect to the notorious Thomistic notion that God has only a "virtual" (rather than a "real") relation to creation,[77] but more likely an exegesis in line with Maritain's speculations, Thomas Weinandy argues to the contrary that, according to Aquinas:

God is actually related, in reality, to the creature, not because of some change in him, but only because the creature is really related to him as he exists in himself as *ipsum esse*. It is because the creature is really related to God that we come to understand God in a new way as Creator. Thus God is in reality Creator and is actually related to the creature, but only because the creature is related to him as he is.[78]

Taking as a point of departure the medieval notion that created otherness is not a deficiency, Balthasar develops reflections on the giftedness of being as revealed in the experience of interpersonal love, phenomenologically examined.[79] To escape from Plotinian Platonism it is necessary

---

[76] Thomas G. Dalzell, *The Dramatic Encounter of Divine and Human Freedom in the Theology of Hans Urs von Balthasar* (New York: Peter Lang, 2000), 290.

[77] Regarding the different kinds of distinctions, see a neoscholastic manual, such as Celestine Bittle, *Ontology: The Domain of Being* (Milwaukee: Bruce, 1939), especially 155–161, on different kinds of logical distinction, particularly "virtual distinction," a term used frequently by other Thomists, such as Garrigou-Lagrange.

[78] Weinandy, *Does God Suffer?*, 136n69. Still, as Weinandy notes there, Aquinas is clear that "it cannot be said, however, that these relations exist as realities outside God" (*SCG* II, 13, 1).

[79] For development of this and related themes, see especially Kenneth L. Schmitz, *The Gift: Creation* (Milwaukee: Marquette University Press, 1982); D. C. Schindler, *Hans Urs von Balthasar and the Dramatic Structure of Truth: A Philosophical Investigation*

to affirm the "positivity" of created being—true, good, and beautiful.[80] Nicholas Healy explains how Thomas conceived the "positivity" of created otherness:

> As Thomas writes, "even the difference between one being and another is a being. Wherefore since God is not the cause of a thing tending to non-being, but is the author of all being, he is not the principle of evil, but he is the cause of multitude" [*De Potentia*, q. 3, a. 16, ad 3]. . . . [*E*]*sse* [which is non-subsistent in creatures] is a unity—it contains all the perfections of being—that, without ceasing to be one, contains a polarity within itself such that it depends on another. Difference is inscribed in the heart of the unity of being as something fundamentally positive.[81]

In other words, multiplicity is no longer conceived, in the Christian tradition, as a necessarily privative reality; both created multiplicity and divine multiplicity are good, even while God alone is perfectly one.[82] Therefore, while God cannot gain anything, strictly speaking, from finite beings, He does make Himself vulnerable to the realities He creates in such a way that His desires for them may either be fulfilled or frustrated.

Nonetheless, Weinandy disputes the related notion that only a triune God would be free not to create, citing Aquinas to the effect that the Creator is most fittingly triune.[83] James Buckley adds: "it is axiomatic for theo-

---

(New York: Fordham University Press, 2004).

[80] Hence, Balthasar states: "[Both Bonaventure and Thomas enunciate the axiom] that (derived, worldly) otherness vis-à-vis God presupposes an (original, Trinitarian) otherness in God, an otherness that, as such, is supreme positivity. We can immediately infer from this basic axiom that anyone who reckons the world's otherness as purely negative in comparison with the sheer divine One will *ipso facto* take a path radically divergent from that of Christianity" (*TL* II, 107 [G 99]).

Giovanni Marchesi notes that this is in contrast to Hegel's conception of the other as a "negative moment," adding that "the positivity of the 'other' in God" is the crucial point central to the *Theodrama* (see *La Cristologia Trinitaria*, 340–341 [my translation]).

[81] Healy, *Being as Communion*, 52.

[82] See Healy, ch. 2; Ratzinger, *Introduction to Christianity* (San Francisco: Ignatius, 2004), 178ff. [*Einführung in das Christentum* (München: Deutscher Taschenbuch, 1971), 165ff.]

[83] See Weinandy, *Does God Suffer?*, 139n75. Alluding to other influences, Weinandy offers the following insights:

> Immutability and impassibility must never be perceived, as Galot and von

logical drama that a non-Trinitarian God could not be Creator (*TD* IV, 54)."[84] Bruce Marshall, pointing to Hegel's influence as the catalyst of such thought, states: "nothing in the contingent history of creation or salvation realizes, perfects, intensifies, or otherwise alters the divine Persons in either their distinction or their unity."[85] Strictly speaking, Marshall is correct, according to perennial Christian doctrine, but the question remains whether there is some sense in which it might be said that the Trinitarian God, already entirely self-sufficient, is super-abundantly fulfilled, as it were, *ad extra,* through His own economic self-expressions in creation, Incarnation, passion-death-descent, Resurrection-ascent, and final judgment (and/or universal consummation).[86] Perhaps another way of stating the same is

---

Balthasar do, as stumbling blocks that need to be overcome, as if, despite being immutable and impassible, God is, nonetheless, in a dialectic fashion, still loving and merciful. Rather, God's immutability and impassibility are the absolute presuppositions and prolegomena for ensuring that he is perfectly loving. Moreover, by attempting to distinguish between God-in-himself and God-for-us, a distinction that is highly dubious in itself, they have placed a breach between God as he truly is and God who relates to us. Such a chasm is not only philosophically unwarranted, but it is also theologically detrimental to biblical revelation and the Christian tradition, which glories in the fact that God actually interacts with and relates to us as he truly is in the fullness of his divinity. God need not "re-fashion" himself in order to interact with us. (*Does God Suffer?,* 163n31)

He cites *ST* I, q. 45, a. 6; see also *ST* I, q. 32, a. 1, ad 1.

[84] "Balthasar's Use of Thomas," 531. Adjudicating the validity of this truth-claim would require a lengthy polemic on the possibility of a "natural theology." For one instance of this debate, see the symposium published in *Nova et Vetera* concerning Thomas Joseph White's *Wisdom in the Face of Modernity: A Study in Thomistic Natural Theology* (Ave Maria, FL: Sapientia Press, 2009), rev. ed. 2016, especially White's "Toward a Post-Secular, Post-Conciliar Thomistic Philosophy: Wisdom in the Face of Modernity and the Challenge of Contemporary Natural Theology," D. C. Schindler's "Discovering the Given: On Reason and God," and White's "Engaging the Thomistic Tradition and Contemporary Culture Simultaneously: A Response to Burrell, Healy, and Schindler," *Nova et Vetera* 10, no. 2 (2012): 521–530, 563–604, 605–623.

[85] Marshall, "The Absolute and the Trinity," 163.

[86] Balthasar apparently agrees with Rahner's opinion that the final judgment occurs at one's own death (*TD* V, 357 [G 326]), which would leave for the end of time only the "consummation of all things." Regardless, it is thanks to the God-man's transformative passion that His timeless love encounters the freedom of every man in the mysterious "moment" of his death (which is thus understood personalistically as an existential event); see my "The Possibility of Universal Conversion in Death." For Maritain, the consummation of all things will follow the final judgment in a progressive manner (see his "Beginning with a Reverie"). As Healy puts it, Christ "undergirds" death by His

to assert that, according to the intimate relationship between economic and immanent dimensions of the God of revelation, there would in fact be no creation if God were not a Trinity of subsistent relations.

It seems that, according to Balthasar's mode of thought, if God were not a Trinity, Hegel and process theology would be right,[87] as Gerard O'Hanlon asserts:

> If God were simply one he would become ensnared in the world-process through the incarnation and cross. But because God is triune, with both poles of difference and unity guaranteed by the Holy Spirit, the difference between Father and Son can accommodate all created differences including that extreme distance shown on the cross which becomes a revelation of the closest togetherness of Father and Son. In this way the ever-greater Trinitarian love of God is the presupposition of the cross.[88]

On the flip side, taking Balthasar's speculations about Trinitarian distance undergirding sinful distance as a point of departure, Richard Barry makes the intriguing claim that without "inter-Trinitarian distance," "there would be no space for genuine otherness (every distance would be collapsed), and there would be no space for finite freedom (every freedom would be overwhelmed), and thus there would be no sin; and there would be no love."[89] In other words, if God were an absolute monad, creation would not exist.[90] On the contrary, if the infinite goodness of the abso-

---

death (see *Being as Communion*, 204).

[87] This follows Bonaventure's persuasive Dionysian argumentation; see *Hexaemeron* XI, 11 (*Opera omnia*, vol. 5 [Quaracchi: Ed. Collegii S. Bonaventurae, 1891]), 381–382. Bonaventure also argues that if God were not a Trinity, He would not be the highest good (i.e., God): see *Itinerarium mentis in Deum*, ch. VI, 1–2 (*Opera omnia*, vol. 5, 310–311); ET, *Itinerarium mentis in Deum*, trans. Philotheus Boehner (St. Bonaventure, NY: Franciscan Institute, 1956), 89–91.

Similarly, Henry of Ghent argues that the world could not have been created with wisdom and freedom if God were not triune; see *Quodlibet* VI, q. 2 (*Opera omnia*, vol. 10, ed. Gordon A. Wilson [Louvain: Leuven University Press, 1987]), 33–40. Balthasar says the same, perhaps most clearly in *Christian Meditation*, trans. Theresilde Skerry (San Francisco: Ignatius Press, 1989), 61.

[88] O'Hanlon, *The Immutability of God*, 27.

[89] Barry, "Retrieving the Goat of Azazel," 23n37.

[90] Against the notion that it would be incoherent to think of God as personal without admitting His Trinitarian nature, see Christopher J. Malloy, "The 'I-Thou' Argument for the Trinity: Wherefore Art Thou?," *Nova et Vetera* [English Edition] 15, no. 1 (2017):

lute One is *diffusivum sui*, then creation would be necessary, unless within Himself being itself is communicated in an infinitely perfect manner, rendering creation almost superfluous. Yet created freedom exists; ergo, it must be fitting for the Trinitarian necessary being to communicate His love *ad extra* with perfect freedom.[91]

When commenting on this notion of "enrichment" in Balthasar's Trinitarian theology, Dalzell for one may not be careful enough to avoid what Marshall designates as the infiltration of Hegelian dialectic into Trinitarian theology, according to which the world is a dialogue partner, as it were, of God's own identity as supreme love:

> Balthasar claims that such receptivity on God's part is made possible by the eternal receptivity in God, the Son's receiving from the Father and the Father's receiving from the Son. . . . It is this positing of an excess (Überfluss) of loving in God that allows Balthasar to save the world's gift to God from being regarded as superfluous. While God's love is ever complete, its ever-greater dimension is perceived as making room for the world's contribution. Rather than the latter being understood as adding to God's love so as to complete it, it is thought to find its place in the ever-greater dimension of that love in such a way that what comes about can even be spoken of as an enrichment (*Bereicherung*) of heaven, a becoming ever-richer (*Je-reicher-Werden*) of the Trinity and an embellishment (*Ausschmuckung*) of the Father's richness.[92]

At the same time, I do not think it can be denied that God in His love is *de facto* incapable of being indifferent toward His own creation and that the self-effusiveness of the good, or the *ek*-static quality of love, is precisely the transcendent sufficient reason for being as a whole (that is, for *ens commune*).

113–159.

[91] I hold a "free inevitable tendency" of God both to create ex nihilo and to relate to His creation through the redemptive Incarnation, a point shied away from by many a Thomist and non-Thomist but essential to understanding how a divine contingent act can be identical to His necessity and how Maritain's understanding of divine permission can be true without introducing any dependency into God.

This free inevitable tendency both to create and redeem may be seen as essential to the constitutive relation of filiation. I cannot develop every element of this position here; hence, many points will have to remain implicit. See, for example, the brief comments of Norris Clarke, favoring Bonaventure over Thomas on the question of freedom in creation (*Explorations in Metaphysics*, 108–109).

[92] Dalzell, "The Enrichment of God," 15.

Dalzell concedes that "it is one thing to use an 'I-Thou' analogy to understand the love in God and another to describe that love, as Balthasar does, in terms of suffering, surprise, and increase."[93] Moreover, it is one thing to speculate on some analogue of receptivity in the divine intra-Trinitarian exchange and another to put such a notion at the center of one's Trinitarian theology, alongside infinite *ek-stasis*, as if one has familiarity with the inner workings of the divine life. It seems the most we can say about God is that in some sense He makes Himself receptive to the reality of evil, that His creative acts flow super-abundantly from His infinitely free love, and that the distinction of hypostases within His own nature is the prototypical origin of creaturely otherness (both as the world relates to its Creator and, derivatively, as finite things relate to one another).[94]

Clearly going beyond the realm of precise speculation, bordering on the mystical (which is necessarily nebulous to the human mind), Dalzell paraphrases some of Balthasar's more eccentric theorizing about the Trinitarian life:

> In letting the Son be, the Father is thought to give himself away to the Son. Indeed, the Father is said *to be* this "giving up movement," holding nothing back for himself. There is then, according to Balthasar, an absolute renunciation in the first divine person of being God alone, a letting go of being God and in that sense a divine Godlessness (*Gott-losigkeit*) out of love which, he proposes, pre-eminently lays a foundation for the very possibility of worldly Godlessness—that of those who have abandoned God but also the "Godlessness" of the one abandoned on the cross. . . . The Father doesn't cease to be God in expropriating himself, for it is precisely in that self-expropriation that the Father is God. . . . [T]he Son's reception of the divinity must, it is argued, include self-gift and this is understood in terms of a readiness to affirm his own being God as a loving response to the original *kenosis* of the Father. Balthasar will even go so far as to suggest that the Father "only" (but eternally) receives himself as Father when the Son "agrees" to be the Son.[95]

---

[93] Dalzell, 7.

[94] Balthasar argues the third point through Thomas and Bonaventure, utilizing particularly the interpretative work of Gustav Siewerth, throughout *TL* II, but especially at 179–186 [G 165–170].

[95] Dalzell, "The Enrichment of God," 6–7. Concerning the Holy Spirit, Dalzell continues:

The talk of godlessness in the Father's self-gift and the godlessness of hell-ish suffering seems more like an equivocation than a genuine analogy, but here we run up against the limits of language again when confronted with the reality of love that is expressed in suffering.

As created otherness mirrors Trinitarian difference for Balthasar, he finds in the Trinity the ground for his theology of the God-man's suffer-ings, expressed dialectically:

> The Son is eternally begotten by the Father: within the infinite divine nature, in other words, one Person is "let be" in absolute Otherness; what deep abysses are here! God has *always* plumbed them, but once a finite world of creatures has been opened up, these depths must be traversed stepwise as forms of alienation. Nonetheless these steps can only be taken as part of a journey already (and always) accomplished in the infinite Trinity. And when the particular mystery of the Son's Incarnation takes place, he traverses—as man and together with all sufferers and on their behalf—the realms of forsakenness that, as God, he has already (and has always) traversed.[96]

Balthasar here ties together everything in his *Theodramatik*, essentially a soteriological eschatology, founded ultimately on the Trinitarian life, which "undergirds" even the very possibility of evil and the redemptive Incarnation that takes it up. While O'Hanlon might be correct that, in some sense, "the Incarnation itself does affect God"—that is, God affects Himself through His own acts, as even God's transitive acts are also nec-essarily intransitive first[97]—nonetheless it goes beyond proper analogical

---

It is this dramatic giving and receiving of love in God that leads Balthasar to characterise the Holy Spirit as the 'correspondence' of fathering gift and filial answering gift. As the identity of giving gift and thanking gift, the Holy Spirit is said to be self-gift in the form of an absolute "We," which not only holds open the infinite difference between the "I" and the "Thou" in God, but eternally bridges it over. ("The Enrichment of God," 7)

For concise criticism of Balthasar's Trinitarian theology, see Bertrand de Margerie, SJ, "Note on Balthasar's Trinitarian Theology," trans. Gregory F. LaNave, *The Thomist* 64 (2000): 127–130.

[96] *TD* V, 502 [G 459] (emphasis original).

[97] Still, I do not see justification for asserting as he does in the same sentence, "its reality is present and effective within the divine event" (*Immutability of God*, 24 [emphasis added]), as if God's being is infinite becoming.

discourse to assert "the incorporation of godforsakenness into the Trinitarian relation of love," as Balthasar himself does.[98]

CONCLUSION

Building on previous argumentation in favor of Maritain's creatively Thomistic position on divine impassibility, I have sought here to engage the best of the secondary literature on Balthasar and his utilization of kenoticism in addressing the problem of the way God relates to moral evil, primarily with respect to the Trinitarian dynamic in his *Theodramatik* as it has been received, critiqued, and defended. Certainly, Balthasar displays significant differences with Hegel and even Moltmann, indubitable differences indeed. Yet that does not negate the fact that throughout his engagement with philosophical modernity he seeks a rapprochement with post-Hegelian theology, not merely a refutation of its misremembrance of Christian tradition, capitulating at least in part on the question of divine impassibility.[99]

Assuming a particular paradigm on the relationship between infinite and finite freedom, Balthasar cannot understand God's relationship to the reality of evil in the same way in which a Thomist such as Maritain does. He must, therefore, revert to reflections from the "death of God" theology, which he nevertheless attempts to temper and modify, in order to account for God's relationship to evil and suffering. The Trinitarian "undergirding" of sin itself points up the intricate connection that exists between Balthasar's implicit theology of evil and his staked-out position on the question of divine impassibility. It also indicates where Balthasar sees the potential resolution of the aporia between God's infinite love and man's final rejection of His glory, namely, in God becoming "sin who knew

---

[98] *Theodramatik*, Band IV, 236; cf. *TD* V, 261, translated more ambiguously by Graham Harrison.

[99] Cyril O'Regan, in his magisterial treatment of Balthasar's engagement with modern (particularly, German) philosophy, admits as much: see *Anatomy of Misremembering*, 241 and 262. He also seems to acknowledge the legitimacy of Thomas Weinandy's "subtle criticism" in *Does God Suffer?* (see 242). However, Rodney Howsare highlights, in his view, Balthasar's constructive engagement with Hegelian thought, despite obvious differences (see his "Why Hegel? A Reading of Cyril O'Regan's *Anatomy of Misremembering*, Volume 1," *Nova et Vetera* [English Edition] 14, no. 3 [2016]: 983–992).

Balthasar's appropriation of (Russian) kenoticism goes hand in hand with the influence Barth's appropriation of Calvinistic Augustinianism exerted on his thought. For more detail on this claim, see my "The Possibility of Refusal: Grace and Freedom in Balthasar," *Josephinum Journal of Theology* 21, no. 2 (Summer/Fall 2014): 342–361.

no sin" (2 Cor 5:21), condemned for our sakes, separating out the good and evil within each person, and incinerating the latter so as to redeem the former.

Without entering into a protracted discussion of the implications Balthasar's own theology draws out of his appropriation of Maritain on evil, I found it fitting here to elucidate both the complex relationship to the dialectical method utilized principally in Hegel that Balthasar exhibits and the vast influence of his attempt to integrate both Maritain and Barth into his own synthetic articulation of divine (im)passibility. Deciphering such influences and how they might fit together in the kenotic perspective on divine suffering, which has pervaded much of contemporary theology, allows one to discern which statements of Balthasar might be validated philosophically (harkening back to Maritain, e.g.) and which statements are unjustified except as mystical utterances devoid of precision and susceptible to rhetorical excess. At the heart of the matter is whether meta-symbolic discourse (as Cyril O'Regan dubs it)[100] has a proper place in theology or if it is less helpful than proper analogical speech aided at times by metaphorical images.

I do not argue that Balthasar's conclusions are dogmatically heterodox, but that they are theologically questionable and in need of a particular "demythologization." The problem is not his utilization of metaphor in theology—indeed, metaphor has a fitting role in theology[101]—but its improper usage, that is, its confusion with proper analogical predication. Conflating metaphor and analogy is fine for a non-theologian (e.g., Adrienne von Speyr), but it does not serve well the clarifying purpose of theology. Without entering into his intriguing spiritual and theological

---

[100] *The Anatomy of Misremembering: Von Balthasar's Response to Philosophical Modernity,* vol. 1, *Hegel* (New York: Herder & Herder, 2014), 228.

[101] As Jean-Hervé Nicolas argues, metaphors function in theology "not only as examples that illustrate the intelligible truth, but also as symbols which contain it" (*Dieu connu comme inconnu* [Paris: Desclée de Brouwer, 1966], 247). But, of course, this is not the full extent of theological discourse, as Nicolas and any metaphysical realist will assert. Hence, pertinent to the nature of philosophical theology, what Yves R. Simon says is also true:

> The use of metaphors in philosophy proper must either be rejected or at least strictly controlled; but in the phase of discovery, in the introduction to a subject, nothing is more natural than to use metaphors. In fact, a rich metaphorical imagination is an indispensible privilege of all creative philosophers. Philosophy will begin when metaphor is transcended, but in the introduction to philosophy we have to use metaphorical analogies. (*Work, Society, and Culture,* ed. Vukan Kuic [New York: Fordham University Press, 1971], 168)

relationship to the mystic Adrienne von Speyr or the legitimacy of the latter's experiences, the potential theological import of her mysticism is certainly difficult to evaluate and reliance upon it is not likely to yield speculative rigor or precision of thought. Hence, absent a detailed psychological and theological interpretation of mystical experience as such,[102] recourse to symbol can only go so far in theological discourse. Arguably, the task of "doing theology on one's knees" does not necessitate importing mystical symbolism into speculative theology.[103] In any case, regardless of Balthasar's influences or methodology, his thoughts have had enormous impact in a number of theological discussions, particularly the significance of naming the divine being "impassible." Thus, the debate rages on concerning the precise relationship between the Trinitarian God of love and the sin-laden world of free creatures, meanwhile divine receptivity remains steadfast in the face of evil.

---

[102] For diverse philosophical interpretations of mysticism as a phenomenon, see Steven T. Katz ed., *Mystical and Philosophical Analysis* (Oxford: Oxford University Press, 1978).

[103] Concerning the relationship between sanctity and theology in Balthasar, see Antonio Sicari, OCD, "Theologie und Heiligkeit," *Wort und Wahrheit* 3 (1948): 881–896; Georges Chantraine, "Théologie et sainteté," *Communio* (French Edition) 14, no. 2 (1989): 54–81; Jacques Servais, "The Ressourcement of Contemporary Spirituality under the Guidance of Adrienne von Speyr and Hans Urs von Balthasar," *Communio* 23, no. 2 (1996): 300–321. Also, for a variety of fair assessments of spirituality in Balthasar's theology, see the entire issue of the *Rivista teologica di Lugano* 6, no. 1 (2001): 9–264.

CHAPTER SIX

Theodramatic Self-Surrender and Analogical Discourse in Balthasar's Trinitarian Theology

As Balthasar impugned Augustine for "knowing too much" about the mysteries of election and reprobation,[1] critics argue that Balthasar seems to know too much about the inner workings of the Trinity.[2] In all fairness, his Trinitarian reflections come from the mystic whom he converted to the Catholic faith, Adrienne von Speyr, whose influence becomes more and more palpable as Balthasar's career progresses.[3] Michele M. Schumacher published in 2014 a savvy defense of Balthasar's Speyrian discourse concerning the Trinity and man's relationship to that supreme mystery in

---

[1] See *Dare We Hope "That All Men be Saved"? With A Short Discourse on Hell*, trans. David Kipp and Lothar Krauth (San Francisco: Ignatius, 1988), 65–69; *Was dürfen wir hoffen?* (Reprint, Einsieldeln: Johannes Verlag, 1989), 52–56; Augustine's *Enchiridion de fide, spe et charitate Liber Unus* [*PL* 40], 27.103, available at http://www.augustinus. it/latino/enchiridion/index.htm.

[2] For criticism of Balthasar's Trinitarian theology, begin with Bertrand de Margerie, SJ, "Note on Balthasar's Trinitarian Theology"; Matthew Levering, *Scripture and Metaphysics*, 120–32; Thomas Joseph White, OP, "Intra-Trinitarian Obedience and Nicene-Chalcedonian Christology," *Nova et Vetera* (English Edition) 6, no. 2 (2008): 377–402; Celia Deane-Drummond, "The Breadth of Glory"; Bruce Marshall, "The Unity of the Triune God: Reviving an Ancient Question," *The Thomist* 74 (2010): 1–32; Guy Mansini, OSB, "Can Humility and Obedience Be Trinitarian Realities?"

[3] Hence, Matthew Lewis Sutton advises caution when attempting to interpret the mystic (*Heaven Opens*, kindle location 716), adding: "When engaging in a Trinitarian theology, especially Trinitarian mysticism, the best word to characterize it might be 'attempt' (*Versuch*), which was a favorite word of von Speyr's" (location 751).

dialogue with contemporary Thomism.[4] Although she is certainly not the only scholar (as will be seen) who has sought to defend Balthasar's approach against traditional objections, her work deserves significant engagement in any treatment of Balthasar's Trinitarian theology. In this chapter, I attempt to evaluate Balthasar's imaginative discourse on the Trinitarian life from a Thomistic perspective in dialogue with some of the best secondary literature available without impugning Speyr's mysticism.

Thus, after analyzing the two most relevant recent works on Balthasar's theodramatic Trinitarian theology—Schumacher's book and a dissertation by Christopher Hadley, SJ—I will attempt to evaluate the metaphysical coherence of the various analogies employed by Balthasar to speak about the Trinity. I will argue that his theodramatic approach to divine realities becomes problematic, from the perspective of systematic theology, when his penchant for meta-symbolic speech usurps proper metaphysical predication. From a Thomistic perspective, when symbolic-metaphorical discourse and phenomenological categories function in place of a robust understanding of the analogy of being, enlightened by the language of divine revelation, analogies are drawn between the Trinitarian life and contingencies that are wholly incommensurable. Economic categories, such as obedience, freedom (as indifference), death, sacrifice, and the like, which are contingent realities contextualized by love in a fallen world, cannot adequately express the essence of divine life itself, which preexists and eminently transcends all contingency. Without entering into the question of analogy proper,[5] I will conclude that Balthasar's Trinitarian theology, particularly in the context of the problem of evil, fails the test of apophasis—he does not adequately take into account the limitations of human experience and speech with regard to the almighty author of all that is good.[6] Finally, I will offer a much-needed tentative assessment

---

[4] Michele M. Schumacher, *A Trinitarian Anthropology*.

[5] This would require the larger task of evaluating the works of Gustav Siewerth and Ferdinand Ulrich, who significantly influenced Balthasar, compared to more traditionally minded Thomists like Cornelio Fabro, Bernard Montagnes, and Thomas Joseph White, even though there are still differences among these diverse thinkers.

   The details of the latter discussion are largely irrelevant to the present task, although benefit would surely be reaped from an examination of Balthasar's choice in his later years to distance himself from Erich Przywara's nuanced account towards Ulrich's personalist-phenomenological reflections, a move for which D. C. Schindler argues in favor (see his *Hans Urs von Balthasar and the Dramatic Structure of Truth: A Philosophical Investigation*, 48–54).

[6] This is not, of course, to deny the important role of affirmation in the *triplex via*; see Mark Johnson, "Apophatic Theology's Cataphatic Dependencies," *The Thomist*

of how to understand Adrienne von Speyr's influence on Balthasar's theology, which is highlighted in recent secondary literature, in light of our evaluation of his (Speyrian) Trinitarian thought.

But before addressing the Trinity as such in Balthasar, we ought not to forget the fundamentally soteriological orientation of his theology, lest his Trinitarian and soteriological concerns be separated. The prism through which he views the Trinitarian life is, of course, the kenosis of Christ, particularly His death and descent for the sake of our redemption. Hence, as the redemptive work of Christ is the Christian's most profound answer to the problem of evil, Balthasar's approach to the Trinitarian mystery always has an eye on the human question: Why is there evil at all? As *ipsum esse* is the answer to the question, "why is there anything at all?," *ipsum amor* is Balthasar's answer to this question of theodicy (a traditionally philosophical field of inquiry that gets theologically transformed into what is now known as soteriology). As lucid an attempt as it is to resolve the problem of evil by recourse to the Trinitarian love of God, there are certainly pitfalls to be avoided in such an endeavor.

Therefore, I will first address recent attempts to justify Balthasar's Trinitarian theology on the basis of theodicy and soteriology before evaluating his theodramatic approach to Trinitarian theology as such with more precision and rigor than is present in his Speyrian resources, which are finally assessed in preliminary fashion.

THEODRAMA AS A RESPONSE TO THE PROBLEM OF EVIL

Jacob Friesenhahn argues that Balthasar offers a better "solution," if you will, to the problem of evil than is found in either contemporary philosophy or scholastic theology via recourse to Trinitarian kenoticism.[7] Proposing that only a Trinitarian approach is capable of offering a satisfactory answer to the question of why there is evil at all (not simply moral evil,

---

62 (1998): 519–531. For a historical investigation of the debate concerning apophasis vs. kataphasis that preceded Thomas Aquinas's own synthetic approach, see Jacob W. Wood, "Kataphasis and Apophasis in Thirteenth Century Theology: The Anthropological Context of the *Triplex Via* in the *Summa Fratris Alexandri* and Albert the Great," *The Heythrop Journal* 57 (2016): 293–311.

[7] Jacob H. Friesenhahn's PhD dissertation on the relationship between the problem of evil and Balthasar's Trinitarian theology, *The Trinitarian Theology of Hans Urs von Balthasar and Theodicy* (Southern Methodist University, 2009) was later published in revised form as *The Trinity and Theodicy: The Trinitarian Theology of von Balthasar and the Problem of Evil* (Burlington: Ashgate, 2011). I rely on the former.

which he sees as the simpler part of the question),[8] Friesenhahn in the process does not offer much clarity on the issue of God's transcendent involvement with the world.

Attempting to distance Balthasar from both Moltmann and Rahner,[9] at one point he states that "The current fad in theology goes to the opposite extreme [of the impassibilists] in depicting God as Himself suffering or caught in a battle with evil that He struggles to win. . . . [Balthasar's theology] does *not* directly predicate suffering of God . . . suffering as such does not exist within God."[10] Yet, at another point, Friesenhahn, following Balthasar, states that "the Cross is fundamentally an inner-Trinitarian event that involves every person of the Trinity, not only the Son,"[11] following John O'Donnell's reference to Balthasar's Cross-centered theology of "the eternal trinitarian drama,"[12] the drama that undergirds every other.[13] The rationale for this is "Balthasar's understanding of the immanent Trinity as kenotic love."[14] This somehow justifies speaking of God "[receiving] human death into eternal life,"[15] presumably a proper predication, and "the mutual exchange of blood between the Persons that . . . is the basis for there being a 'death' in God," presumably metaphorical speech.[16] Hence, Friesenhahn concludes: "divine nature itself does not contain suffering,

---

[8] See *Trinitarian Theology*, esp. 238, 327, and 336. Friesenhahn thinks the lack of a Trinitarian emphasis is the weakness of John Paul II's monumental Apostolic Letter, *Salvifici Doloris* (see §§310–311), but certainly his avoidance of quasi-mythological language (particularly with regard to the Trinity) employed by the mystic Adrienne von Speyr, on whom Balthasar continuously draws, is intentional.

[9] Friesenhahn, *Trinitarian Theology*, 207 and 226. That does not stop him from saying, "both Balthasar and Moltmann convincingly describe the Cross as an essentially trinitarian event," although he prefaces this statement with "a simple formula, that for Moltmann the Cross makes possible the Trinity, but for Balthasar the Trinity makes possible the Cross" (207). Rahner offers a scathing critique of Balthasar's approach to divine impassibility and immutability (see *Karl Rahner in Dialogue,* 126–127).

[10] Friesenhahn, 318.

[11] Friesenhahn, 207.

[12] Friesenhahn, 205, citing Fr. John J. O'Connell, *The Mystery of the Triune God* (New York: Paulist, 1989), 65.

[13] See, e.g., *TD* IV, 327.

[14] Friesenhahn, 318.

[15] *TD* V, 251, cited in Friesenhahn, 319

[16] *TD* V 5, 245, cited in Friesenahn, 326. Discerning when Balthasar is utilizing metaphorical versus proper predication is one of the problems with evaluating the accuracy of his theological claims. Even Balthasar's usage of metaphorical predication is called into question by Kevin Duffy, "Change, Suffering, and Surprise in God"; see also the response by Gerard F. O'Hanlon, SJ, "A Response to Kevin Duffy."

death, or finitude in any univocal sense, but God's essence does contain kenotic relations of love that entail an openness, 'risk,' 'vulnerability,' and even a 'proto-suffering' that becomes actualized when the Son assumes a human nature out of love for man."[17]

In a word, all of Christ's suffering and that of the whole world is encompassed by an original dynamism of self-expropriating love that is expressed paradigmatically in Christ's own descent into the darkness that is hell, death, and sin itself.[18] Thus, it is not entirely accurate to claim that "Balthasar provides a mediating position between a divine nature that *somehow* suffers and an indifferent deity, who remains aloof while Christ suffers in His humanity alone."[19] Rather, he sides with the former option in a nuanced manner. Hence, Friesenhahn states:

> Though, *contra* Moltmann, there is no Hegelian negativity in the divine, human suffering and death are grounded in God in the trinitarian fashion described by Balthasar. The "death" of the Son, both the giving over of Oneself performed by the Son in the immanent Trinity and the historical death of the Incarnate Son upon the Cross, must be seen in light of the "suffering" and "death" of *God the Father*. Balthasar suggests that we understand the Father's original kenosis as the "supra-death" that engenders the Son's imaging reciprocation both as God and as man.[20]

On the brink of Patripassianism,[21] Friesenhahn prefaces this consideration

---

[17] Friesenhahn, *Trinitarian Theology*, 327. Nonetheless, "God's nature [does not] change in any sense of movement from 'potency to act' through contact with the created world. Rather all the drama of the world is possibly only because of the 'theo-dramatic' character of the inner-divine nature" (226).

[18] See, e.g., *TD* V, 252 [G 228]. Aidan Nichols states it this way: "Because the Descent is the final point reached by the Kenosis, and the Kenosis is the supreme expression of the inner-Trinitarian love, the Christ of Holy Saturday is the consummate icon of what God is like" ("Introduction," in Balthasar, *Mysterium Paschale: The Mystery of Easter*, trans. Aidan Nichols [San Francisco: Ignatius, 1990], 7).

[19] Friesenhahn, *Trinitarian Theology*, 229.

[20] Friesenhahn, 324.

[21] Despite Friesenhahn's criticism of Young's *The Shack* as patripassionist (339), it is not clear how his own rendition of Balthasar's Trinitarian theodicy escapes the same point of excess, even if it is only implicit. Thomas Krenski notes that the heresy of patripassianism was a modalist heresy and Balthasar certainly cannot be accused of modalism (see Thomas R. Krenski, *Passio Caritatis: Trinitarische Passiologie im Werk Hans Urs von Balthasars* [Einsiedeln: Johannes Verlag, 1990], 268ff.).

by noting that "the infinite distinction between Father and Son in the immanent Trinity provides the 'space' for the economic event of Christ's abandonment on the Cross."[22]

Balthasar attempts to ground the distance between God and the sinner in the "distance" between the divine persons, particularly the Father and Son.[23] Friesenhahn aptly sums up this dimension of his theology:

> Balthasar regards the evil, the utter alienation from God, of the Cross as encompassed by God's own inner nature. Because the Father and Son are infinitely and eternally distinct persons within the Godhead, the economic separation between Father and Son in the event of the Cross is possible. The Incarnate Son can cry, "My God, my God, why hast thou forsaken me?" (Mt 27:46) economically only because the Son *ad intra* has always been infinitely distinct from the Father. Thus the economic event of the Cross reveals the infinite separation of the three persons of the immanent Trinity from one another.[24]

Thus, Balthasar's ultimate recourse for explaining evil is the irreducible hypostatic difference between persons in the Trinity, which he sees manifest especially in the cry of dereliction. Friesenhahn does not realize that there is a problem here: the kind of difference or distance between, on the one hand, divine innocence and human sinfulness and, on the other hand, that between the persons of the Trinity, even that between the Father who "suffers" the loss of His only-begotten Son and the forsaken One on the Cross, are essentially different—hence, the analogy drawn is actually an equivocation.

While this is historically accurate, conceptually there is little difference between saying the Father suffered on the Cross in the form of the Son and saying that the Father suffered as Father His willing (economic) abandonment of the Son. Perhaps the latter brinks on subordinationism, the opposite Trinitarian heresy—it is easy to shift to Scylla from Charybdis and back again when ontological precision is lacking.

Thus, Ratzinger warns of a "new patripassianism" in Moltmann (see *Behold the Pierced One*, 58n11 [G 50n11]), which would contradict the consensus of the Church Fathers (see Gavrilyuk, *The Suffering of the Impassible God*).

22. Friesenhahn, *Trinitarian Theology*, 324.
23. Hence, Friesenhahn states: "it is possible for the divine Son to become human—to become Other—because the Son is already Other as divine yet *not* the Father. In other words, the greater (infinite) distance between Father and not-Father (Son) renders possible the lesser distance between God and not-God (man)" (*Trinitarian Theology*, 297).
24. Friesenhahn, 314.

Nonetheless, the problem in the background is how this theology operates to undermine the definitiveness of the human refusal of divine grace. Balthasar concludes, as Friesenhahn notes, that "even the 'creature's No, its wanting to be autonomous without acknowledging its origin, must be located within the Son's all-embracing Yes to the Father, in the Spirit.'"[25] Of course, it is Christ's purpose to absorb the human no into His redemptive yes, and yet that does not preclude the possibility of the former's persistence in the face of the latter. Thus, in an otherwise superb work, John Saward avoids the issue when, in answer to his own question, "How can an infinitely good God permit such dangerously fallible freedom?," he concludes (with Balthasar, following Bulgakov): "the analogical kenosis of the divine relations is what makes possible all the other kenoses—creation, covenant, and redemptive Incarnation."[26] The only problem is that sin (i.e., moral evil) cannot be construed as a kenosis and therefore bears no resemblance to the ecstatic diastasis between the divine persons. He explains that, according to Balthasar, because "'the absolute, infinite distance,' between the Father and Son is bridged by and in the Holy Spirit, the Father can not only make creatures to be different but permit them, though of course not will them, to be distant."[27] But, despite the truth that "the Trinity is absolute unity in absolute diversity," and, therefore, "however far a creature may remove himself from God, he is never beyond the loving arms of the Father,"[28] it is quite unbefitting to assert that the godforsakenness into which the Son is plunged—that is, the reality of moral evil and the punishments that accrue to it—is somehow grounded in the distinction, difference, or diversity present among the hypostatic relations that constitute the inner life of *ipsum esse*.[29]

---

[25] Friesenhahn, 200, citing *TD* IV, 328. Likewise, Antoine Birot sums up Balthasar's perspective:

> If the world, created in the Son and subsisting in him, can have no other "locus" but within the difference of the hypostases, then the resounding of the creature's "No" can exist nowhere else but in this very same place (*Stelle*), within the absolute intra-divine difference; and when the Son becomes incarnate and penetrates into the darkness of the world, he is able to "take the place" of darkness and "substitute" (*Stell-vertretung*) himself for it by virtue of his very position in the Trinity. ("God in Christ, Reconciled the World to Himself": 259–285, at 282)

[26] Saward, *Mysteries of March*, 32.
[27] Saward, 32.
[28] Saward, 32.
[29] Even though evil, like nonbeing, is defined precisely in relation to being *qua bonum*, there is no intelligibility to it to be found in God precisely because it merely inheres in

Along the lines of Jacques Maritain, Gerard O'Hanlon, SJ, an eloquent defender of Balthasar, skillfully weaves together the themes of divine impassibility and the finite-infinite freedom interplay that characterizes Balthasar's theodramatic approach:

> By establishing freely this kind of reciprocal relationship between himself and the world God has chosen to be affected by our finite freedom. He has in this sense given us rights over himself, and this divine vulnerability is seen most dramatically in God's relationship to the sinner . . . suffering the salvation of the entire universe. God's sovereignty is not threatened by this drama, in which he chooses to make himself vulnerable, because God is triune. Once again, then, it is the trinitarian event which grounds the possibility of this kind of dialogical relationship between God and us. . . . In his concern to remove any impression that God out-manoeuvres us in a way which destroys our human freedom, Balthasar reminds us that God's eternal omniscience and providence contain a differentiated awareness of human time with its past, present and future. Because of this it is more correct to speak of God creatively (through the Holy Spirit) responding to each human decision and situation as they arise, than to imagine that God's response is "already" always decided. We may express this by using the image of drama which Balthasar so favours: not only does the drama conceived by God require us to be actors in it . . . but also—as was said of Christ's incarnation—it is . . . "an event of

---

the finite good as *privatio*. John Saward is an example of someone who has a tremendous esteem for and understanding of Balthasar's work, but who also accepts Jacques Maritain's interpretation of Thomas Aquinas concerning the divine permission of evil and man's power to nihilate divine (frustrable, i.e., conditional) *auxilium*, but for some odd reason he has not attempted to conjoin the two arenas of discourse.

See, for the former, Saward's *The Mysteries of March*, and for the latter, his "The Grace of Christ in His Principal Members: St. Thomas Aquinas on the Pastoral Epistles," in *Aquinas on Scripture: An Introduction to His Biblical Commentaries*, ed. Thomas G. Weinandy, Daniel A. Keating, and John P. Yocum (New York: T & T. Clark International, 2005), 197–221, at 202–209.

For Maritain, see his *Dieu et la permission du mal* (Paris: Desclée de Brouwer, 1963), in English, *God and the Permission of Evil*, trans. Joseph W. Evans (Milwaukee: The Bruce Publishing Company, 1966); *St. Thomas and the Problem of Evil* (Milwaukee: The Aquinas Lectures, 1942), published originally in English; *Court traité de l'existence et de l'existant* (Paris: Paul Hartmann, 1947), ch. 4, in English, *Existence and the Existent*, trans. Lewis Galantière and Gerald B. Phelan (New York: Pantheon Books, 1948).

total originality, as unique and untarnished as the eternally here-and-now birth of the Son from the Father."[30]

Rather than spin a doctrine of intra-Trinitarian über-suffering that is later manifest in God's becoming vulnerable to the infinite darkness of sin itself, he begins with the insight that God allows Himself to be affected through a dialogical relationship with human freedom.[31] While he does argue for an ultimate ground in God Himself for this relationship to creation, he focuses on Balthasar's occasional insistence against Barth that man is not a cog in a machine of salvation and speculates that divine timelessness is such that He is not in a position so much to *pre*-determine the free decisions of His creatures as to direct them *hic et nunc* by virtue of His own omnipresence within the drama He orchestrates.

Tying together God's infinite intra-Trinitarian freedom and the infinite subtlety of His freedom pervading all things creatively, Balthasar seems to argue that the generation of the Son and the drama of salvation are in some sense equally original "events." Hence, Edward Oakes summarizes the meaning of "theo-drama" as such:

---

[30] O'Hanlon, *The Immutability of God*, 62–64. He continues:

> Rejecting an older approach, which with a certain amazingly cool indifference could assert that God's glory was served equally well by either our eternal happiness or our eternal punishment, Balthasar nonetheless wishes to respect the NT texts concerning the twofold issue of divine judgment, the increasing opposition to the love of God after the event of Christ, and also the freedom of man to make a definitive choice with his life without being forced or overwhelmed by God. In doing so he must reject any simple apocatastasis solution. Obviously, in presenting the matter thus the question about universal salvation is of key concern to us. But it is so because implicit in Balthasar's rejection of the older approach is an acknowledgement that in some way the world does affect God. (*The Immutability of God*, 65)

[31] I would argue that as God is said to will Himself, even though He is Himself necessary, those acts of His which cannot not be (i.e., intra-Trinitarian or self-constitutive ones) may be freely reiterated by the divine essence (and, in fact, probably are confirmed in some sense in every *ad extra* action) and thus called not only "necessary," but also "free" since God transcends the difference between necessity and contingency that comes about in creation itself. But the point made here is that it ought to be clearly stated that God's intra-Trinitarian acts cannot not be and are, therefore, essentially distinct (that is, according to our mode of conceiving them) from His *ad extra* "free" acts (in the sense of notionally contingent).

[A]ccording to his interpretation, in the Triduum of Good Friday, Holy Saturday, and Easter Sunday, *something happens to God*, and this is why this part of the trilogy deserves the title *Theo-Drama* in every sense of the word, being both a subjective as well as objective prefix. Now it is true that one must approach such a statement with considerable care and we shall not be surprised to learn that the drama that Balthasar is talking about must be analogically understood. But that makes his theology even more radical, for of course, in such analogies the *analogatum* is even more true of God than it is of us![32]

Edward Oakes is then able to connect Balthasar's Trinitarian theory summarily not merely to his theology of descent, but also to his perspective on the relationship between divine and human freedom, hinting at its universalist implications:

All attributes that inhere in us must be grounded in God: "the infinite distance between the world and God has its foundation in that original distance between God and God, within God." And that even goes for sin (how daring this man is!); for God's freedom is the presupposition for man's freedom, the very ground of its possibility, including to sin; and giving man freedom must include the risk that he will abuse that freedom in sin. Now of course, Balthasar is not saying that God wills the creature to sin, nor that the "primal image" of sin subsists in God; but he does insist that the experience of separation from God which ensues as a

---

[32] Oakes, *Pattern of Redemption*, 231 (emphasis original). Perhaps, more aptly, Guy Mansini defines theodrama thus: "Theodrama is the drama between God and man reflecting the inner-Trinitarian drama of Father, Son, and Spirit" ("Balthasar and the Theodramatic Enrichment," 499).

Pointing to the preface of the second edition of *Mysterium Paschale*, written after the *Theodrama*, Mansini then summarizes Balthasar's Trinitarian kenotic resolution to the problem of divine impassibility:

While it is true that God does not change by dependence on the world such that without the world there would be something in him there is not, it is nevertheless the case that he does change, with a change already forever "included and outstripped in the eternal event of Love" [*Mysterium Paschale*, ix]. It is this solution, though not always so compactly expressed, and with an appeal to the same clue, that Balthasar develops at length in the *Theodrama* [see *TD* V, 61–65, 75–76]. ("Balthasar and the Theodramatic Enrichment," 501)

direct consequence of sin must be capable of being integrated into the Trinitarian differences—otherwise there is no salvation.[33]

Hence, there is a Trinitarian theology that "undergirds" Balthasar's eschatology, even if it is precisely his understanding of God's relationship to moral evil that has a more direct effect on his eschatology in the direction of a "subjunctive universalism."[34] The Trinitarian "undergirding" of sin itself[35] points up the intricate connection that exists between Balthasar's theology of the finite-infinite freedom interplay (otherwise known as the grace-freedom dynamic) and his staked out position on the question of divine impassibility.[36] It also indicates where Balthasar sees the potential

---

[33] Oakes, *Pattern of Redemption*, 288–289. He continues: "For in the Trinity distance and separation are always positive realities; in the Trinity, and there alone, distance comes to be *because* of love: God the Father's love is so total that there is 'nothing left,' so to speak, when he generates his Son in love; and the Son returns that love so totally, also holding nothing back, that he too is totally 'emptied'" (289).

[34] Hence, for all his speculations, divine *kenosis* serves as the infallible means through which God ensures the attainment of the end for which He created:

> For with the *kenosis* of Christ, eternity has put itself in motion and has passed through time with all of its darknesses. There is no alienating hiatus between the Father's remaining at home and the Son's going forth in pilgrimage, for the "distance" of the *kenosis* is a mode of inner-Trinitarian nearness and of the circumincession of the divine hypostases. In the *kenosis* of the Son, it is true that his innate "form of God" stays back with the Father, is "left behind" with him, both as pledge of his faithfulness to the will of God and as a "reminder" to the Father of how much he himself is committed to the world adventure. In this kind of tension between eternity and time, God is not split apart but more than ever is with himself, for he perfects the free commitment that he began with creation. *It is as if he had wagered with himself that he could do the apparently impossible: create creaturely freedoms that subsist in themselves and yet not let them be lost. (Explorations* IV, 138 [G 131–132], emphasis added)

Nonetheless, what O'Hanlon (among others) notices in Balthasar remains true: "While careful not to flatten everything into some surveyable undramatic *apocatastasis* system, Balthasar does use the descent into hell motif of the *Triduum Mortis* as the basis of a very firm hope for the salvation of all" ("Theological Dramatics," in *The Beauty of Christ*, ed. McGregor and Norris, 92–111, at 98–99). For the term, "subjunctive universalism" and its distinction from "indicative universalism," see Michael Root, "The Hope of Eternal Life," *Ecumenical Trends* 41 (2012): 100.

[35] See, e.g., *TD* IV, 325–27, 333–34 [G 302–304, 310–11].

[36] Balthasar takes a weak position on divine impassibility, according to which the suffering of the world actually exists in a supereminent fashion in God's own being rather than affecting God indirectly as the one who permits finite freedom to nihilate the movements of the "hound of heaven" (i.e., the almost endless graces He offers to each

resolution of the aporia between God's infinite love and man's final rejection of His glory, namely, in God becoming "sin who knew no sin" (2 Cor 5:21), condemned for our sakes, separating out the good and evil within each person, and incinerating the latter so as to redeem the former.[37]

STELLVERTRETUNG AND THEODRAMA

Concerning Balthasar's theodrama, Thomas G. Dalzell states: "While it is important to Balthasar that God takes created freedom seriously, it could be argued that his idea of Christ's descent into hell to accompany those who have damned themselves makes it doubtful that God could lose the human response forever."[38] Along similar lines, Michele M. Schumacher views the relationship between Balthasar's soteriology of representation (or *Stellvertretung*) and the reality of human freedom as problematic, a tension she proposes can be resolved only through the Trinitarian dynamic of free *kenosis*. After noting Balthasar's intention to maintain the integrity of created freedom (in different words), she makes the following insightful comments, even if not entirely accurate (soteriologically):

> [T]he link in his soteriology between the Cross and this conversion [necessary for remission of sins]—which in my view is the final reason for the Cross—remains so obscure that one is left with an arbitrary connection between one's estrangement from God and one's persistence in sin. Since there is little hope for an impasse in the confrontation between an obstinate God and a hardheaded sinner, Balthasar was forced simply to do away with the confrontation through a notion of substitution. . . . Balthasar insists perhaps too unilaterally on a resolution to the problematic from on high. The Creator-creature dynamic is dissolved into the eternal drama between the Father and the Son with the latter's pre-existing obedience tending to "substitute itself for the God-man relation rather than integrating it into itself." Hence it seems that Balthasar must live up to his own demands: the fulfillment of finite freedom requires not only that "the Infinite take the finite into itself (and absorb it)" but also that the finite "be capable of taking the Infinite into itself." Christ's obedient "yes"

---

one of His beloved). See my "God's Relation to Evil."

[37] See *TL* II, 355–59 [G 324–328]; *TD* V, 321 [G 293].

[38] Dalzell, "The Enrichment of God," 15n56.

to the Father cannot simply take the place of our own; it must be appropriated in such a way that the human creature is anchored in God's freedom both objectively, "in God's truthfulness," and subjectively, "in his own attitude of truth," which is to say that "it must commit itself to this truth, which is freely offered to it." In so doing, in letting itself be brought into the realm of infinite freedom, there is no danger that the creature will become alienated from itself, for the simple reason that self-surrender is the very law of trinitarian being; the divine nature "is always both what is possessed and what is given away," the "fullness of blessedness" lying simultaneously in "giving and receiving both the gift and the giver."[39]

Although she notes Balthasar's tendency to undermine finite freedom in order to elevate infinite freedom, she concludes that it is the notion of surrender characterizing Balthasar's Trinitarian theology (borrowed from Speyr) that prevents his soteriology from being deterministic.[40]

She does not investigate Balthasar's understanding of the grace-freedom relationship, except insofar as she displays his general approach to finite freedom as a created mode of infinite freedom (without using exactly these terms).[41] Thus, it remains unclear how understanding redemption as a representative substitution (*Stellvertretung*) on the part of the God-man in the sinner's place might threaten or endanger the integrity of human freedom.[42] But because she discerns a problem with divine freedom becoming

---

[39] Schumacher, "The Concept of Representation in the Theology of Hans Urs von Balthasar," *Theological Studies* 60 (1999): 53–71, at 63–64. She also cites there the following from Balthasar: "[Christ's] whole human substance is 'made fluid' so that it can enter into human beings; but this takes place in such a way that at the same time he also makes fluid the boulders of sin that have formed in resistance to God's fluidity and dissolves them in that experienced godforsakenness of which they secretly consist" (*New Elucidations*, trans. Mary Theresilde Skerry [San Francisco: Ignatius Press, 1986], 116–117, quoted in "The Concept of Representation," 63n54). She elaborates her concerns and proposed resolution to the apparent conflict between human freedom and the substitution model of redemption employed by Balthasar in her magisterial work, *A Trinitarian Anthropology*, especially ch. 5.

[40] See *Trinitarian Anthropology*, 16–17, where Schumacher anticipates her more detailed treatment of the issue in the fifth chapter.

[41] See, e.g., Schumacher, 112, citing *TD* II, 228.

[42] For a concise explanation of Balthasar's understanding of redemption, see John Saward, *Mysteries of March*, 40–41. Ratzinger evidently maintains respect for human freedom, and yet he is even more insistent at times on representative substitution as an exemplary

a substitute for human freedom, that is, in the context of Christ's redemptive work, she opts for a soteriology slightly different from Balthasar's, springing from "a more fitting interpretation of Adrienne's mystical experiences . . . one which does more justice to this Catholic meaning of redemption."[43] According to this interpretation, the Son is not so much abandoned *by* the Father as abandoned (that is, surrendered) *to* the Father and God is revealed in Christ as abandoned by men.[44] Casting doubt upon the possibility that a sinner might definitively refuse divine grace, Schumacher reports that for Balthasar and Speyr, "Christ accompanies the one who willfully refuses the Father's love all the way to the threshold of his or her definitive refusal. It is there–at the moment of the definitive 'Yes or No of finite freedom' to God–that the Spirit of Christ . . . (the Son's 'ultimate surrender to the Father and to us'), solicits finite freedom 'at the very roots of freedom.'"[45]

One might argue that there is typically an alliance between the soteriology of substitution and the Calvinist-Lutheran understanding of the finite-infinite freedom dynamic. Yet there is little or no appearance of such soteriology in Augustine or his closest Catholic adherents (particularly with respect to the grace-freedom dynamic). Perhaps the problem of such an apparent disconnect could be resolved by distinguishing between the soteriology of substitution and the soteriology of representation, although the terminological divide is somewhat artificial—the idea is that the latter allows for participation in the work of redemption on the part of its recipients, whereas the former does not.[46] In any case, Schumacher takes

---

theory of redemption. Regarding the latter, see Ratzinger's entry on "Stellvertretung" in *Handbuch theologischer Grundbegriffe*; see also Christopher Ruddy, "'For the Many': The Vicarious-Representative Heart of Joseph Ratzinger's Theology," *Theological Studies* 75, no. 3 (2014): 564–584.

[43] Schumacher, *Trinitarian Anthropology*, 199.

[44] See Schumacher, 245 and 241.

[45] Schumacher, 245. She goes on to quote from Balthasar's *Epilogue* to the Trilogy: "We do not know whether a human freedom can deny to the very end this offer of the Spirit to give it his own true freedom" (245, citing *Epilogue*, 122).

Speyr, however, does not seem to share this conviction: see Speyr and Balthasar, "L'expérience du Samedi Saint," 65–68; Miles, *Obedience of a Corpse*, 179, 182; Maas, "Das Gaheimnis des Karsamstags," in *Adrienne von Speyr und Ihre Kirchliche Sendung*, ed. Balthasar, Georges Chantraine, and Angelo Scola (Einsiedeln: Johannes Verlag, 1986), 132.

[46] His comments (see, e.g., *TD* V, 272 [G 246]) hint at the distinction between inclusive versus exclusive representation. For the latter, see Albrecht Ritschl, *The Christian Doctrine of Justification and Reconciliation: The Positive Development of the Doctrine*.

up none of these considerations. Hence, the deficiency of her treatment lies in the fact that Balthasar's soteriology of *Stellvertretung* does not preclude the possibility of cooperation between created and uncreated freedom. Nonetheless, Balthasar does tend to view the finite-infinite freedom relationship in Augustinian-Thomistic (almost neo-Bañezian) terms,[47] sometimes even tainted by Barth's Calvinistic perspective and sometimes apparently subordinated to the Eastern synergistic approach he found in Bulgakov and some of the Greek Fathers.[48]

Schumacher, without much protestation or any direct response, notes that Michel Beaudin "recognizes Balthasar as insisting too unilaterally upon a resolution 'from on high.' . . . Everything leads back to a drama between the Father and the Son,"[49] which risks "[substituting] itself for the God-man relation rather than integrating it."[50] Although Beaudin points out Barth's influence in this regard, their concern centers more on how best to understand the redemptive work of Christ than the broader question of how divine and human freedom interact. But it is not as if there is no relationship between the two issues. Schumacher notes with the

---

More precisely, John Saward points out that "The Son's vicarious act of reconciliation is, therefore, both exclusive and inclusive. Insofar as the sinless God-Man does what we cannot do, it is exclusive; but in so far as he stands in for us as our Head, it is inclusive. In other words, mankind, for whose sins he makes satisfaction by his Passion, has been put into a new situation *in its very being*, even before it acknowledges the fact by faith" (*The Mysteries of March*, 42 [emphasis original]).

[47] For example, as early as his *Das Ganze im Fragment*, Balthasar conceives of grace primarily in terms of power: see *A Theological Anthropology*, 198 and 201–202 [G 221 and 225].

[48] Concerning Bulgakov's Eastern synergistic approach to the grace-freedom dynamic, see Aidan Nichols, *Wisdom from Above: A Primer in the Theology of Father Sergei Bulgakov* (Leominster: Gracewing, 2005), 70.

Gregory of Nyssa is probably the most influential Greek Father for Balthasar, at least with regard to this and related questions; see his *Presence et pensée: Essai sur la philosophie religieuse de Gregoire de Nysse* (Paris: Beauchesne, 1942). Nonetheless, Brian Daley argues: "For all its abundant attempts to drop anchor in the text of Gregory of Nyssa, Balthasar's monograph tends to float away from its subject, and suffers from the conceptual structure—an uneasy mixture of Hegel and neo-Thomism—in which he examines Gregory's work" ("Balthasar's Reading of the Church Fathers" in *Cambridge Companion to Balthasar to Hans Urs von Balthasar*, 187–206, at 197).

[49] Schumacher, *Trinitarian Anthropology*, 209.

[50] Beaudin, *Obéissance et solidarité*, 307. Beaudin goes on to anticipate Karen Kilby's critique of Balthasar's approach as too much of a "God's eye view" (*Balthasar*, 163). This precise phrase Kilby takes from Ben Quash (without direct reference): see Quash's essay, "Theodramatics, History, and the Holy Spirit," in the volume he edited, *Theology and the Drama of History* (New York: Cambridge University Press, 2005), 197.

authority of Jean-Pierre Torrell that Thomas Aquinas rarely, if ever, enter-
tains the notion of substitution,[51] and yet it is equally obvious that Aquinas upheld the emphatically anti-Pelagian Augustinian theology of grace
and freedom that Calvinists like Barth exaggerate.[52] One would think
from Schumacher's analysis that there is an alliance between emphatically anti-Pelagian theology and substitution theory. Even though Balthasar
does reflect the influence of Barth in both soteriology and the theology of
grace, it is not so simple.[53]

Not recognizing a precise relationship between one's understanding
of human freedom in relation to God and the theory of representative
substitution (that is, inclusionary substitution or *Stellvertretung*), Schumacher opts for "the image of Christ crucified calling forth from hardened
hearts love in return for (or in response to) love," a kind of moral model
of redemption, in place of Balthasar's image of Christ "assuming our place
of estrangement from God" because the latter seems to be a threat to our
freedom, that is, "man's free response to God's free initiative."[54] Thus, it
is not surprising that Schumacher betrays an approach to the grace-freedom dynamic that is more Molinistic than Balthasar's,[55] even if vaguely so:
"we might best understand the mystery of our redemption not so much in
the identification of Christ with our sinful condition and the subsequent
condemnation of sin in his flesh (cf. Rom 8:3), as in the super-generous
and irrevocable surrender of God's own being to all of humankind in view

---

[51] Schumacher, *Trinitarian Anthropology*, 200n16.

[52] Thomas Joseph White nicely sums up the Augustinian-Thomist view in *Incarnate Lord*,
402–403.

[53] As Ben Quash notes: "Balthasar's introduction to his main discussion of soteriology
in volume iv deliberately eschews any facile reduction of Christ's saving work to one
explanatory theory or metaphoric image. Here, in this pursuit of the meaning of the
Cross into the dark space of Holy Saturday, we see him articulating a doctrine of salvation that has both substitutionary (or representative), and participatory aspects" ("The
theo-drama," in *Cambridge Companion to Hans Urs von Balthasar*, 143–157, at 154).

Balthasar both defends Anselm against popular critiques (see, e.g., *TD* IV, 255ff. [G
235ff.]) and treats Luther's innovative approach very sympathetically (see *TD* IV, 284ff.
[G 263ff.]), even though he critiques aspects of both as well.

Gerard O'Hanlon says, "For Balthasar's discriminating acceptance of the original
theological contribution by Luther to this issue [of the Pauline *pro nobis*], see, *TD*, III,
221–5, 295f. . . . Balthasar's concern is to bring the notions of solidarity and substitution together—see *TD*, III, 245–6. For one-sided treatments of solidarity, see *TD*,
III, 247–62, and of substitution, *ibid.*, 263–91" (*The Immutability of God*, 185n73,76).
Balthasar explicitly links solidarity and representation in *TD* III, 239n35 [G 220n12].

[54] Schumacher, *Trinitarian Anthropology*, 210, citing CCC 2002.

[55] See Schumacher, 210–213.

of our incorporation therein (cf. Jn 17)."[56] Of course, for Balthasar, these putatively Pauline and Johannine perspectives do not stand in conflict. Rather, he conceptualizes the relationship between created and uncreated freedom as analogous to that between the feminine-receptive principle and the masculine-active principle, but ultimately encompassed by the original *diastasis* between the divine persons (particularly the Father and Son), the exemplar of all difference and unity, the *ur-kenosis* that grounds all subsequent *kenosis* (creation, Incarnation, redemption, etc.), and the "primal drama."[57] The eschatological consequence of all this is an—perhaps unwarranted—optimism concerning the end-result of the tragedy that is the conflict between "the sinner's refusal of God and God's refusal of this refusal," as Schumacher aptly puts it.[58]

In support of the possibility (surely abstract) of such a divine tragedy that would be the eternal loss of some of God's free creatures, Balthasar interprets a passage of Speyr thus: "Von Speyr describes hell as a 'preserve' of the Father, in the sense that, as Creator (indeed, as generator of the Son, in whom he has always already conceived every possible world) he foresaw, and took responsibility for, the possibility of the creature's freedom and, given the abuse of this freedom, of its eternal perishing."[59] But he also openly hedges his bets against the definitiveness of such divine loss, at least with respect to human beings.[60] Citing Althaus on the inclusive quality of Christ's representative work of redemption, Margaret Turek, who wrote her dissertation on Balthasar under the direction of Cardinal

---

[56] Schumacher, 214.

[57] See Schumacher, 259ff.

[58] Schumacher, 201n19, citing Balthasar's *Does Jesus Know Us? Do We Know Him?*, trans. Graham Harrison (San Francisco: Ignatius Press, 1986), 35. For just a few of the texts where Balthasar imbues what might be called optative universalism, see Schumacher, *Trinitarian Anthropology*, 368.

[59] *TL* II, 352 [G 321].

[60] Against such a divine tragic loss being definitive, see, e.g., *TD* I, 648 [G 606] and *TD* IV, 149 [G 136–137]. Balthasar himself often explicitly speaks of tragedy in the theodrama, but he also speculates about a divine hope undermining and overcoming the tragedy of human refusal such that the salvific mercy of God has the last word since the latter transcends and undergirds [*unterfassung*] the former (see especially *TD* V, 181, 187, 193–195, 269 [G 160, 166, 173–175, 243]).

Nicholas J. Healy also notes that "[in] Balthasar's proposal for a dramatic eschatology . . . God himself 'hopes for the salvation of the world,'" citing *TD* V, 181–188 (see *Being as Communion*, 2). Hence, Balthasar's overall tendency is to reject (at least implicitly) the possibility that God's creative project may in the end be tragic (i.e., that some are condemned) as infinitely improbable.

Christoph Schönborn, OP, brings together the Trinitarian and dramatic dimensions of Balthasar's perspective on divine-human relations: "it is because the Son's representation of the Father's love underlies the Son's representation of sinners that human freedom, confronted with the form of the Crucified in the 'weakness' of his unreserved surrender, is persuaded to participate in his eternally begotten return of love to the Father—albeit by way of atonement."[61]

Without being able to enter here into the theology of grace, it suffices to say that when Trinitarian theology functions as a theodicy, the temptation to universalism is inevitable, as the impulse to rationalize evil in relation to love predominates. But Balthasar's Speyrian Trinitarian theology is not entirely subsumed by soteriology. Therefore, it is fitting to explore his theodramatic discourse as it pertains directly to the Trinitarian life, as exhibited in Schumacher's work, and yet it will be necessary to circle back to the question of evil's intelligibility in the larger theodramatic schema (particularly by engaging Hadley's analysis).

THEODRAMATIC DISCOURSE ON THE TRINITY: ANALOGY, RECEPTIVITY, AND SELF-SURRENDER

Leaving aside here further consideration of the pertinence of the theology of grace to soteriology and eschatology, other aspects of Schumacher's defense of Balthasar's Trinitarian theology nonetheless deserve further treatment. Since the salvation economy is the sole lens through which Balthasar approaches the immanent life of the Trinity, his theodramatic perspective on the former applies not only to the economy, but also to God Himself. Relying heavily on Adrienne von Speyr, Balthasar proposes a number of questionable images for the Trinitarian life. But before I recapitulate the problematic aspects of Balthasar's analogical speech concerning the Trinitarian life, I will consider Schumacher's attempt to reconcile Balthasar's Speyrian theodramatic Trinitarian theology with the Thomistic Trinitarian theology that tends to dominate Catholic systematic treatises as well as Christopher Hadley's recent defense of Balthasar's Trinitarian thought against critiques offered by Matthew Levering and Karen Kilby.[62]

---

[61] Margaret Turek, *Theology of God the Father*, 201.

[62] See Christopher Hadley, SJ, "The All-Embracing Frame: Distance in the Trinitarian Theology of Hans Urs von Balthasar," (PhD diss., Marquette University, 2015).

In an apparent preemptive defense against any systematic criticism of Balthasar's theodramatic theology, which is clearly intended to encompass and integrate the traditional treatises of Christology, soteriology, Trinitarian theology, theological anthropol-

Utilizing select comments of the foremost Dominican specialist in Trinitarian theology, Gilles Emery,[63] Schumacher rightly argues that Balthasar's opposition to the notion that the Trinitarian processions emanate from the divine essence, as if the nature of God precedes His internal relations, is in line with Aquinas's own articulation.[64] But she seems to recognize that a fundamental difference between Thomistic Trinitarian theology and Balthasar's exists where the former interprets the "greater dissimilitude than similitude" to call for apophasis, while the latter takes

---

ogy, and eschatology, Hadley makes the unargued claim: "[Balthasar] would never call the *Glory of the Lord* and the *Theo-Drama* series 'systematic theology.' . . . Balthasar's slightly more systematic work on the Trinity in TL2 and TL3 presumes the theology of distance established in a more eidetic and literary fashion in GL7, TD4, and TD5" (Hadley, "The All-Embracing Frame," 265).

Certainly, Balthasar does not purport to replace Aquinas's *Summa* with his own or to imitate the medieval model of *quaestiones disputatae*, but that does not mean he makes no claim upon systematic theology. He evidently intends to supersede this type of systematic theology by propounding a literary-aesthetic-dramatic-mystical perspective aimed at grasping the totality of dogma and the exegesis upon which it is based, which of course cannot be devoid of claims bearing on systematic theology (even if "postmodern," in some sense).

I agree, therefore, with what Hadley says a little later on, building on a personal conversation with Peter Henrici:

> Balthasar is always writing eschatology. Balthasar himself leaves a signpost for his readers [*My Work: In Retrospect*, 25]: "Almost my entire work . . . can be understood under this heading as an attempt not to underestimate the utterly mysterious step that revelation takes beyond the eschatology of the Old Covenant (which must be understood prophetically!) into the eschatology of the New and eternal Covenant." This insight is offered in 1955, but he remains true to it through the entire great trilogy to the last volume. ("The All-Embracing Frame," 276)

63 Schumacher relies on Emery's *Trinity in Aquinas* (Ave Maria, FL: Sapientia Press, 2003), which is an excellent compilation of some of his articles (translated by various authors, mostly Matthew Levering), as well as his "*Theologia* and *Dispensatio*: The Centrality of the Divine Missions in St. Thomas's Trinitarian Theology," *The Thomist* 74, no. 4 (2010): 515–561.

But Emery has also authored numerous other trinitarian studies, such as *The Trinitarian Theology of St. Thomas Aquinas*, trans. Francesca Aran Murphy (Oxford: Oxford University Press, 2007); *Trinity, Church, and the Human Person: Thomistic Essays* (Ave Maria, FL: Sapientia Press, 2007); and his doctoral dissertation, *Le Trinité créatrice: Trinité et création dans les commentaires aux Sentences de Thomas d'Aquin et de ses précurseurs Albert le Grand et Bonaventure* (Paris: Vrin, 1995). Schumacher, however, does not highlight the differences between Emery's elucidations of Thomistic trinitarian theology and Balthasar's.

64 See Schumacher, *Trinitarian Anthropology*, 52–53.

it to warrant recourse to mystical language.[65] Balthasar considers the apophatic mode to be delimiting of the Godhead and chooses, instead, to turn the "ever-greater" epistemological claim of the Fourth Lateran Council into an ontological claim about God's own being as "'ever-greater' even [with respect] to himself."[66] Thus, rather than invoke the Dionysian way of eminence, Balthasar speaks of God as super-"x," by which he means to include both the affirmation and negation of the quality; for instance, instead of attributing "absolute immutability" to God, he predicates of Him "super-mutability."[67] None of this is explained by Balthasar, at least, not explicitly. But, as should become clear, this type of approach risks substituting metaphorical-symbolic discourse for proper metaphysical predication.

Perhaps presupposing a Bonaventurian rather than Thomistic theology of revelation and reason,[68] Balthasar prefers a katological approach to the Creator-creature relationship to an analogical one, that is, he tends to view everything as images of an archtypical primal self-surrender, where love precedes knowledge, as Schumacher points out.[69] To designate Balthasar's approach as insufficiently apophatic is a legitimate criticism to anyone who wants to maintain the Fourth Lateran Council's "greater dissimilarity."[70] But some persist in the belief that the economy of divine revelation in history permits such a katalogical perspective. It is not possible to adjudicate here the large-scale debate concerning analogical predication and its import for the view that the economic and immanent dimensions of the Trinity are identical.[71] But Balthasar seems to want it both ways: on the one hand, he objects to Rahner's conflation of the economic and immanent[72]—Rahner is, of course, his favorite sparring partner—but, on

---

[65] See Schumacher, 78.

[66] See Schumacher, 79–80, citing *TD* V, 78.

[67] See Schumacher, 80. Hence, also rather than speak of God's utter transcendence of space and time, He speaks of His "super-space" and "super-time" (see, e.g., *TD* V, 29–32, 250, 310 [G 24–26, 226, 282–283]).

[68] For general familiarity with this difference in medieval theology, see the cursory historical analysis of Ralph McInerny, *Duns Scotus and Medieval Christianity* (Ashland, OR: Blackstone Audio Inc., 2006). Also, Junius Johnson points to Bonaventure's influence on Balthasar's divine discourse in *Christ and Analogy*, 95–97.

[69] See Schumacher, *Trinitarian Anthropology*, 15–16.

[70] Denz. 806 [old numbering: 432].

[71] I have attempted to treat this issue in piecemeal fashion in earlier chapters of this work and elsewhere. For more on this, see, e.g., Dennis W. Jowers, *The Trinitarian Axiom of Karl Rahner: The Economic Trinity is the Immanent Trinity and Vice Versa* (Lewiston, NY: Edwin Mellen Press, 2006).

[72] See Balthasar, *TD* III, 157 [G 143]; *TD* V, 228, 257–258 [G 206, 232–233]. See Rahner,

the other hand, he wants to justify a Speyrian (i.e., God's-eye view) theological vision by "transcending," as it were, the apophatic emphasis of the Fourth Lateran Council, Thomas Aquinas, and Erich Przywara, the formative Jesuit whose treatment of the *analogia entis* Balthasar utilized (and modified) in dialogue with Barth.[73]

Along with Rahner,[74] Balthasar resists the so-called "psychological analogy" for the Trinitarian processions, developed by Augustine and Aquinas.[75] Schumacher highlights Balthasar's Speyrian emphasis on the primordial primacy of love (conceived as self-surrender or "self-expropriation")

"Remarks on the Dogmatic Treatise 'De Trinitate,'" in *Theological Investigations*, vol. 4, *More Recent Writings*, trans. Kevin Smyth (Baltimore: Helicon Press, 1966), 87; *The Trinity*, 22 and 31. Regarding the nineteenth-century origins of this distinction, see Werner Brandle, "Immanente Trinität—Ein 'Denkmal der Kirchengeschichte': Überlegungen zu Karl Rahners Trinitätslehre," *Kerygma und Dogma* 38 (1992): 185–198, at 188–189, cited by Emery, "*Theologia* and *Dispensatio*," 559n133.

For an attempt to iron out the imprecision in Balthasar's treatment of the immanent-economic relationship as it pertains, particularly, to the Father's "self-disappropriation," see Margaret Turek, *Theology of God the Father*, especially 59ff.

[73] For the metaphysics of Przywara, see his newly translated *Analogia Entis: Metaphysics—Original Structure and Universal Rhythm*, trans. John R. Betz and David Bentley Hart (Grand Rapids, MI: Eerdmans, 2014). For background on Przywara's influence on Balthasar, see James Zeitz, "Przywara and von Balthasar on Analogy."

For Balthasar's attempt to reconcile the *analogia entis* with Barth's notion of *analogia fidei*, see especially his *Theology of Karl Barth*. Balthasar later went so far as to accuse Przywara of a tendency toward pantheism or theopanism (see Manfred Lochbrunner, *Hans Urs von Balthasar und seine Theologenkollegen: Sechs Beziehungsgeschichten* [Wurzburg: Echter, 2009], 29–30, 134).

[74] See Rahner, *The Trinity*, especially 18 and 119. For a critique of Rahner on this point, see Jeremy D. Wilkins, "Method, Order, and Analogy in Trinitarian Theology: Karl Rahner's Critique of the 'Psychological' Approach," *The Thomist* 74, no. 4 (2010): 563–592.

[75] See Augustine, *De Trinitate*, Book V; Aquinas, *De Potentia* q. 9, a. 9, ad 7; *ST* I, q. 43, a. 5. The disputable term "psychological analogy," which was picked up by Rahner, was coined by Michael Schmaus (see Emery, *Trinity in Aquinas*, 156). Balthasar tends to avoid the term, but he is also reluctant to utilize the analogy for various reasons (e.g., preference for the language of activity-receptivity and the Bonaventurean primacy he accords to love vis-à-vis truth, which are connected via the notion of self-expropriation).

Rahner more explicitly distances himself from Thomistic Trinitarian theology on scriptural grounds; see Matthew Levering's able response to such criticism in "Wisdom and the Viability of Thomstic Trinitarian Theology," *The Thomist* 64 (2000): 593–618. For a different defense of Aquinas on this score, perhaps too apophatic, see Karen Kilby, "Aquinas, the Trinity, and the Limits of Understanding," *International Journal of Systematic Theology* 7, no. 4 (2005): 414–427.

as the *ratio* constitutive of the Trinitarian processions.[76] She also notes that Aquinas, on the contrary, eventually argues that the Son's generation cannot have its formal reason in love since such would imply an act of the will at the origin of the divine person,[77] and "this is the Arian heresy."[78] It may be difficult to reconcile this argument with the origin of the Holy Spirit in love, which follows upon the Word's generation as image or *verbum* (i.e., Wisdom personified), since the third person proceeds with equal necessity of nature as does the second.[79] But if, as Schumacher argues, Balthasar invokes the "greater dissimilarity" between Creator and creature here to reject the transcendental validity of the principle that what is not known cannot be loved,[80] his application of this dictum is extraordinarily selective to the point of capriciousness. It seems rather odd to claim that thanksgiving and service, for instance, are simpler (or purer) ontological perfections than truth and *intellectus*.[81] Thus, while it is fine to advocate for love as the ultimate *ratio* for the existence of the Trinity, it is problematic to assert (as Balthasar does) that the Son and Spirit proceed by will of the Father,[82]

---

[76] See Schumacher, *Trinitarian Anthropology*, 46–47; Balthasar, *TL* II, 177.

[77] See John F. Boyle, "St. Thomas and the Analogy of *Potentia Generandi*," *The Thomist* 64 (2000): 581–592.

[78] Aquinas, *Super Ioannem* 3, lect. 6, no. 545, cited by Schumacher, *Trinitarian Anthropology*, 47. Emery also notes Aquinas's opposition to "the generation of the Son by will rather than by nature" as Arian heresy, in his commentary on St. John's gospel (*Trinity in Aquinas*, 308).

However, Marchesi notes, citing *TL* III, 133–134 (Italian edition): "With Bonaventure, preceded by Richard of Saint Victor, Balthasar remembers that he needs to keep from defining the procession of the Son as *per modum voluntatis* and that of the Spirit as *per modum voluntatis* or *liberalitatis*, insofar as God—as A. von Speyr affirms—is beyond our categories of necessity and freedom" (*La Cristologia Trinitaria*, 345n60 [my translation]).

[79] Emery even notes: "The doctrine of the procession of the Spirit as Love, by mode of will, is much less clear to our mind [than that of the Word by intellectual mode]" (*Trinity in Aquinas*, 284), commenting on *In Ioannem* 15:26, no. 2064. Aquinas treats the latter, e.g., in his *In Ioannem* 3:35, 5:20, 15:26 (see *Trinity in Aquinas*, 281). See also Aquinas's *In I Sent.*, d. 10, q. 1, a. 1, ad 3, which may shed more light on the difficulty (see Gilles Emery, "Trinity and Creation," in *The Theology of Thomas Aquinas*, eds. Rik Van Nieuwenhove and Joseph P. Wawrykow (Notre Dame: University of Notre Dame, 2010), 58–76, at 64).

[80] See *ST* I, q. 27, a. 3, ad 3; *SCG* IV, ch. 19; IV, ch. 24, no. 3617; *Super Ioannem* 15:16, no. 2064.

[81] Such is implied in *TD* V, 82, as relayed by Schumacher, *Trinitarian Anthropology*, 48.

[82] See *TL* II, 136, 162–164 [G 126–127, 149–151]; *TL* III, 158, 162 [G 145, 149]; *Explorations* IV, 35; *Love Alone is Credible*, 145; all cited by Schumacher, *Trinitarian Anthropology*, 50–51.

given that love presupposes freedom of will, precisely because the love of God transcends the created categories of natural necessity and freedom as it is experienced in this world.

Furthermore, it is precisely his reluctance to found at least the *via eminentiae* upon the prior *via negativa* (or *via remotionis*), opting instead for emphasis upon the *via positiva* (or *via affirmationis*),[83] that facilitates his occasional tendency to speak of the Trinitarian relations in terms of masculinity and femininity, which ends up (in the eyes of many) giving short shrift to femininity.[84] Refuting Tina Beattie's claims of misogyny

---

[83] Acknowledging significant dialogue with Martin Heidegger in Balthasar, D. C. Schindler, relying on Siewerth and Ulrich, argues that Pzywara's rendition of divine naming is more "dialectical" than "analogical" because it hangs too much on the negative moment (particularly, negation of finitude, which itself must be finite). But the alternative Schindler offers cursorily is affirmation of the positivity of finitude, as if super-affirming finite realities of God is better than negating the finitude of every affirmation (see *Dramatic Structure of Truth*, especially 46–56).

Recognizing the limits of human reason, even as enlightened by supernatural faith, would seem to demand emphasis on the determinative significance of the negative moment in the *triplex via* (which culminates in the *via eminentiae*) integral to theological discourse, but I cannot enter here into this aspect of the debate concerning *analogia entis*.

[84] Hence, Balthasar's interpretation of femininity versus masculinity, as well as its implications for Trinitarian theology, has been hotly debated. See, for instance, Linn Marie Tonstad, "Sexual Difference and Trinitarian Death: Cross, Kenosis, and Hierarchy in the *Theo-Drama*," *Modern Theology* 26, no. 4 (2010): 603–631; Aristotle Papanikolaou, "Person, *Kenosis*, and Abuse: Hans Urs von Balthasar and Feminist Theologies in Conversation," *Modern Theology* 19, no. 1 (2003): 41–65; Tina Beattie, "A Man and Three Women: Hans, Adrienne, Mary, and Luce," *New Blackfriars* 79 (1998): 97–105; Agneta Sutton, "The Complementarity and Symbolism of the Two Sexes: Karl Barth, Hans Urs von Balthasar and John Paul II," *New Blackfriars* 87, no. 1010 (2006): 418–433; Barbara K. Sain, "Through a Different Lens: Rethinking the Role of Sexual Difference in the Theology of Hans Urs von Balthasar," *Modern Theology* 25, no. 1 (2009): 71–96; Robert A. Pesarchick, *The Trinitarian Foundation of Human Sexuality as Revealed by Christ according to Hans Urs von Balthasar: The Revelatory Significance of the Male Christ and the Male Ministerial Priesthood* (Rome: Editrice Pontificia Universita Gregoriana, 2000); Kristen Kingfield Kearns, "Love from Above: Analogy and Sexual Difference in the Theology of Hans Urs von Balthasar," (PhD diss., University of Chicago, 2003); David L. Schindler, "Catholic Theology, Gender, and the Future of Western Civilization," *Communio* 20 (1993): 200–239; Anton Strukelj, "Man and Woman under God: The Dignity of the Human Being according to Hans Urs von Balthasar," *Communio* 20 (1993): 377–388; Michelle A. Gonzalez, "Hans Urs von Balthasar and Contemporary Feminist Theology," *Theological Studies* 65 (2004): 566–595; Rachel Muer, "A Question of Two Answers: Difference and Determination in Barth and von Balthasar," *Heythrop Journal* 40 (1999): 265–279; John O'Donnell, SJ, "Man and Wom-

in Balthasar,[85] Schumacher nonetheless does not note the drawbacks of speaking about God in terms of gender difference.[86] In any case, it is simplistic to equate (as Balthasar tends to do) activity with masculinity and receptivity with femininity, given that the sexual difference may be better understood in different categories.

Moreover, Balthasar not only predicates relational receptivity to Son and Spirit,[87] but also attributes receptivity to God as Father. This is a problematic move since Father is origin of Son and Spirit. It makes sense to speak of the activity of the Father with respect to the Son and Spirit as well as of the Son with respect to the Spirit (even if instrumentally),[88] but it ought to

---

an as *Imago Dei* in the Theology of Hans Urs von Balthasar," *Clergy Review* 68, no. 4 (1983): 117–128; Gerard O'Loughlin, "Sexing the Trinity," *New Blackfriars* 79, no. 923 (1998): 18–25, and "Erotics: God's Sex," in *Radical Orthodoxy*, ed. John Milbank et al. (New York: Routledge, 1999), 143–162; Lucy Gardner and David Moss, "Something Like Time: Something Like the Sexes—An Essay in Reception," in *Balthasar at the End of Modernity,* ed. Lucy Gardner et al. (Edinburgh, T&T Clark, 1999), 69–137; Corinne Crammer, "One Sex or Two? Balthasar's Theology of the Sexes," in *Cambridge Companion to Hans Urs von Balthasar,* 93–112; Celia Deane-Drummond, "The Breadth of Glory," *International Journal of Systematic Theology* 12, no. 1 (2010): 46–64, at 59ff.; Antoine Birot, "Le fondement christologique et trinitaire de la difference sexuelle chez Adrienne von Speyr," *Communio* (French Edition) 31 (2006): 123–135; Christopher Hadley, "The All-Embracing Frame," 211ff.; Karen Kilby, *Balthasar*, ch. 6.

85 Schumacher, *Trinitarian Anthropology*, 256–257. In the following pages, she relies largely on Balthasar's essay, "Die wurde der Frau," *Internationale Katholische Zeitschrift "Communio"* 11 (1982): 346–352.

86 See Balthasar, *TD* V, 86, 91 [G 75, 80]; *TD* III, 287–288 [G 264]; *Credo: Meditations on the Apostles' Creed*, trans. David Kipp (Edinburgh: T&T Clark, 1989), 30.

87 See, e.g., *TD* V, 86; Schumacher, *Trinitarian Anthropology*, 86. Compare to Aquinas, *Super Ioannem* 14, lect. 8, no. 1971, available at http://dhspriory.org/thomas/John14.htm. It is interesting to see that even in the former Aquinas is tentative.

88 Emery notes, in the context of the *filioque* controversy, on which both Aquinas and Balthasar are firmly Western: "Thomas does, however, accept references to the Holy Spirit proceeding principally (*principaliter*) from the Father, following Albert who was particularly given to using this Augustinian formula. The procession *principaliter a Patre*, which recalls the theme of Father as '*arche*' in the Greek theological tradition, is also rigorously interpreted in the sense of the order of origin which it designates" (*Trinity in Aquinas*, 218–219). At the same time, with respect to the notion of "*monarchia*" in the Father: "any idea of one person taking priority over another is dispelled (in contrast to Bonaventure, Thomas also refuses to accept references to a 'hierarchy' in the Trinity, in any strict sense), as well as any idea of a 'greater' or a 'lesser': The Holy Spirit does not proceed 'to a greater extent' nor 'more fully' from the Father than from the Son" (218).

For a strange attempt to transcend the *filioque* debate, see Thomas Weinandy, OFM, *The Father's Spirit of Sonship: Reconceiving the Trinity* (Eugene, OR: Wipf & Stock, 1995), the logical result of Rahner's axiom. In contrast, Balthasar developed a doctrine

be added that while active spiration is not a self-subsistent relation, since it is common to two persons of the Trinity, passive spiration is the Holy Spirit Itself.[89] The significance of receptivity as the distinguishing feature of the Spirit is undeveloped in Balthasar, who seems, rather, to want to attribute a mixture of activity and receptivity to each divine person.

Still, Schumacher disputes Nicholas Healy's contention that, according to Balthasar, "God can 'receive' something from the creature."[90] She argues for an interpretation of Balthasar's refusal to identify "the diverse forms of potentiality" with the *dissimilitudines* of creation compared to "divine actuality" in terms of his affirmation of a proportional relationship between the Creator-creature difference and the Father-Son-Spirit difference.[91] But she does not explain how this squares with the final pages of *Das Endspiel* concerning divine self-enrichment, which constitutes the linchpin of Healy's interpretation. There is nothing objectionable about relating various created differences and even the difference between Creator and creature to the inner-Trinitarian distinctions, as Gilles Emery notes that such reasoning is present throughout medieval reflection.[92] The problem comes when one understands this "proportional relation between proportional relations"[93] to imply that mixed perfections (that is, admixtures of act and potency) may be analogously predicated of the divine life.

---

of Trinitarian inversion (see *TL* III, 182–183 [G 166–168]; *TD* III, 183ff. [G 167ff.]); for analysis, see Jean-Noel Dol, "L'inversion trinitaire chez Hans Urs von Balthasar," *Revue Thomiste* 100, no. 2 (2000): 205–237; Matthew Lewis Sutton, "A Compelling Trinitarian Taxonomy: Hans Urs von Balthasar's Theology of the Trinitarian Inversion and Reversion," *International Journal of Systematic Theology* 14, no. 2 (2012): 161–176; Pitstick, *Light in Darkness*, 230–234.

Balthasar desires in the end to transcend the East-West divide on the *filioque* (see *TL* III, 207–218 [G 189–200]), as James Buckley points out, but this does not represent as significant a difference from Aquinas as he suggests (see "Balthasar's Use of Thomas," 536, 539, 544; see *TL* III, 160–161 [G 147–148]).

[89] See Aquinas, *ST* I, q. 40, a. 4. For more on the four divine relations, see also Neil Ormerod, "A Trajectory from Augustine to Aquinas and Lonergan: Contingent Predication and the Trinity," *Irish Theological Quarterly* 82, no. 3 (2017): 208–221.

[90] Healy, *Eschatology*, 25–26; Schumacher, *Trinitarian Anthropology*, 317.

[91] Schumacher, *Trinitarian Anthropology*, 316–317, citing Balthasar, *TL* II, 83, and 316.

[92] See, for instance, Aquinas's *In I Sent.*, d. 26, q. 2, a. 2, ad 2; d. 10, q. 1, a. 1, ad 2; d. 6, q. 1, a. 2. See Emery, "Trinity and Creation: The Trinitarian Principle of the Creation in the Commentaries of Albert the Great, Bonaventure, and Thomas Aquinas on the *Sentences*," in *Trinity in Aquinas*, 33–70. His first major work, *Le Trinité créatrice*, is an even more thorough investigation of this topic.

[93] This quote is from Boethius, *De institutione arithmetica* II, 40 (see Balthasar, *TL* II, 316), cited by Schumacher, *Trinitarian Anthropology,* 317.

It is true that there is something in God analogous to potency *as* a real principle of being and that something is act itself, as act and potency are not equivocally related. But this does not mean that there is something in God properly analogous to act-potency mixtures themselves since the potency limits the act and thus the finite act must be purified of its intrinsic relationship to potency in order to be predicable of the Being that is pure act, which is only possible for spiritual qualities (leaving aside the case of transcendentals).

Schumacher, thus, rightly defends the applicability of the notion of receptivity to the divine, but in doing so she utilizes questionable reasoning, namely, the recruitment of the Thomistic doctrine that the divine hypostases are constitutively distinguished by virtue of their mutual relations.[94] She would be better served to argue that receptivity is a simple perfection, as David Schindler and W. Norris Clarke do, which need not necessitate receptivity to creation as such.[95] Why? Because it is clear that Balthasar prefers the Bonaventurian-Scotist understanding of the Trinitarian identity over Aquinas's. In the former view, "the person is not constituted by the relation but by an absolute reality of the kind that the divine persons are first thought of as absolutes and only secondly as the relations by which they are referred."[96] This certainly sounds more like Balthasar, who routinely speaks of the Son proceeding from the Father's own act of divine self-surrender and, for this reason, is sometimes accused of tending toward tri-theism, as Schumacher notes.[97]

She notes Balthasar's cursory attempt to patch up this division between persons by appeal to the Holy Spirit as the unifying force: "as [personal unity] the Spirit is both 'the heart of the Father's command and the

---

[94] See Schumacher, *Trinitarian Anthropology*, 318, where she invokes Edward Oakes's defense of Balthasar on the matter in *Pattern of Redemption*, 286 (cf. Balthasar, *TD* V, 85).

[95] See references in previous chapter. For the related notion that person is constituted communionally, see Adrian J. Walker, "Personal Singularity and the *Communio Personarum*: A Creative Development of Thomas Aquinas' Doctrine of *Esse Commune*," *Communio* 31 (Fall 2004): 457–479.

[96] See Gilles Emery, *Trinity in Aquinas*, 205n108, citing Scotus, *Lectura in I Sent.*, d. 26, q. 1. (*Opera Omnia*, vol. 17 [Vatican City: Ex typis Polyglottis Vaticanis], 328–337).

[97] Schumacher, *Trinitarian Anthropology*, 333. She does not cite the critics on this point, but see, e.g., Sachs's review of Edward Oakes's *Pattern of Redemption* in *Theological Studies* 56, no. 4 (1995): 787–789; T. J. White, "Kenoticism and the Divinity of Christ Crucified." Other terms used synonymously by Balthasar and Balthasarians are "self-expropriation" and "self-abandonment," the last of which seems to evoke the theme of Christ's suffering more than does the term "self-surrender."

heart of the Son's obedience.'"[98] Again, Balthasar states: "the triune God, who, as God, can command absolutely and obey absolutely and, as the Spirit of love, can be the unity of both."[99] But, strictly speaking, God cannot obey Himself if He is one Being, except insofar as the Incarnate Word *as man* obeys God's commands issued in the name of the Father. The reason Balthasar takes this approach is due to an explicit attempt to go beyond the Cyrillian-Chalcedonian doctrine of the *communicatio idiomatum*,[100] which Schumacher does not mention by name: "Balthasar holds that it is possible 'to apply qualities and attributes of the one nature to the other' precisely because 'both are united in the one person of the Logos.'"[101] In these terms, it becomes possible for Balthasar to speak of God Himself as obedient to Himself as God—yet another manifestation of the dialectic that transcends the analogy of being, for Balthasar. It is his concern in dialogue with Barth to uphold the primacy of Christ over the philosophical notion of analogy as the only bridge across the infinite divide between Creator and creature that lends itself to this type of move.[102]

However, it is not necessary to cast aside the *communicatio idiomatum* to designate Christ as the "concrete *analogia entis*."[103] There is nothing

---

[98] Schumacher, *Trinitarian Anthropology*, 333, quoting *A Theology of History*, 62.

[99] *GL* I, 479, quoted by Schumacher, *Trinitarian Anthropology*, 333; she also cites *GL* I, 409; *TL* II, 354; and *Mysterium Paschale*, 82.

[100] In the context of the chasm between Creator and creature, he states: "it follows that neither the doctrine of grace nor that of the *communicatio idiomatum* between the two natures of Christ is of any avail" (*TD* III, 222 [G 203]).

[101] Schumacher, *Trinitarian Anthropology*, 335, citing *TD* III, 222. Rodney Howsare thinks that Balthasar is able to navigate a *tertia via* between Hegel and "hyper-traditionalism"— an odd, unjustified, and dismissive epithet for the classical position—by simply "[recognizing] the enhypostatic character of [Christ's] suffering" (O'Regan, *Anatomy of Misremembering*, 307; see Howsare, "Why Hegel? A Reading of Cyril O'Regan's *The Anatomy of Misremembering*, Volume 1," *Nova et Vetera* [English Edition] 14, no. 3 [2016]: 983–992, at 991).

Guy Mansini points out that this notion common in kenotic theology derives from Martin Luther (see "Hegel and Christian Theology," *Nova et Vetera* [English Edition] 14, no. 3 [2016]: 993–1001, at 1000). The *en-hypostatic* character of His suffering is affirmed by the Chalcedonian tradition and does not imply anything beyond it, as does Balthasar.

[102] Concerning this question and related questions, see, e.g., Thomas Joseph White, ed., *The Analogy of Being: Invention of the Antichrist or the Wisdom of God?* (Grand Rapids, MI: Eerdmans, 2011). Most relevant to Balthasar's own perspective is Peter Casarella's essay, "Hans Urs von Balthasar, Erich Przywara's *Analogia Entis*, and the Problem of a Catholic *Denkform*," 192–206.

[103] *TD* III, 222 [G 203]; *Theology of History*, 74 [G 53]; *Epilogue*, 89 [G 69].

incompatible between the assertions that what belongs to one of Christ's natures cannot be properly predicated of the other and that Christ is the Incarnation of the commonality (*esse!*) between God and creature. Thus, the receptivity of the Son in generation cannot be conflated with the obedience of the Son Incarnate, even if there is an analogical relationship between the two; hence, the problem comes back to how to understand the distinction made between "economic Trinity" and "immanent Trinity," which Balthasar does not explicitly address.[104]

It is evident that Balthasar wants to thread a very brittle needle, but it does not seem a plausible possibility to mediate successfully (as he attempts) between kenotic theology and classical doctrine. Battling the appearance of tri-theism, Balthasar attempts to clarify his *ur*-kenotic view of the Trinitarian relations, but he does himself no favors:

> The Father strips himself, without remainder, of his Godhead. The Father must not be thought to exist "prior" to this self-surrender (in an Arian sense): he is this movement of self-giving that holds nothing back. This divine act that brings forth the Son, that is, the second way of participating in (and of *being*) the identical Godhead.[105]

It is good that he rules out the Arian sense of priority, which is temporal, but the question is whether he rules out natural or substantial priority (i.e., asserting more than mere logically relational priority). He asserts that the Son proceeds from the Father's own self-expropriation or self-surrender, which implies some kind of ontological priority—that is, not merely the logical priority of Father to Son—but there can no more be a father without a son than a son without a father, as the two terms are mutually defining.[106]

---

[104] Gilles Emery suggests persuasively that this terminology is not helpful, as it tends simplistically to identify the economic with that revealed in the Scriptures (see *Trinity in Aquinas*, 293–294), and he argues effectively that the distinction is methodologically flawed compared to Aquinas's levelheaded treatment of the divine processions and missions (see "*Theologia* and *Dispensatio*," 559–560).

[105] *TD* IV, 323, cited by Schumacher, *Trinitarian Anthropology*, 341–342.

[106] Emery explains Aquinas's reasoning: "What Thomas rejects, here again, is that the suppositum to whom belongs the notional act could be thought in a pre-relational or essential manner (as subsisting essence), independently of his constitution as a person, that is to say independently of his personal relation" (*Trinity in Aquinas*, 192).

Thus, different from Balthasar: "for St. Thomas, this Bonaventurean thesis [of the Father's *primitas*] means that the Father would be in a certain manner constituted as Father prior to his relation of paternity. St. Thomas therefore rejects this thesis because in it he finds a pre-relational conception of the Father" (*Trinity in Aquinas*, 148).

What Balthasar wants to do is to recast the Trinitarian relations in terms of self-surrender, a theme that pervades Schumacher's exposition of his work. Yet responding to criticisms by Alyssa Pitstick, Schumacher denies that Balthasar "mean[s] to identify the divine essence (understood as being or substance) with self-surrender."[107] More accurately reflecting Balthasar's position, I think, Rodney A. Howsare suggests that the divine essence is constituted precisely by self-surrender when he sums up Balthasar's crucicentric Trinitarian theology thus, flirting with mythological transposition:

> In Christ's self-offering to the Father . . . we even get a glimpse of the eternal self-sacrifice that the Father has made in giving his divinity to the Son, without holding anything back. In other words, the self-offering of the Son traces itself all the way back to the self-offering of the Father so that there is no use trying to locate the essence of God anywhere "behind" such self-offering.[108]

Schumacher, instead, invokes Marc Ouellet's keen application of the "greater dissimilitude" to the analogy between the kenosis of the Cross and the mutual self-giving that characterizes the divine persons, a sage move.[109] However, Balthasar himself does not make this move, and Schumacher's complementary citation of "an insight offered by Gilles Emery" causes her own defense of Balthasar to fall under its own weight. Schumacher correctly sums up an aspect of Emery's analysis: "rather than speak of divine 'suffering'—a notion which risks introducing a lack, or defect, into the

---

[107] Schumacher, *Trinitarian Anthropology*, 343. Again, she says: "Balthasar does *not* maintain that surrender is itself the essence of the Godhead" (*Trinitarian Anthropology*, 351n265). But if this is true, what sense does it make to speak of the Trinitarian persons as subsisting acts of "letting-go" or "letting-be" [*gehörenlassen*] (see *TD* V, 86, and *TD* II, 259, cited in *Trinitarian Anthropology*, 351–352)?

[108] Rodney A. Howsare, *Balthasar: A Guide for the Perplexed* (New York: T&T Clark, 2009), 139. Christopher Hadley highlights the significance of *TD* IV, 325 [G 303] for this notion; see "The All-Embracing Frame," 171, 173.

See also *TL* II, 136 [G 126]: "he remains the eternal Father only insofar as he has eternally given over to the Son all that is his, including the divinity. The same applies, analogously, to the Father and the Son in connection with the production of the Holy Spirit, who otherwise could not be the coeternal God. . . . [D]oes not the divine essence become something that is as much 'in motion' as the event of the processions themselves?"

[109] See Ouellet, "The Message of Balthasar's Theology to Modern Theology," *Communio* 23 (1996): 286–299, at 293, cited in Schumacher, *Trinitarian Anthropology*, 344.

absolute perfection of divine being—we should speak instead of God's infinite and unchanging love."[110] In other words, there is an analogical relationship between the mutual self-giving love that constitutes the Trinitarian life and the suffering manifestation of that love in the passion of Christ, but that does not mean it is proper to speak of the processions in terms of a self-sacrificial love, as sacrifice (suffering) cannot exist in the blissful being of *ipsum amor* precisely because it is identical to *ipsum esse*.

Balthasar goes on in the same text to say about the "divine act that brings forth the Son" that it "involves the positing of an absolute, infinite 'distance' that can contain and embrace all the other distances that are possible within the world of finitude, including the distance of sin."[111] Citing the text that immediately follows this as well as a radiobroadcast by Balthasar that was later printed,[112] Schumacher reports:

> [Balthasar] argues that the sinful alienation of the creature is located within the distinction of the hypostases. Similarly, Balthasar argues that "[S]ince the world cannot have any other *locus* but within the distinction between the Hypostases [there is nothing outside God: *Theo-Drama* 2.260–62], the problems associated with it—its sinful alienation from God—can only be solved at this *locus*. The creature's No resounds at the 'place' of distinction within the Godhead" (ibid. 4.333–34).[113]

In fact, the notion of distance is frequently invoked in Balthasar's Trinitarian eschatology, a theme on which much light is shed by the recent dissertation of Christopher Hadley on the topic. Confessedly imitating Kevin Mongrain's heuristic of Irenaean retrieval in Balthasar,[114] Hadley ingeniously discerns a Nyssan retrieval at work,[115] which I think is more prominent. But while Balthasar harnesses his research of Gregory of Nyssa

---

[110] Schumacher, *Trinitarian Anthropology*, 344, citing Emery, "The Question of Evil and the Mystery of God in Charles Journet," *Nova et Vetera* (English Edition) 4, no. 3 (2006): 529–556. I have noted elsewhere a slight difference with Emery's conclusions there.

[111] *TD* IV, 323 [G 301].

[112] *You Crown the Year with Your Goodness*, trans. Graham Harrison (San Francisco: Ignatius Press, 1982), 84–85; *TD* IV, 324–325.

[113] Schumacher, "The Concept of Representation," 60n40.

[114] See Mongrain, *The Systematic Thought*.

[115] See Hadley, "The All-Embracing Frame," 15, 257.

throughout his career, he understands him through a Barthian lens.[116] Appropriating Nyssa for his own purposes, as Balthasar is wont to do with all interlocutors who fulfill some function in his own vision, particularly the patristic and medieval, Balthasar develops a theology of distance that goes beyond Barth's own.[117] Hadley's principal contribution is to enumerate the types of distance referenced in both Nyssa and Balthasar, highlighting how the latter develops an analogical structure to the diverse forms of distance that then pervades his Trinitarian and theodramatic discourse.[118] But Hadley fails to point out the shortcomings of the analogy forged, thinking instead that it is the key to an adequate response to criticisms of Balthasar offered by Kilby, Levering, and others.[119]

Hadley's response to Kilby's critique is more successful than his response to Levering's.[120] Kilby's critique centers on Balthasar's presumption to take "a God's eye view," and Levering focuses on his tendency to find in the Trinitarian life itself an eternal analog for Christ's paschal suffering.[121] While Levering's points are more evaded than addressed, Hadley's reply to Kilby is to say that, with Barth, Balthasar understood theology as necessarily divine in perspective, given the nature of divine revelation as simply beyond the created order.[122] But while it is certainly correct to emphasize the divine origin of theology, it is also true that the divine knowledge (*scientia divina*) imparted to human beings is necessarily received by human beings in a manner that is congruent with the limitations of the latter as finite recipient. *Quidquid recipitur ad modum recipientis recipitur.*

Nonetheless, Kilby pinpoints a significant drawback of Balthasar's overly ambitious systematic project, a concern many share (including Levering), when she asks not merely "whether [Balthasar] has the right to such a vivid picture of the eternal life of God," but also "whether the integration he achieves requires too resolved a vision—too positive a vision, indeed—of suffering and evil."[123] In fact, the fundamental problem with Balthasar's theodramatics is its proclivity to render evil an intelli-

---

[116] See Hadley, 114–121.

[117] See Hadley, 87–92.

[118] See especially the diagram on "The All-Embracing Frame," 36, comparing and relating two types of distance found in Nyssa and four in Balthasar.

[119] See Hadley, especially 23, 137ff.

[120] For the latter, see especially Hadley, 174–179. For the former, see especially 97.

[121] See Hadley, 3, citing Kilby's *Balthasar*, 40, 94, and Levering's *Scripture and Metaphysics*, 121, 126–127. See also Kilby, *Balthasar*, 163 and 65.

[122] See Hadley, 101, 132.

[123] *Balthasar*, 94, cited in Hadley, "The All-Embracing Frame," 3.

gible portion of reality, that is, to do precisely what Balthasar sought to avoid—to over-systematize! Evil is a "surd," as Lonergan says, a "vacuum introduced into the warp and woof of being," as Maritain puts it,[124] or a break in the very fabric of being, similar to a black hole in the space-time continuum.[125] Evil is parasitic upon being, not a quality or relation or "difference" that ought to have some archetype in the inner life of *ipsum esse et amor*.

It is precisely this problematic aspect of Balthasar's theology that Hadley inadvertently highlights in his exposition of the relationship between the four types of difference in Balthasar's theology. The four types of distance found in Balthasar follow: (1) the ontological distance between God and creation; (2) the alienation from God created by sin in free creatures; (3) the distance between "the Father's missioning of the Son within the Trinity and the Son's death on the Cross"; (4) the eternal infinite distinction between persons in the Trinity.[126] The claim that unites the four types of distance is that "distance" here is an analogical reality, not an equivocal term for different realities. Hadley explains how the second and third relate to each other, alluding to Balthasar's interpretation, particularly, of Revelation 13:8: "Balthasar interprets the Lamb who is eternally victorious and yet eternally slain as a sign of the eternal, kenotic, Trinitarian event that is the life of God in the divine processions. The image of the Lamb manifests the triumph of God over all evil contained now within the eternity of God's love after the event of the Cross."[127] On the contrary, if we are to avoid both rooting evil's origin in God and implying that God naturally communicates His intra-Trinitarian love *ad extra*, the economy of creation and salvation must be explained in terms of an utterly free act of divine love, not some sacrificial love that is constitutive of His necessary Trinitarian nature.

Most disconcerting is not so much his use of the metaphor of distance for distinct realities as is the implication that there is an analogical unity between sin and Trinitarian distinction, especially. One might argue that there is an analogy between ontological difference (the first type of

---

[124] See Lonergan, *Insight*, 666–667; *Existence and the Existent*, 92 [F 152].

[125] Hence, there is a need for a philosophy of nonbeing to understand evil as a break in the fabric of being, incommensurable with being as good. See, e.g., Jesús Villagrasa Lasaga, *Realismo Metafísico e irrealidad. Estudio sobre la obra 'Teoría del objeto puro' de Antonio Millán-Puelles* (Madrid: Fundación Universitaria Española, 2008), and *Fondazione di un'etica realista* (Rome: Atheneo Ponficia Regina Apostolorum, 2005).

[126] See especially Hadley's "The All-Embracing Frame," 36.

[127] Hadley, 169.

distance) and Trinitarian distinction (the fourth type of distance), and that perhaps there is an analogical relationship between ontological difference and sin (the second type of distance), although the former does not necessitate the latter. But the similarities between the two pairs of distances are different, that is, there is no analogy between the alienation intrinsic to sin and the distinctions of mutual opposition in the Trinity.[128] Balthasar wants to bridge the gap between the alienating reality of sin and the Trinitarian life of mutual self-giving through the redemptive suffering of Christ, where "God made him who had no sin to be sin for us" (2 Cor 5:21). This is an admirable goal, but in the process we do not want to end up rooting the absurdity of evil in the very love and wisdom of God—a supreme absurdity, if there ever was one.

Redemption is more radical, not less, if sin is conceived as the surd that it is, than if it is construed to be contained analogically in God's own being. While the influence of Barth on Balthasar's "theology of distance" is palpable,[129] the presence of Plotinus in Balthasar's Nyssan retrieval is no less evident.[130] The latter not only inclines toward universalism, following the *exitus et reditus* schema to a fault, it also allows Balthasar to advocate a novel perspective on analogy (which he never explains), which of course helps in his rapprochement with Barth, who is no less universalistic and notoriously designated the *analogia entis* "the Anti-Christ" at one point in his career.[131] Specifically, Balthasar wants to emphasize the rootedness

---

[128] Sometimes the distinctions between the divine persons are called mutual relations of opposition or relative oppositions according to origin, but perhaps the best terminological rendering of the notion involved is opposite relations of origin or mutual relational opposition with respect to origin. Concerning these relations, see especially Aquinas, *ST* I, q. 28, a. 3.

[129] See Balthasar's "Analogie und Dialektik. Zur Klärung der theologischen Prinzipienlehre Karl Barths," *Divus Thomas* 22 (1944): 171–216, analyzed by Hadley, "The All-Embracing Frame," especially 106ff.

[130] See, e.g., Cyrus Olsen, "Exitus-Reditus in H. U. von Balthasar," *Heythrop Journal* 52 (2011): 643–658. Gregory of Nyssa is perhaps the most universalistic of the Fathers; see Brian Daley, *The Hope of the Early Church: A Handbook of Patristic Eschatology* (New York: Cambridge University Press, 1991), 85–89. Barth, likewise, is usually recognized as a universalist, despite his stated intention to avoid the heresy of *apokatastasis* (see *Church Dogmatics* II/II, 417); see Balthasar, *Theology of Karl Barth*, 186.

[131] Karl Barth, *Church Dogmatics* I/1, xiii. The relationship between Barth's dialectics and Balthasar's modest usage of analogy in time is debated. Hadley defends Balthasar's conceptualization of Barth's work into three "moments" against Bruce McCormack's argument for greater continuity in Barth (see "The All-Embracing Frame," 89ff.; McCormack, *Karl Barth's Critically Realistic Dialectical Theology: Its Genesis and Development, 1909–1936* [Oxford: Clarendon, 1995]).

of becoming in being, from which his language of God as event emerges (under Barth's influence):[132]

> The trinitarian diastasis between God (the Father) and "the image of the invisible God" (Col 1:15, the Son) forms the all-embracing frame: at its center is the historical drama of Cross-Resurrection-Church that is acted out within history, in such a way that "becoming" is already lodged safely in "being"; accordingly no opposition can be set up between the process of "being reconciled" and the state of "always having been reconciled."[133]

But is there not a greater dissimilarity than similarity between being and becoming? The infinite distance between them is a positive infinity (that is, an infinite distance between a finite entity and infinite entity), whereas the infinite distance between each and nonbeing is a negative infinity (that is, the relatively infinite distance that exists between an entity and nonentity). Thus, both being and becoming *ex-sist* (i.e., "stand outside of nothing"), but the manners in which they do so are infinitely diverse. In other words, what being and becoming hold in common (their similarity) is infinitesimal—the only thing that can be said of them both is that they are not nothing.

In any case, Balthasar is sympathetic to Barth's dialectic of difference and identity, which he also discerns in Gregory of Nyssa (among other Greek Fathers).[134] The attempt to integrate Barthian dialectic into the practice of Dionysian divine naming (i.e., his emphasis on *via eminentiae*, meanwhile under-emphasizing the *via negativa*) yields a greater focus on relating sin, death, and the like to God's inner life than on the proper

---

[132] *Church Dogmatics* II/1, 263, 271; see also George Hunsinger, "Election and the Trinity: Twenty-Five Theses on the Theology of Karl Barth," *Modern Theology* 24 (2008): 179–198.

[133] *TD* V, 423, cited by Hadley, "The All-Embracing Frame," 31.

[134] See Balthasar, "Patristik, Scholastik und Wir," *Theologie der Zeit* 3 (1939): 65–104; ET, "The Fathers, the Scholastics and Ourselves," *Communio* 24 (1997): 347–396. Gregory is, perhaps, one of the Fathers who falls prey, at least on occasion, to the proto-phenomenalism of Platonic philosophy (a precursor to idealism).

Balthasar's fondness for this type of thought, perhaps a result of his engagement with German idealism, prevents him from privileging proper ontological predication, finding solace in symbolic-metaphorical discourse. Hence, Hadley comments: "Balthasar is rather putting a different emphasis on the human cognition of divine life in terms of a patristic analogy ruled by the logic of symbolic reference" ("The All-Embracing Frame," 233).

analogy that exists between beings as such and the intensive act of being (*ipsum esse*) as the archetypical name for God's essence.[135] Speaking of God in terms of event, *pace* Hadley (basing himself on Barth),[136] is not simply the result of discerning the identity of being and act in God, but of a tendency in modern philosophy (and thus modern theology) to replace the metaphysics of substance with a metaphysics of action ("actualism").[137] For a Thomist, there is nothing necessarily wrong with such a metaphysics of action—Blondel may complement Aristotle—as long as it does not sup-

---

[135] Sutton argues that the Speyrian (aka Balthasarian) approach to God is unlike the *via negativa* of (pseudo-)Dionysius, the anonymous medieval author of *The Cloud of Unknowing,* and Meister Eckhart, and similar to the *via positiva* one finds in Thomas Aquinas (see *Heaven Opens,* locations 2242–2247).

But the dynamic role of these two ways of divine naming, together with the *via eminentiae,* in Aquinas, not to mention the Dionysian influence, is highly debated, and Sutton even cites the contrary Gregory P. Rocca's *Speaking the Incomprehensible God: Thomas Aquinas on the Interplay of Positive and Negative Theology* (Washington, DC: The Catholic University of America Press, 2004).

Sutton also invokes Balthasar's inheritance of Przywara's conceptualization of the *analogia entis,* but neglects to mention Balthasar's explicit attempt to leave behind Przywara's apophatic emphasis (see *TL* II, 95n16 [G 87n16]). In any case, no amount of recourse to the *via eminentiae* (see Sutton, location 2361) justifies forgoing or undermining the apophatic moment in divine naming.

[136] Hadley, "The All-Embracing Frame," 38, 119.

[137] Mark McIntosh mentions actualism in connection with Barth's influence on Balthasar as an "[attempt] to alleviate the metaphysical discomfort with essentialist language in Christology which theologians have felt since Schleiermacher" (*Christology From Within,* 5), as if there is a dichotomy between action and essence.

Cyrus Olsen also defends Barthian actualism in Balthasar's theology:

> The act- and event-character of being in Barth has implications for the being of God as event and happening. The "Reality of God," for Barth, is the unity of being and act held together in divine life, a unit that is meant to prevent being and act from being "torn apart" by the idea of "essence." In fact, however, being and act become too easily identified in Barth's theology as they are related polemically to a reversal of the Scholastic axiom *operari sequitur esse: esse sequitur operari.* . . . Balthasar largely agrees with this pathos and seeks to transfer it into Catholic theology. ("Exitus-Reditus in H. U. von Balthasar," 645–646)

Unfortunately, I cannot critique here the (Kantian) phenomenalism that underlies this unjustified reversal of the scholastic axiom, "action follows being." It suffices to note how this phenomenalist approach, if it were entirely victorious in Balthasar, would result in conflating the loss of the feeling of love with loss of the act of love and the experience of hopelessness (or godforsakenness) with actual hopelessness in His dereliction on the cross. Hence, similarly, identifying mission with identity can only be taken so far—such cannot involve denial of the logical priority of the latter.

plant the metaphysics of substance altogether.

Moreover, equating action (the self-disclosure of being) with being itself leads to an emphasis on "conditions of possibility"—a concept pervasive in Immanual Kant's work—as the *ratio* that relates diverse things, founding the analogical unity of "distance," for instance.[138] But this epistemological notion is not sufficient to establish an ontological analogy. When analogy is rooted in action rather than being, Kant's phenomenalism predominates over Aristotle's "*ousia*-ology," phenomenon supplants foundation, and analogy is merely phenomenological, not ontological.[139] All of this results, perhaps paradoxically, in an onto-theology according to which, "Being is a Super-becoming."[140] But the worst effect of such reasoning is the implication that sin seems necessary, if God is truly to reveal Himself,[141] almost as if the fullness of divine self-communication requires the existence of evil![142] Hadley's most careful argument for Balthasr's analogy between sin and Trinity follows: "The Son thus participates in the sinful state of the human spirit, even if the Son does not share in the sinner's will. Because D3 is an expression of D4, the conditions for hell as D2 therefore exist in God by virtue of the possibility of the sinner's rejection of God's mercy in Christ."[143] The response is simple: Christ's suffering reflects divine love insofar as it is an act of self-giving, but not insofar as it is evil; thus, the evil Christ suffers finds no analog in the love that is expressed through the act of enduring it.

Schumacher notes that the problems Aquinas "seeks to resolve for his

---

[138] Hadley, "The All-Embracing Frame," 30 [emphasis added]. "D2 [the second kind of distance] represents the creature's rejection of the Creator at its own end of the 'polarity' of D1 [the first kind of distance], and therefore finds *the possibility for its existence* in D1."

[139] In this manner, one might argue that Kant via Barth is the source of Balthasar's problematic discourse on God.

[140] Balthasar, *Presence and Thought*, 153. He says much later: "it follows that 'God's being' really 'undergoes development' (E. Jungel). . . . [A] single *being*, while we may not call it *becoming*, is the streaming forth of eternal life, superevent [*Uber-Ereignis*]" (*TD* III, 157, 159 [G 143, 145], original italics).

[141] "The All-Embracing Frame," 152. "This distance between the Father and Son is not merely a 'clean-up job' on D2 [alienation due to sin]. D3 [the third type of distance] reveals to us who God truly is."

[142] To this kind of concern, Hadley has only a disjointed, enigmatic response: see "The All-Embracing Frame," 172. He attempts to exonerate Balthasar of ontologizing sin (see 171) but cannot succeed, due to the force of Balthasar's own analogy: "an absolute, infinite 'distance' that can contain and embrace all the other distances that are possible within the world of finitude, including the distance of sin" (*TD* IV, 323 [G 301]).

[143] Hadley, "The All-Embracing Frame," 194–195.

contemporaries within the perspective of their own language of *ontology*," Balthasar "seeks to resolve for his own contemporaries within the context of their proper language of *freedom*."[144] Of course, Balthasar does not completely leave behind ontology any more than Aquinas fails to address the question of freedom. What she means is that Balthasar approaches the same questions as Aquinas primarily from the perspective of personalist phenomenology. Although a fan of John Paul II, who sought to forge a synthesis of classical metaphysics and personalist phenomenology,[145] she fails to mention how *Fides et Ratio* clearly demarcates the limits of the latter methodology as a preparatory step for proper metaphysical predication.[146] It is precisely Balthasar's tendency to apply descriptive analysis super-eminently to God (i.e., meta-symbolic discourse?) rather than engage in classical analogical naming that yields philosophically problematic statements like the following, cited favorably by Schumacher: "[Christ's death] is the human expression of a shared love-death in a supereminently Trinitarian sense: the One who forsakes is just as much affected (in his eternal life) as the One who is forsaken, and just as much the forsaking and forsaken love that is One in the Holy Spirit."[147]

EVALUATING BALTHASAR'S SPEYRIAN TRINITARIAN ANALOGIES

Now that I have reviewed three of the most recent scholarly works on Balthasar's Trinitarian theology, it is opportune to recapitulate analytically the various images Balthasar applies to the Trinitarian life. One of the most common images that pervades Balthasar's divine discourse is certainly that of "distance," the preferred English translation for various German words (e.g., *Distanz, Abstand, Raum, Trennung*).[148] In the context of var-

---

[144] Schumacher, *Trinitarian Anthropology*, 112 (emphasis original).

[145] See especially his *Persona e Atto*, trans. Giuseppe Girgenti and Patrycja Mikulska (Milano: Bompiani, 2001), which is a better translation of his original Polish manuscript than the English, *The Acting Person*, trans. Anna-Teresa Tymieniecka (Dordrecht, Holland: Springer, 1979).

[146] See the Encyclical Letter at http://w2.vatican.va/content/john-paul-ii/en/encyclicals/documents/hf_jp-ii_enc_14091998_fides-et-ratio.html, §§81–84. For more on this, see especially Villagrasa, *Realismo Metafísico,* 12–13. For a briefer treatment of this work in English, see my "Phenomenology and Metaphysics in *Realismo Metafísico e Irrealidad* by Jesús Villagrasa," *Información Filosófica* 5, no. 11 (2008): 219–237.

[147] *TD* IV, 501; see Schumacher, *Trinitarian Anthropology*, 204.

[148] See Silvia Chichon-Brandmaier, *Ökonomische und immanente Trinität: ein Vergleich der Konzeptionen Karl Rahners und Hans Urs von Balthasars* (Regensburg: Friedrich

ious types of difference (e.g., sexual difference), Rowan Williams trans-
lates the word *Abstand* with "difference" instead of "distance" in a text of
Balthasar's that invokes the notion in regard to the Trinitarian persons.[149]
Christopher Hadley disputes this translation with reliance on personal conversation with Peter Henrici,[150] a philosopher close to Balthasar (a
cousin, in fact). Perhaps one ought not to view the two different attempts
at translation as so distant from one another. I do not think he always understands this language as a spatial analogy because it seems to function as
a rather plastic notion that metaphorically encompasses the almost synonymous usage of difference, distinction, and distance in common parlance.
In fact, Balthasar often uses such language in reference to the distinctions
between the divine persons, irreducible distinctions (relations of opposition!), and one would hope that he does not wish to impose a spatial analogy on the immaterial being of God.

Thomists might as well welcome as a genuine insight the notion that
there is an infinite "difference" [*unterschied*] between the divine hypostases precisely as irreducibly distinct subsistent relations, each nonetheless
mysteriously identical to the divine nature as *esse per essentiam*. Still, such
an analogical term ought to be complemented by the affirmation that the
persons are also infinitely united, which both Speyr and Balthasar clarify.[151] Likewise, it is a profound exercise to speculate that the Trinitarian
difference underlies and permeates the "ontological difference"—to use a
Heideggerian term—or, in scholastic terminology, the "real distinction"
between essence and *esse* in creatures, that is, that the latter difference
presupposes the former.[152] The problem comes when these two types of
"distance" are joined together with the distance between God and the

---

Pustet, 2008), 203–210.

[149] See Williams's "Balthasar and the Trinity," in *Cambridge Companion to Hans Urs von
Balthasar*, 37–50. Interestingly, Emery notes (see *Trinity in Aquinas*, 251) that in one
place Aquinas uses the term *differentia* in reference to the intra-Trinitarian distinctions
(see *De Potentia*, q. 10, a. 4), but rules it out as inappropriate in another place (see *ST* I,
q. 31, a. 2, ad 2).

[150] Hadley, "The All-Embracing Frame," 23.

[151] See Speyr, *World of Prayer*, 66; *John* I, 25; Balthasar, *TD* V, 260–264 [G 235–238].

[152] See especially Balthasar, "Création et Trinité," *Communio* 13 (1988): 9–17. See also Nicholas J. Healy, *Being as Communion*; Martin Bieler, "Meta-anthropology and Christology:
On the Philosophy of Hans Urs von Balthasar," trans. Thomas Caldwell, SJ, *Communio*
20 (1993): 129–146; Angela Franz Franks, "Trinitarian *Analogia Entis* in Hans Urs von
Balthasar," *The Thomist* 62 (1998): 533–559. For the scholastic roots of this notion, particularly in Aquinas's Commentary on Peter Lombard's *Sentences*, see Gilles Emery, *Trinity
in Aquinas*, 60 and 67 (without explicit reference to the essence-*esse* distinction).

sinner in alienation, a distance crossed by the One who became sin without "knowing" it (see 2 Cor 5:21). There is simply no analogical unity between the notions of sinful distance from God and the inner-Trinitarian "distance" between subsisting relations of opposition (that is, irreducibly distinct relations of origin). As Bernard Lonergan says, sin is simply a "surd,"[153] possessing no intelligible relationship to the Absolute Good who wills no evil and cannot do so.[154]

Of course, Speyr and Balthasar are free to try to translate the love of the triune God, which she (presumably) experienced, into terms more understandable to human beings, such as "the giving and receiving of gifts."[155] Nonetheless, somewhat problematic is Speyr's continuous reflection on the characteristics of love as constitutive of the Trinitarian life: availability [*Bereitschaft*], openness, surrender, transparency, and obedience.[156] Strictly speaking, obedience cannot exist between the divine persons because the hypostases are one divine intellect and will.[157] But, since in the created realm and in the salvation economy, particularly exemplified in Christ's passion-death-descent-Resurrection, obedience is a preeminent manifestation and expression of true love of God, she (and Balthasar) tend to understand the love that constitutes the Trinity through such a lens. There is certainly nothing wrong with this as long as one is careful with language when applying this spiritual insight to Trinitarian theology. Hence, Miles clarifies: "*Suscipe.* For von Speyr, love exists in an equation with obedience since obedience is the purest expression of love. . . . Speyr attributes the idea of obedience to the attitudes of all three Persons of the Trinity in the sense of love as pure indifference to one's own desires in preference to the beloved's."[158] Balthasar is often not careful enough, and I hold him to a more critical standard as a professed theologian.

Certainly, Trinitarian reflection need not involve predicating death, suffering, and kenosis as constitutive of the immutable divine essence. Nonetheless, Adrienne von Speyr reflects: "if death is understood to mean the sacrifice of life, then the original image of that sacrifice is in God as

---

153 See Lonergan, *Insight*, 666–667.

154 His impotence for evil is precisely omnipotence for good and vice versa.

155 Miles, "Obedience of a Corpse," 101, citing *John* II, 290–291.

156 See Miles, "Obedience of a Corpse," 90; Speyr, *Confession*, trans. Douglas W. Stott (San Francisco: Ignatius Press, 1985), 67–68.

157 Miles concedes as much in her treatment of Speyr (see "Obedience of a Corpse," 112 [emphasis original]). I have argued in line with Barth elsewhere for an analogous obedience and humility constitutive of the Son's hypostatic relationship to the Father.

158 "Obedience of a Corpse," 105.

the gift of life flowing between Father and Son in the Spirit. For the Father gives his whole life to the Son, the Son gives it back to the Father, and the Spirit is the outflowing gift of life."[159] This sounds like a theological reflection on her own mystical experience (not a report of locutions, that is), to which the theologian must respond: certainly, the Father and Son give life to one another, but giving life is not exactly the same as sacrificing life, and death is not precisely the sacrifice of life, but the loss of life, in which case death is not a proper image to describe the Trinitarian dynamic of self-giving. Hence, as genuine as this reflection might be, it does not meet the criteria for proper analogical predication, even if the metaphor captures something of her grim experiences of God's suffering in Christ.

At times, the two also speak of the Trinitarian processions as if the Father preexists the Son, that is, as if God the Father exists first and then decides to generate the Son. This also is an unintentional theological oversight, I presume.[160] Miles points out: "she [Speyr] attempts to explain eternal concepts in temporal vocabulary,"[161] referencing a text where she attempts to remedy this inevitable shortcoming: "There is no time when the Father is alone in God, still planning the Son—no time prior to the begetting. . . . Similarly, there is no time in God when the Son was still becoming and not yet really fully in being."[162]

Likewise, when she speaks of the intra-Trinitarian self-donation as if it were giving away something so as to lose it and only regain it in such total self-emptying, the theologian can designate such parabolic imagery as rhetorically excessive as far as technical discourse is concerned. Thus, Miles attempts to render such language more intelligible from a theological perspective: "Her concept of Trinitarian *kenosis* and *perichoresis* involves a continual flow of filling and emptying so that there is no 'point in time' in which one of the Persons is isolated from the others or emptied into a vacuum, or a glass. . . . The *kenosis* of the Son in von Speyr does not extinguish or partition the divine essence of love."[163] But Guy Mansini rightly points out that projecting kenosis into the Trinitarian life itself is

---

[159] *John*, vol. 1, *The Word Becomes Flesh*, trans. Lucia Wiedenhover and Alexander Dru (San Francisco: Ignatius Press, 1994), 42–43.

[160] Antonio Lopez attempts to make sense of this kind of language in Balthasar (see "Eternal Happening," 228–229).

[161] Miles, "Obedience of a Corpse," 95.

[162] *The World of Prayer*, 30. Concerning prayer as an analogue for the relationship between the divine persons, Miles points out the Scriptures themselves employ this notion, e.g., in Rom 8:26, 34 (see "Obedience of a Corpse," 101).

[163] Miles, "Obedience of a Corpse," 102.

no way to maintain the unity of the eternal divine will.[164]

Balthasar, following Speyr's mysticism, emphasizes the distinction between the persons over the unity of the divine nature, even though they always evidently intend to maintain the latter. Thus, Thomas Joseph White warns against the potential for tri-theism in both Barth and Balthasar:[165]

> Balthasar also follows Barth unambiguously in ascribing to the Son of God a capacity for obedience even in his divine essence. In fact, Balthasar goes further than Barth does explicitly, in speaking of a divine self-emptying, passivity, or receptivity within the Godhead. This is something distinct from the receptivity of the person of the Son (who receives his personal being from the Father through eternal generation). A notion of receptivity of this kind is traditional and proper to any coherent Trinitarian theology. By contrast, self-emptying or passivity in the essence of the Godhead itself is something else. Such a receptivity would suggest diverse modes of being (as gift on the one hand and receptivity on the other) *within* the simple, immutable, eternal essence of God. Because there is a kind of divine passivity and obedience of the Son that is ascribed to his divine nature, the unity of the person is jeopardized. . . . [T]he divine persons are distinguished only by their relations of origin, while they are considered to be absolutely identical in essence and in "qualities." . . . If the Son is distinct from the Father due not only to his eternal generation (relation of origin) but also due to a quality of passive receptivity that is not present in the Father (or that is present in the Father differently), then the Father possesses qualities of being that are not present in the Son, and vice versa. Trinitarian monotheism is implicitly compromised in this case, however, since there now exists not only a *personal* but also a *natural* ontological plurality within God. Each person has essential or natural attributes that the others do not. Correspond-

---

[164] See "Hegel and Christian Theology," 999–1000. At the same time, O'Regan is on point when, conceding that Balthasar—and the *nouvelle theologie* in general—is too dismissive of neo-scholasticism and "of the value of reason and argument in theology," he asks in response to Mansini: "Granting a greater appreciation of the logical rigor of Scholastic theology, could it not be admitted that Balthasar performs a necessary theological task?" ("Response to Readers of *The Anatomy of Misremembering*, Volume 1 (*Hegel*)," *Nova et Vetera* [English Edition] 14, no. 3 [2016]: 1015–1025, at 1024–1025).

[165] See the problematic passages in Balthasar, *TD* IV, 325–326, 329–330, cited by White, "Kenoticism and the Divinity of Christ Crucified," 36n103.

ingly, there is the absence of a pure unity of essence and identity of being common to the Father and the Son.[166]

While the warning is necessary and Balthasar is sometimes careless with his language in this regard, the criticism needs to be modified. Nowhere does Balthasar attribute passivity or even receptivity to the divine essence as such. Rather, he speculates on the active-receptive interplay between divine persons *as persons*. It is one thing to question the coherence of attributing such "qualities" to the hypostatic relations themselves; it is another to claim that the divine essence itself possesses mutually opposed qualities that are ontologically distinct in the Godhead. Balthasar simply wants to explore the implications for the Trinitarian relations (mutually opposed subsistent relations, each identical to the divine essence) of Christ's human passivity, receptivity, and obedience to the Father and the Spirit. It is, indeed, difficult to avoid the language of three wills in God when we speak of the three relationally distinct subjects of operation subsisting in the one divine being, especially when one is attempting to enumerate relational "qualities" (for lack of a better term) that accompany what distinguishes the three divine persons (paternity, filiation, spiration).[167]

---

[166] *Incarnate Lord*, 432. White also points out that when Balthasar speaks about the Resurrection, he seems to grant only the Father (not the Son) the power to rise him from the dead (see "Kenoticism and the Divinity of Christ Crucified," 38), but one might argue simply that Balthasar is speaking in the mode of appropriation.

In a review of Oakes's *Pattern of Redemption*, John R. Sachs, SJ, a fan of Balthasar's universalism, also expresses severe concern about a "rather strong tri-theism" in Balthasar that he did not perceive when writing his dissertation on Balthasar (789).

Hadley, who seems sympathetic to Kilby's reservations concerning Speyr's influence ("The All-Embracing Frame," 198), also alludes to the Eastern tendency to emphasize the distinction (over unity) of the divine persons and invokes John Zizioulas as support for Balthasar's Trinitarian reflection (particularly, *TD* IV, 326 [G 303]), concluding with the problematic assertion: "The Son and the Holy Spirit have their respective 'freedoms' to exist as hypostases because the Father begets and spirates them as hypostases that are *other than* the Father" ("The All-Embracing Frame," 171n478).

[167] Hence, even Aquinas speaks of "Gift," for instance, as a proper designation of the Spirit and of "Word" or "Image" as appropriate descriptors for the second divine hypostasis. Balthasar, drawing upon this tradition, wants to appropriate receptivity, obedience, etc., in a special manner to the Son, given that He alone became incarnate and suffered death according to the Father's will and the Spirit's guidance.

Étienne Vetö recently advanced the intriguing thesis that the Thomistic emphasis on the unity of the divine nature and the Balthasarian emphasis on the distinction of persons revealed in the economy of salvation may be reconciled by speaking not only of three distinct modes of subsistence (following Rahner), but therefore also of three

Perhaps the most problematic aspects of Balthasar's descriptions of the Trinitarian life are not, in fact, derived from Speyr. As Miles notes, "For von Balthasar, this [intra-trinitarian] giving manifests God's freedom, a concept that von Speyr rarely addresses. . . . He also prefers descriptions of Trinitarian unity and distinctions in terms of freedom and drama rather than the images of marriage and family that von Speyr uses."[168] Hence, Balthasar, as a doctor of German literature, looks at the Trinitarian dynamic (presented in images by the mystic's visions) through the lens of drama as a literary genre particularly adept to exploring the true events of salvation history. But as with every prismatic tool, drama is deficient when it comes to the life of the Trinity—hence, apophasis is counseled here. Similarly, he employs dialogical philosophy when grappling with the Trinitarian personal relations, and one might question whether it is up to the task of describing a singular nature existing in three subjectivities.

Finally, probably most controversial is Balthasar's gendered treatment of the Trinity, which is not entirely without precedent in the tradition, but certainly contentious. There is a glimmer of gender symbolism in the text of the Eleventh Synod of Toledo (675), which proclaims: "One must believe that the Son is begotten and born, not from nothing, nor from some other substance, but from the womb of the Father, that is, from his substance."[169] Thomas Aquinas also discusses the *conceptio* of the eternal *Verbum* in his *Summa Contra Gentiles*. He concludes: "In the generation of the Word Holy Scripture attributes to the Father all those things which in fleshly generation belong separately to the father and to the mother: thus the Father is said both 'to give life to the Son' and 'to conceive and give birth (*concipere et parturire*) to the Son.'"[170] While both Aquinas and

---

corresponding modes of activity, united in the one *operatio* of the triune God; see his *Du Christ à la Trinité: Penser les mystères du Christ après Thomas d'Aquin et Balthasar* (Paris: Les Éditions du Cerf, 2012).

    Perhaps this is a way to overcome such apparently tri-theistic statements of Balthasar, such as the following in his volume on the Holy Spirit: "we must look for the origin of the Spirit's freedom within the Trinity; the freedom of the Spirit must be just as divine as that of Father and Son, yet distinct from it" (*TL* III, 236 [G 218]).

[168] Miles, "Obedience of a Corpse," 103; see also 105.

[169] "Profession of Faith," no. 6 (Denz. 526).

[170] *SCG* IV, ch. 11, nos. 3478–3479. Thus, Speyr uses the image of a mother with child to illustrate the difference-in-union between the divine persons (see *Subjektive Mystik*, 120). Sutton comments: "In this image, von Speyr mutually integrates the difference beween the Latin 'relation of opposition' and the Greek 'relation of origin.' The child relates to the mother both as origin (being generated in her womb) and as opposition (being formed for a life outside his mother)" (*Heaven Opens*, location 2997).

Augustine prefer intrapersonal or "psychological" analogies to interpersonal or familial analogies,[171] this text makes it clear that there are indeed diverse traditions for analogous speech concerning the Trinitarian life that are legitimate. St. Maximilian Kolbe speaks of the Holy Spirit as "the uncreated immaculate conception," that is, the eternal and infinite prototype for the Blessed Virgin Mary.[172] Likewise, Pope St. John Paul the Great popularizes the familial analogy for which Richard of St. Victor was known in the Middle Ages.[173]

Balthasar, in fact, prefers the Richardian (i.e., interpersonal) perspective to the Augustinian (i.e., intrapersonal), even while propounding the necessity to go beyond it into kenotic analogy.[174] Augustine, in his *De Trinitate*,[175] blithely dismisses this perspective and the idea that the Holy Spirit might be considered a feminine principle since He proceeds from the Father, as Eve was taken from the side of Adam, without being son or daughter. Not considering the original Hebrew text, where the "man" created in the image and likeness of the plural God is actually "humanity,"[176] Augustine thinks that Scripture says the male himself was first created in the image of the Trinity and then the female from the male (implying that the male therefore cannot correspond to the Father and the female to the Spirit),[177] and that (because of original sin) "the word 'wife' makes one

---

[171] For a relatively recent discussion of the former, see, e.g., Bernard Lonergan, *Collected Works of Bernard Lonergan*, vol. 12, *The Triune God: Systematics*, trans. Michael G. Shields (Toronto: University of Toronto Press, 2007), 181–189.

[172] See the final written reflection of Kolbe, entitled "Who then are you, O immaculate conception?" on February 17, 1941, available at http://www.piercedhearts.org/hearts_jesus_mary/heart_mary/max_kolbe_immaculate_conception.htm (accessed 11/20/2017).

[173] See his *Man and Woman He Created Them: A Theology of the Body*, trans. Michael Waldstein (Boston: Pauline Books & Media, 2006), 163. St. John Paul II does not mention Richard by name there, but he does so on another matter in conjunction with others on whom he draws throughout the work in 136n3.

[174] See *TD* V, 82 [G 71], and especially *TL* II, 38ff., 62 [G 35ff., 56]. Nonetheless, he warns against "[taking] a naïve construction of the divine mystery after the pattern of human relationships (as Richard of St. Victor attempted by way of a counterblast to Augustine) and make it absolute" (*TD* III, 526–527 [G 481]). Proper interpretation of Richard's familial analogy is an issue of debate; see the English translation of his *De Trinitate*, Ruben Angelici, *Richard of Saint Victor: On the Trinity. English Translation and Commentary* (Eugene, OR: Cascade, 2011).

[175] See ch. 12, sects. 5.5–6.6.

[176] See *Theology of the Body*, 136n2.

[177] Augustine, *De Trinitate* XII.7; see the edition translated by Edmund Hill, OP, *The Trinity* (New York: New City Press, 2012), 326.

think of the corruption of copulation in the beginning of offspring."[178] Obviously, whether one deems the intrapersonal or interpersonal analogy superior, each has its strengths and weaknesses. But it may speak to a deficiency in Balthasar's conception of feminity as well as of the Trinitarian relations themselves that he not only tends to side with Augustine's analysis here, but also seems to reject Matthias Joseph Scheeben's intriguing proposal regarding the femininity of the Spirit, which is in part based upon a more adequate examination of the creation narratives.[179] At the same time, he nonetheless grants that the natural sacrament of marriage "remains, in spite of all the obvious dissimilarities, the most eloquent *imago Trinitatis* that we find woven into the fabric of the creature."[180]

In any case, what is most deficient about Balthasar's insistence on applying the masculine-feminine distinction to all three persons in terms of activity and receptivity, where the Father is the most active and the Spirit is the most receptive, even though each is both in different ways, is precisely the implicit equation of masculinity with activity and femininity with receptivity.[181] While I would defend the view that the male-female rela-

---

[178] Augustine, *De Trinitate* XII.7, 325.

[179] See Scheeben, "Ein hypostatisches Analogon fur den Heiligen Geist und seinen Ursprung auf geschopflichem Gebiet," in *Die Mysterien des Christentums* (1865), 173–181, cited in *TL* II, 60n97 [G 55n97]; for an English translation, see Appendix 1 to Part 1 of *The Mysteries of Christianity*, trans. Cyril Vollert, SJ (St. Louis: B. Herder Book Co., 1946), 181–189.

Balthasar states that "because 'generation' is already exclusively reserved as an analogue for the Father-Son relationship, and because the Son, if anyone, would have to represent the feminine element therein, we cannot legitimately argue from the feminine form of the Hebrew words 'spirit' (*ruach*) and 'wisdom' (*kochma*) that the Spirit is the feminine in God" (*TL* II, 60 [G 55]).

[180] *TL* II, 62 [G 56], drawing on Scheeben, *Mysterien des Christentums*, 572–76.

[181] See *TD* III, 287 [G 264]; *TD* V, 91 [G 80]). There is a good argument for why God is, in the Judeo-Christian tradition, referred to in the masculine rather than the feminine; see Peter Kreeft and Ronald K. Tacelli, *Handbook of Catholic Apologetics: Reasoned Answers to Questions of Faith* (San Francisco: Ignatius Press, 2009), 104–105.

Nonetheless, as Emery notes, citing Aquinas's *SCG* IV, ch. 11, nos. 3478–3479:

The name "Father" must pass through a work of purification in order to be applied to God, since one must exclude corporal generation, the sexual difference, change, aging, and so on. What remains in the notion of *Father*? Two major traits must be retained which constitute the two properties of the first person of the Trinity: (1) the Father is the one from whom the Son is engendered; (2) the Father does not have an origin. (*Trinity in Aquinas*, 145)

Hence, there is no reason to ascribe greater masculinity to the Father than to the Son, for instance, who of course became a male human.

tionship may be accurately characterized by activity-receptivity on some
levels (e.g., physical), on other levels it may be precisely the opposite (e.g.,
social), and thus the couplet is not an adequate framework within which
this dynamic may be comprehended.[182] Likewise, the feminine-masculine
language in regard to the Trinitarian relations is unhelpful in most cases.
There is something to be said of femininity in the Spirit (which Balthasar
does not elucidate). But speaking of the Son's antecedent consent to His
procession and the Father's receptivity to the Son's procession as feminine
is at best not sufficiently apophatic.[183]

Although the notion that anything can consent to its own generation
or procession is confusing, it becomes possible to make some sense of it if
we look at how Speyr applies the notion to creation. Sutton paraphrases:
"Since the world is created out of God's love, the world should respond out
of loving obedience to God. In Genesis, God's creative words of love, 'Let
there be . . .,' are obediently followed by 'and so it was' (Genesis 1). The
creation obeys by letting itself be created."[184] Hence, the consent of the
terminus is subsequent to its actual existence and not causal, but confir-
matory, similar to how God is said to will His own goodness (according
to Aquinas).[185] But perhaps more significantly, obedience here is conceived
as a mode of being, not an act of a preexistent subject. In other words, the
world's own being-created is an act of being-obedient to the divine command. Thus, one might likewise speak of the Son's own being-generated
as an act of obedience in the sense of a pure receptivity or a letting-be
(*gehörenlassen*).[186]

---

[182] For a good conceptualization of the gender difference itself, see John Finley, "The Metaphysics of Gender: A Thomistic Approach," *The Thomist* 79, no. 4 (2015): 585–614;
Jacques Maritain, "Let Us Make for Him a Helpmate Like to Himself," in *Untrammeled Approaches*, 151–164. See also my "A Feminist Argument for a Male-only Priesthood," *Fellowship of Catholic Scholars Quarterly* 39, no. 1/2 (Spring/Summer 2016):
50–52.

[183] See especially *TD* V, 86, 91 [G 75, 80].

[184] Sutton, *Heaven Opens*, locations 3105–3107.

[185] See *SCG* I, chs. 74–77. I prefer this line of explanation to Martin Bieler's: "Balthasar's
view is here in line with Aquinas, who understands the generation (procession) of the
Son as one single act of Father and Son, in which the *potentia generari* of the Son corresponds to the *potentia generandi* of the Father. This view is also shared by Bonaventure"
("God and the Cross," 68). The question here concerns the meaning of consent in the
processions.

[186] For further explanation, see Sutton, *Heaven Opens*, locations 3108–3122.

REGARDING THE INFLUENCE OF ADRIENNE VON SPEYR'S MYSTICISM

In a number of places, Balthasar ties his own theology inextricably to Speyr, the effect of which, arguably, is to elevate it to a higher level of sublimity.[187] Some have persuasively argued that Balthasar needs to be purified of Speyr's influence,[188] but it might just as well be argued that Speyr could be interpreted with greater precision by theologians more systematic than Balthasar, not that he was wholly inadequate to the task (or that anyone would be wholly adequate).[189] In any case, the legitimacy of one's

---

[187] See *First Glance*, 13; *My Work: In Retrospect,* trans. Brian McNeil, Kenneth Batinovich, John Saward, and Kelly Hamilton (San Francisco: Ignatius Press, 1993), 105; *Test Everything: Hold Fast to What is Good*, trans. Maria Shrady (San Francisco: Ignatius Press, 1989), 88; *Our Task*, 13, 39, 44.

[188] This was part of Mongrain's evident purpose in *The Systematic Thought*. Fergus Kerr, OP, emphasizes other influences and wishes to sideline Speyr's, perhaps justly: "Adrienne von Speyr and Hans Urs von Balthasar," *New Blackfriars* 79, no. 923 (1998): 26–32, esp. 28.

Ralph Martin's striking essay, "Balthasar and Speyr: First Steps in a Discernment of Spirits," *Angelicum* 91 (2014): 273–301, points to several red flags. Nonetheless, he notes:

> Even among those now recognized as saints or truly holy persons, it became apparent [in his own study of the mystics and pseudo-mysticism] that a mixture sometimes was present in what was claimed as revelation and sometimes a mixture in those who authoritatively interpreted their revelations. What is very striking in Balthasar's accounts of their relationship is how deeply this was a common project and how little suited Balthasar really was to be an objective evaluator of what was going on in their mutual, symbiotic, deeply entwined, mystical/theological enterprise. . . . Sometimes two genuinely holy people can drift into a situation which is open to deception. When, say, a priest, reaches a point of "total trust" in a woman mystic—or vice versa—while the relationship may be chaste and the two parties genuinely holy and well intentioned, the almost inevitable "mixture" will assert itself and insinuate certain "ideas" that are not from the Holy Spirit. (293–294)

For his study, see *The Fulfillment of All Desire: A Guidebook for the Journey to God Based on the Wisdom of the Saints* (Steubenville, OH: Emmaus Road, 2006). For a very positive assessment of Balthasar's Speyrian mysticism, see Claudia Lee, "The Role of Mysticism within the Church as Conceived by Hans Urs von Balthasar," *Communio* 16 (Spring 1989): 105–126.

[189] Speyr indicates that the mystic herself is inadequate to the task of fully understanding or adequately communicating the content of revelation received because, as Sutton paraphrases, "First, the vision refers to more than what is shown. Second, the vision is more than what the mystic can understand. Finally, the experience for the mystic is more than what he or she can impart to others" (*Heaven Opens*, locations 1915–1917,

mysticism does not render the mystic's theological opinions automatically correct,[190] as mysticism makes not a competent theologian (i.e., it is not a sufficient condition, even if Balthasar is right that it is a necessary one).[191] Hence, her experiences ought to be demythologized,[192] as mystical visions and words of themselves are almost inevitably filtered by or tailored to the recipient's imaginative-estimative faculties, according to the scholastic axiom: *quidquid recipitur ad modum recipientis recipitur.*[193]

Furthermore, since her experiences were dictated to Balthasar, they were most likely filtered through Balthasar's theological vision, even if inadvertently (as I presume). Even Balthasar states in regard to other mystics: "the mystics, describing their experience of the night, necessarily dwell on

---

citing *Subjektive Mystik*, 70).

[190] Even her recent faithful interpreter, Matthew Sutton, expresses disagreement with her in favor of Thomas Aquinas's position on a point of Trinitarian theology, namely, the necessity of each of the divine person's missions. See Sutton, *Heaven Opens*, locations 3437–3445; *Das Angesicht des Vaters* [2nd Edition, Einsiedeln: Johannes Verlag, 1981], 13. It seems unimaginable to Speyr that the missions might be different, and I sympathize with her concern here. I think that while it is necessary, strictly speaking, for *ad extra* divine acts to be common to the divinity as such, one might also argue effectively that the very *ad extra* acts that God willed were chosen inevitably (yet with the freedom that is identical to truth itself), and in this sense, it is almost unintelligible to consider the Father as possibly incarnate, the Son as appropriately the origin of creation, etc.

[191] Hence, even her own understanding of mysticism itself could very well be flawed and yet not delegitimize the authenticity of her own mystical experiences. Concerning her theory of mysticism, treated especially in her posthumously published *Subjektive Mystik* and *Objektive Mystik*, see Sutton's *Heaven Opens*, ch. 2 (or locations 1034–1433).

[192] Schumacher reluctantly hints at the need for what I have called demythologization of Balthasar's theology, which would be a purgation of the metaphorical images imported from Speyr's mysticism (see *Trinitarian Anthropology*, 388–389).

[193] This is not necessarily the case; see Aquinas, *ST* II-II, q. 173 concerning the various modes of prophetic knowledge. But concerning the role of imagination in prophetic vision, see also Aquinas's *Super Ioannem* 4, lect. 6, no. 667. I cannot argue here at length for the prevalent philosophical conceptualization of the mystical phenomenon, according to which the ordinary human faculties of knowledge are not (at least, ordinarily) bypassed in the divine infusion of prophetic species.

The interested reader may see the various philosophical attempts to make sense out of mysticism in Steven T. Katz, ed., *Mysticism and Philosophical Analysis*. Thus, even a mystic as radiant as St. Maria Faustina Kowalska counsels a healthy skepticism with regard to one's personal understanding of one's own mystical experiences when she says in her diary: "O my Jesus, it cannot be helped, but I give priority to the voice of the Church over the voice with which You speak to me," a thought which she later hears Jesus confirm (*Diary: Divine Mercy in My Soul* [Stockbridge, MA: Marians of the Immaculate Conception, 2002], 497). According to Sutton, this ecclesial spirit is in line with Speyr's understanding of mysticism (see *Heaven Opens*, locations 1884ff.).

the feeling of being alone, that's why they do not always avoid the temptation of using the categories of Platonism to describe their experiences."[194]
Therefore, contrary to what is sometimes implied,[195] Speyr's mysticism is
free to be interpreted by theologians in a number of ways, as with any mystic or saint, and not limited to Balthasar's own, albeit intimate, personal
interpretation.[196] The question remains, though, whether it is even possible to locate her own mystical insight apart from Balthasar's theological reception of it and his influence upon her understanding of her own
mystical experiences.[197] Perhaps, even more significantly, "it is impossible
to distinguish how much her interpretations [of Scripture] owe to contemplation received *from above* and how much they depend on her own
prayerful meditation *from below*."[198]

---

[194] *Prayer*, trans. Graham Harrison (San Francisco: Ignatius Press, 1986), 216.

[195] Schumacher states:

> [C]ontrary to the claim of Johann Roten, Balthasar did not understand him-
> self to be Adrienne's interpreter. . . . In fact, Balthasar explicitly proclaims his
> conviction that Adrienne's mission was "not only one of experience, of the dark
> night and other christological states, but also quite expressly one of interpreta-
> tion." Therefore, he appears to have perceived a twofold mystical charism op-
> erative in her dictations: that of vision and that of the interpretation of these
> visions by way of divine inspiration, which is likewise a grace" (*Trinitarian An-
> thropology*, 384, quoting Balthasar's *Our Task*, 18–19).

> At the same time, she affirms: "Balthasar has undoubtedly taken these (the inter-
> pretations) at least one step further" (*Trinitarian Anthropology*, 385). Clearly, Balthasar
> wanted to attribute everything that is good in his work to her "divine inspiration"; see,
> for instance, *Our Task*, 62–63.

[196] Aidan Nichols, OP, a prolific Balthasarian, reports that Balthasar himself, at a Roman
Colloquium in September of 1985, permitted as much, hinting at the fact that the legitimacy of her visions does not guarantee the coherence or precision of her theoretical
reflection on them. See Nichols, "Adrienne von Speyr and the Mystery of the Atonement," *New Blackfriars* 73, no. 865 (1992): 542–553, at 552. The texts of the Colloquium were published as *Adrienne von Speyr und Ihre Kirchliche Sendung*.

[197] Matthew Sutton judges this not to be possible: "[Balthasar] has, of course, done much
on his own, but theologians studying von Balthasar must understand him as the first
interpreter of Adrienne von Speyr. There is much mutual influence between these two.
Their work, especially the Johannesgemeinschaft, was truly a joint task. The reverbera-
tions in their relationship are so intense that the original voice and the echo are too hard
to discern" (*Heaven Opens*, locations 674–76).

[198] Sutton, *Heaven Opens*, location 1629 (emphasis added). While the former would
constitute private revelation, the latter would be intrinsically fallible, even though
well-intentioned. The following words of Gilles Mongeau, SJ, ought to be added: "the
knowledge [the mystics] really have eludes their efforts to express it. It is only over time,
and after much effort of reflection and appropriation of the fruits of the encounter that

Sutton interprets Speyr's Trinitarian mysticism to be in line with "the maximalist interpretation of Rahner's axiom" such that "every moment and every word of the Trinity's activity in the world would correspond to God's immanent triune relations."[199] But the philosophically problematic aspects of Balthasar's Trinitarian predications might ultimately derive from his peculiar perspective on analogical discourse. Since Balthasar's quasi-systematic theology must have influenced Speyr's own understanding of her mystical experience, even though Speyr's mysticism also clearly inspired many of Balthasar's theological insights, the origin of his insufficiently cautious Trinitarian discourse is precisely his philosophical reception of Speyr's Trinitarian ecstasies. It is one thing for a mystic to speak with insufficient precision (from a philosophico-theological standpoint) about her own revelations; it is another for a theologian to attempt to render them more intelligible while utilizing hyperbolic language that lends itself to systematic critique.

CONCLUSION

The reason Adrienne von Speyr has not even been declared venerable, now fifty years after her death (in 1967), could be the dubious nature of her mystical experiences, the difficulty of evaluating the authenticity and reliability of her revelations, the lack of their exemplarity for Christians, or even the impossibility of separating her mysticism from Hans Urs von Balthasar's own peculiar theological vision—likely all of the above. The latter has deep roots in patristic figures from Irenaeus and Maximus the Confessor to Origen and Gregory of Nyssa as well as modern thinkers from Erich Przywara and Karl Barth to Sergei Bulgakov and Vladimir Lossky, not to mention the influence of medieval thinkers from Bonaventure and Aquinas to Meister Eckhart and Richard of St. Victor, John Scotus Eriugena, and Nicholas of Cusa.[200] Hence, Speyr's influence on him, as tremendous as it stands, was inevitably colored by the reflections of numerous diverse historical figures whom he strived to assimilate. Thus, Balthasar's

---

the mystics have been able to articulate approximate understandings gesturing to what happened" ("Human and Divine Knowing of the Incarnate Word," *Josephinum Journal of Theology* 12, no. 1 [Winter/Spring 2005]: 30–42, at 39). The analogies employed by Speyr do not lend themselves to attributing to her what Aquinas attributed to Paul, namely, a rapture that transcends sensible images (see *ST* II-II, q. 175, a. 4).

[199] Sutton, *Heaven Opens*, locations 2337 and 2339.

[200] He ties many of these figures together throughout *TL* II (see, e.g., 192, 217 [G 176, 198]).

project is so incredibly complex that it will take centuries to sift through it fully, and—unfortunately or fortunately—Speyr's legacy will likely be determined by the Church's eventual judgment of Balthasar's, if she decides to tackle such a task.

The legitimacy of establishing a working relationship between mysticism/spirituality and systematic theology ought to be evident to any believer,[201] as faith is not merely reasoned or merely experienced, and yet their proper relationship has to be worked out without fusing the two into one—they are distinctive realities, related surely, but not identical or necessarily mixed homogeneously.[202] For all the beauty that runs throughout his work, there are significant lacunae in Balthasar's treatment and the risk of falling back into a quasi-mythological type of divine discourse. Philosophical precision ought not to diminish when appropriating the insights of diverse figures throughout history. When metaphorical-symbolic language dominates theological treatises, theology becomes reducible to spirituality. Spiritual experience can certainly aid theology, but theology encompasses more than just the believer's individual (even mystical) experiences.

The Trinity, the ultimate mystery of the Christian faith, is not simply a mystical phenomenon susceptible to human spiritual experience, but a reality that transcends all contingent categories and yet remains hidden within everything that is good, especially the Paschal Mystery. Natural human reason, enlightened by revealed faith, has access to even the most sublime of divine realities not simply through mystical ecstasy, but also through the rich wisdom contained in the reflections of minds gifted with particular insight. It is the analogy of being that allows the human intellect to discern the difference between diverse types of predication. The rules of intelligible discourse are not suspended when it comes to Trinitarian theology, even if the limits of language are strained. If even evil becomes analogous with the infinite life constitutive of the divine processions, the limits of theological language are strained to the point of relative incoherence. The Trinity is the supremely ecstatic union of love, and the truth of love cannot be essentially sorrowful, sacrificial, or moribund.

I have argued, in accord with the lion's share of Christian tradition,

---

[201] Balthasar practically states this as his purpose in *TD* II, 57 [G 50–51].

[202] Mark A. McIntosh, for instance, has dedicated several works to this task. In his book on Balthasar, *Christology from Within*, while failing to recognize the problematic aspects of Balthasar's project (see especially 112), he excellently displays how Balthasar's spirituality—largely Ignatian, which arguably gives primacy to the imagination—informs his theological reflection.

that one of the Trinity has suffered, yes, but the origin and end of this suffering—the foundation of the phenomenon of suffering—entirely transcends the suffering itself; that is, the foundation transcends the phenomenon, even if it is the phenomenon that reveals the foundation: *amor ipsum est esse ipsum! Benedicta sit sancta Trinitas!*

Conclusion

WHAT I HAVE SOUGHT to do in this book is to engage, however cursorily, the speculative thought of Hans Urs von Balthasar on the topic of divine suffering in dialogue with other Catholic systematic theologies, especially contemporary Thomism. The theology of divine suffering is an attempt to resolve the perennial problem of evil from the perspective of divine revelation, and yet that revelation is inevitably received by human minds with their own proclivities and dispositions, the best of which are philosophical habits of correct reasoning—that is, rigorous, precise, and profound reasoning. The claims of divine revelation certainly go beyond anything human reason can hope to obtain on its own or to grasp fully. But, as theology is "faith seeking understanding,"[1] systematic theology is an arduous, well-ordered, and meticulous attempt to articulate the contents of such faith in a manner that is both intrinsically intelligible and potentially intelligible for contemporary people. Systematic theology is consequential for contemporary life precisely because it is intelligible, even in a world that suffers the unintelligible in such an evident fashion, where polarizing extremes manifestly increase without an intelligible end in sight. In this world, one of the few intrinsic goods left, but unrecognized, is speculative inquiry concerning the meaning of it all in the eternal limelight. Therefore, I will highlight what I deem to be an essentially philosophical defect underlying Balthasar's theology of divine suffering before offering a final reflection on the evil of suffering and how it relates to the eternal life of

---

[1] This phrase of Augustinian inspiration is commonly attributed to St. Anselm of Canterbury, even as the original subtitle of his *Proslogion*; see G. Sohngen, *Lexikon für Theologie und Kirche*, ed. J. Hofer and K. Rahner, *Faith and Order—Hannibaldis*, vol. 4, 2nd ed. (Freiburg: Herder, 1960), 119–120; F. Cayre, *Patrologie et histoire de la théologie*, vol. 2, 4th ed. (Paris: Desclée, 1947), 395.

the triune God, utilizing another luminary of the twentieth century.

QUASI-PHILOSOPHICAL POSTSCRIPT

In the opinion of this reader, Balthasar's theology would have been better served by less retrojection of contemporary proclivities into the history of thought and more serious engagement with giants like Thomas Aquinas and the full force of the Thomistic tradition. Thus, I have sought in this book to force Balthasar into dialogue with contemporary Thomistic theology, leaning on others who have attempted to do the same. It has become evident to this student of Balthasar and of Aquinas (among others) that the former's theology of divine suffering is at the epicenter of his thought overall, and that, despite containing significant insights, it also betrays a fundamental flaw, not at all manifest at first glance (or even after many years of arduous study), that pervades much of Balthasar's theological speculation concerning God. The fundamental flaw is an implicit—whether intentional or not—privileging of phenomenological description over proper ontological predication.[2] In the words of Pope St. John Paul

---

[2] I recently discovered that Rosenberg made a similar observation:

> Balthasar's fluid use of both metaphorical and ontological terms [is] so fluid that it is often difficult for the reader to distinguish which world of discourse Balthasar is employing. . . . Our purpose has only been to point out instances which suggest in Balthasar's [sic] a kind of "symbolic mentality." He privileges, at least in his writings on the cross, the metaphorical over the ontological. ("Theory and Drama," 214)

Lonergan defines the term "symbolic mentality" as "a way of understanding, judging, and speaking that obeys the laws of imagination rather than the logic developed by the Greeks and diffused through Hellenistic culture" (*De Verbo Incarnato*, 534; cf. Rosenberg, 231–232). Rosenberg's interpretation of Balthasar's *theologia crucis*, though, seems to be overly influenced by Alyssa Pitstick's *Light in Darkness*. I do not see as much space between Balthasar's and Lonergan's respective understandings of the redemption as Rosenberg does, even though their modes of conceptualization are obviously distinct; Rosenberg admits congruence (see 299) in *TD* III, 164 [G 150] and *TL* II, 246 [G 223].

For what it is worth, Fr. Matthew Lamb, a close student, scholar, and follower of Lonergan, told me in conversation before his death that Lonergan pointed to Balthasar as indicative of the future of Catholic theology; perhaps, then, the two were not as far apart as some may assume. I have found no citations of Balthasar by Lonergan, but apparently, they became aware of each other late in their careers; at least, Balthasar cites Lonergan's *De Deo Trino* in *TL* III, 131, 136n19 [G 120, 125n19], which Rosenberg notes (see "Theory and Drama," 5n8).

It is odd that Balthasar cites Lonergan's Trinitarian work, given that Lonergan certainly would not have found Balthasar's dramatic analogies particularly fitting, even if

the Great, he does not transition sufficiently "from phenomenon to foundation," that is, from personalist phenomenological language to properly metaphysical discourse.[3] In the language of Bernard Lonergan, he does not entirely transcend the level of common sense into the level of theory.[4] In

the dramatic may be integrated into an explanatory framework:

> Lonergan's conception of the intra-trinitarian relationship excludes this mode of understanding [namely, Father as Author, Son as Actor, Spirit as Director] as based on a metaphor that is intrinsically conditioned by space and time, namely, the theater. However, can we ground this within the explanatory framework of Doran's aesthetic-dramatic or psychic operator in human consciousness, inasmuch as psychic conversion enables an explanatory understanding of symbolic meaning? Within the framework of elemental meaning, perhaps Balthasar's integration of the roles of author, actor, and director becomes explanatory in so far as it illuminates the three roles in relation to one another and as mediating dramatic meaning to the audience. (Rosenberg, "Theory and Drama," 291–292)

It is noteworthy, however, that in some of his later writings, Lonergan also seems to let the existential-phenomenological trend of thinking usurp the perennial foundation of classical metaphysics.

[3] Personalist phenomenology is admirable as far as it goes, but as its great practitioner, Pope St. John Paul, reminds us: it is necessary to transition "from *phenomenon to foundation*" (Encyclical Letter *Fides et Ratio*, §83 [emphasis original]).

[4] Lonergan, *Insight*, 225–242. In accordance with this Lonerganian distinction, Rosenberg's dissertation explores the possibility of integrating Balthasar's dramatic approach into a higher, more systematic (Lonerganian) viewpoint in the course of correcting his reticence to grant Christ the beatific vision in life and death.

Building on Robert Doran's work, Rosenberg "advances the possibility of a subaltern place in systematic-theological discourse for dramatic categories . . . [giving] priority to a theoretically controlled discourse," but he notes at the same time:

> Proposing a systematic significance for the dramatic analogy in psychic conversion does not automatically eliminate the theological issues that may be connected to this analogy [drama] on the level of elemental meaning. The Father's "kenosis," "letting go," "god-lessness," "powerlessness" are uncontrolled expressions that may obscure of [sic] the mysteries of faith articulated in the Christological and Trinitarian dogmas. So perspectives drawn from psychic conversion, drama, or paradox in relation to the Father's kenosis do not mitigate its potential problems and do not answer further questions which could be given control and coherence by theoretical categories. ("Theory and Drama," 295–296)

I agree that the realm of common sense ought not to be dismissed but sublated by the higher function of theory. He also points to places where Lonergan speaks of "the mystical pattern of experience" (*Insight*, 410), the "special categories" of religious experience (*Method in Theology* [Toronto: University of Toronto, 2007], 290), and warns of the "potential hazards of transposing one's symbolic apprehension into explanatory categories" ("Theory and Drama," 306–307; see Lonergan, *De Verbo Incarnato*, 535).

contemporary Thomistic terms, he does not reach the full level of abstraction found in the method of *resolutio*.[5]

Balthasar's intention is to refocus theology in Christ as the concrete *analogia entis* in dialogue primarily with Karl Barth, but in the process, he tends to immanentize the transcendent by importing the economic category of kenosis to the immanent identity of *ipsum esse*. In other words, Balthasar tends to overlook the apophatic limits of analogical naming that are intrinsic to all *theo*-logy, succumbing to cataphatic excess in the form of meta-symbolic discourse, which risks an anthropomorphization of God Himself.[6] Without proper analogical predication there is only univocity

---

Thus, Rosenberg also leaves open the possibility that such an integration or transposition may not be feasible. In this regard, namely, whether or not "a place for the dramatic approach in systematic-theological discourse [may] be salvaged," he concludes:

> The key to an *affirmative* answer is Robert Doran's account of "permanent elemental meaning" and the aesthetic-dramatic operator in human consciousness. If there is room in systematic theology for descriptive, symbolic, and dramatic apprehension of the mysteries of faith (or an explanatory grasp of this apprehension), as well as a theoretial and explanatory understanding, then the emphases of Balthasar (descriptive, symbolic, dramatic) and Lonergan (theoretical, explanatory) can complement each other in providing a fuller understanding of the mystery. The key to a *negative* answer is an appropriation of Lonergan's methodological idea of functional specialization that distinguishes within theology among Foundations, Doctrines, Systematics, and Communications. ("Theory and Drama," 309–310).

I am not keen on the latter, and Rosenberg also seems to tend toward the former option (see 311, 314). Finally, I agree with him when he comments on Tad Dunne's suggestion that "from the point of view of theory, God is unchanging; but from the point of view of common sense, God changes" and "in the intellectual pattern of experience, we should not conceive of God as changing, but in the dramatic pattern of experience we ought to imagine God as changing" (Dunne, *Lonergan and Spirituality: Towards a Spiritual Integration* [Chicago: Loyola University Press, 1985], 215), by clarifying: "if [this] is useful, it should only have a subalternate place in systematic discourse. Ultimately, as Dunne implies, such commonsense and dramatic discourse would need to be refined or controlled by the theoretical, intellectual pattern of experience" ("Theory and Drama," 312). Thus, Rosenberg also revises O'Hanlon's view that metaphorical and ontological discourse are mutually complementary (see "Theory and Drama," 313; cf. O'Hanlon, *Immutability of God*, 141–142).

5   See Jan A. Aertsen, "Method and Metaphysics: The *via resolutionis* in Thomas Aquinas," *The New Scholasticism* 63, no. 4 (1989): 405–418; Eileen C. Sweeney, "Three Notions of *Resolutio* and the Structure of Reasoning in Aquinas," *The Thomist* 58, no. 2 (1994): 197–243; Jesus Villagrasa, "La *resolutio* come metodo della metafisica secondo Cornelio Fabro," *Alpha Omega* 4, no. 1 (2001): 35–66.

6   Karl Rahner's own critique of Balthasar's theology as tending toward Gnosticism hits

and equivocity—Balthasar, thus, struggles to navigate between the two extremes (Scylla and Charybdis), in effect succumbing to aspects of both, although he explicitly rejects the former (Hegel's post-Kantian route) and exercises caution with regard to the latter (Heidegger's route).[7] Balthasar's theological discourse attempts both to remain at the level of phenomenon and to transcend it. But Balthasar's recourse to symbol in place of proper analogical predication is symptomatic of Kantian phenomenalism,[8] which Rahner at least openly embraces (à la Joseph Maréchal). Yet Balthasar's divine discourse is susceptible even to Heidegger's critique of onto-theology because, as for Heidegger any theology that is not meta-theology is onto-theology, but more pertinently because Balthasar tends to ontologize phenomena. Hence, whoever rejects the Aristotelian-Dionysian-Thomistic doctrine of analogy inevitably ends up either conflating God and creation or suspending access to the former.[9] When human access to the divine via

---

essentially the same point: see *Karl Rahner in Dialogue*, 126–127. Nonetheless, Cyril O'Regan displays voluminously how Balthasar intends a fundamentally anti-Gnostic posture: see *The Anatomy of Misremembering*.

[7] Balthasar rejects Hegel, Scotus, and Suarez's positions on the *analogia entis* (see *GL* V, 588, 16–19 [G 919, 377–380]; *TD* IV, 383 [G 357]), but nonetheless ultimately fails to draw the proper conclusions from Aquinas's doctrine in the midst of dialogue with Barth's dialectical Christology. For one account of Balthasar's relationship to Heidegger, particularly in comparison to Rahner, see Vincent Holzer, "'Analogia Entis' Christologique et pensée de l'être chez Hans Urs von Balthasar," *Theophilyon* 4, no. 2 (1999): 463–512; and Fergus Kerr, "Balthasar and Metaphysics," in *The Cambridge Companion to Hans Urs von Balthasar*, 224–240.

[8] This is most likely due to the influence of Karl Barth, who betrays the common working assumption that Kant's critique of substantialist metaphysics is definitive (see, e.g., *Church Dogmatics* II/1, 263), as do the so-called post-liberal theologians, who purport to transcend propositional (objectivist!) and expressivist (subjectivist!) conceptions of divine revelation through the cultural-linguistic lens inherited from Wittgenstein and analytic philosophy. Investigation of this issue must also be left for another work.

Cyril O'Regan attempts to exonerate Balthasar of any hint of Hegelianism by arguing with an erudite display of diction that he was fundamentally as anti-Hegelian as he was anti-Gnostic, given that Hegel is the modern prototype of Gnosticism. However, Guy Mansini points to passages where O'Regan lauds Balthasar's attempt to appropriate Hegel's "dynamic view of God" and the related "critique of the metaphysical tradition" (O'Regan, *Anatomy of Misremembering*, 226) by transcending analogical predication into the realm of symbolic discourse, where "such meta-symbolic names are also 'un-names'" (Mansini, "Hegel and Christian Theology," 996), and "the Christian meaning of such symbols [suffering and immutability] 'cannot be tied exclusively to Greek metaphysics and its regime of binary oppositions of an ontological sort' (229)" (Mansini, 997, quoting O'Regan). See O'Regan's recourse to "meta-symbolism" also on 307.

[9] For a good, exposition of the former, see Alan Philip Darley, "Predication or Partici-

proper predication (i.e., philosophical theology) is suspended, discourse on God is either scrapped altogether (Kant, Heidegger, Wittgenstein) or engaged only mystically (Eriugena, Eckhart, Huxley).[10]

Consciously or not, Balthasar attempts to return to a modern (pseudo-) monastic style of doing theology, rather than embrace the development of scholastic theology, thanks to an attachment to literary-aesthetic catego-

---

pation? What is the Nature of Aquinas' Doctrine of Analogy?," *Heythrop Journal* 57, no. 2 (2016): 312–324. See also Ignacio Eugenio Maria Andereggen, *La Metafisica de Santo Tomas en la "Exposicion" sobre el "De Divinis Nominibus" de Dionisio Areopagita* (Buenos Aires: Editorial de la Universidad Catolica Argentina, 1989).

[10] Lucy Gardner and David Moss, conceding without criticism that Balthasar displays significant influence from Heidegger (see *Balthasar at the End of Modernity*, 73–74n14), argue nonetheless that it is "philosophically naïve" to charge Balthasar with "offering metaphor in place of metaphysics, picture in the place of argument" and that "[the fundamental grammar of Balthasar's theology] is determined by a fundamental commitment to the analogical knowledge of being as precisely reflection upon the event of the absolute *identity-in-difference* of world and God" (76).

Attempting to clarify what this enigmatic statement means, they add: "It is our contention that Balthasar . . . offers not a God beyond metaphysics [alluding explicitly to Jean Luc Marion's *God Beyond Being*] but rather a God freed from any ancient binary creaturely marking which would seek to marshal the multiple differences of creation against an absolute oppositional limit" (76).

But Cyril O'Regan (*Anatomy of Misremembering*, 228), Anthony Sciglitano ("Death in Cyril O'Regan's *The Anatomy of Misremembering*," 1011), and others manifestly argue for the interpretation Gardner-Moss attempt to evade. Hence, Balthasar's mixture of analogical predication, metaphorical discourse, mystical symbolic description, and Barthian dialectic simply bespeaks a confusing syncretism rather than a precise synthesis or rigorous methodology.

For Balthasar's influence on Jean-Luc Marion, see Robyn Horner, "A Theology of Distance," in *Jean-Luc Marion: A Theo-Logical Introduction* (Aldershot: Ashgate, 2005). Rosenberg also discerns a discourse similar to Marion in Balthasar (see "Theory and Drama," 192), citing Marion's *The Idol and Distance: Five Studies*, trans. Thomas A. Carlson (New York: Fordham University Press, 2001).

Nonetheless, Marion says Balthasar is "a promising if insufficient practitioner of theological phenomenology" (*In Excess: Studies in Saturated Phenomena* [New York: Fordham University Press, 2002], 29). Balthasar returns the favor, as it were: "J.-L. Marion seems in his two works, *L'idole et la distance* (Paris: Grasset, 1979) and *Dieu sans l'être* (Paris: Fayard, 1982) to concede too much to the critique of Heidegger and others and to disregard the passages where Siewerth and even Thomas define *bonum* as the intrinsic 'self-transcending' of *esse*" (*TL* II, 134–135n10 [G 125–126n10]; cf. *TL* II, 177n9 [G 163n9]; *TD* V, 105 [G 93]).

For analysis of Balthasar's and Marion's respective appropriations of Dionysius's mystical theology, see Tamsin Jones, "Dionysius in Hans Urs von Balthasar and Jean-Luc Marion," *Modern Theology* 24, no. 4 (2008): 743–754.

ries, which is the lens through which he receives Speyr's mysticism.[11] Despite the truth-value of mystical discourse, it is certainly disputable whether it is beneficial to employ it in the context of a theology that attempts to articulate theological truth in any *systematic* manner. In fact, Balthasar at times substitutes mystical discourse for properly theological discourse, mystical symbolism for systematic theology, raw mysticism for theological reason. This is the perennial trap of fideism versus rationalism, of subject versus object, of phenomenological description versus ontological metaphysics. The history of philosophical thought may be summed up in terms of this ongoing conflict,[12] which finds its resolution only in an adequate synthesis of these diverse elements of reality that the human person experiences.[13] But one element that is intractably resistant to any attempt

---

[11] See his "Theologie und Spiritualitat," *Gregorianum* 50 (1969): 571–587; ET, "Spirituality," in *Explorations* I, 211–226. Nonetheless, I do not impugn Speyr herself for Balthasar's theological deficiencies, since she—in the words of Joseph Ratzinger—provided "'the charismatic, prophetic impulse' that made Balthasar's work 'a truly living theology,'" as Schumacher reports (see *Trinitarian Anthropology*, 70, citing Ratzinger's "Das Problem der christlichen Prophetie: Neils Christian Hvidt im Gesprach mit Joseph Kardinal Ratzinger," *Internationale katholische Zeitschrift "Communio"* 28 [March–April 1999]: 183).

[12] There is also, of course, the perpetual apparent conflict between religion and science, which is another form of the dualism of faith-reason, phenomenon-*intellectus*, subject-object, which is yearning for synthesis, but which will never be fully achieved short of the *eschaton*.

[13] The only thinker to attempt this synthesis aptly and self-consciously is Karol Wojtyla, who (perhaps not coincidentally) became Pope St. John Paul the Great. But, alas, exploration of how his thought is a unique and necessary attempt to overcome this perpetual dichotomy that fundamentally characterizes the history of philosophical thought must be left for another work.

See especially his *Persona e Atto*, trans. Giuseppe Girgenti and Patrycja Mikulska (Milano: Bompiani, 2001), and is also contained within the Italian compilation of most of his philosophical work (as well as his doctoral dissertation in theology), called *Metafisica della Persona: Tutte le opera filosofiche e saggi integrative*, ed. Giovanni Reale and Tadeusz Styczen (Milano: Bompiani, 2003).

See also the compilation of some of his articles in English translation, called *Person and Community*. His lectures at the Catholic University of Lublin, unavailable in English, are published in German translation, *Lubliner Vorlesungen*, trans. Anneliese Danka Spranger and Edda Wiener (Stuttgart-Degerloch: Seewaldverlag, 1981) and in two volumes in Spanish translation, *Lecciones de Lublin*, trans. Rafael Mora Martin (Madrid: Palabra, 2014).

Finally, see his brief reflections on the modern turn in philosophy, which allude to his own attempted synthesis of the philosophies of being and consciousness (i.e., medieval and modern), in his last book, *Memory and Identity: Conversations at the Dawn of a Millennium* (New York: Rizzoli International, 2005), 8, 10, 12.

at synthesis is the reality of evil, which occupies the center of Balthasar's theological concerns. The question, then, becomes: How might his mysticism in the face of evil be tempered by *scientia divina*?

A RESOLUTION TO THE PROBLEM OF EVIL?

At the center of any philosophically informed theology and of theology as such (*theos-logos*) is the problem of evil ("theodicy"), which is the only lasting existential objection in the heart of every human being to the notion of an omnipotent, omni-benevolent God. Why, if God loves His creatures, is there so much suffering? Why, if God became man, suffered, and rose from the dead for our sakes, does the world not seem any better off for it all? It seems technology is the only reason humanity is better off today than it was in centuries past, and yet it also contributes exponentially to human suffering (e.g., weapons of mass destruction and pornography). Consider for a moment how many billions of people today suffer hunger, thirst, cold, disease, and violence, while a very small percentage basks in the immense luxuries produced by the riches they have created or inherited and hoarded for themselves, for the most part, to their own moral peril and that of many others. Compare the leisure experienced in the developed (or "first") world today, despite constant complaint of want, to the millennia past of human beings who spent every waking hour preoccupied with procuring life's essentials. Imagine the intensity of evil that pervades the hearts of those involved in human trafficking, the sex trade, the abortion industry, and the many unimaginable sexual perversions that proliferate the modern world. I am skeptical of the claim that all things were hunky-dory in the Christian empire of the so-called Middle Ages. Grotesque infidelity to the promises of consecrated life existed then too. Perversions of all types have existed in the human heart since the dawn of time (or, at least, the moment right after man's fall). The proliferation of the mass media of communication, one of many technological advances invented by the human intellect, simply renders the evil that is ever-present in the world of human history all the more evident to the watchful human mind.

Does it suffice to say that Christ, the eternally begotten Son of God the Father, willingly entered into this evil world in order to suffer it all in a way unimaginable to finite beings? Balthasar's answer to the problem of evil is not only that Christ suffered all things, but that God ("One of the Trinity"!) Himself takes evil itself up into His own infinite being most especially simply by being Trinity. In other words, evil finds its mysterious origin in the eternal ontological relationship between the divine persons—God does not will evil, but evil has a *raison d'être* and it exists in the depths of love itself as infinite self-expropriation, self-surrender, selflessness, self-sacrifice. I find this attempt to resolve this perennial question to be severely misguided, but it is the logical result of a *particular* understanding of reality as intelligible. I propose, instead, that evil as such has no *raison d'être*—it is utterly absurd, a true rupture in the fabric of being, which alone is intelligible. God chose to bear the brunt of this absurdity in the flesh along with us out of love, which is not ultimately self-sacrifice, but self-gift.[14]

It is not that the infinite goodness that constitutes the triune identity of God *had to* overflow into a distinct and therefore imperfect reality that He, nonetheless, purifies in the end to become perfectly one with His glory. Rather, God had no reason other than Himself to create a world where intelligibility and unintelligibility are inevitably intertwined, a world that not only did not need to be, but might as well not have been, a reality that is good because it is created by Him, but is not any better than the real possibility of evil never having existed by never having a finite good in which to inhere, except insofar as it is actual. Jesus says about Judas, "it would have been better for him if he had never been born" (Matt 26:24). Likewise, it might have been better for the world if it had never existed. But that does not mean it would have been better, *simpliciter*, if the world had never existed. It would not have been better or worse. It just is. Why? Because there exists a God who has willed it. He has not willed the evil, but the good alone, and the finite good has created evils.[15] God has taken

---

[14] Without entering into the debates concerning feminist theology, the fact that *kenosis* by itself is not an adequate or just message, particularly, for victims of violence reflects the truth that love does not need to be expressed in suffering, even if it often takes advantage of it—and powerfully so.

[15] Could free creatures have chosen never to introduce moral evil into the world? Theoretically. But in actuality, it seems inevitable (not necessary) that finite freedom eventually defect from moral perfection, given that it necessarily possesses the potency to do so and, provided infinite time, that potency (if it is real, indeed) must at some point become actualized (albeit freely, that is, with finite defectible freedom).

   This argument I have presented for the inevitability of the fall borrows a premise from Aquinas's illustrious "third way" of demonstrating God's existence. Certainly, God could have prevented this natural potency from being actualized, given infinite time, but I am assuming that there would be no reason for Him to do so, as finite freedom is being considered in accord with its nature precisely as finite and therefore capable of defection.

   Would it make sense for God to create such freedom only to contradict the inherent

upon Himself all evil not in order to create a perfect world, but in order to love.

It remains true, then, that enduring evil is the greatest act of love, if undertaken virtuously. But it cannot be concluded that, therefore, evils exist *in order for* love to be expressed, only that love takes advantage of the already absurd existence of evil to create meaning by enacting good, by fighting to overcome evil, by suffering it with virtue, by conquering precisely in loving. As Paul says, "overcome evil with good" (Rom 12:21). God has given us the opportunity to participate in the act of self-giving, which in the face of evil takes the form of self-sacrifice. But eternity is not self-sacrifice since evil is inherently finite—parasitic upon the finite, in fact; evil is not eternal precisely because it is conquered by the mere existence of the infinite good, which gives itself infinitely. Finite freedom will become itself fully by being split apart into the utter lack of freedom, on the one hand, and perfect union with the infinite freedom of love itself, on the other.[16]

As I have argued elsewhere, Balthasar would not have felt the need to project an exemplar form of suffering into the inner life of the Godhead if it were not for his lack of an adequate theology of the divine permission of moral evil (i.e., grace, freedom, predestination).[17] The inherited framework with which he sought to understand grace and freedom seems to have led to his approach to divine impassibility because, absent a more adequate grasp of this dynamic, defining the Trinity in terms of *ur-kenosis* is the only way to respond to the demands of the soteriological problem. In other words, where there is no acknowledgement of the role of nihilation in the free creature's causation of evil, a dichotomy arises: either God must take the responsibility for evil or empathy must constitute His very being—he opts for the latter. When God is empathy itself, there is no problem locating—in fact, it is necessary in this case to locate—the root of all evil somehow in His infinite being, a perplexing notion that yields

---

nature (i.e., potency) of the thing created? Of course, this does not in the least make God responsible for evil, except insofar as He created the finite realities that made evil possible.

[16] This is not so much a dualism as it is a triadology: good, evil, *relatio*; true, false, *relatio*; subject, object, *relatio*; being, nonbeing, *relatio*; Creator, creature, *relatio*; etc. Balthasar seems, instead, to opt for a monism, where unity is the supremely operative transcendental (see, e.g., his derision of Teilhard de Chardin's eschatological "dualism" as "Jewish" in *TD* V, 167 [G 147]).

[17] I have explored the latter thoroughly in "God's Relation to Evil."

problematic conclusions in eschatology as well.[18] On the contrary, when one grapples with the problem of evil in terms of the reality of "nihilation" initiated by finite freedom, it is possible to discern the affective receptivity of the Creator to such without departing from Thomistic principles.[19] In this more refined approach, God becomes empathetic with our suffering through the Incarnation, thanks to the sympathy His love knows in divine receptivity to the free initiative of sinfulness in creatures.

Finally, the most profound reflection on how God Incarnate, Love embodied, eternal Wisdom ensconced in temporal absurdity, gives intelligibility to the unintelligible, rendering suffering meaningful on a supernatural level (i.e., salvific or redemptive), is Pope St. John Paul the Great's Apostolic Letter, *Salvifici Doloris*.[20] Emphasizing the need to go beyond description to the level of explanation, John Paul points to love enfleshed in the person of the "suffering servant" of God as the only possible source of meaning for the human experience of evil.[21] Without evil, there is no suffering; without suffering, there is no redemption; without evil and suffering, there is no need for redemption, and thus God's love would not be expressed through the acts of humility, obedience, and surrender (trust in God's will) that characterized Christ and that characterizes the authentic Christian, culminating in the holy death (i.e., one imitative of His). There is no necessity for divine love to be expressed through created virtues or for free creatures to participate in this living out of love in a sin-laden world. Yet it is so—and there is a certain beauty to the actual economy of creation and salvation. It is counterfactual, counterproductive, and marginally useless to speculate about the possibility or fittingness of a creation without evil and suffering. Evil exists, but God has brought forth good from evil; in fact, He has redeemed suffering itself.[22] Still, no answer to the problem of evil satisfies the human heart completely in this life. As John Paul explains:

> The one to whom [the human person] puts the question is himself suffering and wishes to answer him from the Cross, from the

---

[18] See, e.g., *Dare We Hope*, 61, 96 [G 49, 78]. I deal extensively with this problematic dimension of Balthasar's project in another volume.

[19] See Jacques Maritain, "Quelques réflexions sur le savoir théologique."

[20] The text is available on the Vatican Website, at https://w2.vatican.va/content/john-paul-ii/en/apost_letters/1984/documents/hf_jp-ii_apl_11021984_salvifici-doloris.html (accessed 12/27/2017).

[21] See *Salvifici Doloris*, §§5, 13–19.

[22] See *Salvifici Doloris*, §19.

heart of his own suffering. Nevertheless, it often takes time, even a long time, for this answer to begin to be interiorly perceived. For Christ does not answer directly and he does not answer in the abstract this human questioning about the meaning of suffering. Man hears Christ's saving answer as he himself gradually becomes a sharer in the sufferings of Christ. The answer which comes through this sharing, by way of the interior encounter with the Master, is in itself something more than the mere abstract answer to the question about the meaning of suffering. . . . A source of joy is found in the overcoming of the sense of the uselessness of suffering, a feeling that is sometimes very strongly rooted in human suffering.[23]

Suffering has become a means of sanctification because the Holy One Himself has embraced it with love, thus transforming it from the mere result of evil into a means for good.[24] The infinite wisdom of infinite love knows all things, bears all things, and endures all things with us and for us (see 1 Cor 13:7). *O felix culpa quae talem et tantum meruit habere redemptorem*!

---

[23] See *Salvifici Doloris*, §§26–27.
[24] See *Salvifici Doloris*, §20.

APPENDIX: CRUCIAL DIFFERENCES BETWEEN BALTHASAR AND RATZINGER

THE FORMATIVE INFLUENCE of the thought of Hans Urs von Balthasar on the theology of Joseph Ratzinger is common knowledge.[1] Ratzinger pays tribute to him on more than one occasion.[2] There are two theological novelties that rush to the mind of any student attempting to characterize Balthasar's peculiar thought: (1) his doctrine of Holy Saturday, or the descent of Christ into the hell of the damned,[3] and (2) his quasi-universalist ar-

---

[1] Ratzinger's allegiance to the *nouvelle theologie* with Henri de Lubac and Hans Urs von Balthasar, among others, is, perhaps, most evident in his article, "Gratia praesupponit naturam: Erwägungen über Sinn und Grenze eines scholastischen Axioms," in *Einsicht und Glaube*, ed. Heinrich Fries (Freiburg: Herder Verlag, 1962): 151–165, English translation available in *Dogma and Preaching: Applying Christian Doctrine to Daily Living*, unabridged ed. (San Francisco: Ignatius Press, 2011).

But, interestingly enough, Ratzinger bases his position on the nature-grace relation (common to the *Communio* school) upon Bonaventure rather than Thomas, thus he is not subject to much of the critique directed toward the position as it appears in Lubac. Moreover, his relationship to Lubac's position is further complicated by his laudatory comments on M. J. Marmann's *Praeamubla ad gratiam: Ideengeschichtliche Untersuchung* über *die Entstehung des Axioms 'Gratia praesupponit naturam'* (unpublished dissertation, Regensburg, 1974); see the appendix to Ratzinger's *In the Beginning: A Catholic Understanding of the Story of Creation and the Fall*, trans. Boniface Ramsey, OP (Grand Rapids, MI: Eerdmans, 1995), (originally published *Konsequenzen des Schopfungsglaubens* [Regensburg: Univ. A. Pustet, 1979]), nos. 1 and 19.

Finally, his mature thought on the subject is further distinguishable from Lubac's, however still only implicitly, in Pope Benedict XVI's Encyclical Letter, *Deus Caritas Est*; see Serge-Thomas Bonino, OP, "'Nature and Grace' in the Encyclical *Deus Caritas Est*," *Nova et Vetera* (English Edition) 5, no. 2 (2007): 231–248, originally "'Nature et grace' dans l'encyclique *Deus Caritas Est*," *Revue Thomiste* 105 (2005): 531–549, trans. Shannon Gaffney.

[2] Most notably, in his memoirs, he says: "meeting Balthasar was for me the beginning of a lifelong friendship I can only be thankful for. Never again have I found anyone with such a comprehensive theological and humanistic education as Balthasar and de Lubac, and I cannot even begin to say how much I owe to my encounter with them" (*Milestones*, 143).

See also Cardinal Joseph Ratzinger, "Homily at the Funeral of Hans Urs von Balthasar," in *His Life and Work*, and Pope Benedict XVI, "Papal Message for Centenary of von Balthasar's Birth: Reflections on the Swiss Theologian," available online at http://www.ignatiusinsight.com/features2005/benxvi_praiseshub_oct05.asp (accessed 27 March 2014).

[3] He frequently speaks of Christ's descent in terms of the Old Testament *Sheol*, but his

gument in favor of a theological hope for the salvation of all men. There is a third dimension of Balthasar's thought that takes up these two features into a higher plane, as it were: the infinite love of the Trinity itself is *ur-kenotic*. In other words, central to his theology is the dual claim that the descent of Christ into hell is the most perfect reflection of the self-surrender that constitutes the Trinitarian life and that it is most fitting for the triune God to embrace (by first "undergirding") hell in all its New Testament horror (i.e., the "second death" of Rev 20–21), freely surrendering impassibility in the economy of salvation, wherein the second person of the Trinity "becomes sin."[4]

Ratzinger also reflects on the painful descent of Christ and its impact upon the reality of damnation, but it remains to be seen to what extent he may agree with the most radical points of Balthasar's theology and how much (or little) influence the Trinitarian thought of the latter had upon him. I will assert that even if Ratzinger is likewise reticent to proclaim divine impassibility unqualifiedly, the descent for him, although understood in a very similar way to Balthasar, relates to damnation and the Trinity in a way that is fundamentally different from the way these three elements interact functionally in Balthasar's theology.[5]

---

identification of the latter with *Gehenna* allows him to affirm that although Christ cannot be said to have suffered the New Testament hell proper, his hell encompasses the eschatological no and the deepest possible suffering. See *MP*, 172–173 [G 246–247]; *TD* V, 199, 354 [G 178, 323].

[4] For the Cross as revelation of the Trinity, see *TD* V, 510–511, 259–260 [G 466–467, 234–235].

[5] Therefore, I disagree with Edward Oakes's assertion that "The most obvious proponent of this view that the Trinity is fully engaged in the event of Christ's descent into hell is of course Hans Urs von Balthasar. . . . [H]is most important ally on this theologoumenon will surely prove to be Joseph Ratzinger, whose career shows a remarkable consistency when he comes to discuss the connection between Christ's vicarious, atoning suffering and his descent into hell" ("*Descensus* and Development" 12); he then quotes *Introduction to Christianity*, 297, 301, *Eschatology* 217–218, and *Jesus of Nazareth* I, 20, all of which reflect remarkably on the descent-sufferings of Christ's passion and death, but say nothing about the Trinity or even Christ's relationship to the Father as such (see Oakes, "*Descensus* and Development," 12–14).

Nevertheless, Ratzinger appears to broach Balthasar's position on impassibility in his *Schauen auf den Durchbohrten*, although it is difficult to judge precisely where he falls in the spectrum between Adrienne von Speyr's mystical excess, as it were (adopted by Balthasar), and Maritain's moderately Thomistic approach. He is certainly more careful than Balthasar, but he does not say enough for one to draw out clearly a precise formulation of his position on the matter (see *Behold the Pierced One*, 56ff. [G 48ff.]), except insofar as he invokes ultimately John Paul II's *Dives in Misericordia* §52 (see §59n11).

Rather than attempt to summarize Balthasar's detailed treatment of each of the terms in this relation and then develop Ratzinger's relationship to that treatment, I will briefly take up in chronological order what in each of their major works directly pertains to damnation and its relationship to the triune God.[6] It will become clear that while Balthasar's eschatological concerns cause his understanding of the triune God to center on the hellish passion of Christ and his being-dead on Holy Saturday, Ratzinger understands Christ's vicarious descent on the Cross in terms of the Son's economic "being-for," which proceeds from His own being-from the Father (and the two are one in the unifying gift of being-with that is the Holy Spirit). Ratzinger's Trinitarian thought is therefore an ontology of relation, comprising at once a "negative theology" and a foundation for a more disciplined soteriology and eschatology than is exhibited in Balthasar. This contrast is a significant one that no one, to my knowledge, has exposed as of yet, given that many of Ratzinger's admirers also, if not primarily, consider themselves disciples of Balthasar and therefore do not wish to drive a wedge between the two thinkers. While some may want to turn a blind eye to differences between the two thinkers, it is imperative to recognize Ratzinger's theology for what it really is, namely, something entirely distinct from, even though very influenced by, the theology of his senior theological confrere and close friend, Hans Urs von Balthasar.

RATZINGER'S NUANCED RELATION TO BALTHASAR'S CONTROVERSIAL THESES

Many may not realize that not only did Balthasar's thought on these matters not receive definitive shape until the 80s with the publication of the final volumes of the *Theodramatik*, but it is not at all clear that Balthasar's earliest formulations of the significance of Christ's descent preceded

---

[6] I may, therefore, overlook minor works. Overall, I did not find Oakes's article particularly illuminating. In fact, he concludes the section on *Spe Salvi* with a comment that is clearly Balthasarian without evidence of such a position in Ratzinger/Benedict: "[T]he outcome of final judgment must remain unknown, precisely so that hope may be given its proper room and not be trumped by certainty" (249–250).

This is the position advocated in Balthasar's *Was dürfen wir hoffen?* But I will show that it is not necessarily shared by Ratzinger. In fact, his words in *Spe Salvi* §§45–46 claim that some are in fact beyond the point of conversion, lost in egoism, even if the number of lost is less than the number destined for purgatory; if one admits the existence of an irreversible egoism that does in fact culminate in damnation, then he cannot have a *theological* hope for the salvation of all men.

Ratzinger's earliest comments on the same, as is commonly assumed by those who emphasize Balthasar's influence on Ratzinger.[7] Therefore, I will turn first to Ratzinger's *Introduction to Christianity* before I compare its remarks to Balthasar's *Mysterium Paschale*. Commenting on a thought presented by Jean Daniélou, a common source along with Henri de Lubac for both Ratzinger and Balthasar on this matter,[8] Ratzinger says:

> In the last analysis pain is the product and expansion of Jesus Christ's being stretched out from being in God right down to the hell of "My God, why have you forsaken me?" Anyone who has stretched his existence so wide that he is simultaneously immersed in God and in the depths of the God-forsaken creature is bound to be torn asunder, as it were; such a one is truly "crucified." But this process of being torn apart is identical with love; it is its realization to the extreme (Jn 13:1) and the concrete expression of the breadth it creates.[9]

Alluding to the dark night of the mystics as a participation in the suffering

---

[7]   Balthasar's German essay "Mysterium Paschale" in 1969. Ratzinger's *Einführung in das Christentum* (*Introduction to Christianity* in the English) was published originally in 1968. Balthasar does briefly reflect on the Holy Saturday doctrine in his *Verbum Caro (Skizzen zur Theologie I)* in 1960 (in English, *Explorations in Theology* I). His most significant remark there appears on 263–264 [G 285–286]. He does not yet bring the Trinity into the discussion; he will do so in the fourth volume of his *Explorations*. He does treat universalism in the first volume, but he does not explicate any clear relationship between Christ's descent into hell and the prospect of universal hope. He, nevertheless, anticipates here Ratzinger's development of the theme of the "dark night" as the hell embraced by mystics (in solidarity with Christ and sinners); see *Explorations* I, 249–250, 268–269 [G 269–270, 290–291]).

     Moreover, Ratzinger notes in his "Reflections on the Origin of My Meditations on Holy Week" that he "had taught Christology for the first time at the university in Freising and explored the meaning of this article ['He descended into hell') which at the time was rather at the margin of theological consciousness" before he "was asked in the summer of 1956 to review a new book of Hans Urs von Balthasar (*Die Gottesfrage des heutigen Menschen*, Vienna, Herder, 1956)" (*Sabbath of History*, 21). This work of Balthasar is the first in which he offers controversial reflections on the descent, about which Ratzinger had misgivings.

[8]   Ratzinger cites Daniélou's *Essai sur le mystère de l'histoire* (Paris: Les Éditions du Seuil, 1953). Martin Bieler notes that Henri de Lubac's 1938 *Catholicisme: Les aspects sociaux du dogme* likely served as Balthasar's original source on Holy Saturday and Christ's "lonesomeness among the lonesome," for which Balthasar made a German translation in 1970 ("God and the Cross," 64).

[9]   Ratzinger, *Introduction to Christianity*, 290 [G 212].

inherent to Christ's love, a common connection drawn by Ratzinger, he acknowledges a hell of sorts in the cry of dereliction, but his understanding of it focuses upon the person of Christ, how He is simultaneously in full communion with God's inner life and immersed in the darkness of the human sinfulness He wished to take upon Himself in the passion for our sakes. The suffering embraced by Christ is an expression of God's love for us:

> The New Testament is the story of the God who of his own accord wished to become, in Christ, the Omega—the last letter—in the alphabet of creation. It is the story of the God who is himself the act of love, the pure "for," and who therefore necessarily puts on the disguise of the smallest worm (Ps 22:6 [21:7]). It is the story of the God who identifies himself with his creature and in this *contineri a minimo*, in being grasped and overpowered by the least of his creatures, displays that "excess" that identifies him as God.[10]

The Cross does not function here as the perfect image of God's own life, but it reveals the love God has for a sinful mankind:

> The truth about man is that he is continually assailing truth; the just man crucified is thus a mirror held up to man in which he sees himself unadorned. But the Cross does not reveal only man; it also reveals God. God is such that he identifies himself with man right down into this abyss and that he judges him by saving him. In the abyss of human failure is revealed the still more inexhaustible abyss of divine love. The Cross is thus truly the center of revelation, a revelation that does not reveal any previously unknown principles but reveals us to ourselves by revealing us before God and God in our midst.[11]

So, the Cross does reveal something about God, but these comments do not indicate anything about the *immanent* life of God (i.e., the Trinity); rather, it reveals God's loving response to man's rejection of truth, and this revealed love both judges and saves mankind.

Notice that for Ratzinger the descent of God into the "abyss" takes

---

[10] *Introduction to Christianity*, 291–292 [G 213].
[11] *Introduction to Christianity*, 293 [G 214].

place on the Cross and that it does not function as a launching pad for speculation about the secret recesses of the Trinity itself, even if certainly, the triune God is love itself and the passion of Christ is a response of divine love to human sinfulness. The question remains: What is the relationship between the descent and the hell of the damned? Ratzinger answers this question in the following manner:

> [T]he Old Testament has only one word for hell *and* death, the word *sheol*; it regards them as ultimately identical. Death is absolute loneliness. But the loneliness into which love can no longer advance is—hell. . . . This article [of the Creed] thus asserts that Christ strode through the gate of our final loneliness, that in his Passion he went down into the abyss of our abandonment. Where no voice can reach us any longer, there is he. Hell is thereby overcome, or, to be more accurate, death, which was previously hell, is hell no longer. Neither is the same any longer because there is life in the midst of death, because love dwells in it. Now only deliberate self-enclosure is hell or, as the Bible calls it, the second death (Rev 20:14, for example). But death is no longer the path into icy solitude; the gates of *sheol* have been opened.[12]

Christ has done the impossible of separating death from hell; he suffered the depths of human loneliness and abandonment, but "the second death" replaces the hell that existed prior to His redemptive work—the hell due those who finally reject God's love is not embraced by Christ, but is rather a possibility consequent to His triumph over the hell that is death.[13] However, it is not this simple—there is a tension present in Ratzinger's thought, where he appears to say something closer to what Balthasar will claim later:

> [T]his article of the Creed turns our gaze to the depths of human existence, which reach down into the valley of death, into the zone of untouchable loneliness and rejected love, and thus embrace the dimension of hell, carrying it within themselves as one of their own possibilities. Hell, existence in the definitive re-

---

[12] *Introduction to Christianity*, 301 [G 220–221].
[13] In *Spe Salvi* §37, Pope Benedict, similarly, reflects on the "hell" into which Christ descends not in terms of damnation proper, but in terms of dark human experiences and the mystical expressions of the Psalmist.

jection of "being for," is not a cosmographical destination but a dimension of human nature, the abyss into which it reaches at its lower end. We know today better than ever before that everyone's existence touches these depths. . . . Christ, the "new Adam," undertook to bear the burden of these depths with us and did not wish to remain sublimely unaffected by them; conversely, of course, total rejection in all its unfathomability has only now become possible.[14]

Thus, "definitive rejection of 'being for'" is a fundamental dimension of every man's existence and the abyss into which Love descends in the form of Christ's passion, but even though God lets Himself be affected by our rejection of His love (our resistance to His grace), it is this divine act of vulnerability that makes "total rejection" (definitive refusal) of God truly possible. Perhaps he wants to say that prior to Christ man could issue final refusal of God's love and that this refusal, which affects every man as part of the same body of humanity, is borne by Christ in the descent, and yet this divine event brings about the reality of still a more profound possibility for self-exclusion from God's love.

In fact, Ratzinger is consistently reticent to embrace fully Balthasar's treatment of the descent into hell, at least in part because of its potential eschatological implications. As he reports in 1997, his reluctance to endorse in full this element of his theology, which is its center, and "[to allow] the unknowable to remain in the unknowable," spans his entire theological career, which exhibits greater "modesty" (as he says):

I was asked in the summer of 1956 to review a new book of Hans Urs von Balthasar (*Die Gottesfrage des heutigen Menschen*, Vienna, Herder, 1956) in which the author shifts the article on the descent into hell to the center of Christian faith and life. According to Balthasar, Christ participated himself in hell, in the deepest sense of the word; only in the last level of his descent did redemption penetrate into the deepest abyss, that is to say, hell. At the time I did not want to adopt this thesis that Balthasar later (1969) developed again in a grand and impressive way in his *Theology of the Three Days*. I have to admit that even today, as in 1956 and 1967, I find it difficult fully to concur with the great Swiss theologian with whom I developed a close friendship. I prefer to leave

---

[14] *Introduction to Christianity*, 311–312 [G 229–230].

this mysterious sentence, which leads from the historical world into the hiddenness of death, in its mysterious obscurity. . . . Yes, Jesus died, he "descended" into the mysterious depths death leads to. He went to the ultimate solitude where no one can accompany us, for "being dead" is above all loss of communication. It is isolation where love does not penetrate. In this sense Christ descended "into hell" whose essence is precisely the loss of love, being cut off from God and man. But, however, wherever he goes, "hell" ceases to be hell, because he himself is life and love, because he is the bridge which connects man and God and thereby also connects men among themselves. And thus the descent is at the same time also transformation. The final solitude no longer exists—except for the one who wants it, who rejects love from within and from its foundation, because he seeks only himself, wants to be from and for himself.[15]

Thus, for Ratzinger, the possibility of self-enclosure, the opposite of Christ's complete self-sacifice, remains a possibility for the human being!

There is certainly a tension, however, between Ratzinger's understanding of the community of man in terms of an all-pervading *relatio* and the reality of damnation. It is unclear how heaven can be heaven "above" a hell, how it is tolerable for the elect (and for God!) that some of Christ's body be lost forever. He does not attempt a resolution to this perplexing dilemma, perhaps out of a fear of falling into the trap of over-systematizing the faith by positing the necessity of a hope-filled response to a concealed promise that God's desire for universal salvation cannot be impeded even by a merely finite freedom. He seems, rather, to believe that man is created with the capacity to reject definitively any and all grace that God could offer him or, at least, that God may not offer Himself ordinarily in an irresistible fashion. But it remains a mystery for Ratzinger how precisely this apparent frustration of God's will ought to be understood.[16] Therefore,

---

[15] "Reflections on the Origins of My Meditations on Holy Week," in *The Sabbath of History*, 17–23, at 21–22. Edward Oakes, unfortunately, decides to ignore precisely this excerpt from Ratzinger's "Reflections" (see *Infinity Dwindled to Infancy*, 380).

On the other end of the spectrum, Bruce D. Marshall mischaracterizes Benedict XVI's citation of Balthasar and Moltmann together in his *Jesus of Nazareth* II, 306 [G 326–327], as if Ratzinger suddenly reversed his interpretation of the cry of dereliction as a true experience of godforsakenness (see his "Reading the Gospels").

[16] For exploration of this question, see my *My Grace is Sufficient for You: A Contemporary Thomistic Theology of Grace and Freedom* (forthcoming).

more than Balthasar, Ratzinger reveres the Creator's intractable respect for the radical freedom of the human person to refuse His love definitively.[17]

Kenoticism in Balthasar's Earlier Work

Ratzinger's reflections here clearly do not go as far as Balthasar's in *Mysterium Paschale*, even if Balthasar later undermines this book as "a quickly written work" that did not fully appropriate the mystical insights of Adrienne von Speyr.[18] Rather, the latter serves to radicalize his interpretation of the descent doctrine in a quasi-mythological direction. Relevant to the topic of the Trinity's involvement in Christ's condemnation and consequent relation to the hell of the damned, Balthasar seems to take a position directly in opposition to that of his friend, Ratzinger:

> [T]he real object of a theology of Holy Saturday does not consist in the completed state which follows on the last act in the self-surrender of the incarnate Son to his Father—something which the structure of every human death, more or less ratified by the individual person, would entail. Rather does that object consist in something unique, expressed in the "realisation" of all Godlessness, of all the sins of the world, now experienced as agony and a sinking down into the "second death" or "second chaos," outside of the world ordained from the beginning by God. And so it is really God who assumes what is radically contrary to the divine, what is eternally reprobated by God, in the form of the supreme obedience of the Son towards the Father, and, thereby, in Luther's words, *sub contrario* discloses himself in the very act of his self-concealment.[19]

---

[17] Hence, in *Spe Salvi* §§45–46, he says that some are in fact beyond the point of conversion, lost in egoism, even if the number of lost is less than the number destined for purgatory. If one admits the existence of an irreversible egoism that does in fact culminate in damnation, then he cannot have a *theological* hope for the salvation of all men, which runs contrary to the fundamental argument of Balthasar's *Dare We Hope*.

[18] See his *TL* II, 345n75 [G 315n1]; Steffen Lösel, "A Plain Account," 150n54. Alberto Espezel argues that his treatment of the descent becomes more precise and coherent in his later works, such as the *Theo-Drama*, than in his earlier *Glory of the Lord* and *Mysterium Paschale* (see "Quelques aspects de la soteriologie de Hans Urs von Balthasar," *Nouvelle Revue Théologique* 112 [1990]: 80–92).

[19] *MP* 51–52 [G 160–161].

Hence, for Balthasar there is a dialectical struggle between the loving self-surrender of Son to Father, on the one hand, and the "second death" or reprobation that man brings upon himself in rejecting such—the latter is the hell into which Christ descends in order to reveal the solidarity of God with the godless.

The redemptive Incarnation for Balthasar is not merely a renunciation of divine immutability,[20] but, more so, it reflects an eternal sacrifice in the triune God:

> The truth which intervenes between [divine immutability and divine mutability] concerns the "Lamb slain before the foundation of the world" (Apocalypse 13, 8; cf. 5, 6, 9, 12) . . . . [The "slaying"] designates, rather, the eternal aspect of the historic and bloody sacrifice of the Cross (Apocalypse 5, 12)—as indeed Paul everywhere presupposes. Nevertheless what is indicated here is an enduring supratemporal condition of the "Lamb" . . . a condition of the Son's existence co-extensive with all creation and thus affecting, in some manner, his divine being. Recent Russian theology . . . was right to give this aspect a central place . . . that basic idea of [Bulgakov] which we agreed just now to give a central place high on our list of priorities. The ultimate presupposition of the Kenosis is the "selflessness" of the Persons (when considered as pure relationships) in the inner-Trinitarian life of love. . . . And since the will to undertake the redemptive Kenosis is itself indivisibly trinitarian' . . . God the Father and the Holy Spirit are for Bulgakov involved in the Kenosis in the most serious sense: the Father as he who sends and abandons, the Spirit as he who unites only through separation and absence.[21]

The effect of such a position can be no other than precisely a strong presumption in favor of the salvation of all men since the godlessness of those who reject divine mercy is itself taken up into the *kenosis* of Christ, ren-

---

[20] Balthasar holds divine immutability in principle (see *TD* II, 278 [G 253]; *TD* III, 523 [G 479]; *TD* V, 222 [G 200]), but the "Greek" notion (as he says) has little effect on his understanding of divine impassibility—God, in his estimation, wills to become passible (see *TD* V, 234 [G 211]) and suffers not merely in the human nature of Christ (as his *ur-kenotic* theory of the Trinity makes clear). See his ambivalence toward immutability in *MP* 34 [G 152]); *TD* II, 9, 280, 293 [G 9, 255, 266–267]; *TL* II, 352n131 [G 321n57]. See also Gerard O'Hanlon, *The Immutability of God*, 24.

[21] *MP* 34–35 [G 152–153].

dering such rejection a mere moment in the dialectic of love and sin, which itself functions as a most fitting expression of the original *kenosis* that constitutes the Trinitarian life. He expresses the relationship between Trinity and hell when he states:

> Christ takes the existential measure of everything that is sheerly contrary to God, of the entire object of the divine eschatological judgment, which here is grasped in that event in which it is "cast down" (*hormemati blethesetai*, Apocalypse 18, 21; John 12, 31; Matthew 22, 13). But at the same time, this happening gives the measure of the Father's mission in all its amplitude: the "exploration" of Hell is an event of the (economic) Trinity.[22]

Although here he includes the qualification "economic," he reports without rebuke the view of Bulgakov, which he acknowledges as indebted to "a perspective borrowed from the philosophies of Schelling and Hegel," that "the economic Trinity is 'from time immemorial assumed' in the immanent Trinity."[23] This relationship is developed in his later writings, but even here, while expressing reticence about "temptations of a Gnostic or Hegelian sort" in the "sophiological presuppositions" of Bulgakov,[24] he is, nonetheless, not shy about appropriating Russian kenoticism.

Here is a glimpse into the kenotic view he adopted of the Trinitarian persons:

> Lossky interprets the Kenosis as a revelation of the entire Trinity. This permits one to grasp how, on occasion, the thought arises, tentatively and obscurely, that when the Creator first made man the ideal Image he had in mind was the Incarnate Son as our Redeemer. If one takes seriously what has just been said, then the event of the Incarnation of the second divine Person does not leave the inter-relationship of those Persons unaffected. Human thought and human language break down in the presence of this mystery: namely, that the eternal relations of Father and Son are focused, during the "time" of Christ's earthly wanderings, and in

---

[22] *MP* 174–175 [G 248].

[23] *MP* 35 [G 153]. Yet, he appears later to align Bulgakov with Rahner concerning the immutability of the triune God (see *TD* IV, 277–278 [G 256–257]). But, in the same work, he expresses fundamental agreement with Bulgakov's Trinitarian "doctrine of redemption" (see *TD* IV, 313–314 [G 291–292]).

[24] *MP* 35 [G 153].

a sense which must be taken with full seriousness, in the relations between the man Jesus and his heavenly Father, and that the Holy Spirit lives as their go-between who, inasmuch as he proceeds from the Son, must also be affected by the Son's humanity.[25]

Hence, not only the descent into hell but every redemptive act of Christ is truly a window into the Trinitarian relations, as "the entire Trinity" has willed to be affected by the events of the economic order.[26]

BALTHASARIAN DEVELOPMENTS

After Balthasar's piece in *Mysterium Salutis* and before Ratzinger's *Eschatologie*, Balthasar published the fourth volume of his *Skizzen zur Theologie* (in the English, *Explorations in Theology*), entitled *Pneuma und Institution*, the concluding section of which treats the descent into hell and eschatological themes together.[27] At points in this work I notice a transition

---

[25] *MP* 30 [G 152]. See also Edward T. Oakes, *Patterns of Redemption*, 243.

[26] His justification for such a move is both scriptural and methodological. He interprets Philippians 2, on grammatical grounds, to be indicating a self-emptying that takes place in God Himself, not simply in Christ Jesus (see *MP* 23–24 [G 143–144]). Mansini presents Thomas's interpretation of this text very cogently and concisely, relying upon his *Super Epistolam ad Philippenses Lectura*, ch. 2, lect. 2, no. 57 (see "Can Humility and Obedience Be Trinitarian Realities?," 94–95). Defending Balthasar's understanding of *kenosis*, Antoine Birot argues against Thomas on the Incarnation: see his "The Divine Drama," 421–422n23.

It is not very clear whether Birot thinks such a "depositing" of divine nature without loss coheres well or not with the Thomistic doctrine of analogy, but the latter is certainly something Balthasar did not wish to abandon (only to modify); in any case, this will not be a question here explicitly addressed.

Pitstick characterizes Balthasar's position as follows: "Since [Christ's] human nature is incapable of bearing the punishment of all sins, 'the whole superstructure of the Incarnation' is removed in his descent. . . . Thus, since the Incarnation is suspended in his descent, his redemptive suffering after death is a suffering as divine Son" ("Development of Doctrine or Denial," 133).

She bases her reading on *TD* III, 228; *TD* IV, 335 and 495; *TD* V, 221–222 and 277; *Explorations* IV, 138, 411–412; *GL* VII, 205–206, 213 and 231; cf. *Light in Darkness*, 117–122, 131–133, 148–158, 190–203, 235–239, 288, 302–308 (cited in "Development of Doctrine or Denial," 133 nn. 12–14 and 143n54).

Steffen Lösel adds a comment on *Theologik* II, 324: "The agony of the cross increases upon the Son's death, when the Son enters the emptiness of hell, or what Balthasar calls the dwelling-place of 'sin having become already amorphous'" ("Murder in the Cathedral," 434).

[27] See *ET* IV, Part Three. The original German text was published in 1974.

in Balthasar from understanding the descent into hell through Eastern tradition and Christology toward his own Trinitarian eschatology that borders on mysticism but does not quite reach the intensity it will later under the cumulative influence of Adrienne von Speyr's life and work.[28] For example, he says: "[T]he experience of the abyss he undergoes is both entirely in him (insofar as he comes to know in himself the full measure of the dead sinner's distance from God) as well as at the same time entirely outside of him, because what he experiences is utterly foreign to him (as the eternal Son of the Father): on Good Friday he is himself entirely alienated from himself."[29] This self-alienation begun on the Cross and culminating in his being-dead on Saturday (whether the events of the two days are conceived as temporally distinct or as an existential unit celebrated in two phases)[30] certainly involves an alienation from the Father. After im-

---

[28] Even though he met her early on in his career, her visions, which he helped put into writing, had an increasing influence on his own thought after her death in 1967. Geoffrey Wainwright corroborates the interpretation of Balthasar's development on this question:

> The notion of Christ's "solidarity with the dead" as set forth in [*Mysterium Paschale*] . . . [is] a compromise that would eventually give way to the even more radical idea that in his descent into hell Jesus underwent—vicariously of course—*the full fate of the damned*. In his later writings, Balthasar begins to lean ever more heavily for his eschatology on the mystical experiences of his collaborator Adrienne von Speyr, whose meditations on this theme were privately published. . . . A short, resumptive article of Balthasar's on "The Descent into Hell" dates from 1970, and already a shift in emphasis from *Mysterium Paschale* of a year earlier can be detected" ("Eschatology," in *Cambridge Companion to Hans Urs von Balthasar*, 117 [emphasis original]).

> Nonetheless, there is an enduring continuity throughout his writing, as Andrew Louth points out in comparing his *Heart of the World*, written five years after meeting von Speyr in Basel, and his *Theodramatik* (see "The Place of *Heart of the World* in the Theology of Hans Urs von Balthasar," in *The Analogy of Beauty*, 154–155).

[29] *ET* IV, 409 [G 395]. Likewise, he says:

> By going all the way to the outermost alienation, God himself has proven to be the Almighty who also is able to safeguard his identity in nonidentity, his being-with-himself in being lost, his life in being dead. And so the Resurrection of Christ and of all who are saved by him can be seen as the inner consequence of his experience on Holy Saturday. There is no "reascent" after the descent; the way of love "to the end" (Jn 13:1) is itself love's self-glorification. (413 [G 399])

[30] There are occasional indications in Balthasar that he does not conceive the events of "Holy Saturday" as temporally distinct from his suffering on the Cross, and there are occasions where he seems to envision the descent as a continuance of the passion after the "moment" of His death. At times in *Explorations* IV he seems to relegate His suffering proper to Friday (e.g., see 406 [G 392]), while *Mysterium Paschale* (his "quickly

plying that the hell of the damned is itself taken up by Christ's descent,[31] he explains in what way this alienation plays into the relationship between Father and Son:

> [T]he most ultimate ground of all is the Trinitarian difference between Father and Son: the Father's surrender of the Son and the Son's being surrendered in the unity of the Trinitarian agreement. The path is one of total self-alienation, for the triad of death-Hades-Satan is the summation of everything that resists God's way, that cannot be united to God and is, as such, rejected by God. This path is trod in "obedience" (Phil 2:7-11) to the surrendering will of the Father in a willingness that is itself "power" (Jn 10:18) but which lets itself be available even in the ultimate powerlessness of dying and being dead. The perfect self-alienation of the experience of hell is the function of the incarnate Christ's obedience, and this obedience is once more a function of his free love for the Father. . . . [T]his truly being dead is a function of the total surrender of the Son.[32]

The Trinitarian move seems to be necessary in order to bolster the claim that Christ's death-descent "undergirds" and is thus capable of destroying from within any creaturely attempt to exclude oneself from the superior freedom of God's infinite love.[33] Hence, he links the Father-Son relationship to the "the farthest reaches of hell."[34] The universalist implications of his position become apparent already at this stage when he says:

> [T]here is, on Holy Saturday, the descent of the dead Jesus into hell: that is (speaking very simplistically), his solidarity in non-time with those who have been lost to God. For these people, their choice is definitive, the choice whereby they have chosen their "I" instead of God's selfless love. Into this definitiveness (of death) the Son descends. . . . [T]he sinner who wants to be "damned" by God now rediscovers God in his loneliness—but this time he rediscovers God in the absolute impotence of love. For now God has placed himself in solidarity with those who have

---

written work") seems to assert a distinction between the passion of Friday and its continuation on Saturday (e.g., see 164 [G 240]).
[31] See *ET* IV, 410 [G 395–396].
[32] *ET* IV, 410–411 [G 396–397].
[33] See *ET* IV, 422 [G 408–409].
[34] *ET* IV, 412 [G 397–398].

damned themselves, entering into nontime in a way we could never anticipate. . . . [E]ven the battle cry "God is dead"—that self-asserting *diktat* of the sinner who is finished with God—gains a whole new meaning that God himself has established. Creaturely freedom is respected but is still overtaken by God at the end of the Passion and once more undergirded ("*inferno profundior*," as Pope Gregory the Great put it). Only in absolute weakness does God want to give to each freedom created by him the gift of a love that breaks out of every dungeon and dissolves every constriction: in solidarity, from within, with whose [sic] who refuse solidarity.[35]

Here we see an undermining of human freedom. Nevertheless, the structure of this "undergirding," that is, how Christ's alienation is already somehow present in the distinction of divine persons, is not fully expressed until the *Theodramatik*.

RATZINGER AND BALTHASAR ON DIVINE SUFFERING

Before Balthasar presented his more developed soteriology, eschatology, and Trinitarian theory, particularly in the *Das Endspiel* volume of his *Theodramatik*, Ratzinger published his *Eschatologie: Tod und ewiges Leben* in 1977. There it is clear that one of the fundamental notions pervading Ratzinger's thought, which is already present in *Introduction to Christianity*,[36] is that of being as relation (or the transcendentality of *relatio*).[37] Developing what he acknowledges as Origen's "mythological expression" on "the indestructible relation" which obtains between the lives of men and their intra-historical destination, according to which the joy of the blessed and of Christ is incomplete for as long as members of His body are "missing," Ratzinger reflects on how Christ (and the saints derivatively)

---

[35] *ET* IV, 422 [G 408–409].

[36] Invoking Augustine's *De Trinitate* (5, 5, 6) [*PL* 42:913f.], Ratzinger states: "*relatio* stands beside the substance as an equally primordial form of being" (*Introduction to Christianity*, 182 [G 125]). On the absolute subsistence of relation alone in God as Trinity, see Aquinas's *Commentary on Peter Lombard's Sentences*, Book I, d. 26, q. 1, a. 2. The analogical relationship between *relatio* in the divine and *relatio* in created being is the subject of complex metaphysical debate.

[37] Ratzinger, Eschatology: Death and Eternal Life, 155 [*Eschatologie: Tod und ewiges Leben*, in *Joseph Ratzinger: Gesammelte Schriften*, Band 10, *Auferstehung und ewiges Leben* (Reprint, Freiburg: Herder Verlag, 2012), 166]: "A being is the more itself the more it is open, the more it is in relationship."

fulfills the myth of the Bodhisattva:

> The nature of love is always to be "for" someone. Love cannot, then, close itself against others or be without them so long as time, and with it suffering, is real. No one has formulated this insight more finely than Therese of Lisieux with her idea of heaven as the showering down of love towards all. But even in ordinary human terms we can say, How could a mother be completely and unreservedly happy so long as one of her children is suffering? And here we can point once again to Buddhism, with its idea of the Bodhisattva, who refuses to enter Nirvana so long as one human being remains in hell. By such waiting, he empties hell, accepting the salvation which is his due only when hell has become uninhabited. Behind this impressive notion of Asian religiosity, the Christian sees the true Bodhisattva, Christ, in whom Asia's dream became true. The dream is fulfilled in the God who descended from heaven into hell, because a heaven above an earth which is hell would be no heaven at all.[38]

Hence, love for him is a relational category (and the person is constituted by his capacity to love),[39] which creates a problem when one is faced with the reality of damnation. He wants to indicate that God descended upon earth in order to rescue it from the darkness of rejecting love, where man lives the self-contradiction of "Sheol-existence."[40]

While Ratzinger, even after *Mysterium Paschale*, does not drag the Trinity into the realm of the damned (à la Christ's descent),[41] he does in

---

[38] Ratzinger, *Eschatology*, 188 [G 193–194].

[39] Ratzinger, *Eschatology*, 259 [G 274–275]): "This abidingness [human being's eternal relationship to the eternal], which gives life and can fulfil [sic] it, is truth. It is also love. Man can therefore live forever, because he is able to have a relationship with that which gives the eternal. 'The soul' is our term for that in us which offers a foothold for this relation. Soul is nothing other than man's capacity for relatedness with truth, with love eternal."

[40] See Ratzinger, *Eschatology*, 156–157 [G 167].

[41] Balthasar, on the other hand, even in his *TL* II describes hell with Adrienne von Speyr as a "trinitarian event": "For her, hell is a trinitarian event. She describes at length the trinitarian form of sin. . . . [O]n Holy Saturday, the Son (as man and redeemer) is initiated into the dark mystery of the Father. . . . 'The Father is never more present than in this absence on the Cross'" (*TL* II, 352 [G 321]).

Matthew Levering, citing this passage in his *Predestination: Biblical and Theological Paths* (New York: Oxford University Press, 2011), comments: "Far from cutting off

the "Afterword to the English Edition" of *Eschatology* compliment the final volume of Balthasar's *Theodramatik*, published in 1983, as "a foundational contribution to a deepening of the eschatology theme."[42] In this volume Balthasar's theory of the Trinitarian processions in terms of the suffering, death, and descent of Christ becomes fully developed. Perhaps overreacting to the anthropocentric approach of Karl Rahner,[43] his oppo-

---

persons from God's presence, then, hell places persons inescapably at the heart of the Trinity" (165–166).

Balthasar also quotes Speyr stating:

"If you take hell away, the Word has no more foundation in the Father. However dreadful hell is, for the history of salvation it, so to say, lays the foundation of the relationship of Father, Son, and Spirit. It is out of this darkness that the Cross can be light in the first place" (ibid. [*Kreuz und Hölle* II], 233). . . . This gives rise to "the question whether hell, which is the eternal night of sin, is so included in the mystery of the Trinity that the sin vanquished on the Cross is ultimately used to solidify what (at the Cross) still remains of the world's shaken structure" (KH 1, 207–8). (*TL* II, 346n79 [G 316n5])

Therefore, Edward Oakes notes: "[F]or Balthasar other antinomies and paradoxes besides those purely Christological ones have compelled him to look at the ultimate moment of God's self-emptying: when the Second Person of the Blessed Trinity descended into hell for the sake of the damned. In that way, hell becomes for Balthasar not just a Christological place but above all a moment in the life of the Trinity" ("'He descended into hell,'" 232). Oakes also says, "[for Balthasar] the entire event of the Triduum is seen as an inherently trinitarian event" (*Pattern of Redemption*, 241).

[42] Ratzinger, *Eschatology*, 262 [G 277]. He says the "concern" for the "aspects of eschatology" manifest in Balthasar's "profound analysis of the essence of Christian hope, of the pain of God, of judgment and the consummation" "could well release the subject [of eschatology] from a narrowly anthropological concept of its own task."

This comment, written in 1987, need only be taken as an endorsement of the Trinitarian approach to eschatology as an effective tool against the anthropological approach of theologians like Karl Rahner; it does not imply that he accepts everything said about these themes in the work or that he agrees with Balthasar's Trinitarian theory itself.

[43] Balthasar's polemic with Rahner on this point is already seen in *MP* 140, 147n106 [G 226, 223–224n1]. He opposes Karl Rahner's "anthropocentric tendency" by turning to "the Trinitarian background of the Cross" (140 [G 226]).

Celia Deane-Drummond criticizes Balthasar's Trinitarian theology as "[leaning] towards tri-theism and thereby parsing of the God/human analogy too far in an anthropocentric direction" because it is based on "peculiarly *human* experiences of sin and reconciliation" ("The Breadth of Glory," 52 [emphasis original]).

Acknowledging his indebtedness to Bulgakov, she also criticizes him for characterizing the Trinity "through such drastic separation of persons . . . [breaking] up the unity of the Trinity, but also [straining] any analogical understanding of the Trinity to breaking point" (51), citing as her support Matthew Levering's *Scripture and Metaphysics*, 132.

sition to the latter's identification of economic and immanent trinities,[44] nevertheless, incorporates a qualified passibilist position. For him "'economic' reality is only the expression of something 'immanent' in the Trinity,"[45] and yet "The Son has been offering his sacrifice to the Father from the very beginning."[46] Since "the ontic possibility for God's self-emptying in the Incarnation and death of Jesus lies in God's eternal self-emptying in the mutual self-surrender of the Persons of the Trinity,"[47] "[t]he Judgment that takes place within the Trinity can be understood only in terms of the suffering love between Father and Son in the Spirit."[48] Hence, Balthasar seeks in the inner life of God a "foundation" or "ground" for the privative character of Christ's passion.[49] Since the descent to hell is at the center of Christ's suffering experiences, he goes so far as to say with von Speyr that "the Father allows the Son to experience the most intimate thing that he possesses: his darkness"[50] and with Ferdinand Ulrich that "pain and death are eternally the language of his glory."[51]

For Balthasar the passion, especially the cry of dereliction, provides the believer with a glimpse into the mutual self-giving that constitutes the very life of God and, particularly, reveals the distinction of persons that flows from divine *ek-stasis*. He wants to affirm infinite distance between the persons as persons but maintain also their inextricable union as divine[52]—hence the "separation" between the divine persons that is experienced on the Cross becomes a "mode of union."[53] "[T]he distance between the Persons, within the dynamic process of the divine essence,

---

[44] He states that he fundamentally agrees with tightly binding the two dimensions together, but he does not subscribe to a simple identification (or convertibility) of the two dimensions (e.g., see *TD* III, 508 [G 466]).

[45] *TD* V, 258 [G 233].

[46] *TD* V, 510 [G 467]. This is a quote from Adrienne von Speyr's *Kath. Briefe*, vol. 2. He says in the introductory note to the volume that "I quote her to show the fundamental consonance between her views and mine on many of the eschatological topics discussed here" (13 [G 11]). Indeed, I have not found one place where he expresses disagreement with her.

[47] *TD* V, 243 [G 220]. This is an approving quote from H. Schurmann's *Jesu ureigner Tod* (Herder, 1975).

[48] *TD* V, 278 [G 252].

[49] For development of this point, see Antoine Birot, "'God in Christ," 281–282.

[50] *TD* V, 267 [G 242].

[51] *TD* V, 246 [G 222].

[52] See, for example, *TD* V, 513, 517–518 [G 469, 473–474].

[53] See *TD* V, 257 [G 232].

is infinite."[54] Furthermore, concerning their distinction, he says: "[T]he Father was never more distinct, never more earnest, than at this hour of the Cross. . . . [T]he distinction of the Persons has never been more clearly revealed than in the relationship between the Son who is abandoned and the Father who abandons him."[55] Not only does Christ's experience of abandonment reveal the Father and Son as distinct persons, but there is an actual rupture that occurs in the economic order and that reflects the infinite distance there is between the persons precisely as hypostatically distinct. The suffering of Christ points to something analogous within the Trinitarian life: "there is nothing hypothetical about the 'pre-sacrifice' of the Son (and hence of the Trinity)."[56] Hence, "The Son's death is the exemplification of the supreme aliveness of triune love."[57]

Whereas for Balthasar, the generation of the Son occurs because the Father totally surrenders the Godhead, constituting an *ur-kenosis* in the immanent Trinity,[58] Ratzinger is generally hesitant to speak, as Balthasar does, of any "interweaving of Christ's suffering and the suffering of the Trinity."[59] A notable exception to such apparent reticence are the more modest words in *Behold the Pierced One: An Approach to a Spiritual Christology*, where he restates Origen's bold idea that "the Father suffers in allowing the Son to suffer, and the Spirit shares in this suffering."[60] Even

---

[54] *TD* V, 245 [G 221].

[55] *TD* V, 517 [G 473].

[56] *TD* V, 510 [G 467].

[57] *TD* V, 327 [G 298].

[58] *TD* V, 245 (G 221): "[The self-giving of the divine persons] is a total surrender of all possessions, including Godhead . . . [T]he Father's generation of the Son gives him an equally absolute and equally free divine being." Balthasar also states, "[T]he Father who sends him, the Father who, in doing so, surrenders himself" (*TD* V, 327 [G 297]).

   There are many questions that arise from Balthasar's words: is it not, more properly, the Son who surrenders himself to the Father? Is not the subsistent relation of paternity concomitant with that of filiation (rather than prior)? Does the category of *kenosis* really do justice to the entirety of love's essence?

   In answer to the second point, Ratzinger says: "[T]he first Person does not beget the Son as if the act of begetting were subsequent to the finished Person; it *is* the act of begetting, of giving oneself, of streaming forth. It is identical with the act of self-giving. Only as this act is it person, and therefore it is not the giver but the act of giving" (*Introduction to Christianity*, 184 [G 127]).

[59] *TD* V, 245 [G 221].

[60] These words first appeared in a paper he delivered on the mystery of Easter to the Sacred Heart Congress in Toulouse, 1981, collected in the volume, *Schauen auf den Durchbohrten*, translated by Graham Harrison as *Behold the Pierced One*, 57–58 [G 49–50]. He also refers to Origen and Gregory Nazianzen in interpretation of the groaning of the

though he cites Balthasar's *Das Ganze in Fragment* for interpretation of Origen and Gregory Nazianzen, in the final footnote to this text he clarifies: "This must be made absolutely clear, lest the way be opened for a new Patripassianism, as J. Moltmann seems to be proposing," a charge of which he nevertheless exonerates Balthasar's *Zu einer christicher Theologie der Hoffnung.*[61] He also indicates there his admiration for comments

---

Spirit in Rom 8:26f., depending again on Balthasar's *Das Ganze im Fragment*, as well as Heinrich Schlier's *Der Romerbrief* (see *Behold the Pierced One*, 58n9 [G 50n9]).

But the texts merely indicate the usage of "passion" as a term of love, even if the Father and Spirit are in some way associated with the Son's historical suffering (*the passion*). Steffen Lösel cites this note in Ratzinger (see "Murder in the Cathedral," 438n66) among the support for his proposal that the Spirit's procession is as kenotic as the Son's (438–439). Lösel notes that Balthasar is particularly modest in this regard, to a fault, in his opinion:

> Notice that both in the economic and the immanent Trinity, the Spirit is merely the bond of love who keeps open and bridges over the painful distance between Father and Son; as such, the Spirit itself cannot be said to suffer. At this point Balthasar's trinitarian drama of suffering love reveals itself as merely *binitarian*. Neither the Son nor the Father, but rather the Holy Spirit is the true victim in Balthasar's theo-drama; denied to suffer, the Spirit is "murdered in the cathedral" of Balthasar's theology. ("Murder in the Cathedral," 438)

And yet he notes in a later article that "[Balthasar] adopts Adrienne von Speyr's term 'pre-sacrifice' (*Voropfer*) to describe the mutual self-giving relationship of Father, Son, and Holy Spirit" ("A Plain Account," 163).

In fact, Balthasar states in an early work:

> The Holy Spirit anticipates all the tragedy of the sinful world, not only by being beyond it in a cloudless heaven, but also by being in its innermost heart. Thus, the divine Spirit which implants itself in humanity can have infinite compassion and, through love, infinite knowledge, without necessarily on that account succumbing to the tragedy of not-loving. It is precisely the freedom from all not-loving and paralysis of the heart which makes possible that intimacy and ultimate knowledge and involvement which characterize the Spirit. If this is so, then the conquest through the Holy Spirit of man's tragic incompleteness in the ordering of existence is truly ensured if the Spirit does not stand out against impotent humanity as the one fully potent force. (*A Theological Anthropology*, 73 [G 94])

Lösel does not present any analysis of Ratzinger's work in either article, and I would argue that Ratzinger is at least as modest as Balthasar on this point as well. For the dangerous implications of a misconceived pneumatological kenosis, see my "Pneumatologies of Christian Division: A Catholic Critique of Ephraim Radner's Kenotic Ecclesiology," *Angelicum* 92, no. 2 (2015): 165–194.

61 See *Behold the Pierced One*, 58n11 [G 50n11]. However, in 1985, Balthasar quotes approvingly the following words of Adrienne von Speyr from *Kreuz und Hölle*: "hell is a

made in an article by Jacques Maritain on divine "com-passion,"[62] which in fact provide some of the least radical reflections utilized by Balthasar as a launching pad for his own.[63]

While Ratzinger is clearly not a strict impassibilist,[64] he speaks of God as revealed in man (with Christ as the exemplar) in terms of being-for, being-from, and being-with.[65] He does subtly link *theologia crucis* with the revelation of the Trinity, but in a very different way from Balthasar. In

---

'Cross' for the Father" (*TL* II, 352n135 [G 321n61]). For a balanced approach, along Maritain's line, Ratzinger cites John Paul II's *Dives in Misericordia* §52 as "highly significant" (59n11).

[62] See Maritain, "Quelques réflexions sur le savoir théologique."

[63] See *TD* V, 242 [G 218]. Along these lines the following words of Adrienne von Speyr's might also be interpreted:

> If the Son is forsaken by the Father, then no one is to think that the Father in turn is not forsaken by the Son: for, if the Son loses his access to the Father, it is impossible for the Father still to have his access to the Son. The Father too is forsaken on the Cross and is separated from the Son who is separated from him. This is so, because love is a unity, and it is not possible in love for one to be affected without the other being affected too. Thus the Father and the Son together bear witness to the one, forsaken love. (*John* II, 162–163).

In other words, "forsaken love" here must mean something like "the (cognitional) potential for suffering inherent to love," and by *perichoresis* such may be analogously attributed to the Trinity of persons insofar as the life that constitutes their relational identities is precisely love itself. In other words, it is true by metaphorical analogy that the Father suffers as the humanity of Christ is literally subject to suffering, which is hypostatically united to the divine essence in the person of the Word.

Hence, "Speyr would be aware of Patripassionism. . . . [S]he certainly does not mean or indicate that she believes the Father suffered on the Cross. It seems much more likely and more consistent with her thought that she reflects on the image of a loving parent embracing the child's suffering from afar or from outside the surgery theater. There is no question of feeling the physical pain but the empathic pain of the parent can be just as real" (Miles, "Obedience of a Corpse," 155).

[64] Ratzinger certainly does not fall prey to the notion that impassibility is Greek and therefore subject to dismissal, as may be charged of Balthasar: "Historic Christianity rests on a fusion of the biblical inheritance with Greek thought" (*Eschatology*, 247 [G 263]). His nuanced (and brief) treatment of this question does contrast the "God of the philosophers" and the "God of faith," but it also emphasizes the unity of the two in historical Christian revelation (see *Introduction to Christianity*, 118–119, 145, 147–148 [G 74–75, 96, 98]). Compare this to *TD* V, 213, 217f., 235 [G 291, 195f., 212].

[65] Ratzinger says, "Man is God's image precisely insofar as being 'from,' 'with,' and 'for' constitute the fundamental anthropological pattern" ("Truth and Freedom," *Communio* 23, no. 1 [Spring, 1996]: 16–35, at 16). It will become clear how this triadic structure of man reflects God's own life.

the first volume of *Jesus of Nazareth*, he says both that John the Baptist's "reference to the Lamb of God interprets Jesus' Baptism, his descent into the abyss of death, as a theology of the Cross"[66] and that at Jesus' baptism "together with the Son, we encounter the Father and the Holy Spirit. The mystery of the Trinitarian God is beginning to emerge, even though its depths can be fully revealed only when Jesus' journey is complete."[67] Hence, he sees the entirety of Jesus's life, culminating in His Resurrection and ascent, as revelation of the Trinity, but he does not presume to envision the mystery in such detail as it is relayed to Balthasar by the alleged visionary, Adrienne von Speyr. Ratzinger appears to take the interpretation he develops there of the descent through the event of Jesus's baptism from a page in Balthasar's *Explorations* IV,[68] which depends on Daniélou's patristic research. But he skillfully weaves together the "strong man" tradition deriving from Matthew 12:29 and Luke 11:22, a "triumphant" interpretation of the descent that Balthasar undermines,[69] and the Jonah motif, which Balthasar esteems,[70] in his reflections on the descent as represented in the baptism.[71] Jesus as Lamb of God is also "the Servant of God who bears the sins of the world by his vicarious atonement.... 'By the expiatory power of his innocent death he blotted out ... the guilt of all mankind.'"[72] The harmonious balance of Ratzinger's exegesis leaps off the page.[73]

A running theme in both Balthasar and Ratzinger's understanding of redemption is the replacing of the influential "much-coarsened version of St. Anselm's theology of atonement"[74] in the so-called "satisfaction theory"

---

[66] Pope Benedict XVI, *Jesus of Nazareth* I, 22 [G 49]; each volume of this series will be subsequently designated by the respective Roman numeral.

[67] *Jesus of Nazareth* I, 23 [G 50].

[68] See *ET* IV, 406 [G 392].

[69] For his take on the "strong man" perspective of Christ as "chaining" and "robbing" Satan, see *ET* IV, 407 [G 393].

[70] See *ET* IV, 412–413n29 [G 398–399n29]. Apparently, he thinks the Jonahan hermeneutic superior to the "strong man" interpretation since he portrays it as unfortunate that it became "minor."

[71] See especially *Jesus of Nazareth* I, 18–19 [G 44–46].

[72] *Jesus of Nazareth* I, 21–22 [G 48]. He points there to Joachim Jeremias's observation that the Hebrew word *talia* probably used by John the Baptist at Christ's baptism can mean "lamb," "boy," or "servant."

[73] See *Jesus of Nazareth* I, 17, 20 [G 44, 46].

[74] *Introduction to Christianity*, 281 [G 204]. Interestingly, Balthasar appears to impugn Ratzinger as too harsh on Anselm in the midst of a critique of Bultmannian exegesis: "Kessler continues the (now customary) frontal attacks on Anselm's doctrine of satisfaction (K. Rahner, J. Ratzinger, L. Bouyer, et al.)" (*TD* III, 107n29 [G 97n29]). Referring later to this text he omits Ratzinger's name: "We have already observed that it is

with emphasis on the dimension of vicarious representation in Christ's passion.[75] As early as *Introduction to Christianity* he expresses his reservation regarding Anselm's perspective on the redemption together with his preferred conceptualization of the redemption in terms of being-for.[76] While Balthasar is in fact more appreciative of Anselm than many would like to admit,[77] Ratzinger gradually appears less critical of the satisfaction model.

In his late work, *Jesus of Nazareth: Holy Week*, Ratzinger seems not only more appreciative of Anselm's approach, but also reticent toward the more radical dimension of Balthasar's soteriology, particularly his appropriation of the contemporary death of God theology.[78] His treatment there of Christ's death as atonement or reconciliation certainly borrows from Anselm and Thomas.[79] Yet such is not to deny his earlier view of redemption as vicarious representation (shared by Balthasar). Hence, he still warns against the "coarsened version" of Anselmic soteriology:

> The reality of evil and injustice that disfigures the world and at the same time distorts the image of God—this reality exists, through our sin. It cannot simply be ignored; it must be addressed. But here it is not a case of a cruel God demanding the

---

currently fashionable to campaign against Anselm's so-called 'satisfaction theory' [note 36: In addition to Rahner, cf. Küng, Duquoc, Kessler, Schillebeeckx, Bouyer, etc.]" (*TD* III, 240 [G 220]).

[75] Ratzinger early on wrote a compelling article propounding this model of redemption, which extends to the Church's role in the world as the "little flock" and "light to the nations" and includes an alternative to Rahner's notorious notion of "anonymous Christianity," entitled "Stellvertretung" in *Handbuchtheologischer Grundbegriffe*, in English, "Vicarious Representation." Christopher Ruddy elaborates on some aspects of Ratzinger's approach to the redemption throughout his theological career in "For the Many."

Also, in *Introduction to Christianity*, Ratzinger expresses his reservation regarding Anselm's perspective on the redemption (see 233 [G 166–167]). In his late work, *Jesus of Nazareth*, vol. 2, *Holy Week: From the Entrance into Jerusalem to the Resurrection*, trans. Vatican Secretariat of State (San Francisco: Ignatius, 2011), he still seems to favor the model of redemption as vicarious representation (shared by Balthasar) over the Anselmic satisfaction model on 232 [*Jesus von Nazareth: vom Einzug in Jerusalem bis zur Auferstehung* (Herder, Freiburg, 2011), 256].

[76] See *Introduction to Christianity*, 233 [G 166–167].

[77] See, e.g., *TD* III, 240ff [G 220ff]; *TD* IV, 255ff. [G 235ff.])

[78] In the "Bibliography" section of *Jesus of Nazareth* II, there is a note corresponding to his criticism of "modern theologies of God's pain" as "too narrowly individualistic" (215 [G 238]) in chapter eight, which refers the reader to Moltman's *The Crucified God* and Balthasar's *TD* V as examples (see 306 [G 326–327]).

[79] See *Jesus of Nazareth* II, 229–240 [G 254–264].

infinite. It is exactly the opposite: God himself becomes the locus of reconciliation, and in the person of his Son takes the suffering upon himself. God himself grants his infinite purity to the world. God himself "drinks the cup" of every horror to the dregs and thereby restores justice through the greatness of his love, which, through suffering, transforms the darkness.[80]

Finally, in the second volume, oddly enough, while treating "Jesus' cry of abandonment," he does not develop the same Balthasarian theology of the descent that he had entertained as late as the first volume of *Jesus of Nazareth*; instead, he relies primarily upon Augustine's theology of corporate personality.[81] Nonetheless, in his Apostolic Exhortation *Verbum Domini*, Benedict reflects briefly on "the experience of the distance of the almighty Father" in Christ's passion, no doubt a Balthasarian theme.[82]

Like Balthasar, Ratzinger interprets Jesus' mission (action) and identity (being) in terms of "pro-existence," a heuristic he attributes to Heinz Schurmann,[83] even while Balthasar attributes it to Norbert Hoffmann.[84] It is clear that for Ratzinger one's understanding of the redemption must go hand-in-hand with the category of "being-for."[85] The couplet being-for and being-from come to the fore in Ratzinger's conception of how the Christological economy and the immanent life of God relate:

> The event of the crucifixion appears [in Johannine theology] as a process of opening, in which the scattered man-monads are drawn into the embrace of Jesus Christ, into the wide span of his outstretched arms, in order to arrive, in this union, at their goal,

---

[80] *Jesus of Nazareth* II, 232 [G 256].

[81] See *Jesus of Nazareth* II, 213ff. [G 237ff.]. See also Bruce Marshall, "Reading the Gospels with Benedict XVI: How the Pope Finds Jesus in the Bible," *First Things* (October 2011), available at https://www.firstthings.com/article/2011/10/reading-the-gospels-with-benedict-xvi.

[82] Pope Benedict XVI, *Verbum Domini*, §21, available at http://w2.vatican.va/content/benedict-xvi/en/apost_exhortations/documents/hf_ben-xvi_exh_20100930_verbum-domini.html (accessed on 5/31/18); see also his Encyclical Letter, *Deus Caritas Est*, §12, also available on the Vatican Website.

[83] See Pope Benedict XVI, *Jesus of Nazareth* II, 174 [G 197].

[84] See *TD* V, 244 [G 220].

[85] See also his homily, "Sin and Salvation," in *In the Beginning*, 59–78 (originally published *Im Anfang schuf Gott* [Freiburg: Erich Wewel, 1986]), for development of the notion of sin as a rupture in relationality (i.e., assertion of autonomy) and Christ the Redeemer as the antithesis (i.e., utter dependence, selflessness, surrender, being-for).

the goal of humanity. But if this is so, then Christ as the man to come is not man for himself but essentially man for others; it is precisely his complete openness that makes him the man of the future . . . [T]he future of man lies in "being for." This fundamentally confirms once again what we recognized as the meaning of the talk of sonship and, before that, as the meaning of the doctrine of three Persons in one God, namely, a reference to the dynamic, "actual" existence, which is essentially openness in the movement between "from" and "for." And once again it becomes clear that Christ is the completely open man, in whom the dividing walls of existence are torn down, who is entirely "transition" (Passover, 'Pasch'). . . . [A]fter the piercing with a spear that ends his earthly life, his existence is completely open; now he is entirely "for"; now he is truly no longer a single individual but "Adam," from whose side Eve, a new mankind, is formed. . . . The fully opened Christ, who completes the transformation of being into reception and transmission, is thus visible as what at the deepest level he always was: as "Son."[86]

RATZINGER'S TRINITARIAN THEOLOGY

One can extrapolate from Ratzinger's reflections here and elsewhere that the notions of being-for, being-from, and being-with offer us a glimpse into the Trinitarian life, but he does not push the parallelism so far that each corresponds directly with a divine person, although it is apparent that in the immanent Trinity these are most fittingly appropriated to Father, Son, and Spirit, respectively. As Jesus is literally God-with-us, so the Spirit is the God who dwells within us. But God and being are not simply convertible such that one can then say Christ is being-with-us and the Spirit is being-in-us. He says not only that "Son" means being-from-another, but also that the Son defines Himself on earth completely in terms of His Father; thus, He is being-for by mission because He is in Himself "being-from" the Father.[87] Therefore, when a Christian strives to unite himself fully to Christ, he replaces his own individuality with "pure, unreserved being 'from' and 'for.'"[88] Hence, the Incarnate Word also inculcates being-for, being a transparent window into the Father and even an example for men of pater-

---

[86] *Introduction to Christianity*, 240–241 [G 172–173].
[87] *Introduction to Christianity*, 186–187 [G 128–129].
[88] *Introduction to Christianity*, 187 [G 129].

nal virtue. But it is the Father who is the very act of self-giving in God.[89] Again, "'Father' is purely a concept of relationship. Only in being for the other is he Father."[90] Moreover, the "completely open being" of Christ's being-from or being-toward, which does not stand on its own, must be "pure relation (not substantiality) and, as pure relation, pure unity."[91]

Finally, speaking of "spirit" generically but in the context of this Trinitarian theology, he prepares the way by means of analogy for the traditional appropriation of unity and love to the third divine person: "pure oneness can only occur in the spirit and embraces the relatedness of love."[92] Earlier he had stated the following regarding the Spirit:

> This new experience [of God as "I" and "You" in the dual nature of the God-with-us ("Emmanuel")] is followed finally by a third, the experience of the Spirit, the presence of God in us, in our inner-most being. And again it turns out that this "Spirit" is not simply identical either with the Father or the Son, nor is he yet a third thing erected between God and us; it is the manner in which God gives himself to us, in which he enters into us, so that he is *in* man yet, in the midst of this "indwelling," is infinitely *above* him.[93]

The Holy Spirit is the continuation in history of God-with-us by dwelling in man insofar as he is a member of Christ's body and therefore a spiritual agent in history.[94] The Church is the created mirror of the Spirit because the Spirit herself is receptive, as the divine exemplar of what it means to listen and to remember. Ratzinger says the following in *The Nature and Mission of Theology*:

---

[89] *Introduction to Christianity*, 184 [G 127].

[90] *Introduction to Christianity*, 183 [G 126].

[91] *Introduction to Christianity*, 187 [G 129].

[92] *Introduction to Christianity*, 188 [G 130].

[93] *Introduction to Christianity*, 164 [G 111].

[94] *Introduction to Christianity*, 332–333 [G 246]: "[T]he Holy Spirit [is] the power through which the risen Lord remains present in the history of the world as the principle of a new history and a new world." For the sacramental and institutional Church as the locus of the Spirit's presence, see 334ff [G 247ff.].

He also declares, "[I]n our Creed the Church is understood in terms of the Holy Spirit, as the center of the Spirit's activity in the world" (335 [G 248]). He also develops this point in his essay, "The Holy Spirit as Communion: On the Relationship between Pneumatology and Spirituality in the Writings of Augustine," in *Pilgrim Fellowship of Faith: The Church as Communion*, ed. Stephan Horn and Vinzenz Pfnur, trans. Henry Taylor (San Francisco: Ignatius, 2005).

A further characteristic of the Spirit is listening: he does not speak in his own name, he listens and teaches how to listen. In other words, he does not add anything but rather acts as a guide into the heart of the Word, which becomes light in the act of listening. . . . [T]he Spirit effects a space of listening and remembering, a "we."[95]

The Spirit is, therefore, the principle of communion among men, but only because He is first the *communio* of Father and Son, the One who unites the two, who reveals their unity.

He conceives pneumatology as the link between Christology and ecclesiology, as a theology of the Spirit precisely of Christ, according to which the Son is the revelation (*logos*) of God in history. It is understood that "deposit of faith" reveals little about the Holy Spirit in Himself.[96] He, nevertheless, speaks in his essay on the "The Holy Spirit as Communion" of self-giving as the very being of the Spirit as well, who as *datus* opens up the Son as *natus* to the world as *factus*. The doctrine of the Spirit provides the link between the economic and immanent dimensions of the Trinity—the Spirit bridges the gap between salvation history and the *logos* behind creation.[97] The Spirit is the unity of the being-for and being-from of God; He shares in the being-from of the Son and yet communes equally with the Father's being-for[98]—He joins the being-from of the Son to the being-for of the Father in the being-with that is the love of God.[99] Flowing from this identity, the Spirit in history acts as the "wholly other" dimension of God at the core of every religious experience,[100] which provides a kind of portal into eternity, the realm of abiding love.[101] The Church is the gift of God to the world, the very image of the Spirit, who is God as gift.[102] From the

---

[95] Joseph Ratzinger, *The Nature and Mission of Theology: Essays to Orient Theology in Today's Debates*, trans. Adrian Walker (San Francisco: Ignatius Press, 1995), 55.

[96] See *Introduction to Christianity*, 331ff. [G 245ff.].

[97] See *Pilgrim Fellowship*, 48–49.

[98] *Jesus of Nazareth* II, 98 [G 115]: "[T]his characteristic identity of the Son [namely, being from the Father] is extended to include the Holy Spirit: 'He will not speak on his own authority, but whatever he hears he will speak' (16:13). The Father sends the Spirit in Jesus' name (14:26); Jesus sends him from the Father (15:26)."

[99] See *Pilgrim Fellowship*, 41.

[100] See *Pilgrim Fellowship*, 43.

[101] See *Pilgrim Fellowship*, 45.

[102] See *Pilgrim Fellowship*, especially 51 and also 49.

crucified Christ the divine power of living and moving in *agape* flows forth and "enlightenment about what the Holy Spirit is" may only then come.[103]

While the Spirit in His "being-with" the Father and the Son (and thus is the continuation of the Emmanuel's presence), the being-from of Christ's identity is the reason for His mission of being-for;[104] Christ is a "being-for" others in time precisely because He is wholly one with the Father from eternity. Hence, Ratzinger affirms that "'Mission' theology is again theology of being as relation and of relation as mode of unity.... [T]hrough the concept of the mission, being is interpreted as being 'from' and as being 'for.'"[105] Thus, the category (or rather, transcendental) of *relatio* is revealed to us in the economy of creation and salvation history as a window into the inner life of God as well as into man as His image.[106]

---

[103] See *Pilgrim Fellowship*, 46–47.

[104] This connection is not entirely clear in his later work, where a focus on the "pro-existence" or being-for of Christ seems to elevate the economic dimension to identity with the immanent dimension of the Son's divine being:

> Recently theology has rightly underlined the use of the word "for" . . . a word that may be considered the key . . . to the figure of Jesus overall. His entire being is expressed by the word "pro-existence"—he is there, not for himself, but for others. This is not merely a dimension of his existence, but its innermost essence and its entirety. His very being is a "being-for." If we are able to grasp this, then we have truly come close to the mystery of Jesus. (*Jesus of Nazareth* II, 134 [G 154])

Again, he states, "Jesus' 'substantial' being is as such the entire dynamic of 'being for'; the two are inseparable" (88 [G 106]). But he also says: "Jesus, the Holy One of God, is the one sent by God. His whole identity is 'being sent.' . . . He lives totally 'from the Father,' and there is nothing else, nothing purely of his own, that he brings to the Father" (97–98 [G 115]). Hence, it may be that he simply wants to maintain the inseparability of *processio* and *missio*. See also *Introduction to Christianity*, 165 [G 112].

[105] *Introduction to Christianity*, 188–189 [G 130–131].

[106] For Ratzinger's understanding of *relatio* in terms of Augustine's Trinitarian theology, itself also a theological anthropology: see *Introduction to Christianity*, 182–184 [G 125–127]. Notwithstanding his inept characterization there of "accidents" in Aristotle, he clearly wants to elevate *relatio*, on the basis of God's ontological identity as mutually subsisting relations, to the point of having equal status with substance, sitting alongside each other, as it were, distinct in creatures but neither subordinate to the other.

In support of *relatio* as transcendental, he could have also quoted the following from Augustine: "So we are left with the position that the Son is called being by way of relationship, with reference to the Father. And this leads us to the most unexpected conclusion that being is not being, or at least that when you say being you point not to being but to relationship" (*De Trinitate* 7, 2 [see *The Trinity*, 2nd ed. Trans. Edmund Hill (Hyde Park: New City, 2012), 220]).

The triadic theme of being-for, being-from, and being-with appears in subtle ways throughout most of Ratzinger's writings, but the relative infrequency of these terms compared with other more common theological expressions does not undermine the almost programmatic function of this profound triad in his work. It plays the role of uniting his anthropology, which conceives the person as essentially relational and thus called to a *communio* of love, with his understanding of God's revealed being, where Christ is the bridge between the inner-divine exchange and the person as the center of the cosmos.[107] Balthasar, instead, approaches the mystery of God impetuously, extrapolating from the revelation of Christ's descent into hell (begun on the Cross) a sort of topography of God's inner life.

CONCLUSION

Ratzinger shares with Balthasar a similar vision of the profundity and extremity of the descent,[108] but he explicitly limits it to the suffering of Christ

---

[107] Hence, even in his liturgical theology the theme makes an appearance with the following words:

> And now the challenge is to allow ourselves to be taken up into [Christ's] being "for" mankind, to let ourselves be embraced by his opened arms, which draw us to himself. He, the Holy One, hallows us with the holiness that none of us could ever give ourselves. We are incorporated into the great historical process by which the world moves toward the fulfillment of God being "all in all." (*The Spirit of the Liturgy*, trans. John Saward [San Francisco: Ignatius, 2000], 59)

Furthermore, he speaks of the Eucharistic consecration in terms of divine action in the world and reflects: "For a moment the world is silent, everything is silent, and in that silence we touch the eternal—for one beat of the heart we step out of time into *God's being-with-us*" (212, emphasis added).

[108] In his early work, Ratzinger interprets Christ's passion, like Balthasar, in terms of two traditionally minimized scriptural passages: "[Christ's] holiness expressed itself precisely as mingling with the sinners whom Jesus drew into his vicinity; as mingling to the point where he himself was made 'to be sin' and bore the curse of the law in execution as a criminal—complete community of fate with the lost (cf. 2 Cor 5:21; Gal 3:13)" (*Introduction to Christianity*, 342 [G 253]).

In his much later work, *Jesus of Nazareth* I, Ratzinger emphasizes Christ's death on the Cross as the culmination of His *kenosis*, even appearing to discourage an understanding of the descent into hell that would separate it temporally from His suffering on Friday: "God descends, to the point of death on the Cross. And precisely by doing so, he reveals himself in his true divinity. We ascend to God by accompanying him on this descending path. . . . [T]he man who is God . . . who, precisely because he is God, descends, empties himself, all the way to death on the Cross" (95, 99 [G 126, 130]).

on the Cross (culminating in his death)[109] and he does not extrapolate from this event an eschatology or a theology of suffering in the Trinity. While Balthasar conceptualizes the Trinitarian God almost exclusively in terms of *kenosis*, where the descent of Christ into hell is its economic culmination, Ratzinger opts instead to reflect on the transcendental relationality of divine being, as revealed in the redemptive Incarnation as such.[110] As the Paschal Mystery is, for Balthasar, a perfect reflection of the self-surrender constitutive of the infinitely distinct but united divine hypostases, the divine "undergirding" of sin and death penetrates even "the second death." Instead of associating the economic Trinity with the hell of the damned à la Christ's descent, Ratzinger's more disciplined approach discerns in every dimension of Christ's life a "being-for" that points to His being-from the Father, united by the being-with of the Spirit. The Trinitarian eschatology of Balthasar, which relies on a dramatic understanding of the grace-freedom dynamic and a brutal interpretation of Holy Saturday,[111] clearly acts to undermine the real possibility of damnation for men. Ratzinger distances himself from Balthasar's sympathies with the Origenist *misericordia* tradition, while at the same time reflecting deeply on the implications for an objectively redeemed humanity of Christ's descent into *Sheol*, the utter darkness of human loneliness and *Angst* proper to sin and death.

---

[109] See, for example, *Introduction to Christianity*, 290, 293, 297–298, 300–301 [G 212, 214, 217–218, 220–221].

[110] I believe Balthasar has at least Ratzinger in mind when he says late in his career: "Those who are reluctant to import such concepts into God (preferring to stay at the level of the equation *relatio = persona*) ought to remove these imperfect likenesses from the world" (*TL* III, 241 [G 222–223]). He, then, reflects with Hegel and Feuerbach on life and love as death.

[111] Balthasar was convinced early on in his career that "the Eastern Church" provides the light needed by the West on both of these issues, the theology of grace and the theology of Holy Saturday (see *The God Question*, 127–134). "Brutal" here is not intended in a derogatory manner, as it is sometimes understood. For a defense of the Father's innocence in predestining His Son to such a gruesome death, see Nicholas Lombardo, OP, *The Father's Will: Christ's Crucifixion and the Goodness of God* (Oxford: Oxford University Press, 2014).

BIBLIOGRAPHY

WORKS BY HANS URS VON BALTHASAR AND ADRIENNE VON SPEYR

TRANSLATIONS

Balthasar, Hans Urs von. *A Theological Anthropology*. Translated by Benziger Verlag. New York: Sheed and Ward, 1967.

———. *A Theology of History*. Reprint, San Francisco: Ignatius Press, 1994.

———. *Christian Meditation*. Translated by Mary Theresilde Skerry, SSpSAP. San Francisco: Ignatius Press, 1989.

———. *Convergences: To the Source of Christian Mystery*. Translated by E. A. Nelson. San Francisco: Ignatius Press, 1983.

———. *Credo: Meditations on the Apostles' Creed*. Translated by David Kipp. Edinburgh: T&T Clark, 1989.

———. *Dare We Hope "That All Men be Saved"? With A Short Discourse on Hell*. Translated by David Kipp and Lothar Krauth. San Francisco: Ignatius Press, 1988.

———. *Does Jesus Know Us? Do We Know Him*? Translated by Graham Harrison. San Francisco: Ignatius Press, 1986.

———. *Epilogue*. Translated by Edward T. Oakes. San Francisco: Ignatius Press, 2004.

———. *Explorations in Theology*. Vol. 1, *The Word Made Flesh*. Translated by A. V. Littledale and Alexander Dru. San Francisco: Ignatius Press, 1989.

———. *Explorations in Theology*. Vol. 2, *Spouse of the Word*. Translated by A. V. Littledale and Alexander Dru. San Francisco: Ignatius Press, 1991.

———. *Explorations in Theology*. Vol. 3, *Creator Spirit*. Translated by Brian McNeil, CRV. San Francisco: Ignatius Press, 1993.

———. *Explorations in Theology*. Vol. 4, *Spirit and Institution*. Translated by Edward T. Oakes. San Francisco: Ignatius, 1995.

———. *First Glance at Adrienne von Speyr*. Translated by Antje Lawry and Sergia Englund, OCD. San Francisco: Ignatius Press, 1981.

———. "General Introduction to the Posthumous Works." In Adrienne von Speyr, *Book of All Saints*. Translated by D. C. Schindler. San Francisco: Ignatius Press, 2008.

————. *God Question and Modern Man*. Translated by Hilda Graef. New York: Seabury Press, 1967.

————. *Heart of the World*. Translated by Erasmo Leiva-Merikakas. San Francisco: Ignatius Press, 1979.

————. *Love Alone is Credible*. Translated by D. C. Schindler. San Francisco: Ignatius Press, 2004.

————. *My Work: In Retrospect*. Translated by Brian McNeil, Kenneth Batinovich, John Saward, and Kelly Hamilton. San Francisco: Ignatius Press, 1993.

————. *Mysterium Paschale: The Mystery of Easter*. Translated by Aidan Nichols. San Francisco: Ignatius Press, 1990.

————. *New Elucidations*. Translated by Mary Theresilde Skerry, SSpSAP. San Francisco: Ignatius Press, 1986.

————. "On the Concept of Person." *Communio* 13, no. 1 (Spring 1986): 18–26.

————. "On the Tasks of Catholic Philosophy in Our Time." *Communio* 20, no. 1 (Spring 1993): 147–187.

————. *Prayer*. Translated by Graham Harrison. San Francisco: Ignatius Press, 1986.

————. *Presence and Thought: An Essay on the Religious Philosophy of Gregory of Nyssa*. Translated by Mark Sebanc. San Francisco: Ignatius Press, 1995.

————. *Razing the Bastions*. Translated by Brian McNeil. San Francisco: Ignatius Press, 1993.

————. "The Fathers, the Scholastics and Ourselves." *Communio* 24 (1997): 347–396.

————. *The Glory of the Lord: A Theological Aesthetics*, Vol. 1, *Seeing the Form*. Translated by Erasmo Leiva-Merikakis. Edited by Joseph Fessio, SJ, and John Riches. San Francisco: Ignatius Press, 1982.

————. *The Glory of the Lord: A Theological Aesthetics*. Vol. 7, *Theology: The New Covenant*. Translated by Brian McNeil. Edited by John Riches. San Francisco: Ignatius Press, 1989.

————. *The Moment of Christian Witness*. Translated by Richard Beckley. San Francisco: Ignatius Press, 1994.

————. *The Theology of Karl Barth*. Translated by Edward T. Oakes, SJ. San Francisco: Ignatius Press, 1992.

————. *The Von Balthasar Reader*. Edited by Medard Kehl and Werner Loser. New York: Crossroads, 1982.

————. *The Way of the Cross*. Translated by Rodelinde Albrecht and Maureen Sullivan. New York: Herder and Herder, 1969.

————. *Theo-Drama: Theological Dramatic Theory.* Vol. 2, *The Dramatis Personae: Man in God.* Translated by Graham Harrison. San Francisco: Ignatius Press, 1990.

————. *Theo-Drama: Theological Dramatic Theory.* Vol. 3, *The Dramatis Personae: The Person in Christ.* Translated by Graham Harrison. San Francisco: Ignatius Press, 1993.

————. *Theo-Drama: Theological Dramatic Theory.* Vol. 4, *The Action.* Translated by Graham Harrison. San Francisco: Ignatius Press, 1994.

————. *Theo-Drama: Theological Dramatic Theory.* Vol. 5, *The Final Act.* Translated by Graham Harrison. San Francisco: Ignatius Press, 1998.

————. *Theo-Logic: Theological Logical Theory.* Vol. 2, *Truth of God.* Translated by Adrian J. Walker. San Francisco: Ignatius Press, 2004.

————. *Theo-Logic: Theological Logical Theory.* Vol. 3, *The Spirit of Truth.* Translated by Graham Harrison. San Francisco: Ignatius Press, 2005.

————. *Truth is Symphonic: Aspects of Christian Pluralism.* Translated by Graham Harrison. San Francisco: Ignatius Press, 1987.

————. *You Crown the Year with Your Goodness.* Translated by Graham Harrison. San Francisco: Ignatius Press, 1982.

Balthasar and Angelo Scola, *Test Everything: Hold Fast to What Is Good.* Translated by Maria Shrady. San Francisco: Ignatius Press, 1989.

Balthasar and Jacques Servais, *To the Heart of the Mystery of Redemption.* Translated by Anne Englund Nash. San Francisco: Ignatius Press, 2010.

Speyr, Adrienne von. *John.* Vol. 1, *The Word Becomes Flesh.* Translated by Lucia Wiedenhover and Alexander Dru. San Francisco: Ignatius Press, 1994.

————. *John.* Vol. 2, *The Discourses of Controversy.* Translated by Brian McNeil. San Francisco: Ignatius Press, 1993.

————. *John.* Vol. 3, *The Farewell Discourses.* Translated by E. A. Nelson. San Francisco: Ignatius Press, 1987.

————. *John.* Vol. 4, *The Birth of the Church.* Translated by David Kipp. San Francisco: Ignatius Press, 1991.

Original Texts

Balthasar, Has Urs von. "Analogie und Dialektik. Zur Klärung der theologischen Prinzipienlehre Karl Barths." *Divus Thomas* 22 (1944): 171–216.

————. *Au coeur du mystère rédempteur.* Paris: Chambray-Tours, 1980.

————. *Cordula oder der Erstfall.* Einsiedeln: Johannes Verlag, 1966.

————. "Création et Trinité." *Communio* (French Edition) 13 (1988): 9–17.

————. *Das Ganze im Fragment*. Einsiedeln: Benziger Verlag, 1963.

————. *Die Gottesfrage des heutigen Menschen*. Vienna: Herder, 1956.

————. "Die Metaphysik Erich Przywara." *Schweizer Rundschau* 33 (1933): 489–499.

————. *Du kronst das Jahr mit deiner Huld: Radio-predigten*. Einsiedeln: 1982.

————. *Epilog*. Einsiedeln: Johannes Verlag, 1987.

————. *Herrlichkeit. Eine theologische Ästhetik*. Band I: *Schau der Gestalt*. Einsiedeln: Johannes Verlag, 1988.

————. *Herrlichkeit: Eine Theologische Ästhetik*, Band III: *Im Raum der Metaphysik*. Teil 1: *Altertum*. Einsiedeln: Johannes Verlag, 1965.

————. *Herrlichkeit: Eine Theologische Ästhetik*. Band III: *Theologie*. Teil 2: *Neuzeit*. Einsiedeln: Johannes Verlag, 1969.

————. *Karl Barth: Darstellung und Deutung seiner Theologie*. Reprint, Einsiedeln: Johannes Verlag, 1976.

————. *Kleiner Diskurs* über die Höll, *Apokatastasis*. Reprint, Einsiedeln: Johannes Verlag, 2013.

————. *Mein Werk—Durchblicke*. Einsiedeln: Johannes Verlag, 1990.

————. "Mysterium Paschale." In *Mysterium Salutis: Grundriss heilsgeschichtlicher Dogmatik*, Band III: *Das Christusereignis*, Teil 2. Edited by Johannes Feiner and Magnus Lohrer. Einsiedeln: Benziger Verlag, 1969: 133–326.

————. *Presence et pensée: Essai sur la philosophie religieuse de Gregoire de Nysse*. Paris: Beauchesne, 1942.

————. *Schliefung der Bastionen: Von der Kirche in Dieser Zeit*. Einsiedeln: Johannes Verlag, 1952.

————. *Skizzen zur theologie*, Band I: *Verbum Caro*. Einsiedeln: Johannes Verlag, 1960.

————. *Skizzen der Theologie*, Band IV: *Pneuma und Institution*. Einsiedeln: Johannes Verlag, 1974.

————. *Theodramatik*, Band II: *Die Personen des Spiels*, Teil I: *Der Mensch in Gott*. Einsiedeln: Johannes Verlag, 1976.

————. *Theodramatik*, Band II: *Die Personen des Spiels*, Teil II: *Die Personen in Christus*. Einsiedeln: Johannes Verlag, 1978.

————. *Theodramatik*, Band III: *Die Handlung*. Einsiedeln: Johannes Verlag, 1980.

————. *Theodramtik*, Band IV: *Das Endspiel*. Einsiedeln: Johannes Verlag, 1983.

―――. "Theologie und Spiritualitat." *Gregorianum* 50 (1969): 571–587.

―――. *Theologik*, Band II: *Wahrheit Gottes*. Einsiedeln: Johannes Verlag, 1985.

―――. *Theologik*, Band III: *Der Geist der Wahrheit*. Einsiedeln: Johannes Verlag, 1987.

―――. *Was dürfen wir hoffen?* Reprint, Einsieldeln: Johannes Verlag, 1989.

Chantraine, Georges, and Angelo Scola. *Adrienne von Speyr und Ihre Kirchliche Sendung* Einsiedeln: Johannes Verlag, 1986.

Speyr, Adrienne von, and Hans Urs von Balthasar. "L'expérience du Samedi Saint." *Communio: Revue Catholique Internationale* 6 (Janvier–Février 1981): 63–68.

Speyr, Adrienne von. *Das Angesicht des Vaters*. 2nd ed. Einsiedeln: Johannes Verlag, 1981.

―――. *Das Buch vom Gehorsam*. Einsiedeln: Johannes Verlag, 1966.

―――. *Das Wort und die Mystik*, Teil 1: *Subjektive Mystik*. Einsiedeln: Johannes Verlag, 1970.

―――. *Das Wort und die Mystik,* Teil II: *Objektive Mystik*. Einsiedeln: Johannes Verlag, 1970.

―――. *Der Grenzenlose Gott*. 2nd ed. Einsiedeln: Johannes Verlag, 1981.

―――. *Die Magd des Herrn: Ein Marienbuch*. Einsiedeln: Johannes Verlag, 1969.

―――. *Die Nachlasswerke*, Vol 11, *Ignatiana*. Edited by H. U. von Balthasar. Einsiedeln: Johannes Verlag, 1974.

―――. *Die Passion von Innen*. Einsiedeln: Johannes Verlag, 1981.

―――. *Kreuz und Holle*. Einsiedeln: Johannes Verlag, 1966.

Works by Joseph Ratzinger / Pope Benedict XVI

Benedict XVI. Angelus Address, November 5, 2006, available on Vatican Website.

―――. Apostolic Exhortation *Verbum Domini*, available on Vatican Website.

―――. Encyclical Letter *Deus Caritas Est*, available on Vatican Website.

―――. Encyclical Letter *Spe Salvi*, available on Vatican Website.

―――. *Jesus of Nazareth*, Vol. 1, *From the Baptism in the Jordan to the Transfiguration*. Translated by Adrian J. Walker. New York: Double-Day, 2007.

————. *Jesus of Nazareth*, Vol. 2, *Holy Week: From the Entrance into Jerusalem to the Resurrection*. Translated by Vatican Secretariat of State. San Francisco: Ignatius, 2011.

————. *Jesus of Nazareth*, Vol. 3, *The Infancy Narratives*. New York: Random House, 2012.

————. *Jesus von Nazareth*, Teil I: *von der Taufe im Jordan bis zur Verklarung*. Freiburg: Herder, 2007.

————. *Jesus von Nazareth*, Teil II: *vom Einzug in Jerusalem bis zur Auferstehung*. Freiburg: Herder, 2011.

————. "Papal Message for Centenary of von Balthasar's Birth: Reflections on the Swiss Theologian," available online on Ignatius Insight Website.

Ratzinger, Joseph. *Behold the Pierced One: An Approach to a Spiritual Christology*. Translated by Graham Harrison. San Francisco: Ignatius, 1986.

————. "Bewusstsein und Wissen Christi: Zu E. Gutwengers gleichnamigen Buch." *Munchener theologische Zeitschrift* 12 (1961): 78–81.

————. "Biblical Interpretation in Conflict: On the Foundations and the Itinerary of Exegesis Today." In *Opening Up the Scriptures: Joseph Ratzinger and the Foundations of Biblical Interpretation*. Edited by José Granados, Carlos Granados, and Luis Sánchez-Navarro. Translated by Adrian Walker. Grand Rapids, MI: William B. Eerdmans Publishing Co., 2008.

————. "Concerning the Notion of Person in Theology." *Communio* 17, no. 3 (1990): 439–454.

————. "Das Problem der christlichen Prophetie: Neils Christian Hvidt im Gesprach mit Joseph Kardinal Ratzinger." *Internationale katholische Zeitschrift 'Communio'* 28 (March–April 1999).

————. *Dogma and Preaching: Applying Christian Doctrine to Daily Living*. Unabridged Edition, San Francisco: Ignatius Press, 2011.

————. *Einfuhrung in das Christentum*. München: Deutscher Taschenbuch, 1971.

————. *Eschatologie: Tod und ewiges Leben*. Regensburg: Friedrich Pustet, 1977.

————. *Eschatologie: Tod und ewiges Leben*. In *Joseph Ratzinger: Gesammelte Schriften*. Band 10, *Auferstehung und ewiges Leben*. Reprint, Freiburg: Herder Verlag, 2012.

————. *Eschatology: Death and Eternal Life*. Translated by Michael Waldstein. Washington, DC: The Catholic University of America Press, 1988.

————. *Fundamentals of Catholic Theology: Building Stones for a Fundamental Theology.* Translated by Mary Frances McCarthy, SND. San Francisco: Ignatius Press, 1987.

————. "Gratia praesupponit naturam: Erwägungen über Sinn und Grenze eines scholastischen Axioms." In *Einsicht und Glaube.* Edited by Heinrich Fries. Freiburg: Herder Verlag, 1962: 151–165.

————. "Homily at the Funeral of Hans Urs von Balthasar." In *Hans Urs von Balthasar: His Life and Work.* Edited by David L. Schindler. San Francisco: Ignatius, 1991.

————. *Im Anfang schuf Gott.* Freiburg: Erich Wewel, 1986.

————. *In the Beginning: A Catholic Understanding of the Story of Creation and the Fall.* Translated by Boniface Ramsey, OP. Grand Rapids, MI: William B. Eerdmans Publishing Co., 1995.

————. *Introduction to Christianity.* Translated by J. R. Foster. San Francisco: Ignatius Press, 2004.

————. *Konsequenzen des Schopfungsglaubens.* Regensburg: Univ. A. Pustet, 1979.

————. *Meditationen zur Karwoche.* Freising: Kyrios–Verlag, 1969.

————. *Milestones: Memoirs 1927–1977.* Translated by Erasmo Leiva-Merikakis. San Francisco: Ignatius Press, 1998.

————. *Perche' siamo ancora nella chiesa.* Collana: Rizzoli, 2008.

————. *Pilgrim Fellowship of Faith: The Church as Communion.* Translated by Henry Taylor. Edited by Stephan Horn and Vinzenz Pfnur. San Francisco: Ignatius, 2005.

————. *Schauen auf den Durchbohrten.* Einsiedeln: Johannes Verlag, 1984.

————. "Schriftauslegung im Widerstreit: Zur Frage nach Grundlagen und Weg der Exegese Heute." In *Wort Gottes: Schrift–Tradition–Amt.* Edited by Peter Hünermann and Thomas Söding. Freiburg: Herder, 2005: 83–116.

————. "Stellvertretung." In *Handbuchtheologischer Grundbegriffe.* Vol. 2. Edited by Heinrich Fries. Munich: Kosel Verlag, 1962–1963.

————. *The Nature and Mission of Theology: Essays to Orient Theology in Today's Debates.* Translated by Adrian Walker. San Francisco: Ignatius Press, 1995.

————. *The Sabbath of History.* Translated by John Rock. Edited by William Congdon. District of Columbia: The William G. Congdon Foundation, 2000.

313

———. *The Spirit of the Liturgy.* Translated by John Saward. San Francisco: Ignatius, 2000.

———. "Truth and Freedom." *Communio* 23, no. 1 (Spring 1996): 16–35.

———. "Vicarious Representation." Translated by Jared Wicks. *Letter & Spirit* 7 (2011): 209–220.

Secondary Literature on Balthasar and Speyr

Barry, Richard. "Retrieving the Goat of Azazel: Balthasar's Biblical Soteriology." *Nova et Vetera* 15, no. 1 (2017): 13–35.

Beattie, Tina. "A Man and Three Women: Hans, Adrienne, Mary, and Luce." *New Blackfriars* 79 (1998): 97–105.

Beaudin, Michel. *Obéissance et solidarité: Essai sur la christologie de Hans Urs von Balthasar.* Québec: Corporation des Éditions Fides, 1989.

Bieler, Martin. "Causality and Freedom." *Communio* 32 (Fall 2005): 407–434.

———. "God and the Cross: The Doctrine of God in the Work of Hans Urs von Balthasar." *Communio* 42 (Spring 2015): 61–88.

———. "Meta-anthropology and Christology: On the Philosophy of Hans Urs von Balthasar." Translated by Thomas Caldwell, SJ. *Communio* 20 (1993): 129–146.

Birot, Antoine. "'God in Christ, Reconciled the World to Himself': Redemption in Balthasar." *Communio* 24, no. 2 (1997): 259–285.

———. "Le fondement christologique et trinitaire de la difference sexuelle chez Adrienne von Speyr." *Communio* (French Edition) 31 (2006): 123–135.

———. "The Divine Drama, from the Father's Perspective: How the Father Lives Love in the Trinity." *Communio* 30 (Fall 2003): 406–429.

Blankenhorn, Bernhard, OP. Review of *Light in Darkness: Hans Urs von Balthasar and the Catholic Doctrine of Christ's Descent into Hell* by Alyssa L. Pitstick. In *Nova et Vetera* (English Edition) 6, no. 4 (2008): 951–955.

Brotherton, Joshua R. "Damnation and the Trinity in Ratzinger and Balthasar." *Logos* 18, no. 3 (2015): 123–150.

———. "God's Relation to Evil: Balthasar and Maritain on Divine Impassibility." *Irish Theological Quarterly* 80, no. 3 (August 2015): 191–211.

———. Review of *Christ's Descent into Hell: John Paul II, Joseph Ratzinger, and Hans Urs von Balthasar on the Theology of Holy Saturday* by Alyra Pitstick. In *Nova et Vetera* (English Edition) 16, no. 2 (2018): 665–669.

————. "The Possibility of Refusal: Grace and Freedom in Balthasar." *Josephinum Journal of Theology* 21, no. 2 (Summer/Fall 2014): 342–361.

————. "The Possibility of Universal Conversion in Death: Temporality, Annihilation, and Grace." *Modern Theology* 32, no. 3 (Summer 2016): 307–324.

————. "Universalism and Predestinarianism: A Critique of the Theological Anthropology that Undergirds Catholic Universalist Eschatology." *Theological Studies* 77, no. 3 (2016): 603–626.

Buckley, James J. "Balthasar's Use of the Theology of Aquinas." *The Thomist* 59 (1995): 517–545.

The Cambridge Companion to Hans Urs von Balthasar. Edited by Edward T. Oakes, SJ, and David Moss. Cambridge: Cambridge University Press, 2004.

Campodonico, Angelo. "Hans Urs von Balthasar's Interpretation of the Philosophy of Thomas Aquinas." *Nova et Vetera* 8, no. 1 (2010): 33–53.

————. "Il pensiero filosofico di Tommaso d'Aquino nell'interpretazione di H. U. Von Balthasar." *Medioevo* 18 (1992): 187–202.

Carabine, Deirdre. "The Father's: The Church's Intimate, Youthful Diary." In *The Beauty of Christ: An Introduction to the Theology of Hans Urs von Balthasar.* Edited by Bede McGregor, OP, and Thomas Norris. New York: T&T Clark, 1994.

Chantraine, Georges. "Théologie et sainteté." *Communio* (French Edition) 14, no. 2 (1989): 54–81.

Chapp, Larry. "Revelation," in *Cambridge Companion to Hans Urs von Balthasar,* 11–23.

Chichon-Brandmaier, Silvia. *Ökonomische und immanente Trinität: ein Vergleich der Konzeptionen Karl Rahners und Hans Urs von Balthasars.* Regensburg: Friedrich Pustet, 2008.

Cirelli, Anthony. "Re-assessing the Meaning of Thought: Hans Urs von Balthasar's Retrieval of Gregory of Nyssa." *The Heythrop Journal* 50 (2009): 416–424.

Daley, Brian E. "Balthasar's Reading of the Church Fathers," in *Cambridge Companion to Hans Urs von Balthasar,* 187–206.

Dalzell, Thomas G. *The Dramatic Encounter of Divine and Human Freedom in the Theology of Hans Urs von Balthasar.* New York: Peter Lang, 2000.

————. "The Enrichment of God in Balthasar's Trinitarian Eschatology." *Irish Theological Quarterly* 66 (2001): 3–18.

Deane-Drummond, Celia. "The Breadth of Glory: A Trinitarian Eschatology for the Earth through Critical Engagement with Hans Urs von Balthasar." *International Journal of Systematic Theology* 12, no. 1 (2010): 46–64.

Dol, Jean-Noel. "L'inversion trinitaire chez Hans Urs von Balthasar." *Revue Thomiste* 100, no. 2 (2000): 205–237.

Donneaud, Henry, OP. "Hans Urs von Balthasar contre saint Thomas d'Aquin sur la foi du Christ." *Revue Thomiste* 97, no. 2 (1997): 335–354.

Doyle, Brian, OP. "'He descended into hell': The Theology of Hans Urs von Balthasar and Catholic Doctrine." *Nova et Vetera* (English Edition) 14, no. 3 (2016): 845–878.

Duffy, Kevin. "Change, Suffering, and Surprise in God: Von Balthasar's Use of Metaphor." *Irish Theological Quarterly* 76, no. 4 (2011): 370–387.

Dulles, Avery Cardinal. "Responses to Balthasar, Hell, and Heresy," *First Things* (March 2007).

Espezel, Alberto. "Quelques aspects de la sotériologie de Hans Urs von Balthasar." *Nouvelle Revue Théologique* 112 (1990): 80–92.

Facolta di Teologia di Lugano. *Rivista teologica di Lugano* 6, no. 1 (2001): 9–264.

Flannery, Kevin L., SJ. "How to Think about Hell." *New Blackfriars* 72, no. 854 (1991): 469–481.

Franks, Angela Franz. "Trinitarian *Analogia Entis* in Hans Urs von Balthasar." *The Thomist* 62 (1998): 533–559.

Friesenhahn, Jacob H. *The Trinitarian Theology of Hans Urs von Balthasar and Theodicy.* PhD diss., Southern Methodist University, 2009.

————. *The Trinity and Theodicy: The Trinitarian Theology of von Balthasar and the Problem of Evil.* Burlington: Ashgate, 2011.

Gardner, Lucy, David Moss, Ben Quash, and Graham Ward, editors. *Balthasar at the End of Modernity.* Edinburgh: T&T Clark, 1999.

Gonzalez, Michelle A. "Hans Urs von Balthasar and Contemporary Feminist Theology." *Theological Studies* 65 (2004): 566–595.

Griffiths, Paul. "Is There a Doctrine of the Descent into Hell?" *Pro Ecclesia* 17, no. 3 (2008): 257–268.

Hadley, Christopher. "The All-Embracing Frame: Distance in the Trinitarian Theology of Hans Urs von Balthasar." PhD diss., Marquette University, 2015.

Hauke, Manfred. "'Sperare per tutti?' Il ricorso all'esperienza dei santi nell'ultima grande controversia di Hans Urs von Balthasar." *Rivista teologica di Lugano* 6, no. 1 (2001): 195–220.

Healy, Nicholas J. *The Eschatology of Hans Urs von Balthasar: Being as Communion.* New York: Oxford University Press, 2005.

Holzer, Vincent. "'Analogia Enti' christologique et pensée de l'être chez

Hans Urs von Balthasar." *Theophilyon* 4, no. 2 (1999): 463–512.

—————. "La kénose christologique dans la pensée de Hans Urs Von Balthasar: Une kénose christologique étendue à l'être de Dieu." *Theophilyon* 9, no. 1 (2004): 207–236.

Horner, Robyn Horner. "A Theology of Distance." In *Jean-Luc Marion: A Theo-Logical Introduction*. Aldershot: Ashgate, 2005.

Howsare, Rodney A. *Balthasar: A Guide for the Perplexed*. New York: T&T Clark, 2009.

—————. *Hans Urs von Balthasar and Protestantism: The Ecumenical Implications of His Theological Style*. New York: T&T Clark International, 2005.

—————. "Why Hegel? A Reading of Cyril O'Regan's *Anatomy of Mis-remembering*, Volume 1," *Nova et Vetera* (English Edition) 14, no. 3 (2016): 983–992.

Hunt, Anne. "Psychological Analogy and Paschal Mystery in Trinitarian Theology." *Theological Studies* 59 (1998): 197–218.

Johnson, Junius. *Christ and Analogy: The Christocentric Metaphysics of Hans Urs von Balthasar*. Minneapolis, MN: Fortress Press, 2013.

Jones, Tamsin. "Dionysius in Hans Urs von Balthasar and Jean-Luc Marion." *Modern Theology* 24, no. 4 (2008): 743–754.

Kearns, Kristen Kingfield. "Love from Above: Analogy and Sexual Difference in the Theology of Hans Urs von Balthasar." PhD diss., University of Chicago, 2003.

Keating, James F., and Thomas Joseph White, OP, eds. *Divine Impassibility and the Mystery of Human Suffering*. Grand Rapids, MI: William B. Eerdmans Publishing Co., 2009.

Kerr, Fergus, OP. "Adrienne von Speyr and Hans Urs von Balthasar." *New Blackfriars* 79, no. 923 (1998): 26–32.

—————. "Balthasar and Metaphysics," in *Cambridge Companion to Hans Urs von Balthasar*, 224–238.

Kilby, Karen. *Balthasar: A (Very) Critical Introduction*. Grand Rapids, MI: William B. Eerdmans Publishing Co., 2012.

—————. "Balthasar and Karl Rahner," in *Cambridge Companion to Hans Urs von Balthasar*, 256–268.

Krenski, Thomas R. *Passio Caritatis: Trinitarische Passiologie im Werk Hans Urs von Balthasars*. Einsiedeln: Johannes Verlag, 1990.

Lauber, David Edward. "Towards a Theology of Holy Saturday: Karl Barth and Hans Urs von Balthasar on the *descensus ad inferna*." PhD diss., Princeton Theological Seminary, 1999.

Lee, Claudia. "The Role of Mysticism within the Church as Conceived by

Hans Urs von Balthasar. *Communio* 16 (Spring 1989): 105–126.

Levering, Matthew. "Balthasar on Christ's Consciousness on the Cross." *The Thomist* 65 (2001): 567–581.

———. "Juridical Language in Soteriology: Aquinas's Approach." *Angelicum* 80 (2003): 309–326.

Lochbrunner, Manfred. *Hans Urs von Balthasar und seine Theologenkollegen: Sechs Beziehungsgeschichten.* Wurzburg: Echter, 2009.

Long, D. Stephen. *Saving Karl Barth: Hans Urs von Balthasar's Preoccupation.* Minneapolis, MN: Fortress Press, 2014.

Lopez, Antonio. "Eternal Happening: God as an Event of Love." *Communio* 32 (Summer 2005): 214–245.

Lösel, Steffen. "A Plain Account of Christian Salvation? Balthasar on Sacrifice, Solidarity, and Substitution." *Pro Ecclesia* 13, no. 2 (2004): 141–171.

———. "Murder in the Cathedral: Hans Urs von Balthasar's New Dramatization of the Doctrine of the Trinity." *Pro Ecclesia* 5, no. 4 (1996): 427–439.

———. "Unapocalyptic Theology: History and Eschatology in Balthasar's Theo-Drama." *Modern Theology* 17, no. 2 (2001): 201–225.

Loser, Werner. *Im Geiste der Origines: Hans Urs von Balthasar als Interpret der Theologie des Kirchenvater.* Frankfurt: Josef Knecht Verlag, 1976.

Luy, David. "The Aesthetic Collision: Hans Urs von Balthasar on the Trinity and the Cross." *International Journal of Systematic Theology* 13, no. 2 (2011): 154–169.

Mansini, Guy, OSB. "Balthasar and the Theodramatic Enrichment of the Trinity." *The Thomist* 64 (2000): 499–519.

———. "Can Humility and Obedience Be Trinitarian Realities?" In *Thomas Aquinas and Karl Barth: An Unofficial Catholic-Protestant Dialogue.* Edited by Bruce L. McCormack and Thomas Joseph White, OP. Grand Rapids, MI: William B. Eerdmans Publishing Co., 2013.

———. "Hegel and Christian Theology." *Nova et Vetera* (English Edition) 14, no. 3 (2016): 993–1001.

———. "Rahner and Balthasar on the Efficacy of the Cross." *Irish Theological Quarterly* 63 (1998): 232–249.

———. "Understanding St. Thomas on Christ's Immediate Knowledge of God." *Thomist* 59 (1995): 91–124.

Marchesi, Giovanni. *La Cristologia Trinitaria di Hans Urs von Balthasar: Gesu Cristo pienezza della ivelazione e della salvezza.* Brescia, Italia: Queriniana, 2003.

Margerie, Bertrand de, SJ. "Note on Balthasar's Trinitarian Theology."

Translated by Gregory F. LaNave. *The Thomist* 64 (2000): 127–130.

Martin, Ralph. "Balthasar and Speyr: First Steps in a Discernment of Spirits." *Angelicum* 91 (2014): 273–301.

———. *Will Many Be Saved? What Vatican II Actually Teaches and Its Implications for the New Evangelization.* Grand Rapids, MI: William B. Eerdmans Publishing Co., 2012.

Martin, Regis. *Suffering of Love: Christ's Descent into the Hell of Human Hopelessness.* San Francisco: Ignatius Press, 2006.

McGregor, Bede, OP, and Thomas Norris, eds. *The Beauty of Christ: An Introduction to the Theology of Hans Urs von Balthasar.* New York: T&T Clark, 1994.

McIntosh, Mark A. "Christology," in *Cambridge Companion to Hans Urs von Balthasar,* 24–36.

———. *Christology from Within: Spirituality and the Incarnation in Hans Urs von Balthasar.* Notre Dame, IN: University of Notre Dame Press, 1996.

Menke, Karl-Heinz. *Stellvertretung.* Einsiedeln: Johannes Verlag, 1991.

Miles, Lois M. "An Introduction to Adrienne von Speyr." *First Things,* November 7, 2013.

———. "Obedience of a Corpse: The Key to the Holy Saturday Writings of Adrienne von Speyr." PhD diss., University of Aberdeen, 2013.

Mongrain, Keven. *The Systematic Thought of Hans Urs von Balthasar: An Irenaean Retrieval.* New York: The Crossroad Publishing Co., 2002.

Mooney, Hilary. *The Liberation of Consciousness: Bernard Lonergan's Theological Foundations in Dialogue with the Theological Aesthetics of Hans Urs von Balthasar.* Frankfurt: Josef Knecht, 1992.

Muer, Rachel. "A Question of Two Answers: Difference and Determination in Barth and von Balthasar." *Heythrop Journal* 40 (1999): 265–279.

Narcisse, Gilbert. OP. *Les raisons de Dieu. Argument de convenance et ésthetique théologique selon saint Thomas d'Aquin et Hans Urs von Balthasar.* Fribourg: Éditions Universitaires Fribourg, 1997.

Nichols, Aidan, OP. "Adrienne von Speyr and the Mystery of the Atonement." *New Blackfriars* 73, no. 865 (1992): 542–553.

———. *A Key to Balthasar: Hans Urs von Balthasar on Beauty, Goodness, and Truth.* Grand Rapids, MI: Baker Academic, 2011.

———. *Divine Fruitfulness: A Guide through Balthasar's Theology beyond the Trilogy.* Washington, DC: Catholic University of America Press, 2007.

————. *From Newman to Congar: The Idea of Doctrinal Development from the Victorians to the Second Vatican Council.* Edinburgh: T&T Clark, 1990.

————. "Introduction." In Balthasar, *Mysterium Paschale: The Mystery of Easter.* Translated by Aidan Nichols. San Francisco: Ignatius, 1990.

————. *No Bloodless Myth: A Guide Through Balthasar's Dramatics.* Washington, DC: Catholic University of America Press, 2000.

————. *Say It Is Pentecost: A Guide through Balthasar's Logic.* Edinburgh: T&T Clark, 2001.

————. *Scattering the Seed: A Guide Through Balthasar's Early Writings on Philosophy and the Arts.* Washington, DC: Catholic University of America Press, 2006.

————. "The Theo-logic," in *Cambridge Companion to Hans Urs von Balthasar,* 158–174.

————. *The Word Has Been Abroad: A Guide Through Balthasar's Aesthetics.* Edinburgh: T&T Clark, 1998.

————. *Wisdom from Above: A Primer in the Theology of Father Sergei Bulgakov.* Leominster: Gracewing, 2005.

Oakes, Edward T, SJ. "Balthasar's Critique of the Historical-Critical Method." In *Glory, Grace, and Culture: The Works of Hans Urs von Balthasar.* Edited by Ed Block, Jr. Mahwah, NJ: Paulist, 2005.

————. "*Descensus* and Development: A Response to Recent Rejoinders." *International Journal of Systematic Theology* 13, no. 1 (2011): 3–24.

————. "*Envoi*: the future of Balthasarian theology," in *Cambridge Companion to Hans Urs von Balthasar,* 269–274.

————. "'He descended into hell': The Depths of God's Self-Emptying Love on Holy Saturday in the Thought of Hans Urs von Balthasar." In *Exploring Kenotic Christology: The Self-Emptying of God.* Edited by C. Stephen Evans. New York: Oxford University Press, 2006: 218–245.

————. *Infinity Dwindled to Infancy: A Catholic and Evangelical Christology.* Grand Rapids, MI: William B. Eerdmans Publishing Co., 2011.

————. *Pattern of Redemption: The Theology of Hans Urs von Balthasar.* New York, Continuum Publishing Co.: 1997.

Oakes, Edward T., SJ, and Alyssa L. Pitstick, "Balthasar, Hell, and Heresy: An Exchange." *First Things* (December 2006).

Oakes, Edward T., SJ, and Alyssa L. Pitstick, "More on Balthasar, Hell, and Heresy." *First Things* (January 2007).

Oakes, Edward T., SJ, and David Moss, eds. *The Cambridge Companion to Hans Urs von Balthasar.* Cambridge: Cambridge University Press, 2004.

O'Donnell, John, SJ. *Hans Urs von Balthasar.* Collegeville, MN: Liturgical Press, 1992.

———. "Man and Woman as *Imago Dei* in the Theology of Hans Urs von Balthasar." *Clergy Review* 68, no. 4 (1983): 117–128.

O'Hanlon, Gerard F., SJ. "A Response to Kevin Duffy on von Balthasar and the Immutability of God." *Irish Theological Quarterly* 78, no. 2 (2013): 179–184.

———. *The Immutability of God in the Theology of Hans Urs von Balthasar.* New York: Cambridge University Press, 2007.

O'Loughlin, Gerard. "Sexing the Trinity." *New Blackfriars* 79, no. 923 (1998): 18–25.

———. "Erotics: God's Sex." *Radical Orthodoxy.* Edited by John Milbank, Graham Ward, and Catherine Pitstock. New York: Routledge, 1999: 143–162.

Olsen, Cyrus. "Exitus-Reditus in H. U. von Balthasar." *Heythrop Journal* 52 (2011): 643–658.

O'Regan, Cyril. "Balthasar: Between Tubingen and Postmodernity." *Modern Theology* 14, no. 3 (1998): 325–353.

———. "Response to Readers of *The Anatomy of Misremembering*, Volume 1 (*Hegel*)." *Nova et Vetera* (English Edition) 14, no. 3 (2016): 1015–1025.

———. *The Anatomy of Misremembering: Von Balthasar's Response to Philosophical Modernity*, Vol. 1, *Hegel*. New York: Herder & Herder, 2014.

———. "Von Balthasar and Thick Retrieval: Post-Chalcedonian Symphonic Theology." *Gregorianum* 77 (1996): 227–60.

Ouellet, Marc. "The Message of Balthasar's Theology to Modern Theology." *Communio* 23 (1996): 286–299.

Palakeel, Joseph. *The Use of Analogy in Theological Discourse: An Investigation in Ecumenical Perspective.* Roma: Pontificia Universita Gregoriana, 1995.

Papanikolaou, Aristotle. "Person, *Kenosis*, and Abuse: Hans Urs von Balthasar and Feminist Theologies in Conversation." *Modern Theology* 19, no. 1 (2003): 41–65.

Pesarchick, Robert A. *The Trinitarian Foundation of Human Sexuality as Revealed by Christ According to Hans Urs von Balthasar: The Revelatory Significance of the Male Christ and the Male Ministerial Priesthood.* Rome: Editrice Pontificia Universita Gregoriana, 2000.

Pidel, Aaron, SJ. "The Consciousness and Human Knowledge of Christ according to Lonergan and Balthasar." *Lumen et Vita* (Jun 2011): 1–25.

Pitstick, Alyssa L. *Christ's Descent into Hell: John Paul II, Joseph Ratzinger, and Hans Urs von Balthasar on the Theology of Holy Saturday.* Grand Rapids, MI: William B. Eerdmans Publishing Co., 2016.

———. "Development of Doctrine, or Denial? Balthasar's Holy Saturday and Newman's *Essay.*" *International Journal of Systematic Theology* 11 (2009): 131–145.

———. *Light in Darkness.* Grand Rapids, MI: William B. Eerdmans Publishing Co., 2007.

———. "*Lux in Tenebris*: The Traditional Catholic Doctrine of Christ's Descent into Hell and the Theological Opinion of Hans Urs von Balthasar." PhD diss, Angelicum University, 2005.

———. "Response to Webster and Lauber." *Scottish Journal of Theology* 62, no. 2 (2009): 211–216.

Quash, Ben. "Between the Brutely Given, and the Brutally, Banally Free: Von Balthasar's Theology of Drama in Dialogue with Hegel." *Modern Theology* 13, no. 3 (1997): 293–318.

———. "The Theo-drama," in *The Cambridge Companion to Hans Urs von Balthasar,* 143–157.

———. "Theodramatics, History, and the Holy Spirit." In *Theology and the Drama of History.* Edited by Ben Quash. New York: Cambridge University Press, 2005.

Rémy, Gérard. "La déréliction du Christ: Terme d'une contradiction ou mystère de communion?" *Revue Thomiste* 98 (1998): 39–94.

———. "La substitution: Pertinence ou non-pertinence d'un concept théologique." *Revue Thomiste* 94 (1994): 559–600.

Riches, John, ed. *The Analogy of Beauty: The Theology of Hans Urs von Balthasar.* Edinburgh: T&T Clark Ltd., 1986.

Rosenberg, Randall S. "Christ's Human Knowledge: A Conversation with Lonergan and Balthasar." *Theological Studies* 71 (2010): 817–845.

———. "Theory and Drama in Balthasar's and Lonergan's Theology of Christ's Consciousness and Knowledge: An Essay in Dialectics." PhD diss, Boston College, 2008.

Sachs, John R., SJ. "Current Eschatology: Universal Salvation and the Problem of Hell." *Theological Studies* 52 (1991): 227–254.

Sain, Barbara K. "Through a Different Lens: Rethinking the Role of Sexual Difference in the Theology of Hans Urs von Balthasar." *Modern Theology* 25, no. 1 (2009): 71–96.

Sara, Juan M. "*Descensus ad Inferos*, Dawn of Hope. Aspects of the Theology of Holy Saturday in the Trilogy of Hans Urs von Balthasar." *Communio: International Catholic Review* 32 (Fall 2005): 541–572.

Saward, John. *The Mysteries of March: Hans Urs von Balthasar on the Incarnation and Easter.* London: Collins Religious Publishing, 1990.

Schenk, Richard, OP. "The Epoche of Factical Damnation?: On the Costs of Bracketing Out the Likelihood of Final Loss." *Logos: A Journal of Catholic Thought and Culture* 1, no. 3 (1997): 122–154.

Schindler, David L. "Catholic Theology, Gender, and the Future of Western Civilization." *Communio* 20 (1993): 200–239.

———, ed. *Hans Urs von Balthasar: His Life and Work.* San Francisco: Ignatius Press, 2011.

Schindler, D. C. *Hans Urs von Balthasar and the Dramatic Structure of Truth: A Philosophical Investigation.* New York: Fordham University Press, 2004.

Schmidt, William. *The Sacrament of Confession as "Sequela Christi" in the Writings of A. von Speyr.* PhD diss, Pontifical Lateran University, Rome, 2001. Available from Dissertation.com.

Schrijver, Georges de. *Le merveilleux accord de l'homme et de Dieu: Étude de l'analogie de être chez Hans Urs von Balthasar.* Leuven: Leuven University Press, 1983.

Schumacher, Michele M. *A Trinitarian Anthropology: Adrienne von Speyr and Hans Urs von Balthasar in Dialogue with Thomas Aquinas.* Washington, DC: Catholic University of America Press, 2014.

———. "The Concept of Representation in the Theology of Hans Urs von Balthasar." *Theological Studies* 60 (1999): 53–71.

Sciglitano, Anthony C., Jr. "Death in Cyril O'Regan's *The Anatomy of Misremembering.*" *Nova et Vetera* (English Edition) 14, no. 3 (2016): 1003–1014.

Servais, Jacques. "The Ressourcement of Contemporary Spirituality under the Guidance of Adrienne von Speyr and Hans Urs von Balthasar." *Communio* 23, no. 2 (1996): 300–321.

Sicari, Antonio, OCD. "Theologie und Heiligkeit." *Wort und Wahrheit* 3 (1948): 881–896.

Spence, Brian J. "The Hegelian Element in Von Balthasar's and Moltmann's Understanding of the Suffering of God." *Toronto Journal of Theology* 14, no. 1 (1998): 45–60.

Strukelj, Anton. "Man and Woman under God: The Dignity of the Human Being according to Hans Urs von Balthasar." *Communio* 20 (Summer 1993): 377–388.

Sutton, Agneta. "The Complementarity and Symbolism of the Two Sexes: Karl Barth, Hans Urs von Balthasar and John Paul II." *New Blackfriars* 87, no. 1010 (2006) 418–433.

Sutton, Matthew Lewis. "A Compelling Trinitarian Taxonomy: Hans Urs von Balthasar's Theology of the Trinitarian Inversion and Reversion." *International Journal of Systematic Theology* 14, no. 2 (2012): 161–176.

————. *Heaven Opens: The Trinitarian Mysticism of Adrienne von Speyr.* Minneapolis, MN: Fortress Press, 2014.

Tonstad, Linn Marie. "Sexual Difference and Trinitarian Death: Cross, Kenosis, and Hierarchy in the *Theo-Drama*." *Modern Theology* 26, no. 4 (2010): 603–631.

Turek, Margaret. "Dare We Hope 'That All Men Be Saved' (1 Tim 2:4)?: On von Balthasar's Trinitarian Grounds for Christian Hope." *Logos* 1 (1997): 92–121.

————. *Towards a Theology of God the Father: Hans Urs von Balthasar's Theodramatic Approach.* New York: Peter Lang, 2001.

Vetö, Etienne. *Du Christ à la Trinité: Penser les mystères du Christ après Thomas d'Aquin et Balthasar.* Paris: Les Éditions du Cerf, 2012.

Vogel, Jeffrey A. "The Unselfing Activity of the Holy Spirit in the Theology of Hans Urs von Balthasar." *Logos: A Journal of Catholic Thought and Culture* 10, no. 4 (Fall 2007): 16–34.

Wainwright, Geoffrey. "Eschatology," in *Cambridge Companion to Hans Urs von Balthasar*, 113–130.

Webster, John. "Balthasar and Karl Barth," in *Cambridge Companion to Hans Urs von Balthasar*, 241–255.

White, Thomas Joseph, OP. "Jesus' Cry on the Cross and His Beatific Vision." *Nova et Vetera* (English Edition) 5, no. 3 (2007): 555–582.

————. "Von Balthasar and Journet on the Universal Possibility of Salvation and the Twofold Will of God." *Nova et Vetera* (English Edition) 4, no. 3 (2006): 633–666.

————. "Did Christ Descend into Hell? The Mystery of Holy Saturday." In *The Incarnate Lord: A Thomistic Study in Christology.* Washington, DC: Catholic University of America Press, 2015.

Wigley, Stephen. *Balthasar's Trilogy: A Reader's Guide.* New York: T&T Clark, 2010.

————. *Karl Barth and Hans Urs von Balthasar: A Critical Engagement.* New York: T&T Clark, 2007.

Williams, Rowan. "Balthasar and the Trinity," in *Cambridge Companion to Hans Urs von Balthasar*, 37–50.

Yeago, David Stuart. "The Drama of Nature and Grace: A Study in the Theology of Hans Urs von Balthasar." PhD diss., Yale University, 1992.

Yocum, John. "A Cry of Dereliction? Reconsidering a Recent Theological Commonplace." *International Journal of Systematic Theology* 7, no. 1 (2005): 72–80.

Zeitz, James. "Przywara and von Balthasar on Analogy." *The Thomist* 52 (1988): 473–498.

Other Works Cited

Aertsen, Jan A. "Method and Metaphysics: The *via resolutionis* in Thomas Aquinas." *The New Scholasticism* 63, no. 4 (1989): 405–418.

Andereggen, Ignacio Eugenio Maria. *La Metafisica de Santo Tomas en la "Exposicion" sobre el "De Divinis Nominibus" de Dionisio Areopagita.* Buenos Aires: Editorial de la Universidad Catolica Argentina, 1989.

Angelici, Ruben. *Richard of Saint Victor: On the Trinity. English Translation and Commentary.* Eugene, OR: Cascade, 2011.

Aquinas, Thomas. *De Potentia.* Available on Dominican House of Studies Priory Webpage.

———. *In Symbolum Apostolorum Expositio.* In *Opuscula Theologica*, Vol. 2. Edited by Raimund Spiazzi, OP. Rome: Marietti, 1954.

———. *In I Sententiae.* Available on Dominican House of Studies Priory Webpage.

———. *Quaestiones disputatae de fide.* Available on Dominican House of Studies Priory Webpage.

———. *Summa Contra Gentiles.* Vol. 4. Available on Dominican House of Studies Priory Webpage.

———. *Summa Theologiae.* Available on Dominican House of Studies Priory Webpage.

———. *Super Epistolam ad Philippenses Lectura.* Available on Dominican House of Studies Priory Webpage.

———. *Super Evangelium S. Ioannis Lectura.* Available on Dominican House of Studies Priory Webpage.

———. *The Sermon-Conferences of St. Thomas Aquinas on the Apostles' Creed.* Translated by Nicholas Ayo, CSC. Notre Dame: University of Notre Dame Press, 1988.

Athanasius. *De Incarnatione.* Available on Christian Classics Ethereal Library.

Augustine of Hippo. *De Civitate Dei.* Available at www.augustinus.it/.

———. *De Trinitate.* Available online at www.augustinus.it/.

———. *Enchiridion de fide, spe et charitate Liber Unus.* Available at www.augustinus.it/.

———. *The Trinity*. Translated by Edmund Hill, OP. New York: New City Press, 2012.

Aulen, Gustaf. *Christus Victor: A Historical Study of the Three Main Types of the Idea of the Atonement*. Translated by A. G. Hebert. New York: Macmillan Co, 1951.

Barth, Karl. *Church Dogmatics*. Vol. 1, *The Doctrine of the Word of God*, Part 1: *The Word of God as the Criterion of Dogmatics; the Revelation of God*. Translated by G. W. Bromiley and T. F. Torrance. New York: Continuum, 2004.

———. *Church Dogmatics*. Vol. 2, *The Doctrine of God*, Part 1: *The Knowledge of God*. Translated by G. W. Bromiley and T. F. Torrance. New York: T&T Clark: 2000.

———. *Church Dogmatics*. Vol. 2, Part 2: *The Election of God, The Command of God*. Translated by G. W. Bromiley and T. F. Torrance. New York: T&T Clark, 1957.

———. *Church Dogmatics*. Vol. 4, *The Doctrine of Reconciliation*, Part 1: *The Subject-Matter and Problems of the Doctrine*. Translated by G. W. Bromiley and T. F. Torrance. New York: T&T Clark, 1961.

———. *Church Dogmatics*. Vol. 4, *The Doctrine of Reconciliation*, Part 2: *Jesus Christ, the Servant as Lord*. Translated by G. W. Bromiley and T. F. Torrance. New York: Bloomsbury, 2004.

Benedict XII. *Benedictus Deus*. Available on the EWTN Library Website.

Blair, George A. "On *Esse* and Relation." *Communio* 21, no. 1 (1994): 162–164.

Boethius. *De Institutione Arithmetica*. Available on the Smithsonian Library Website.

Bonaventure, *Itinerarium mentis in Deum*. Translated by Philotheus Boehner. St. Bonaventure, NY: Franciscan Institute, 1956.

———. *Opera omnia*. Vol. 5. Quaracchi: Ed. Collegii S. Bonaventurae, 1891.

Bonino, Serge-Thomas, OP. "Le role de l'image dans la connaissance prophétique d'après saint Thomas d'Aquin." *Revue Thomiste* 89, no. 4 (1989): 533–568.

———. "'Nature and Grace' in the Encyclical *Deus Caritas Est*." Translated by Shannon Gaffney. *Nova et Vetera* (English Edition) 5, no. 2 (2007): 231–248.

———. "'Nature et grace' dans l'encyclique *Deus Caritas Est*." *Revue Thomiste* 105 (2005): 531–549.

Boyle, John F. "St. Thomas and the Analogy of *Potentia Generandi*." *The Thomist* 64 (2000): 581–592.

Brandle, Werner. "Immanente Trinität—Ein 'Denkmal der Kirchengeschichte': Überlegungen zu Karl Rahners Trinitätslehre." *Kerygma und Dogma* 38 (1992): 185–198.

Brotherton, Joshua R. "A Feminist Argument for a Male-only Priesthood." *Fellowship of Catholic Scholars Quarterly* 39, no. 1/2 (Spring/Summer 2016): 50–52.

———. "Development(s) in the Theology of Revelation: From Francisco Marin-Sola to Joseph Ratzinger." *New Blackfriars* 97, no. 1072 (2016): 661–676.

———. "Phenomenology and Metaphysics in *Realismo Metafisico e Irrealidad* by Jesús Villagrasa." *Información Filosófica* 5, no. 11 (2008): 219–237.

———. "Pneumatologies of Christian Division: A Catholic Critique of Ephraim Radner's Kenotic Ecclesiology." *Angelicum* 92, no. 2 (2015): 165–194.

———. "Revisiting the *Sola Scriptura* Debate: Yves Congar and Joseph Ratzinger on Tradition." *Pro Ecclesia* 24, no. 1 (Winter 2015): 85–114.

Calvin, John. *Institutes of the Christian Religion.* Translated by Henry Beveridge. Grand Rapids, MI: Christian Classics Ethereal Library, 2002.

Catechism of the Catholic Church. Vatican City: Libreria Editrice Vaticana, 2000.

The Catholic Encyclopedia: An International Work of Reference on the Constitution, Doctrine, and History of the Catholic Church. Vol. 2. Edited by Charles G. Herbermann, Edward A. Pace, Conde B. Pallen, Thomas J. Shahan, and John J. Wynne, SJ. New York: Robert Appleton Co., 1907.

Cayre, F. *Patrologie et histoire de la théologie,* Vol. 2. 4th ed. Paris: Desclée, 1947.

Clarke, W. Norris, SJ. *Explorations in Metaphysics: Being–God–Person.* Notre Dame: University of Notre Dame Press, 1994.

———. *Person and Being.* Milwaukee: Marquette University Press, 1998.

———. "Person, Being, and St. Thomas." *Communio* 19, no. 4 (1992): 601–618.

———. "Response to Blair's Comments." *Communio* 21, no. 1 (1994): 170–171.

———. "Response to David Schindler's Comments." *Communio* 20, no. 3 (1993): 593–598.

———. "Response to Long's Comments." *Communio* 21, no. 1 (1994): 165–169.

Congregation for the Doctrine of the Faith, *Notification on the Works of*

Father Jon Sobrino, SJ. Available on the Vatican Website.

Cooper, Adam G. "Hope, A Mode of Faith: Aquinas, Luther and Benedict XVI on Hebrews 11:1." *Heythrop Journal* 53 (2012): 182–190.

Culpepper, Gary. "'One Suffering in Two Natures': An Analogical Inquiry into Divine and Human Suffering," in *Divine Impassibility and the Mystery of Human Suffering*, ed. James F. Keating and Thomas White, 77–98.

Daley, Brian. *The Hope of the Early Church: A Handbook of Patristic Eschatology.* New York: Cambridge University Press, 1991.

Daniélou, Jean. *Essai sur le mystère de l'histoire.* Paris, 1953.

Darley, Alan Philip. "Predication or Participation? What is the Nature of Aquinas' Doctrine of Analogy?" *Heythrop Journal* 57, no. 2 (2016): 312–324.

Denzinger, Heinrich. *Compendium of Creeds, Definitions, and Declarations on Matters of Faith and Morals.* Edited by Robert Fastiggi and Anne Englund Nash. 43rd. ed. San Francisco: Ignatius Press, 2012.

Diepen, H.-M. "La critique du basilisme selon saint Thomas d'Aquin." *Revue Thomiste* 50 (1950): 515–562.

———. "La psychologie humaine du Christ." *Revue Thomiste* 50 (1950): 515–562.

Doran, Robert M. *What is Systematic Theology?* Toronto: University of Toronto Press, 2005.

Dulles, Avery. *Magisterium: Teacher and Guardian of the Faith.* Ave Maria, FL: Sapientia Press, 2010.

Dunne, Tad. *Lonergan and Spirituality: Towards a Spiritual Integration.* Chicago: Loyola University Press, 1985.

Dyer, George J. *Limbo: Unsettled Question.* New York: Sheed and Ward, 1964.

Egan, Harvey D., SJ. "Hell: The Mystery of Eternal Love and Eternal Obduracy." *Theological Studies* 75, no. 1 (2014): 52–73.

Elert, Werner. *Der Ausgang der altkirchlichen Christologie. Eine Untersuchung uber Theodor von Pharan und seine Zeit als Einfuhrung in die alte Dogmengeschichte.* Berlin: Lutherisches Verlagshaus, 1957.

Emery, Gilles. *Trinity in Aquinas.* Ave Maria, FL: Sapientia Press, 2003.

———. "*Theologia* and *Dispensatio*: The Centrality of the Divine Missions in St. Thomas's Trinitarian Theology." *The Thomist* 74, no. 4 (2010): 515–561.

———. *The Trinitarian Theology of St. Thomas Aquinas.* Translated by Francesca Aran Murphy. Oxford: Oxford University Press, 2007.

———. *Trinity, Church, and the Human Person: Thomistic Essays*. Ave Maria, FL: Sapientia Press, 2007.

———. *Le Trinité créatrice: Trinité et création dans les commentaires aux Sentences de Thomas d'Aquin et de ses précurseurs Albert le Grand et Bonaventure*. Paris: Vrin, 1995.

———. "The Question of Evil and the Mystery of God in Charles Journet." *Nova et Vetera* (English Edition) 4, no. 3 (2006): 529–556.

Finley, John. "The Metaphysics of Gender: A Thomistic Approach." *The Thomist* 79, no. 4 (2015): 585–614.

Gaine, Simon Francis, OP. *Did the Saviour See the Father? Christ, Salvation, and the Vision of God*. New York: Bloomsbury T&T Clark, 2015.

———. "Is There Still a Place for Christ's Infused Knowledge in Catholic Theology and Exegesis?" *Nova et Vetera* 16, no. 2 (2018): 601–615.

Galot, Jean, SJ. "De la science du Christ. Science, préscience et conscience, méme prépascales du Christ Rédempteur," *Doctor Communis* 36 (1983): 12–58.

———. *La Conscience de Jesus*. Paris: Duculot, 1971.

———. *La Rédemption: mystère d'alliance*. Paris: Bruges, 1965.

———. "Le Christ terrestre et la vision." *Gregorianum* 67, no. 3 (1986): 429–450.

———. "Problèmes de la conscience du Christ." *Esprit et vie* 92 (1982): 145–152.

———. *Who is Christ? A Theology of the Incarnation*. Translated by M. A. Bouchard. Rome: Gregorian University Press, 1980.

Garrigou-Lagrange, Reginald, OP. *Beatitude: A Commentary on Thomas' Theologica Summa, IaIIae, qq. 1-54*. Translated by Patrick Cummins, OSB. Ex Fontibus Co., 2015.

———. *Christian Perfection and Contemplation: According to St. Thomas Aquinas and St. John of the Cross*. Charlotte, NC: TAN Books, 2010.

———. *Les trois ages de la vie intérieure prélude de celle du ciel. Traité de théologie ascétique et mystique*. Paris: Cerf, 1938.

Garrigues, Jean Miguel. "La conscience de soi telle qu'elle était exercée par le Fils de Dieu fait homme." *Nova et Vetera* (French Edition) 79, no. 1 (2004): 39–51.

———. "L'instrumentalité rédemptrice du libre arbitre du Christ chez saint Maxime le Confesseur." *Revue Thomiste* 104 (2004): 531–550.

Gathercole, Simon. *Defending Substitution: An Essay on Atonement in Paul*. Grand Rapids, MI: Baker Academic, 2015.

Gavrilyuk, Paul L. *The Suffering of the Impassible God: The Dialectics of Patristic Thought*. Oxford: Oxford University Press, 2006.

Gilson, Étienne. *Spirit of Medieval Philosophy*. Translated by A. H. C. Downes. South Bend, IN: University of Notre Dame Press, 1991.

Gondreau, Paul. *The Passions of Christ's Soul in the Theology of St. Thomas Aquinas*. Scranton, PA: University of Scranton Press, 2009.

Gregory of Nyssa. *Catechetical Orations*. Edited by James Herbert Srawley. Cambridge: Cambridge University Press, 1903.

———. *The Life of Moses*. Translated by Abraham J. Malherbe and Everett Ferguson. New York: Paulist, 1978.

Grensted, Laurence William. *A Short History of the Doctrine of the Atonement*. New York: Longmans, Green & Co., 1920.

Hart, David Bentley. "No Shadow of Turning: On Divine Impassibility." *Pro Ecclesia* 11, no. 2 (2002): 184–206.

Hayes, Zachary. "Heaven." In *The Modern Catholic Encyclopedia*. Edited by Michael Glazier and Monika K. Hellwig. Collegeville, MN: Liturgical Press, 2004.

Healy, Nicholas J., Jr. "*Simul viator et comprehensor:* The Filial Mode of Christ's Knowledge." *Nova et Vetera* (English Edition) 11, no. 2 (2013): 341–355.

Hefling, Charles. "Another Perhaps Permanently Valid Achievement: Lonergan on Christ's (Self-)Knowledge." *Lonergan Workshop* 20 (2008): 127–164.

———. "A Perhaps Permanently Valid Achievement: Lonergan on Christ's Satisfaction." *Method: Journal of Lonergan Studies* 10 (1992): 51–76.

Henry of Ghent, *Opera omnia*. Vol. 10. Edited by Gordon A. Wilson. Louvain: Leuven University Press, 1987.

Hildebrand, Dietrich von. *The Heart: An Analysis of Human and Divine Affectivity*. Edited by John F. Crosby. South Bend, IN: St. Augustine's Press, 2007.

Hunsinger, George. "Election and the Trinity: Twenty-Five Theses on the Theology of Karl Barth." *Modern Theology* 24 (2008): 179–198.

Hunt, Anne. *The Trinity and the Paschal Mystery*. Collegeville, MN: Liturgical Press, 1997.

Imhof, Paul, and Hubert Biallowons. *Karl Rahner in Dialogue: Conversations and Interviews, 1965–1982*. Translated by Harvey D. Egan. New York: Crossroad, 1986.

International Theological Commission. "The Consciousness of Christ Concerning Himself and His Mission." *Communio* 14, no. 3 (1987): 316–325.

John of the Cross, *Dark Night of the Soul*. Translated by David Lewis. London: Baker, 1908.

John Paul II, *A Catechesis on the Creed*, Vol. 2 of *Jesus: Son and Savior*. Reprint, Boston: Pauline Books & Media, 1996.

————. Apostolic Letter *Novo Millenio Ineunte*. Available on the Vatican Website.

————. Apostolic Letter *Salvifici Doloris*. Available on the Vatican Website.

————. Encyclical Letter *Dominum et Vivificantem*. Available on the Vatican Website.

————. Encyclical Letter *Fides et Ratio*. Available on the Vatican Website.

————. *Man and Woman He Created Them: A Theology of the Body*. Translated by Michael Waldstein. Boston: Pauline Books & Media, 2006.

Johnson, Mark. "Apophatic Theology's Cataphatic Dependencies," *The Thomist* 62 (1998): 519–531.

Journet, Charles. *The Meaning of Evil*. Translated by Michael Barry. New York: P. J. Kennedy & Sons, 1963.

Jowers, Dennis W. *The Trinitarian Axiom of Karl Rahner: The Economic Trinity is the Immanent Trinity and Vice Versa*. Lewiston, NY: Edwin Mellen Press, 2006.

Katz, Steven T. *Mystical and Philosophical Analysis*. Oxford: Oxford University Press, 1978.

Keating, James F. and Thomas Joseph White, eds. *Divine Impassibility and the Mystery of Human Suffering*. Grand Rapids, MI: William B. Eerdmans Publishing Co., 2009.

Kilby, Karen. "Aquinas, the Trinity, and the Limits of Understanding." *International Journal of Systematic Theology* 7, no. 4 (Oct 2005): 414–427.

————. *Rahner: Theology and Philosophy*. London: Routledge, 2004.

King, J. Norman, and Barry L. Whitney. "Rahner and Hartshorne on Divine Immutability." *International Philosophical Quarterly* 22, no. 3 (1982): 195–209.

Kolbe, Maximilian. "Who Then Are You, O Immaculate Conception?," February 17, 1941. Available on the Pierced Hearts Website.

Kreeft, Peter, and Ronald K. Tacelli. *Handbook of Catholic Apologetics: Reasoned Answers to Questions of Faith*. San Francisco: Ignatius Press, 2009.

Kowalska, St. Maria Faustina. *Diary: Divine Mercy in My Soul*. Stockbridge, MA: Marians of the Immaculate Conception, 2002.

Langdon, Adrian. "Confessing Eternity: Karl Barth and the Western Tradition." *Pro Ecclesia* vol. 21, no. 2 (Spring 2012): 125–144.

Leemans, J., and L. Jocqué, eds. *Corpus Christianorum Latina.* Xenium natalicium: 1953–2003. Turnhout, Belgium: Brepols, 2003.

Levering, Matthew. *Christ's Fulfillment of Torah and Temple: Salvation according to Thomas Aquinas.* Notre Dame, IN: University of Notre Dame Press, 2002.

———. *Predestination: Biblical and Theological Paths.* New York: Oxford University Press, 2011.

———. *Sacrifice and Community: Jewish Offering and Christian Eucharist.* Oxford: Blackwell Publishing, 2005.

———. *Scripture and Metaphysics: Aquinas and the Renewal of Trinitarian Theology.* Malden, MA: Blackwell, 2004.

———. "Wisdom and the Viability of Thomstic Trinitarian Theology." *The Thomist* 64 (2000): 593–618.

Lewis, Alan. *Between Cross and Resurrection: A Theology of Holy Saturday.* Grand Rapids, MI: William B. Eerdmans Publishing Co., 2001.

Loke, Andrew Ter Ern. Review of *Did the Saviour See the Father? Christ, Salvation, and the Vision of God* by Simon F. Gaine, OP. *Journal of Theological Studies* 68, no. 1 (2017): 465–468.

Lombardo, Nicholas, OP. *The Father's Will: Christ's Crucifixion and the Goodness of God.* Oxford: Oxford University Press, 2014.

———. *The Logic of Desire: Aquinas on Emotion.* Washington, DC: Catholic University of America Press, 2011.

Lonergan, Bernard J. F., SJ. *Collected Works of Bernard Lonergan.* Vol. 1, *Grace and Freedom: Operative Grace in the Thought of St. Thomas Aquinas.* Edited by Frederick E. Crowe, SJ, and Robert M. Doran, SJ. Reprint, Toronto: University of Toronto, 2000.

———. *Collected Works of Bernard Lonergan.* Vol. 7, *The Ontological and Psychological Constitution of Christ.* Translated by Michael Shields. Toronto: University of Toronto Press, 2002.

———. *Collected Works of Bernard Lonergan.* Vol. 12, *The Triune God: Systematics.* Translated by Michael G. Shields. Edited by Robert Doran, SJ, and H. Daniel Monsour. Toronto: University of Toronto Press, 2007.

———. *Collected Works of Bernard Lonergan.* Vol. 19, *Early Latin Theology.* Edited by Robert Doran, SJ, and H. Daniel Monsour. Translated by Michael Shields. Toronto: University of Toronto Press, 2011.

———. *De Verbo Incarnato.* 3rd ed. Rome: Gregorian University, 1964.

———. *Insight: A Study of Human Understanding.* New York: Harper & Row, 1978.

————. *Method in Theology*. Reprint, Toronto: University of Toronto, 2007.

Long, Steven A. "Divine and Creaturely 'Receptivity': The Search for a Middle Term." *Communio* 21, no. 1 (1994): 151–161.

Luther, Martin. *Luther's Works*. Vol. 7, *Lectures on Genesis, Chapters 38–44*. Edited by Jaroslav Pelikan. Translated by Paul D. Pahl. St. Louis: Concordia Publishing House, 1965.

————. *Luther's Works*. Vol. 26, *Lectures on Galatians 1535: Chapters 1–4*. Edited by Jaroslav Pelikan. Translated by Walter A. Hansen. St. Louis: Concordia Publishing House, 1964.

————. *Luther's Works*. Vol. 35. Edited and Translated by E. Theodore Bachman. Philadelphia: Fortress Press, 1960.

————. *Sermons of Martin Luther: The House Postils*. Vol. 2. Edited by Eugene Klug. Translated by Erwin W. Koehlinger. Grand Rapids, MI: Baker, 1996.

Maas, Wilhelm. *Gott und die Holle: Studien zum Descensus Christi*. Einsiedeln: Johannes Verlag, 1979.

Malloy, Christopher J. "The 'I-Thou' Argument for the Trinity: Wherefore Art Thou?" *Nova et Vetera* (English Edition) 15, no. 1 (2017): 113–159.

Maréchal, Joseph. *Le point de départ de la métaphysique: leçons sur le développement historique et théorique du problème de la connaissance*. 5 Vols. Bruges-Louvain: Charles Beyaert, 1922–1947.

Margerie, Bertrand de. "De la science du Christ. Science, préscience et conscience, même prépascales du Christ Rédempteur." *Doctor Communis* 36 (1983): 123–158.

Marion, Jean-Luc. *In Excess: Studies in Saturated Phenomena*. New York: Fordham University Press, 2002.

————. *The Idol and Distance: Five Studies*. Translated by Thomas A. Carlson. New York: Fordham University Press, 2001.

Maritain, Jacques. *Approaches sans entraves*. Paris: Librairie Arthem Fayard, 1973.

————. *Court traité de l'existence et de l'existant*. Paris: Paul Hartmann, 1947.

————. *De la grace et de l'humanité de Jesus*. Bruges: Desclée de Brouwer, 1967.

————. *Dieu et la permission du mal*. Paris: Desclée de Brouwer, 1963.

————. *Distinguer pour unir; ou, Les degrés du savoir*. Paris: Desclée de Brouwer, 1946.

————. *Existence and the Existent*. Translated by Lewis Galantière and

Gerald B. Phelan. New York: Pantheon Books, 1948.

—. *God and the Permission of Evil.* Translated by Joseph W. Evans. Milwaukee: The Bruce Publishing Company, 1966.

—. *La souffrance de Dieu.* Paris: Le Centurion, 1975.

—. *Neuf leçons sur les notions premières de la philosophie morale.* Paris: P. Téqui, 1951.

—. *On the Grace and Humanity of Jesus.* Translated by Joseph W. Evans. New York: Herder & Herder, 1969.

—. "Quelques réflexions sur savoir théologique," *Revue Thomiste* 69, no. 1 (1969): 5–27.

—. *St. Thomas and the Problem of Evil.* Milwaukee: The Aquinas Lectures, 1942.

—. *The Collected Works of Jacques Maritain,* Vol. 20, *Untrammeled Approaches.* Translated by Bernard Doering. Notre Dame, IN: University of Notre Dame Press, 1997.

—. *The Degrees of Knowledge.* Translated by Gerald B. Phelan. Notre Dame, IN: University of Notre Dame Press, 1995.

Maritain, Jacques and Raïssa. Œuvres complètes. Vol. 14. Fribourg: Éditions Universitaires; Paris: Editions St.-Paul, 1993.

Marmann, M. J. *Praeamubla ad gratiam: Ideengeschichtliche Untersuchung* über *die Entstehung des Axioms "Gratia praesupponit naturam,"* Unpublished Dissertation. Regensburg, 1974.

Marshall, Bruce D. "Jesus' Human Knowledge: A Test for Theological Exegesis." Lecture for Thomistic Institute on October 2, 2015.

—. "Reading the Gospels with Benedict XVI: How the Pope Finds Jesus in the Bible." *First Things* (October 2011). Available on the First Things Website.

—. "The Absolute and the Trinity." *Pro Ecclesia* 23, no. 2 (2014): 147–164.

—. "The Unity of the Triune God: Reviving an Ancient Question." *The Thomist* 74 (2010): 1–32.

Martin, Ralph. *The Fulfillment of All Desire: A Guidebook for the Journey to God Based on the Wisdom of the Saints.* Steubenville, OH: Emmaus Road Publications, 2006.

McCormack, Bruce. *Karl Barth's Critically Realistic Dialectical Theology: Its Genesis and Development, 1909–1936.* Oxford: Clarendon, 1995.

McInerny, Ralph. *Duns Scotus and Medieval Christianity.* Ashland, OR: Blackstone Audio Inc., 2006.

Migne, Jacques-Paul. *Patrologia Latina*: 1944–1855. Available at patristica.net/latina/.Molnar, Paul D. "A Response: Beyond Hegel with Karl

Barth and T. F. Torrance." *Pro Ecclesia* 23, no. 2 (2014): 165–173.

Mondello, Geoffrey K. *The Metaphysics of Mysticism: A Commentary on the Mystical Philosophy of St. John of the Cross* (2010). Available at http://johnofthecross.com/.

Mongeau, Gilles, SJ. "Human and Divine Knowing of the Incarnate Word." *Josephinum Journal of Theology* 12, no. 1 (Winter/Spring 2005): 30–42.

Most, William G. *The Consciousness of Christ*. Front Royal, VA: Christendom College Press, 1980.

Newman, Cardinal John Henry. *Discourses Addressed to Mixed Congregations*. London: Longman, 1891.

Nicolas, Jean-Hervé. *Dieu connu comme inconnu*. Paris: Desclée de Brouwer, 1966.

Nieuwenhove, Rik van, and Joseph Wawrykow, eds. *The Theology of Thomas Aquinas*. Notre Dame: University of Notre Dame Press, 2005.

O'Connell, John J. *The Mystery of the Triune God*. New York: Paulist, 1989.

Ormerod, Neil. "A Trajectory from Augustine to Aquinas and Lonergan: Contingent Predication and the Trinity." *Irish Theological Quarterly* 82, no. 3 (2017): 208–221.

Pannenberg, Wolfhart. *Systematic Theology*, Vol. 2. Translated by Geoffrey W. Bromiley. Grand Rapids, MI: William B. Eerdmans Publishing Co., 1994.

Pearson, J. B., ed. *Patrologiae Graecae*. Vol. 77, *Cyril of Alexandria, Theodotus of Ancyranus, et al.* Paris: J.-P. Migne, 1859.

Pesch, O. H. "Existential and Sapiential Theology—The Theological Confrontation between Luther and Thomas Aquinas." In *Catholic Scholars in Dialogue with Luther*. Edited by J. Wicks. Chicago: Loyola University Press, 1970: 59–81.

Pius X. *Lamentabili Sane*. Available online at papalencyclicals.net.

Pius XII. *Haurietis Aquas*. Available online at papalencyclicals.net.

———. *Mystici Corporis*. Available online at papalencyclicals.net.

Przywara, Erich. *Analogia Entis: Metaphysics—Original Structure and Universal Rhythm*. Translated by John R. Betz and David Bentley Hart. Grand Rapids, MI: William B. Eerdmans Publishing Co., 2014.

Rahner, Karl. "Remarks on the Dogmatic Treatise 'De Trinitate.'" In *Theological Investigations*. Vol. 4, *More Recent Writings*. Translated by Kevin Smyth. Baltimore: Helicon Press, 1966.

————. "The Intermediate State." In *Theological Investigations*. Vol. 17, *Jesus, Man, and the Church*. Translated by Margaret Kohl. London: Darton, Longman & Todd, 1981.

————. *Theological Investigations*. Vol. 1, *God, Christ, Mary, and Grace*. Baltimore: Helicon, 1961.

————. *The Trinity*. Translated by Joseph Donceel. New York: The Crossroad Publishing Company, 1970, 1997.

Riestra, Jose Antonio. "Experiencia Mistica y Vision Beatifica en Cristo, segun Santo Tomas." *Studi Tomistici* 44 (1991): 318–325.

Rigney, J. F. "Communication of Idioms." In *New Catholic Encyclopedia*. Vol. 4. Second Edition, Detroit: Gale, 2003.

Ritschl, Albrecht. *The Christian Doctrine of Justification and Reconciliation: The Positive Development of the Doctrine*. Edited by A. B. Macaulay. Translated by H. R. Mackintosh. Clifton, NJ: Reference Book Publishers, 1966.

————. *The Creeds of Christendom, with a History and Critical Notes*. Vol. 2, *The Greek and Latin Creeds*. New York: Harper and Brothers, 1877.

Rocca, Gregory P. *Speaking the Incomprehensible God: Thomas Aquinas on the Interplay of Positive and Negative Theology*. Washington, DC: Catholic University of America Press, 2004.

Root, Michael. "The Hope of Eternal Life." *Ecumenical Trends* 41 (2012): 100.

Rosato, Andrew V. "Aquinas and Maritain on Whether Christ's Habitual Grace Could Increase." *Nova et Vetera* 15, no. 2 (2017): 527–546.

Ruddy, Christopher. "'For the Many': The Vicarious-Representative Heart of Joseph Ratzinger's Theology." *Theological Studies* 75, no. 3 (2014): 564–584.

Sachs, John, SJ. Review of *Pattern of Redemption,* by Edward T. Oakes, SJ. *Theological Studies* 56, no. 4 (Dec 1995): 787–789.

Saward, John. "The Grace of Christ in His Principal Members: St. Thomas Aquinas on the Pastoral Epistles." In *Aquinas on Scripture: An Introduction to His Biblical Commentaries*. Edited by Thomas G. Weinandy, Daniel A. Keating, and John P. Yocum. New York: T & T Clark International, 2005: 197–221.

Schaff, Philip, ed. *Nicene and Post-Nicene Fathers of the Christian Church*. Vol. 1, *The Confessions and Letters of St. Augustine*. Reprint, Grand Rapids, MI: William B. Eerdmans Publishing Co., 1988.

Scheeben, Matthias J. *Die Mysterien des Christentums: Wesen, Bedeutung und Zusammenhang derselben nach der in ihrem übernatürlichen*

Charakter gegebenen Perspektive dargestellt. Matthias-Grünewald-Verlag, 1925.

———. *The Mysteries of Christianity.* Translated by Cyril Vollert, SJ. St. Louis: B. Herder Book Co., 1946.

Schindler, David L. "Norris Clarke on Person, Being, and St. Thomas." *Communio* 20, no. 3 (1993): 580–592.

———. "The Person: Philosophy, Theology, and Receptivity." *Communio* 21, no. 1 (1994): 172–190.

Schindler, D. C. "Discovering the Given: On Reason and God." *Nova et Vetera* 10, no. 2 (2012): 563–604.

Schmitz, Kenneth L. "Selves and Persons: A Difference in Loves?" *Communio* 18, no. 2 (1991): 183–206.

———. "The Geography of the Human Person." *Communio* 13, no. 1 (1986): 27–48.

———. *The Gift: Creation.* Milwaukee: Marquette University Press, 1982.

Schmitz, Rudolf M. "Christus Comprehensor: Die 'Visio Beatifica Christi Viatoris' bei M. J. Scheeben." *Doctor Communis* 36 (1983): 347–359.

Schurmann, H. *Jesu ureigner Tod.* Frieburg: Herder, 1975.

Scotus, Duns. *Opera Omnia,* Vol. 17. Vatican City: Ex typis Polyglottis Vaticanis, 1950–2013.

Simon, Yves R. *Work, Society, and Culture,* edited by Vukan Kuic. New York: Fordham University Press, 1971.

Sohngen, G. *Lexikon für Theologie und Kirche,* Vol. 4, *Faith and Order—Hannibaldis.* Edited by J. Hofer and K. Rahner. Second edition. Freiburg: Herder, 1960.

Stewart, Jon. *Kierkegaard's Relations to Hegel Reconsidered.* New York: Cambridge University Press, 2003.

Sweeney, Eileen C. "Three Notions of *Resolutio* and the Structure of Reasoning in Aquinas." *The Thomist* 58, no. 2 (1994): 197–243.

Tschipke, Theophil. *Die Menschheit Christi als Heilsorgan der Gottheit.* Freiburg im Breisgau, 1939.

———. *L'humanité du Christ comme instrument de salut de la divinité.* Fribourg: Academic Press Fribourg, 2003.

The Liturgy of the Hours. Vol. 2. New York: Catholic Books Publishing, 1976.

Torrell, Jean-Pierre, OP. *Le Christ en ses mystères,* Vol. 2, *La Vie et L'Œuvre de Jésus selon Saint Thomas d'Aquin.* Paris: Desclée de Brouwer, 1999.

———. *Pour nous les hommes et pour notre salut: Jésus notre rédemption.* Paris: Les Éditions du Cerf, 2014.

————. *Recherches sur la théorie de la prophétie au moyen âge, xiie–xive siécles: études et textes*. Fribourg: Éditions Universitaires Fribourg Suisse, 1992.

————. "S. Thomas d'Aquin et la science du Christ." In *Saint Thomas au XXe siècle*. Edited by Serge-Thomas Bonino, OP. Paris: Éditions St. Paul, 1994: 394–409.

Villagrasa, Jesús Lasaga. *Fondazione di un'etica realista*. Roma: Atheneo Ponficia Regina Apostolorum, 2005.

————. "La *resolutio* come metodo della metafisica secondo Cornelio Fabro." *Alpha Omega* 4, no. 1 (2001): 35–66.

————. *Realismo Metafísico e irrealidad. Estudio sobre la obra "Teoría del objeto puro" de Antonio Millán-Puelles*. Madrid: Fundación Universitaria Española, 2008.

Vorgrimler, Herbert. "Christ's Descent into Hell—Is It Important?" *Concilium: An International Review of Theology* 1, no. 2 (1966): 75–81.

Walker, Adrian J. "Personal Singularity and the *Communio Personarum*: A Creative Development of Thomas Aquinas' Doctrine of *Esse Commune*." *Communio* 31 (Fall 2004): 457–479.

Weinandy, Thomas G., OFM. *Does God Suffer?* Edinburgh: University of Notre Dame Press, 2000.

————. *In the Likeness of Sinful Flesh: An Essay on the Humanity of Christ*. Edinburgh: T&T Clark, 1993.

————. "Jesus' Filial Vision of the Father." *Pro Ecclesia* 13, no. 2 (2004): 189–201.

————. "The Beatific Vision and the Incarnate Son: Furthering the Discussion." *The Thomist* 70, no. 4 (2006): 605–615.

————. *The Father's Spirit of Sonship: Reconceiving the Trinity*. Eugene, OR: Wipf & Stock, 1995.

White, Thomas Joseph, OP. "Dyotheletism and the Instrumental Human Consciousness of Jesus." *Pro Ecclesia* 17, no. 4 (2008): 396–422.

————. "Engaging the Thomistic Tradition and Contemporary Culture Simultaneously: A Response to Burrell, Healy, and Schindler." *Nova et Vetera* 10, no. 2 (2012): 605–623.

————. "Intra-Trinitarian Obedience and Nicene-Chalcedonian Christology." *Nova et Vetera* (English Edition) 6, no. 2 (2008): 377–402.

————. "Kenoticism and the Divinity of Christ Crucified." *The Thomist* 75 (2011): 1–41.

————, ed. *The Analogy of Being: Invention of the Antichrist or the Wisdom of God?* Grand Rapids, MI: William B. Eerdmans Publishing Co., 2011.

———. "The Infused Science of Christ." *Nova et Vetera* 16, no. 2 (2018): 617–641.

———. "The Voluntary Action of the Earthly Christ and the Necessity of the Beatific Vision." *The Thomist* 69, no. 4 (2005): 497–534.

———. "Toward a Post-Secular, Post-Conciliar Thomistic Philosophy: Wisdom in the Face of Modernity and the Challenge of Contemporary Natural Theology." *Nova et Vetera* 10, no. 2 (2012): 521–530.

———. *Wisdom in the Face of Modernity: A Study in Thomistic Natural Theology.* Ave Maria, FL: Sapientia Press, 2009.

Wicks, Jared, SJ. "Christ's Saving Descent to the Dead: Early Witnesses from Ignatius of Antioch to Origen." *Pro Ecclesia* 17, no. 3 (2008): 281–309.

Wilkins, Jeremy D. "Method, Order, and Analogy in Trinitarian Theology: Karl Rahner's Critique of the 'Psychological' Approach." *The Thomist* 74, no. 4 (2010): 563–592.

Wojtyla, Karol. *Faith in St. John of the Cross.* San Francisco: Ignatius Press, 1981.

———. *Lecciones de Lublin.* Translated by Rafael Mora Martin. Madrid: Palabra, 2014.

———. *Lubliner Vorlesungen.* Translated by Anneliese Danka Spranger and Edda Wiener. Stuttgart-Degerloch: Seewaldverlag, 1981.

———. *Memory and Identity: Conversations at the Dawn of a Millennium.* New York: Rizzoli International, 2005.

———. *Metafisica della Persona: Tutte le opera filosofiche e saggi integrative.* Edited by Giovanni Reale and Tadeusz Styczen. Milano: Bompiani, 2003.

———. *Persona e Atto.* Translated by Giuseppe Girgenti and Patrycja Mikulska. Milano: Bompiani, 2001.

———. *Person and Community: Selected Essays.* Translated by Theresa Sandok. New York: Peter Lang, 1993.

———. *The Acting Person.* Translated by Anna-Teresa Tymieniecka. Dordrecht, Holland: Springer, 1979.

Wood, Jacob W. "Kataphasis and Apophasis in Thirteenth Century Theology: The Anthropological Context of the *Triplex Via* in the *Summa Fratris Alexandri* and Albert the Great." *The Heythrop Journal* 57 (2016): 293–311.

Aertsen, Jan A. 268

Aquinas, Thomas 1, 2, 17, 18, 19, 29, 42, 43, 44, 45, 50, 51, 52, 54, 57, 59, 61, 62, 65, 71, 74, 75, 79, 81, 83, 84, 87, 89, 90, 92, 93, 94, 97, 98, 108, 112, 115, 116, 122, 123, 125, 131, 132, 136, 149, 152, 165, 169, 173, 177, 179, 191, 201, 202, 203, 204, 206, 207, 213, 215, 220, 226, 228, 233, 234, 236, 237, 240, 255, 256, 257, 270, 277, 288, 291, 299, 300, 302, 304

Athanasius 19, 29, 112

Augustine 17, 18, 19, 50, 54, 61, 65, 71, 74, 75, 122, 123, 169, 173, 177, 213, 226, 233, 237, 256, 275, 291, 300, 302, 304

Aulen, Gustaf 31

Barry, Richard 54, 67, 205

Balthasar, Hans Urs von *passim*

Barth, Karl 9, 15, 22, 25, 27, 30, 51, 54, 56, 64, 70, 75, 79, 80, 141, 143, 144, 145, 146, 147, 148, 152, 163, 165, 167, 168, 180, 181, 188, 189, 193, 199, 201, 209, 210, 221, 227, 228, 233, 235, 239, 243, 245, 246, 247, 248, 251, 253, 262, 268, 269, 270

Beaudin, Michel 56, 227

Benedict, Pope 8, 22, 24, 58, 101, 105, 120, 124, 125, 175, 277, 279, 282, 284, 298, 300

Bieler, Martin 53, 147, 182, 250, 258, 280

Birot, Antoine 26, 33, 34, 148, 151, 152, 161, 191, 219, 236, 288, 294

Blankenhorn, Bernhard 80, 196, 199, 200

Boethius 237

Bonaventure 123, 193, 203, 205, 206, 207, 231, 232, 233, 234, 236, 237, 258, 262, 277

Bonino, Serge-Thomas 132, 277

Boyle, John F. 234

Buckley, James J. 2, 203, 237

Calvin, John 18, 19, 22, 30, 34, 45, 46, 52, 64, 75, 109, 148, 209, 226, 227, 228

Clarke, W. Norris 7, 19, 158, 201, 206, 238

Cooper, Adam G. 125

Culpepper, Gary 152, 163, 164, 165

Daley, Brian 179, 227, 245

Dalzell, Thomas 183, 195, 199, 201, 202, 206, 207, 224

Daniélou, Jean 280, 298

Darley, Alan Philip 269

Diepen, H.-M. 86, 97, 102

Donneaud, Henry 124, 125

Doran, Rober 8, 171, 267, 268

Doyle, Brian 23, 61, 62, 63

Duffy, Kevin 179, 180, 195, 196, 197, 198, 199, 216

Dulles, Avery 68, 71

Dyer, George J. 16

Egan, Harvey D. 161

Emery, Gilles 231, 233, 234, 236, 237, 238, 240, 241, 242, 250, 257

Fabro, Cornelio 214, 268
Flannery, Kevin L. 71
Franks, Angela Franz 250
Friesenhahn, Jacob H. 215, 216,
 217, 218, 219
Gaine, Simon Francis 80, 87, 103,
 104, 119
Galot, Jean 49, 86, 87, 88, 89, 91,
 97, 98, 102, 106, 144, 148,
 149, 203
Garrigou-Lagrange, Reginald 87,
 98, 202
Garrigues, Jean Miguel 97
Gavrilyuk, Paul L. 17, 218
Gondreau, Paul 83, 87, 91, 92, 93,
 94, 103
Gregory of Nyssa 29, 61, 71, 125,
 169, 190, 227, 243, 245, 246,
 262
Gregory Nazianzen 125, 295, 296
Gregory 146, 291
Griffiths, Paul J. 67, 68, 69
Hadley, Christopher 214, 230,
 231, 236, 241, 242, 243, 244,
 245, 246, 247, 248, 250, 254
Hart, David Bentley 163, 169,
 170, 171, 182, 233
Hauke, Manfred 4
Healy, Nicholas J. 5, 82, 144, 161,
 167, 188, 201, 203, 204, 229,
 237, 250
Hefling, Charles 18, 90, 119
Heidegger, Martin 2, 170, 171,
 235, 269, 270
Hildebrand, Dietrich von 173, 174
Holzer, Vincent 28, 185, 269
Howsare, Rodney 19, 20, 209,
 239, 241
Hunsinger, George 246
Hunt, Anne 190, 192, 200

John Paul II 26, 61, 72, 73, 74,
 75, 84, 86, 107, 108, 175, 216,
 235, 249, 256, 266, 267, 271,
 275, 278, 297
Johnson, Mark 214
Johnson, Junius 193, 232
Journet, Charles 3, 27, 32, 156,
 242
Jowers, Dennis W. 232
Keating, James F. 145
Kerr, Fergus 179, 187, 259, 269
Kilby, Karen 19, 48, 50, 55, 179,
 183, 227, 230, 234, 243, 254
Kreeft, Peter 257
Krenski, Thomas R. 200, 217
Lauber, David Edward 30, 49, 54,
 56, 69, 70, 71, 168
Levering, Matthew J. 16, 31, 42,
 53, 54, 73, 74, 81, 113, 131,
 132, 178, 187, 213, 230, 231,
 243, 292, 293
Lewis, Alan 27
Lochbrunner, Manfred 233
Lombardo, Nicholas 103, 104,
 306
Lonergan, Bernard 8, 18, 82, 86,
 88, 89, 90, 95, 96, 97, 102,
 103, 117, 118, 119, 120, 171,
 192, 237, 244, 251, 256, 266,
 267, 268
Long, D. Stephen 79, 188
Long, Steven A. 201
Lopez, Antonio 192, 193, 194,
 195, 252
Lösel, Steffen 26, 27, 32, 33, 47,
 53, 149, 161, 167, 183, 285,
 288, 296
Loser, Werner 29
Luther, Martin 17, 18, 19, 20, 21,
 22, 24, 26, 29, 30, 34, 46, 52,

64, 125, 147, 148, 175, 186, 226, 228, 239, 285

Maas, Wilhelm 72, 226

Malloy, Christopher 205

Mansini, Guy 54, 81, 89, 90, 92, 93, 161, 168, 169, 177, 190, 213, 222, 239, 252, 253, 269, 288

Marchesi, Giovanni 187, 188, 203, 234

Maréchal, Joseph 179, 180, 269

Margerie, Bertrand de 87, 116, 208, 213

Marion, Jean-Luc 270

Maritain, Jacques 9, 87, 88, 89, 97, 103, 114, 115, 117, 134, 135, 142, 143, 144, 145, 147, 148, 149, 150, 154, 155, 156, 157, 158, 159, 161, 162, 163, 164, 165, 167, 169, 172, 173, 174, 176, 181, 182, 201, 202, 204, 206, 209, 210, 220, 244, 258, 275, 278, 297

Marshall, Bruce 28, 50, 81, 86, 104, 105, 187, 189, 204, 206, 213, 284, 300

Martin, Regis 56

Martin, Ralph, 62, 259

McCormack, Bruce 163, 165, 167, 168

McInerny, Ralph 232

McIntosh, Mark 55, 178, 247, 263

Menke, Karl-Heinz 21

Miles, Lois M. 38, 44, 46, 53, 63, 65, 68, 69, 70, 82, 109, 114, 120, 126, 127, 134, 226, 251, 252, 255, 297

Mongrain, Kevin 80, 180, 242, 259

Most, William G. 88

Narcisse, Gilbert 132

Newman, John Henry 19, 53, 56, 71

Nichols, Aidan 1, 2, 23, 33, 71, 185, 187, 193, 217, 227, 261

Nicolas, Jean-Hervé 210

Nicolas, M.-J. 116

Oakes, Edward T. 2, 3, 4, 7, 18, 19, 21, 24, 41, 53, 55, 61, 62, 66, 71, 72, 73, 79, 131, 132, 161, 178, 181, 221, 222, 254, 278, 279, 284, 288, 293

O'Donnell, John 20, 31, 32, 216, 235

O'Hanlon, Gerard F. 5, 21, 153, 160, 161, 167, 172, 179, 181, 184, 189, 190, 191, 192, 193, 194, 195, 196, 198, 199, 205, 208, 216, 220, 221, 223, 228, 268, 286

Olsen, Cyrus 245, 247

O'Regan, Cyril 28, 66, 179, 180, 185, 186, 190, 193, 197, 209, 210, 239, 253, 269, 270

Ormerod, Neil 237

Ouellet, Marc 241

Pannenberg, Wolfhart 21

Pesch, O. H. 22

Pidel, Aaron 118, 119

Pitstick, Alyssa L. 15, 19, 41, 46, 47, 49, 53, 54, 55, 56, 57, 58, 59, 60, 66, 67, 68, 69, 70, 71, 72, 73, 74, 80, 104, 113, 120, 126, 190, 237, 241, 266, 288

Pius X 86

Pius XII 86, 119

Przywara, Erich 187, 188, 214, 233, 247, 262

Quash, Ben 21, 28, 47, 56, 167, 187, 189, 227, 228

Rahner, Karl 1, 6, 8, 20, 31, 64, 65, 85, 101, 111, 112, 141, 143, 145, 159, 160, 161, 171, 178, 179, 197, 204, 216, 232, 233, 236, 249, 254, 262, 265, 268, 269, 287, 293, 298, 299

Ratzinger, Joseph 8, 16, 21, 22, 24, 35, 39, 40, 58, 59, 60, 61, 63, 64, 66, 67, 71, 74, 75, 93, 106, 115, 137, 156, 175, 176, 201, 203, 218, 225, 226, 271, 277, 278, 279, 280, 281, 282, 283, 284, 285, 286, 288, 290, 291, 292, 293, 294, 295, 296, 297, 298, 299, 300, 301, 302, 303, 304, 305, 306

Rémy, Gérard 44

Riches, John 7, 21, 23, 106, 121, 167, 179

Ritschl, Albrecht 21, 226

Rocca, Gregory 247

Root, Michael 125, 223

Rosenberg, Randall S. 8, 18, 49, 59, 80, 82, 89, 90, 97, 100, 110, 111, 119, 120, 121, 266, 267, 268, 270

Sachs, John R. 43, 44, 238, 254

Sara, Juan 48, 54

Saward, John 7, 43, 53, 107, 108, 219, 220, 225, 227, 259, 305

Scheeben, Matthias J. 97, 257

Schenk, Richard 4

Schindler, David 38, 201 235, 238

Schindler, D. C. 76, 180, 202, 204, 214, 235

Schmidt, William 29

Schmitz, Kenneth L. 201, 202

Schrijver, Georges de 188

Schumacher, Michele M. 79, 189, 213, 214, 224, 225, 226, 227, 228, 229, 230, 231, 232, 233, 234, 236, 237, 238, 239, 240, 241, 242, 248, 249, 260, 261 271

Sciglitano, Anthony C. 197, 270

Servais, Jacques 24, 30, 31, 116, 211

Spence, Brian J. 182

Speyr, Adrienne von 8, 26, 27, 29, 37, 38, 39, 44, 46, 48, 49, 54, 55, 56, 62, 63, 65, 68, 69, 70, 75, 76, 79, 80, 81, 82, 106, 109, 117, 120, 121, 125, 126, 127, 128, 134, 135, 137, 141, 142, 146, 147, 163, 176, 178, 183, 189, 194, 199, 200, 210, 211, 213, 214, 215, 216, 225, 226, 229, 230, 234, 236, 247, 249, 250, 251, 252, 253, 254, 255, 257, 258, 259, 260, 261, 262, 263, 271, 278, 285, 289, 292, 293, 294, 296, 297, 298

Sutton, Matthew Lewis 38, 54, 65, 69, 79, 117, 127, 128, 213, 236, 247, 255, 258, 259, 260, 261, 262

Torrell, Jean-Pierre 49, 87, 91, 92, 94, 97, 98, 99, 103, 106, 134, 228

Turek, Margaret 25, 61, 161, 200, 230, 233

Vetö, Etienne 254

Villagrasa, Jesús 244, 249, 268

Vogel, Jeffrey A. 167

Wainwright, Geoffrey 289

Walker, Adrian 28, 53, 93, 238, 303

Webster, John 49, 69, 70, 79, 188, 189

Weinandy, Thomas G. 26, 49, 84,

86, 94, 95, 96, 97, 100, 101,
102, 106, 136, 144, 181, 182,
202, 203, 209, 220, 236
White, Thomas Joseph 3, 22, 27,
32, 41, 42, 43, 44, 45, 46, 49,
51, 52, 55, 63, 64, 75, 81, 83,
84, 85, 88, 93, 95, 97, 98, 99,
100, 101, 102, 103, 116, 131,
145, 168, 169, 204, 213, 214,
228, 238, 239, 253, 254
Wicks, Jared 21, 22, 66, 67
Wigley, Stephen 19, 79
Wilkins, Jeremy D. 233
Williams, Rowan 179, 180, 185,
199, 250
Wojtyla, Karol 59, 174, 271
Wood, Jacob W. 215
Yeago, David Stuart 110, 111
Yocum, John 26, 27, 50, 66, 187,
220
Zeitz, James 187, 233